Writing Themselves into History

WRITING THEMSELVES INTO HISTORY

Emily and Matilda Bancroft in Journals and Letters

KIM BANCROFT

HEYDAY

Heyday, Berkeley, California
The Bancroft Library, University of California, Berkeley, California

Library of Congress Cataloging-in-Publication Data

Names: Bancroft, Kim, author. | Bancroft Library, issuing body.
Title: Writing themselves into history : Emily and Matilda Bancroft in journals and letters / Kim Bancroft.
Description: Berkeley, California : Heyday : The Bancroft Library, University of California, [2022] | Includes bibliographical references and index.
Identifiers: LCCN 2022014039 (print) | LCCN 2022014040 (ebook) | ISBN 9781597145886 (hardcover) | ISBN 9781597145916 (epub)
Subjects: LCSH: Bancroft, Emily, 1834-1869. | Bancroft, Matilda, 1848-1910. | Bancroft, Hubert Howe, 1832-1918--Family. | Historians' spouses--California--Biography. | Women--California--Social conditions--19th century. | California--History--1850-1950. | California--Biography.
Classification: LCC F866 .B195 2022 (print) | LCC F866 (ebook) | DDC 979.4/04092 [B]--dc23/eng/20220506
LC record available at https://lccn.loc.gov/2022014039
LC ebook record available at https://lccn.loc.gov/2022014040

Cover Design: Marlon Rigel
Interior Design/Typesetting: Rebecca LeGates

Published by Heyday
P.O. Box 9145, Berkeley, California 94709
(510) 549-3564
heydaybooks.com

Printed in East Peoria, Illinois, by Versa Press, Inc.

10 9 8 7 6 5 4 3 2 1

CONTENTS

PART I

Emily Ketchum Bancroft: A Life in Letters

PART II

Matilda Coley Griffing Bancroft: A Writer in Her Own Right

Introduction

> We had an excellent sermon from Dr. [Wadsworth] yesterday.
> ... He spoke first of the spiritual state of California, that the
> eyes of the whole world are upon a country whose rocks were
> silver & her dust gold. He likened us to the ancient city of
> Palestine—said we are destined to become as great, unless
> God in his wrath for our worldliness & sinfulness, should
> cause an earthquake to entirely overthrow us. (July 13, 1864, to
> her parents)

So Emily Bancroft captured a vision of California in 1864 from the pulpit of a prominent preacher of San Francisco who saw the state as both rife with the dangers of greed and ripe with potential grandeur. During the 1860s, Emily Ketchum Bancroft (1834–1869), the first wife of Hubert Howe Bancroft (1832–1918), historian of the West, wrote nearly daily letters to her parents and sister in Buffalo, New York. For ten years until her early death, Emily depicted the life of her family and of the young, striving society of California. Emily's letters provide a window that enables us to peek into a long-gone world, helping us understand our journey from that past to the present.[1]

My opportunity to engage with these letters came during a time of crisis in my life. In 2008, I turned fifty and had spent nearly three decades as a writing instructor, providing thick commentary on my students' compositions. I'd taught both in high schools and colleges in the US and Mexico, with up to 150 students at a time. Determined that they should learn the fine points of writing, from the use of commas to the logic of evidence, I'd spend evenings and weekends burdened by stacks of papers that I annotated closely with rules and encouragement. I loved my students, but my duty overwhelmed me. So I left that editing swamp to find other ways to edit manuscripts not destined for the "circular file."

My simmering crisis over my future serendipitously met with an inspired new direction through the unsuspecting intervention of Theresa Salazar, the curator of Western Americana at UC Berkeley's Bancroft Library. Hubert Howe Bancroft, the founder of that renowned library, is my great-great-grandfather. I had attended a few events at The Bancroft Library over many years; however, perpetually busy with my teaching work, I'd never perused its extensive archives.

On the inauguration of the library's grand new facilities after seismic renovations in 2008, I entered a handsome wood-paneled seminar room where Theresa was showing a few archived items pulled out for public display. There under a Plexiglas box lay a thick leather diary, open to a page of careful cursive script. It was the journal that H. H. Bancroft's second wife, my great-great-grandmother Matilda Griffing Bancroft (1848–1910), had written about the early years of her marriage and travels with her husband between 1876 and 1878. I'd never seen it before, nor did I know very much about Matilda beyond smatterings of family lore from my father, Paul "Pete" Bancroft III.

"You know, Kim," Theresa fairly chastised me, "you really ought to come in and look at some of your great-great-grandmother's work here. She was a writer in her own right."

Indeed she was, I would learn. Theresa's suggestion stimulated me to return that summer to begin reading and copying from several of Matilda's diaries, including those written about each of her four children, along with her travelogue of the family's trip to Mexico in 1891.

Who were all these people and what were these places Matilda described? I finally sought yet another source to learn about this family, *my* family: H. H. Bancroft's 1890 autobiography, *Literary Industries*. In prior years, I'd leafed through his eight-hundred-page memoir, but I never persevered through his erudite and rambling Victorian exegesis.

When I finally did read H.H.'s story, I was surprised to learn for the first time of his first wife, Emily Ketchum. After marrying in 1859 in her hometown of Buffalo, the couple came to San Francisco, where in 1852 H.H. had already embarked on a career as a bookseller. Amazed, I read Bancroft's poignant account of Emily's death in 1869, how crushed he was by losing her. With more historical sleuthing, I discovered that two thick volumes of Emily's letters sent home to her sister and parents in Buffalo had been bound and were stored in the Special Collections & Archives at UC San Diego.

So began my peregrinations to The Bancroft Library in Berkeley, to UCSD's Special Collections, and to other libraries and archives. Both Emily's and Matilda's words sang out to me. Theresa Salazar was correct: both these women were writers, with detailed stories and descriptions that portrayed their lives for families far away, in Emily's case, or, in Matilda's case, for her children in "memory books." Although women's private letters and diaries were generally not deemed suitable for publishing in their entirety, H. H. Bancroft himself used parts of Matilda's 1876 diary in his own descriptions of the West for his histories. He also championed the importance of saving private documents—including those of his wives—for posterity, in order to illuminate the past.

Collecting archives that would capture the story of the West became H. H. Bancroft's passion. He had left his farming family in Granville, Ohio, in 1848 at age sixteen to work in his brother-in-law's bookstore in Buffalo, New York. There, as an autodidact, he learned to love books and the knowledge they offered, an enchantment that continued throughout his life. In 1852, Bancroft arrived in San Francisco at age nineteen to work with his father in the gold fields while awaiting a cargo of books from his brother-in-law, who sought to capitalize on new markets created by the gold rush. With hard work, young Bancroft established his San Francisco bookstore in 1856, and expanded into printing and publishing enterprises.

Meanwhile, he became fascinated by the rapid changes that California and the entire West were undergoing. In 1859, he sought to prepare an almanac for immigrants still coming west by land, so he gathered all the books and pamphlets on the topic of California in his store as source material. This initial act of collecting led to a "bibliomania," as he called it. Over time, he was driven to collect every document he could find and every oral history he could capture about the history of the "Pacific Slope," from Indigenous grammars and baptismal records hidden away in Spanish missions, to the stories of early Mexican *Californios*, to early American settlers' accounts of their covered-wagon trails and trials, along with maps, posters, newspapers, government records, and much, much more.

By the 1870s, Bancroft had hired a small army of assistants to travel from Alaska to Mexico on collecting excursions. Then he hired a phalanx of writers to help compose what became thirty-nine volumes on the history of the Pacific West, collectively titled *Bancroft's Works*, each book eight hundred pages in length. The last volume of his *Works* was his 1890 memoir, *Literary Industries*, meant, as he said, to explain "the history of my history." In 1905, Bancroft sold the sixty thousand items he had amassed in his collection to the University of California. The Bancroft Library today contains more than sixty million items in its collections—surely H. H. Bancroft's greatest legacy.

When I finally picked up *Literary Industries*, I found myself enjoying H.H.'s often lively style and the analysis he applied to his own life. I commented as much one day to the then director of The Bancroft Library, Charles Faulhaber, who replied, "I've always said there's a good short book in H.H.'s memoir." His idea sparked another opportunity in that time of change for me: I edited Bancroft's memoir to create a narrative that best represented his life's journey and the labor that ultimately led to his histories and his library. The resulting abridged version was published in 2014 by Heyday Books, with illustrations from The Bancroft Library collections.[2]

H.H. and his *Works* were both lauded and critiqued in his day.[3] Meanwhile, as in many families that honor their illustrious men, the women in Bancroft's family received little attention. I had heard nothing about H.H.'s first wife and daughter, Emily and Kate, and very little about his second daughter, Lucy, by his second wife, Matilda. I certainly didn't know that either wife had left behind extensive writings. By contrast, the stories of his three sons, Paul, Griffing, and Philip, had been recounted many times over in my family's lore.

Until the most recent women's movement, we've taken for granted that our history books rarely reported on notable achievements by women. Societies have typically measured achievement in terms of public contributions to government, science, commerce, and culture—nearly exclusive domains of men—despite noteworthy but isolated women writers, warriors, artists, judges, scientists, and queens. In fact, one set of books H. H. Bancroft published was called *Chronicles of the Builders of the Commonwealth*, seven volumes about those who made important contributions to early California and the West. Not a single woman was included.

Like many men of his time and since, Bancroft thought women's role should be limited to the domestic world. He insisted that women lacked the fortitude to become writers. Only one woman ever worked in his 1870–1880s workshop of researchers and writers. He said of women's role in society,

> Hard work, the hardest of work, is not for frail and tender woman. It were a sin to place it on her. Give her a home, with bread and babies; love her, treat her kindly, give her all the rights she desires, even the defiling right of suffrage if she can enjoy it, and she will be your sweetest, loveliest, purest, and most devoted companion. But life-long application, involving life-long self-denial, involving constant pressure on the brain, constant tension of the sinews, is not for women, but for male philosophers or—fools. So, long since, I forswore petticoats in my library; breeches are sometimes bad enough, but when unbefitting they are disposed of somewhat more easily.[4]

Though H.H. refused to let women in general join his staff, he readily noted that he relied on his wife Matilda to take dictations and to help edit his work. But such acknowledgments were few.

Seventy years later in the 1960s, a wave of feminism erupted, simultaneous with interest in ethnic and labor studies and social history. As a result, we've learned how women's concerns and contributions, though often relegated to the private sphere, also have historical significance. Women's letters and diaries are ever more a source for understanding the richness of family life, the challenges of domestic work, the nature of childhood and aging, and private perspectives on public affairs.

I certainly found such rich material and more as I opened the figurative family cedar chest of letters and diaries from the wives of H. H. Bancroft, preserved by him and later generations. I thank my great-great-grandfather for his perspicacity in saving the hundreds of letters and dozens of diaries now tucked away in library archives. I thank, too, his descendants and their spouses who took it upon themselves to be sure that some of the documents stored in their attics made it to a library for safekeeping.

This book, then, focuses on the women who, in their swishing long dresses, bustled about their husbands and fathers and took steel-nibbed pens to onionskin paper and leather-bound volumes to share their own stories. In revealing words previously ignored as a result of a dominating male point of view, this volume sheds light on the nuances of women's experiences that wove the fabric of their lives and that of their children. Furthermore, these archives illuminate aspects of social history of the West from 1860 to 1890, the years in which Emily and Matilda wrote about what they experienced in burgeoning California and beyond. This book, then, also celebrates the rich archives typically forgotten in libraries but so worthy of investigation.

Part I

Emily Ketchum Bancroft: A Life in Letters

Letters that H. H. Bancroft's first wife, Emily Ketchum, wrote to her sister and parents back in Buffalo were saved by her family, as were letters from her parents, now in bound volumes in UC San Diego's Special Collections & Archives. An additional volume of over one hundred letters to Emily from her friends is stored in The Bancroft Library, called *General Letters to My Mother from Friends*.[5] Emily's daughter, Kate Bancroft Richards (1869–1945), may have had H.H. preserve these letters. They are arranged chronologically from 1851 to 1859, with the last twenty having no date (or are out of order). Only a handful come from the period after Emily became "Mrs. Bancroft" in 1859.

Emily died tragically in late 1869, at the age of thirty-five. The attending doctor believed she had kidney disease. She was pregnant, due in February 1870, but she had been warned in 1864 not to have more children following the death of her newborn daughter. Her then unnamed disease was causing her to waste away and posed significant enough danger that her pregnancy likely precipitated her death.

Bookbinder and archivist that he was, H. H. Bancroft ensured that the hundreds of letters exchanged between Emily and her sister and parents in Buffalo were mostly arranged in chronological order and bound into two volumes. A third volume contained letters from her parents to Emily. A fourth contains letters of Kate Bancroft to her father, H.H. Some of Kate's descendants ended up living near San Diego. Through the efforts of various relatives, the four volumes of correspondence from and to Emily and daughter Kate arrived at the Special Collections & Archives at UC San Diego for safe storage and public use.[6] Tucked among Emily's collected letters home was also a letter from H.H. to his in-laws, regarding the death of his newborn girl in 1864.

Incidentally, I found no letters from Emily to her husband in any of these collections. Perhaps she sent letters to him at his San Francisco business. If so, Emily's letters stored there may have been destroyed in 1886 when Bancroft's entire store burned to the ground, a dreadful loss that he described movingly in *Literary Industries*.

Emily referred to her letters as a "journal," an almost daily rendering of various facets of her life: what she was sewing and cooking; where she and Hubert traveled together or apart; how their baby girl, Kate, was born and developing; her efforts to get good help; how she coped with her terrible headaches; reactions to events of national importance, such as the Civil War; and her concerns about her parents and family three thousand miles away. Emily's letters capture the quality of life of a middle-class woman in San Francisco's still rough society in the 1860s, when the city lay at the far edge of the continent. In one letter, in fact, Emily referred to a visitor coming from "the States." We see her quiet struggles as a young woman adapting to life without her beloved family far away across the country.

Emily's letters also reveal a private side of H. H. Bancroft. In the 1860s, he was simply a printer and bookseller, though he had quietly begun his collecting campaign. Emily described his character as generous with her and others, concerned for her health, hardworking, and driven to learn.

In her letters of ten to fifteen pages, Emily noted the day of the week and then scribbled two paragraphs or two pages at a time, often between tasks. While sitting by the fire or next to an oil lamp, she offered a sense of her life for family back home in Buffalo. One letter might include a list of foods she served for dinner, the presents received from her husband, and a steamship's tragic loss off a California coast. Here she described to her parents the terrible drought in November 1864 (with her original punctuation and capitalization):

> We are having a little rain for the second time only this fall.
> H. says money never was so hard to get. You see miners
> cannot get out the gold without water. . . . The want of water
> affects all kinds of business. . . . Friday: We've had a splendid
> rain today. if it would only last a week, it would be worth a
> million dollars to Cal!

In just a few words, she conveyed life in California for her rain-drenched family in upstate New York. The "want of water" is ever more at the forefront in California today. What else must we forgo, like the miners abandoning gold, if we are to survive? As with other stories Emily told, her views on life 150 years ago are relevant today in examining where we have been and where we want to go as a society.

Emily surely did not see herself as a writer, but she did commit herself to writing, even expressing sorrow when she let a day or more go by without sitting down with her "journal." In her effort to save space on the page, Emily crammed in her stories, at times not even allowing for new paragraph indentations. Her parents also sought to save paper by writing first in one direction and then writing crosswise over what they had already written, making their words exceedingly difficult to decipher.

Given the richness of the two volumes of Emily's letters home, I concentrated on transcribing those and mined them to capture how she portrayed her life. I organized her work around themes that recur in her writing, both to examine more fully the topics that Emily herself raised in her letters and to put them in context. This approach provides perspective not only on her life with H. H. Bancroft but also on the historical place and time in which they lived. As much as possible, I've retained her original spelling, punctuation, and capitalization.

The first of the five chapters on Emily focuses on her description of coming to San Francisco and her early home life with her husband and child. The second moves into how Emily managed her household, including multiple Bancroft family relatives who came to the Bay Area and formed part of the couple's life. Also relevant to a focus on home was Emily's discussion of servants who worked for them, household finances, and the homes they lived in. H. H. Bancroft was always on the move!

In chapter 3 we see Emily taking her readers even further afield into the Bancrofts' social and public worlds, from friendships to religious topics, the Civil War as they experienced it in California, and innovations influencing their lives. Chapter 4 covers their travels, including months in Europe on their grand tour. During that time, Emily's mother died; her letters poignantly reveal the deep split she felt between her commitment to her husband and her regret over being absent from her mother's bedside.

The last chapter recounts Emily's struggle with her unnamed illness, including "the sick headache"—now called migraines—mentioned throughout her letters; the death of one baby; the fear of another pregnancy; her diminishing eyesight and increasing "wasting," all leading to her ultimate demise.

At the top of each letter, Emily usually wrote the name of the city she was in and the date, mostly but not always including a year. However, she never wrote an address on her letters and rarely noted streets, so finding out exactly where she and her husband lived has proved difficult. Some letters on which she did not note the year were tucked in with other letters and bound together, but clearly referred to events that hint as to when the letter had been written.

Emily always addressed her letters to her sister Kate "My dear Kate" and to her parents as "Dear Pa and Ma." But often the letters to her sister ended up in the volume to her parents, and vice versa. Should any reader hope to find the same letter again, I've included its date with the excerpt and indicated the recipient as a means of following the archival trail.

Part II

Matilda Griffing Bancroft:
A Writer in Her Own Right

"Her life was one continuous sparkle. Her face was as a lovely landscape, brightly serene, warmed by all melting sympathy, and lighted by the glow of intellect." With this loving description, Hubert Howe Bancroft captured the attractions of his fiancée, Matilda Coley Griffing, upon their courtship in 1876. Importantly, he was captivated by her intelligence, which became a crucial feature in the dynamics of their shared family goals and in the historical work of H. H. Bancroft.

Upon Theresa Salazar's admonition to investigate Matilda's literary industries, I delved into her many diaries and letters. They provide portals not only into the life of H. H. Bancroft but also into a deep appreciation of the complexity of ambitious women living within the strictures of Victorian society.

Matilda first wrote a diary about the initial two years of her marriage, including her ruminations on the fast-growing city of San Francisco in 1876 (population around two hundred thousand), descriptions of the couple's new life together, and stories of their journey as far north as Vancouver in 1878 on one of H.H.'s historical collecting missions. There Matilda enjoyed conducting an oral history for the first time.

Matilda's next works include the four "Childhood Memory Books" she wrote for her children, 250 to 350 beautifully handwritten pages each. Three are preserved at The Bancroft Library. (Unfortunately, the book written for my own great-grandfather, Paul Sr., is nowhere to be found.) These diaries richly describe each child's life from babyhood to age ten. Matilda also incorporated many aspects of their father's work and endeavors, the family's activities, and the many places they traveled and lived. She told stories about their homes, the public events they celebrated, and the rigorous homeschooling she ensured her children received. Also filling these pages were reports on her stepdaughter, "Sister Kate," along with other family members and the important people H.H. had befriended in his literary ventures.

Matilda's four children—Paul, Griffing, Philip, and Lucy—were born in a six-year period between 1877 and 1882. How astounding it is, then, that a mother of four young children so close in age wrote a book for each with dense descriptions of their individual developments and family ventures, all while actively managing the children's education at home in their first thirteen years, as well as family travels and some of the family real estate.

Matilda wrote a diary of the family's trip to Mexico in December 1891, called *Our Winter in Mexico*, complete with photographs taken by her son Paul.[7] Finally, Matilda created a genealogical record of both sides of her children's family, going back six generations, with extensive stories copied from various historical sources. Her dedication to telling family history went far beyond outlining a family tree but rather became a celebration of ancestors.[8]

In addition to these books, over sixty of Matilda's letters were preserved in The Bancroft Library, along with letters from H.H. to Matilda and to their sons. These records—what Matilda and H.H. reported to each other and what H.H. wrote about her to his family—help create an elaborate portrait of a woman who remained in her time an invisible power behind the throne of the grand family patriarch.

Visionary in his ambitions, H. H. Bancroft contributed to early West Coast literary culture through his bookstore, before expanding into publishing and collecting ventures. By 1870 Bancroft had gathered sixteen thousand Western Americana archival artifacts. The 1870s mark the initiation of his research and writing, which continued throughout his life, as did his collecting, making possible his history of the Pacific West, published between 1874 and 1890. Ultimately even more valued is Bancroft's then private library, subsequently a tremendous resource for historians and researchers down to the present. The man is rightly lauded for the grandiosity of his vision and his determination to achieve it.

But Bancroft did not accomplish all that alone. He had tremendous help from the "Men on the Fifth Floor" of his library—and one female writer, Frances Fuller Victor—to whom he gave credit in his memoir. There he also glowingly acknowledged Matilda in a few references, but from some of Matilda's papers we see even more strongly the vital role she played behind the scenes of her husband's success.

The chapters devoted to Matilda here recount the stories she told as she brilliantly served her husband, family, and society as a mother, teacher, oral historian, writer, and editor, and even home builder and real estate manager. One chapter focuses on her relationship with her husband; through Matilda's writing and H.H.'s letters to her, we see more of his character, contradictions and all. As we have already seen, H.H. had very prescriptive ideas of what he thought a woman—and especially a now upper-class wife—could and should do, including in the arena of writing. Yet he also prized Matilda's intellect and valued her services and contributions, not just for their family's well-being but also for his histories and real estate schemes. H.H. even wrote to her in 1887, "It makes you feel smart to be called a better man than your husband, doesn't it? Well you deserve it all and I am not jealous" (Feb. 21).[9]

In fact, through her writing, we see how Matilda provided H.H. with attractive ideas in relation to what her husband and later her sons might do with their real estate interests and careers, such as starting a "colony" for poor Italian immigrants or creating a health sanitarium.

She encouraged her son Griffing to pursue leads she provided for his business and writing. One can imagine that Matilda had to divert what would have been her own career potential into opportunities for her husband and sons. However, she never exhibited regret about such limitations, and her husband ensured her a wealth of opportunities within their marriage to utilize her capacious skills.

––––––

In pairing the writing of the two wives of H. H. Bancroft, one sees not only how differently the two women wrote about their experiences but also the difference in lifestyles they each had with the same man, because Bancroft himself was in such different phases of his life during these marriages.

In 1859, Emily had married a rather humble bookseller and stationer whose business enterprise grew exponentially over their ten years together. By 1866, H.H. had succeeded enough to take Emily on a grand tour of Europe. H.H. also became rich enough to spend a portion of his wealth on collecting for his library, including buying precious archival documents and hiring agents to scour distant sources and scribes to copy archives for his collection. However, on Emily's death in 1869 and for a few years thereafter, H.H.'s sense of purpose languished. He was not yet a public man beyond his enormous business on Market Street in San Francisco.

For her part, Emily was a disciplined and elaborate writer of letters. In missives sent home, she described the world around her as she experienced it. She was surely conscious of her audience, albeit small; sometimes she would write "Private" on the top of a letter to ensure that the recipient would not share it with anyone else, given that others were interested in her stories of life on the coast three thousand miles away.

By contrast, Matilda married a very public man. By 1876, H.H. had produced five volumes titled *Native Races*. He knew exactly what kind of wife he now needed as a man with important public and private work to carry out: he wanted a true helpmate in his growing ventures, especially if she could serve as a writer and editor for his work. Even better, Matilda also provided "dictations," or oral histories, as did some of his other assistants. But when it came to getting interviews from female members of the Church of Jesus Christ of Latter-day Saints about the history of Utah, having a woman interview women was far more appropriate than having a "gentile" or non-Mormon man do the interviewing. Matilda served.

Of course, with H.H.'s obsessive focus on collecting historical archives, he expected his wife to be producing her own, helping preserve his family's history. In complying with her husband's vision and exigencies, Matilda wrote herself into history as well, but in the private voice of wife and mother.

Would either of these women ever have imagined that their descendants would preserve their letters and books in order to create a new understanding of life during their time, how they had experienced their husband, children, community? What do any of us imagine for "private" writing—our own or others'—when we scribble in our diaries or journals, or carefully set aside letters received?

Now 150 years later, the intricacies of these two women's lives lived long ago can be glimpsed and pondered, offering a view into the private challenges and opportunities of so many women like Emily and Matilda who helped support and form the men who built the commonwealth of communities everywhere. The contributions of women once little appreciated for the talents they brought to a marriage and family can now be revealed in the stories of these late-nineteenth-century women who were indispensable to the growth of one intellectual giant and his industries.

PART I

Emily Ketchum Bancroft: A Life in Letters

Portrait of Emily Ketchum Bancroft, no date, courtesy of Ruth Swisher

CHAPTER ONE

Emily, Hubert, and Daughter Kate at Home

"I've got just the best kindest husband in the world. Isn't it strange. I like him better every day," wrote Emily Ketchum Bancroft from New York City to her older sister, Kate, in Buffalo, New York, a few days after her marriage to Hubert Howe Bancroft on October 27, 1859.[1] Emily's news on November 4 was surely gratifying to Kate, since Emily had known her new husband for only a relatively short time in person. The very next day, she would board a ship to make a new life in California, leaving behind her family in Buffalo. In those days, such a journey could mean no return.

The newlyweds took the six-week steamer trip to San Francisco with an overland crossing at the Isthmus of Panama. In San Francisco, Hubert's home and thriving bookstore and printing business awaited Emily.

In that first letter from New York City to her sister, Emily marveled at her experiences in the huge metropolis, including an exciting visit to the opera. Emily herself loved to sing and had a beautiful voice, as verified by her husband in his memoir years later. But Emily also conveyed to Kate her ambivalent feelings about the momentous changes looming ahead.

> I've wanted to write you before so much, but I had not a bit
> of time. . . . We've had a nice time, going, and seeing company

constantly.... I cannot realize that we are to set out on so long a journey tomorrow & perhaps it's just as well I do not dread it as much as I did.... How my heart will yearn for you all. Em (Nov. 4, 1859)

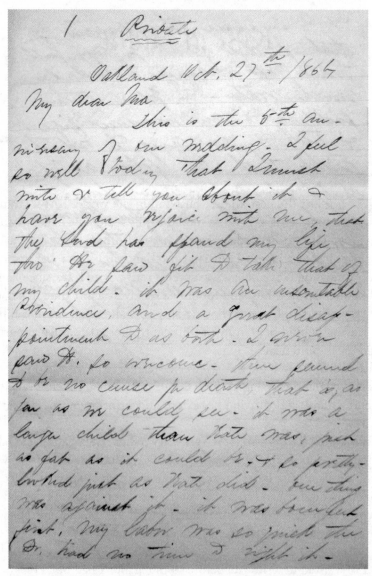

Letter from Emily Ketchum Bancroft, courtesy of the Special Collections & Archives, UC San Diego

Throughout the next ten years of missives to Buffalo, Emily, like many young brides who traveled to the still-new state of California, expressed both abiding love for her husband and deep yearning for her beloved family. Although becoming a wife and parting from one's family were conventional, accompanying a new husband three thousand miles to the other coast of the nation was not, and brought great emotional cost. Letters from both her mother and her dearest friend prior to Emily's wedding signal how wrenching her departure would also be for her loved ones.

Emily's letters touched on all aspects of her new life as a young wife, torn from home and hungering to maintain connections with her family. At a time when cross-country letter writing itself was an uncertain practice, Emily's depiction of her new life illustrates how young women in the still-nascent West contended with their challenges. That Emily wrote often about her husband's kindness, generosity, and humor offers a private aspect of the public man that H. H. Bancroft would be. Closely bound to her family, Emily also sought, through rich descriptions of her child's personality and antics, to convey her daughter's life for the family left behind.

The Man Emily Married

In 1857, when Hubert Howe Bancroft met Emily Ketchum, he owned a bookstore and printing shop in San Francisco. He had learned the business after his sister Cecilia (or Celia) married George Derby, a bookstore owner who hired the lad at age sixteen in 1848. Bancroft had followed Celia to Buffalo from their family's home in Granville, Ohio, and went to work in Derby's store.

When news of California's gold discovery captivated the world in 1849, Derby saw the financial possibilities of a bookstore in San Francisco. He sent young Hubert and Bancroft's friend George Kenny to sell books for him there. The two young men arrived in San Francisco in 1852. Bancroft worked hard to become an independent and profitable merchant, returning every two years or so to Ohio and to Buffalo to visit his family and his book supplier. After George Derby's sudden death, H.H.'s sister invested in a cargo of books for Bancroft's business. On a visit back to Buffalo in the fall of 1857, Bancroft met Emily Ketchum. He had just opened his business on San Francisco's Merchant

Street, right across from what is now the Transamerica Pyramid. He was doubtlessly hoping for a wife to match his own intellectual and cultural curiosity. His writing indicates that he admired Emily; she had an "above the average female intellect" and a "cultivated" mind.[2] He said he wooed her with determination, including through letters in his absence. They wed two years later.

That same year of their marriage in 1859, Hubert had begun collecting works on the history and geography of California to create a guide for people trekking by wagon train from Missouri. The transcontinental railroad was still ten years in the future. His "bibliomania" eventually entailed the work of numerous research assistants to help him collect and analyze more than sixty thousand items for his library and for his history of the Pacific West.

Emily in Her Family Setting

The 1850 census for Buffalo indicates that Emily Brist Ketchum's father, William (1798–1876), was himself a merchant, dealing in furs, with about $15,000 in real estate (equivalent to about $525,000 in 2021), making Ketchum part of Buffalo's upper-middle class. He had even served as its mayor (1844–1845). William and his wife, Lamira Callendar (1804–1866), had three children: Catherine (called Kate, born in 1829), George B. Ketchum (born in 1832), and Emily B. Ketchum (born in 1834).

William Ketchum also studied history. His two-volume history of Buffalo was published by the Buffalo Historical Society in 1864, to which Emily referred in her letters. William and H.H. surely discussed common interests in commerce and history, in addition to the future of Mr. Ketchum's younger daughter.

Part of the plan for the Ketchum daughters may well have been developing their intellectual capacity. Emily's older sister, Kate, was among the first students at Miss Porter's School in Farmington, Connecticut, opened by Sarah Porter in 1843 and still thriving today. In 1846, twelve-year-old Emily wrote one of her earliest extant letters to her sister, then attending the school. Emily's lively personality shows in her report that she was enjoying parties and had been told she excelled at "catching the beaux" (July 7, 1846, located in the volume of letters to her parents). In mentioning two boys whom she found particularly

GENEALOGY COLLECTION

HISTORY OF BUFFALO,

WITH SOME ACCOUNT OF

ITS EARLY INHABITANTS, BOTH SAVAGE AND CIVILIZED,

COMPRISING

HISTORIC NOTICES OF THE SIX NATIONS OR IROQUOIS INDIANS, INCLUDING
A SKETCH OF THE LIFE OF SIR WILLIAM JOHNSON, AND OF
OTHER PROMINENT WHITE MEN, LONG RESIDENT
AMONG THE SENECAS.

ARRANGED IN CHRONOLOGICAL ORDER,

IN TWO VOLUMES.

BY WILLIAM KETCHUM.

VOL. II.

BUFFALO, N. Y.
ROCKWELL, BAKER & HILL, PRINTERS.

———

1865.

An Authentic and Comprehensive History of Buffalo by William Ketchum,
published in 1864 by the Buffalo Historical Society

attractive, Emily noted, "They both are perfect gentlemen and have been through college," which suggests that she was eager to marry a well-bred, accomplished, and intellectual companion.

When Emily attended Miss Porter's herself a few years later, becoming one of the school's "scholars,"[3] she described her rigorous schedule and lessons in music, French, and astronomy. At age sixteen, she reported from Farmington to her parents: "I must fly to bed for it is after nine. We get up at half past five every morning, have prayers at half past six, and breakfast at seven" (June 2, 1851).

In addition to the Ketchums' interest in books and business, the family was also devoutly Presbyterian. An interesting set of letters indicates how those values were tested in a playful and unconventional friendship with Fred B. Perkins. One letter from Perkins, dated from Hartford, October 12, 1851 (after Emily had graduated from school), shows an intriguing aspect of women's opportunities in the 1850s.[4] In his letter, Perkins's play with language and ideas seemingly seeks to delight Emily while contravening strict convention. He raises questions about the morally ambiguous position in which Emily's interchange of familiar letters with him, a young unmarried man, could place her, especially since Emily came from a strictly religious family: "I don't exactly understand about your being afraid of me & liking me too & that in spite of yourself. . . . Why shouldn't you & I write to one another if we choose? Tho' I suppose that many people would say that is improper." Perkins admitted that if he appeared to like anyone with "more than a transitory liking," as in her case, "perhaps Mr. & Mrs. Wm. K. would make a conflistication"—a deliberate play on the idea of a conflagration in the Ketchum home should this flirtatious friendship between a man and a woman by mail be known.

Most tellingly, Perkins added:

> You speak of your being dissatisfied with the insipidity of your life at Buffalo. . . . If I were a young lady & insipidly situated I would study alone a year or two years, & then go & teach school for three years. I can assure you that after that course of training, intelligently performed, all insipidity is gone forever. . . . But I have very often reflected that young women were not pleasantly put in society now—there are many of their years which are only frittered; & I am sure if I were a woman, that I would, under present circumstances,

either cut my throat or go to teaching school, or get married
(if I could) in a month. (Oct. 12, 1851)

Perkins sharply captures the limited opportunities for young,
middle-class, and even partially educated women like Emily in the
1850s: teach school, get married, or kill themselves! Surely he jested
in saying that were he to face "frittered" years in such circumstances,
he'd commit suicide, but in so saying, he anticipates the frustrations of
early feminists in the 1860s who agitated for increasing women's rights
and choices, from speaking publicly in the struggle against slavery to
wearing bloomers.

This "Fred B. Perkins" is probably Frederic Beecher Perkins (1828–
1899), making this friendship with Emily all the more interesting.
He was a member of the famous Beecher family of ministers and
social reformers, including Henry Ward Beecher and his sister Harriet Beecher Stowe, whose novel *Uncle Tom's Cabin*, in portraying the
oppression of slavery, helped instigate white readers' passions against
the "peculiar institution." Fred Perkins entered Yale in 1846, but left
after two years. From 1848 to 1851, when he was writing to Emily, he was
working in his father's Hartford law office until he was admitted to the
Connecticut bar in 1851. Perkins became a writer, editor, and librarian,
eventually serving as head of the San Francisco Public Library.

Perkins later became the father of Charlotte Perkins Gilman
(1860–1935), the author of the protofeminist novella *The Yellow Wallpaper* (1892), concerning a woman diagnosed with hysteria, a common
middle-class woman's "ailment" of the Victorian era that committed
the patient to bed rest instead of allowing meaningful work and mental
stimulation. The novel's protagonist, confined to bed, loses her mind,
imagining she must free a woman trapped in the wallpaper. It is not
far-fetched that the father of such a writer as Charlotte would, in his
own youth, already be defending women's right to a liberated life.

Fred's playfulness and intellectual propensities are again evident in
a letter dated August 12, 1851, that sheds light on Emily's recent gradu-
ation from Miss Porter's School. Fred refers to her pending departure
for "the great metropolis of Bisontown." He continues, "<u>Are</u> you an
unsophisticated school girl?—Not <u>now</u> are you? I tho't that now or
forthwith you were 'once & for aye' emancipated from all tutors &
governors—free to roam all abroad among books & work & health-
ful play at your own sweet will." Finally, he asks, "what do you think

of the Science of Correspondences?" He is referring to the esoteric set of divine principles devised by the eighteenth-century theologian Emmanuel Swedenborg.

That Emily was able to capture the attention of this burgeoning intellectual and engender his playfulness as well as his wide-ranging curiosity about society and ideas says much about Emily herself, a young woman hoping to avoid a life of "insipidity" by putting her mind to some advantage. When a dashing young bookseller and autodidact intellectual from San Francisco entered her quiet life in Buffalo, wishing to take her off to a frontier city, Emily was primed for adventure.

The Marriage of Emily and Hubert

In his memoir, Hubert described his courtship of Emily at length:

> While stopping in Buffalo once more I made the acquaintance of Miss Emily Ketchum, daughter of a highly respected and prominent citizen of the place, and of whom my sister Mrs Palmer was loud in praise. Her face was not what one would call beautiful, but it was very refined, very sweet. She was tall, with light hair and eyes, exquisitely formed, and very graceful. Her mind was far above the average female intellect, and well cultivated; she was exceedingly bright in conversation, and with a ready wit, possessed keen common-sense. Her well trained voice in singing was one of the sweetest I ever heard. I was captivated and soon determined to marry her—if I could. My time was short; I must return to my affairs immediately. We had not met half a dozen times before I called one afternoon to say good-by. She was entirely unconscious of having aroused any special interest in me and as a matter of course I could not then make a proposal.
>
> What to do I did not know. I could not leave matters as they were and go back to California to be absent perhaps for years, and yet I could not speak my heart. I dared not even ask if I might write, lest I should frighten her. At last fortune came to my relief. The young woman had lately become deeply interested in religion, was a new convert, as she said, though her whole life had been one of the strictest religious

training. Naturally she was keen for proselytes, and evidently took me for a heathen, one of the worst sort, a California heathen. Zealously she attacked me, therefore, her eyes sparking, her cheeks glowing, her whole soul lit with inspiration in proclaiming the blessedness of her faith. I listened attentively; I could have listened had she been demonstrating a problem in Euclid, or talking of Queen Victoria's new bonnet. After a three hours' session, during which by dropping here and there a penitent word, the fire of her enthusiasm had been kept ablaze, I rose to take my leave.

"Absorbed in business as I am," I said, "away from home and its hallowing influences, worship is neglected and piety grows cold. Had I you to remind me of my duty now and then, I might do better."

"Would that I could be of such assistance to you," she replied.

"You can."

"How?" she asked.

"Write me occasionally."

"I will," was the prompt response.

It was enough, more than I had expected, better than I could have hoped for: I had her promise to write—little cared I what she wrote about—and then, of course, I could write to her. My heart was light, the barrier of conventionalism was broken.

Nor did I forget her sermon. I remembered it on the railway journey to New York; I remembered it on the steamer deck, down in the tropics, as I gazed up into the starlit sky and thought of her and her sweet words. And I vowed to be a better man, one more worthy of her. I remembered it when on reaching San Francisco I put my brains in my pocket and joined the good people of Calvary church in their march heavenward. I remembered it at the Sabbath-school where I taught, at the prayer-meetings which I attended. All through the religious life which for the next ten years I so strictly led I never forgot her, for she was with me, with her holy living and that dear love and fond devotion of which in part she robbed God to bestow on me.

In truth I was earnest in my profession both of love and of godliness; and my love was crowned with success, for I married Emily Ketchum. In the spring of 1859 I again visited the east, and in the autumn of that year my marriage took place, which was in this wise: The sacred correspondence had long since been cut off. To the parents the device was altogether too transparent. On reaching Buffalo I immediately presented myself and found the lady amiable and tractable. I told her I had come to marry her; in reply she declared herself willing, but feared her parents would object to her going so far from them. That night I left for Ohio, to give time for consideration. In three weeks I returned and asked her if she was ready. For herself, yes, but she would not leave her father and mother without their full and free assent; so to the father and mother I went. They sighed and hesitated; I desired a "yes" or "no," and receiving neither that night I left for New York. This time I remained away six weeks, and on returning, all was happiness. In due time the ceremony was performed and we sailed for California.[5]

Bancroft's sardonic remark of "putting his brains in his pocket" underscores what churchgoing meant for him, but his desire for Emily's "holy living and dear love" was evidently worth partaking in the church.

The question of how dear Emily was to Hubert, and he to her, gets a twist when viewed through the lens of *General Letters to My Mother from Friends*, the letters collected by Emily's daughter, Kate.[6] One boarding-school friend in particular, Sarah Brandegee, wrote over fifty letters. Her spirited tone suggests that Emily reciprocated. They wrote in French or signed their letters with funny pseudonyms. Sarah made her love for Emily plain. Sometime in 1851, after they had graduated, Sarah wrote, "It seems to me that I have never loved you or thought of you so much as I have since I left school." Anticipating a visit, she added, "Em Ketchum I can't hardly believe that I am going to see you Thursday. How I so long for the day to come." Such openly passionate friendships were typical of young women's lives in the nineteenth century.[7] These letters from Sarah to Emily, from age sixteen until Emily's marriage at age twenty-five on October 20, 1859, represent a wealth of interdependent connection.

Given their closeness, Sarah's letter of October 7, 1859, indicates how heartbreaking was their pending separation thousands of miles apart across the country, with concomitant weeks or months between letters. Actual traveling across that divide could happen rarely or never. So we can understand Sarah's grief when she learns of Emily's imminent marriage—all the more so since she did *not* learn about it from Emily herself.

Sarah complained, "I will not attempt to tell you how badly I have felt to hear from various quarters that you were preparing for a momentous change, and to have no intimation from you was really cruel." Having "considered us best of friends," she was shocked to hear suddenly that "now . . . you are 'in love' and going to California. . . . Was I surprised? When it came as a statement of facts, I was astounded, but not at all surprised that Mr Bancroft fancies and charms you as that you should be willing to go with him even to California." "Even to California" demonstrates how far away the place seemed, how far one might go for love. That Emily revealed she was "in love" with "Mr Bancroft" added fairy-tale charm to the image of her new life in a distant land.

Sarah continued, "I am the last one to laugh at you." Perhaps Emily had expressed her fear that she'd appear foolish for this rash decision and her swift departure. Curiously, Sarah also wrote, "if I never marry it may be because I am too earnest a devotee," though it is not clear to what. She and Emily were both around age twenty-five at this time, already "old" for marrying, and may have thought their chances gone. Finally, Sarah concludes, "I cannot bear to think of you going dear Em. I shall indeed feel myself miserably bereaved. . . . [But] I do believe he is worthy of your love and will make you happy."

The coda to this tale of Emily's marriage and parting comes from Emily's mother. Lamira Ketchum, writing on September 10, 1859, a little over a month before her daughter's wedding, delicately criticized the "hurried" nature of the nuptials, while also bemoaning the loss of her last child still at home.

I was homesick last night . . . felt so sad at the prospect of being left so soon all alone in our old age. As for your going the 20th I shall not hear an other word of it, I think we will set our own time, and not inconvenience you ourselves [which date meant is unclear, but perhaps Hubert and Emily were seeking to marry on September 20th]. . . I think there is

> somebody to be considered besides the young gentleman. . . .
> It is bad enough for him to take you off without hurrying you
> and us so. . . .
>
> . . . I am going to help you until we get ready to let you go.
> just inform your young gentleman of it—as for your being
> hurried off, I have no idea of it.
>
> Do you expect to go to Ohio before sailing. Mrs. P said the
> other day H. wanted to take you to New Haven before you
> leave. I am thinking if you are going to so many places first
> you'll not get away before December after all.

This parent's pitiable perspective on the wedding diverges from
H. H. Bancroft's description. It was convenient and perhaps even
necessary for him to hurry the wedding, as he had a business back in
San Francisco. He'd been away since the spring. But a bit of emotional
blackmail seems apparent in H.H.'s explanation of his courtship. He
recounts his multiple trips to Buffalo with increasingly lengthy absences
between them, to gain first Emily's consent, then her parents', and
blithely concludes, "In due time the ceremony was performed and we
sailed for California." H.H. skipped over the hardship of others around
him, for surely Lamira's one letter from September barely scratches the
surface of her loss.

Emily's own letters from California convey the pain of her separation, but they also demonstrate her effort to deliver stories that might
assuage her family's longing for a lost sister and daughter by regaling
them with details of her new home and daily life.

The Nature of Letter Writing in the Still-Wild West

Having accomplished his goal of winning the heart of this smart and
cultured young woman, Hubert brought her to San Francisco, a city
only ten years old in its new role as the most significant port on the far
West Coast. Emily's only connection to her family now was through
the often irregular postal system, going mostly by ship.

Emily referred to her letters and those received from her sister as
"journals," alluding to the way the two women aimed to share *daily*
accounts of their lives. Written on brittle onionskin paper, often twelve

The steamer *Brother Jonathan*, courtesy of The Bancroft Library

or fourteen pages in length, a letter might start with one date, such as Monday, March 18, 1861, and continue with an additional report, labeled Tuesday, Wednesday, and another on Friday, March 22. Then suddenly she would express a great rush to finish the letter because the steamer was leaving that very day. The steamship arrived and departed only every ten days, so she would face a long wait before a letter arrived—*if* it did—on the next steamer. These letters were eagerly awaited and prized, read again and again, including to gathered family.

As on the long voyage Emily had taken to reach San Francisco, a US Mail steamer would leave New York City for Cuba and then Colón on the east coast of the Isthmus of Panama. There, until 1855, passengers, freight, and mail would transfer to the west coast of the Isthmus by canoe and muleback. In 1859, however, Emily would have boarded the Panama Railroad in Colón and taken it across the Isthmus to Panama City on the west coast, and there caught a Pacific Mail steamer for San Francisco. The coordination of passengers, freight, and mail across the Isthmus did not always go smoothly, as Emily noted in this letter to her parents: "It is quite a long time since I've heard from you, as the Steamer did not connect last time at the Isthmus. I must now wait until the next Steamer" (Apr. 5, 1865).

Mail delivery via the Overland Stage Line from St. Joseph, Missouri, to Sacramento was also vulnerable to delay: "The overland mails have been interrupted. I presume you've not received my letters very regularly" (Jan. 22, 1863). In a couple of letters, Emily specifically noted that the interruption came from "Indian unrest," as in this letter to her parents (June 8, 1863): "I have thought I would have a letter from some of you before this, but none has come yet. the mails have again been disturbed by Indians."

How detached Emily, like many Americans, seems from news of "Indian unrest." In reality, vicious battles against Native Americans raged across the West, including across and deep into California's rural terrain, with the aim of Indian removal, if not annihilation of those who refused to be marched off to a reservation. Indigenous people were losing their lands and lives, and the resources for their survival. They retaliated against white settlers and the perceived tools of pioneer invasion, such as stagecoaches with mail. In towns distant from "Indian disturbances," people such as Emily presumed the Manifest Destiny of their ownership of the whole country, and so little noticed these tragic struggles.[8]

The delivery of mail did represent a heroic effort, whether overland or by ship, and was probably better appreciated in those days than in ours. Emily's comments on mail delivery problems accentuate her dependence on this vital link to her family. Emily reiterated her appreciation of Kate's letters, as in this note to her sister:

> Hubert came up about 11 ½ this forenoon . . ., bringing two
> such nice letters from Pa, Ma [& you]. . . . I'm very much
> afraid Kate that you've an idea that your journals are not
> appreciated by me, which I assure you is not the case. I know
> it is a tax to write every day, but if you knew the pleasure your
> journals afforded me, I believe you would feel fully repaid.
> (Mar. 26, 1861)

Letters from home also served as entertainment. Emily remarked to her parents, "H brought me a nice long letter from you last night. . . . It took me from H's supper time until I went to bed to read it. Read it aloud. H is as much interested as I am. It is real pleasant to us both to have you keep a journal & tell us everything" (July 6, 1864).

Writing letters encouraged Emily to be a storyteller who intended a sense of narrative when possible. To her sister she wrote, "Monday morning. I was going to have such a nice 'sit down' with you in this letter but so long a time has intervened and so much has happened in the meantime that I've lost the thread of my narrative" (Mar. 23, 1860).

Early in these "journals" to her sister, Emily struggled to describe her new world in San Francisco, compared to Kate's known world in Buffalo. "You are a good girl to write me so regularly and so often.... I can assure you ... a journal from home is so much more interesting to me than I think one from here can be to you for you know I used to see you every day, and knew all that was going on with you, and know all about the persons you speak of" (May 28, 1860). Writing her story required work, but valued work, to let her family know of the people and places in her new life, so that her family could feel as connected to her as she felt to them.

Giving Up the Homeland for a Husband

The joy Emily expressed in her brand-new husband even before leaving the East Coast with him was a pleasure she reiterated in years to come. Several months after arriving in San Francisco, Emily said of Hubert to her sister, "He is the best old soul.... I believe he makes it a rule to be as good and kind to me as he can be" (Mar. 6, 1860). What a relief that mutual affection must have been for Emily, given how isolated she was in California and how dependent on her husband.

Still, Emily remained uneasy about abandoning her parents. She added in the same letter, "I would have just perfect times Kate if not for the remembrance of Pa & Ma.... I never shall feel easy until ... [I have] them out here." Her campaign for her family to visit in California continued unabated.

In the same letter, Emily complained that the cold of San Francisco was somehow more chilling than the winters in Buffalo. "I think it is too cold to be truly delightful even during the pleasant winter.... I would wish myself out of it if my husband did not like it, and it was not of interest to be here ... but you must not think me dissatisfied. I like [it] and find it very much pleasanter than I expected." She struggled to adapt for her husband's sake, wishing to appear content, despite problems encountered.

Throughout her years away, Emily always manifested this longing for home, as well as a desire to help her parents. Here, still early in her life in San Francisco, she grumbled to her sister,

> You are a real good girl to write me so regularly, but you give
> such poor accounts of Pa, of their loneliness, and [with] the
> slow arrival of my letters to them, it makes me blue. I wish
> they were with me, where they ought to be, yesterday I was
> homesick but what's the use! I can't drop in and see you for a
> little while and vice versa. (Mar. 23, 1860)

A year after moving to San Francisco, Emily told her sister and
brother-in-law that she was still not entirely reconciled with her new
community. She used the word "country" as though California were
not part of the United States but rather an alien land.

> I don't like this country at all. . . . I find it rather hard to
> accustom myself with my present way of living, surrounded as
> I am constantly by so many strangers, so small a house, and so
> few conveniences. . . . Everyone has some trials, and a married
> woman should be thankful . . . she has a kind good husband,
> and happy too, [even] if her situation and all around her is
> not just what she would like. (Dec. 4, 1860)

Eventually, Emily *did* express satisfaction with her life out West,
writing to her parents in 1863,

> I know you will be glad to learn that I like it here better than
> I did at first. It seems more like home to me and I think I
> am going to be more contented than ever before. The city
> has improved very much. . . . Hubert seems very well satisfied
> with his business. (Jan. 20, 1863)

For easterners, the dry summers in California also took getting used
to, a phenomenon still true today. To her sister, Emily reported in April:

> They tell me the summer weather is now floating in, tho wind
> and dust are annihilating most [everything], it already looks
> as if it had not rained in months. I suppose it will not rain
> now until Sept. or Oct. and I think it is forlorn. If you wish
> to know my opinion, I would much rather take the cold and

snow of our winters at home and have our pleasant summers than the weather we have here. (Apr. 16, 1860)

Despite these disappointments, Emily's letters are filled with many other happy and curious details about her life in California, most especially her appreciation of her husband, Hubert. To Kate, Emily explained: "Hubert sits here reading still as a mouse. . . . His week's work is done & he's had his bath. The gentlemen all use the public baths here & [he] looks so clean as a pin—he's a good find!" (Feb. 11, 1860). If she was thrilled that he had bathed, one can imagine what so many other women tolerated!

In her day, many women married less for love and more to benefit others: to unload the burden of a girl at home who could not pay her keep, or to provide a wife to an older widower with children. Finding fulfilling romantic love in marriage was a privilege, not the rule. In fact, many women who went west in the 1850s were "mail-order brides" for lonely settlers. Some sought to escape the confines of gender expectations back East in exchange for adventure on the frontier, taking jobs as teachers or agreeing to marry a near stranger. But they could not necessarily expect love in such an arranged marriage. Emily was lucky to count herself loved. In this note to her sister discussing a friend's upcoming marriage, she concluded by affirming the love in her own marriage: "She [the friend] will love her husband, as he seems to love her. it must be a miserable life without the love. I wouldn't want to try it" (Mar. 23, 1860).

Four years into her San Francisco sojourn, Emily blossomed with contentment. She expressed her continued tenderness for her husband, his desire to spend time with her, and their shared sense of humor.

I am growing more & more contented here, perhaps it is only like other married ladies. I am contented where my husband is. He has been more with me this week, actually came up to dinner. After dinner came up stairs & read more than an hour. (San Francisco, Jan. 12, 1863, to her sister)

H. says it is so much warmer and pleasanter than at the store he thinks he will spend his time here. I tell him if he <u>behaves</u> he may. (San Francisco, Jan. 20, 1863, to her parents)

I'm sitting on a stool in the door of my cottage, waiting for my beloved. It is after 7 pm, most time for the [horse-drawn street] cars to be in. (Oakland, June 8, 1864, to her parents)

Evening: I hear the cars which are to bring my husband. the lamp is lighted & the fire burning in my room, & his slippers are waiting. (Oakland, Apr. 5, 1865, to her parents)

In setting the scene of a sewing project, Emily wittily explains collaborating on her husband's Christmas gift with her visiting mother-in-law, Lucy Howe Bancroft.

Mother B. and I have both been hard at work on the dressing gown, it will be very handsome. I locked H. out of my room tonight so I could sew. he concluded he was in the wrong house. (Dec. 17, 1864)

While her contentment with her husband would be constant throughout her short life, Emily never stopped longing for home and for detailed stories from home. She lauded her sister's letters, which Kate sometimes wrote on a visit at their father's home: "Your letters from his house are the most interesting of any, for you enter into particulars a little more. You are a real good girl to write me so regularly. I do want to see you so much sometimes, it seems as if I would fly. It is too bad we have to live so far apart. It seems a waste of time to live here" (May 21, 1869). Of course, Emily could never imagine that actually *flying* home across the country to one's family in a journey of one day would ever be a reality.

Over time, like her abiding love for her husband, Emily's appreciation of her new home state also grew. Speaking of her hope to travel to Yosemite, Emily said, "I am just waking up a little to the beauties and wonders of this country. As the mode of travelling improves, I shall go about more and <u>may</u> become an enthusiastic Californian" (June 30, 1869).

A Generous Husband

Emily clearly enjoyed offering love and humor to her husband, and he
returned her care. H. H. Bancroft must have believed in making his
wife happy by sharing the largesse of his growing prosperity. Early in
her marriage, Emily wrote to her sister: "Found $10 in my purse the
other morning which I knew nothing of. Hubert puts something into
my purse I guess every Saturday night. $10 here go about as far as $3 at
home" (Mar. 8, 1860). Emily felt fortunate in Hubert's support of her
needs and desires. She describes his offer to buy her a new dress, her
"first," she calls it. "I concluded last night that I wanted a new dress, so
I asked H. for my first dress. He seemed so willing, I shall have no com-
punction another time" (May 27, 1861). Accomplished seamstress that
she was, Emily did much of her own sewing, describing the fabric she
was working with, the colors, textures, and styles. But a year-and-a-half
into her marriage, she was happy to have a store-bought dress at last.

To her sister, Emily explained another aspect of Hubert's generosity:
his patience.

> I have good times shopping with H. which is not very often.
> I make him go to all the stores, stop at all the windows, and
> "loaf" generally. And he looks as if he was on pins & needles,
> but is very patient and does'nt say anything. (May 12, 1860)

Even today, partners who do not enjoy shopping and find themselves
stationed on the "husbands' bench" in the lobby will identify with
Hubert's forbearance.

Hubert often marked special dates in distinctive ways:

> This is the fourth anniversary of our wedding day. H. told
> me to come over & he would buy me <u>something</u>. I've been
> talking about a purple woolen dress, cloak & parasol like it, so
> he went with [me] to every store we knew of to find a purple
> dress to match my bonnet. . . . He presented me with a hand-
> some bouquet Saturday. (Oct. 27, 1863)

For Christmas in 1864, Hubert gave her a sable fur cape—an expensive gift that also indicates the success of his business. In writing to her
parents, Emily expressed a sense of suspense and surprise.

—and—and—and—a sable fur cape from my husband! What
do you think of that!! it is very large, fits me perfectly—you
know I've always wanted a fur cape & H. did'nt want me
to have one unless it was nice. I am delighted with it. only I
think it was too expensive a present for H. to make. he says
I mustn't expect anything for the next ten Christmas' but a
bouquet, that I can't have anything new again for a long long
time. It is Russian sable and so deep behind that I sit on it. It
is a pelerine cape, very fine.

Hubert also lavished gifts on Emily for no apparent reason: "Yesterday I had a present from my husband of a beautiful set of jewelry, pin &
ear-rings, [and] pearls set in a round piece of jet, with a heavy engraved
gold edge" (Feb. 13, 1863, to her parents).
    Sometimes the gift was simply a surprise to share a joyful experience.

It was a lovely day and somehow I felt like riding, but nothing
had been said about it. H. came up to dinner & I told him
how much I wanted to go. he did'nt say anything. finished
his dinner and started off. I went out into the hall to bid him
good bye as usual, found him looking out the door & there
stood two nice horses, one with a side saddle on!!

She added that she quickly got dressed and ready to go.

H. said he never saw me look so well! I believe he made up his
mind in the course of the p.m. to buy me a nice horse, saddle,
bridle, whip, & hat, the very nicest rig he can find. he told it to
me the next day as a great secret. says I'm not half so fond of
getting them now he has told me as before. (Jan. 18, 1863)

H.H. also liberally provided help for Emily at home. Although having a servant was typical in a middle-class home, Emily noted that
having a "girl" came from Hubert's desire to put her at ease. Emily
explained to her sister how he found *two* women to help at home,
though normally they had just one or none: "[We] pay them good, full
wages, they have an easy time and a pleasant home. . . . H. has'nt so

much money to spend, but he does it just to make it comfortable and pleasant for me" (May 27, 1861).

In the early 1860s, when Bancroft was just making his mark as a merchant and beginning his explorations as a collector and scholar, he helped out others as best he could. For instance, Emily reported to Kate that the Calvary Presbyterian Church they attended in San Francisco "took up a collection for the Chinese. . . . I paid $5. . . . [Hubert] said he would have put down $10 as he tho't it a good cause" (Feb. 11, 1860). As Hubert's business expanded, making him ever more financially comfortable, he continued to aid others, especially his extended family and Emily's. She wrote to her parents,

> This is a rather private letter & you needn't say anything about it. H. said he put $25 into a letter I sent off yesterday "that the Lord had given him a better business this last month, than ever before since he has been in business & he could'nt devote it to a better cause than funding you a little." . . . It is all for you. (Nov. 4, 1863)

Writing elsewhere about Hubert's relatives, Emily contrasted Hubert's sense of responsibility for his family with his cousins' treatment of their parents. Emily spoke of the Hillyers, cousins on his mother's side who lived in Auburn, California.

> Their sons have the reputation of being very rich, spend $1000 per month & live a great deal more handsomely than we do, but they don't do for their parents what they promised to do more than a year ago. & what my husband did for his parents without any promising & without saying a word to any one. . . . I do not think parents get much from their children after they are once married. One's children are a slim dependence usually I think, don't you find it so? (May 17, 1865)

Even as she praised her husband for taking care of his parents, Emily's own guilt at having abandoned hers likely came into play here.

One last example from a letter to her parents:

> You have been in my thoughts continually lately, more particularly because from letters I received yesterday I know

you are feeling badly. . . . I showed both your letter & Kate's
to H. and without my asking a word, he brought me up the
enclosed in the evening. You may be sure he would willingly
share his last penny with you. in fact, I think he would help
most any one he knew was needy, if they were in the decline
of life. I hope you will tell me just how much money you have
always. (Mar. 1, no year)

Hubert's generosity to others—from invitations to employees for
a home-cooked meal, to offering a home for his brother Albert and
nephew Will, to the best care he could provide for his wife and daughter—represents the best in the young H.H.

Life with Daughter Kate

On August 21, 1860, ten months after Emily and Hubert's marriage,
Katherine Ketchum Bancroft was born in San Francisco. Nine days
later, on August 30, 1860, Emily wrote to her mother about her "sickness," a term that pathologizes childbirth compared to our modern
celebration of it. For women of Emily's time, however, the vulnerability and the problems that often accompanied childbirth could indeed
seem like a sickness.

In fact, throughout her letters Emily referred to women's misfortune
in childbearing. To her sister Kate, who was expecting a baby, Emily
recounted this terrible, yet surely common, childbirth news.

By the time this reaches you, I hope you will have a little baby
two months old. One of my neighbors Mrs. May Woods, a
sweet woman, lost last week a little baby. She was taken with
convulsions, lay delirious for three days & in that time her
baby was born dead. She has suffered so much, poor woman!
Last spring she had very much the same experience. I hope
you may never know anything like it. (Mar. 7, 1865)

In May 1865, Emily described spending a morning with her friend
Mrs. Hudson who had had a miscarriage after waiting seven years since
her prior pregnancy. Then in July 1865, Emily reported:

I was terribly shocked on coming home to hear one of my
neighbors' (Mrs. Hawley) little boy had suddenly died, was
perfectly well in the morning and was dead at 2 pm, had a
convulsion, it is the third child they have lost, have only one
left, and are extraordinarily fond of children. I feel very sorry
for them.

Risks to a mother during childbirth and to a fetus, to a newborn,
and to very young children were all keenly in the minds of childbearing
women and their families.

Fortunately, the birth of Emily's first baby went well. At the top of
her letter to her mother on August 30 (a letter located in the volume of
letters to her sister), Emily wrote, "No one must see this but yourself.
You must burn it." Obviously, Mrs. Ketchum did not burn the letter,
so we are privileged to see how Emily reported on her first birth. She
included the role played by Albert, Hubert's younger brother, who had
been living with them for most of the year.

My dear ma—I know you would like to know all the details
of my sickness and as I feel so well now and the family are at
breakfast, and the nurse in the next room dressing herself, and
the baby is asleep on her bed, I've taken some paper out of the
drawer of the stand which is by my bedside, found a pencil
and propose to write & send tomorrow. In the first place you
know I was sick just a month sooner than I expected to be.
Went to church with Hubert on Sunday at his urgent request.
He said I needn't go again. Felt very well but Monday was
troubled all day with a diarrhea, and early Tuesday morning
was awakened by severe pain . . . in my stomach, "choleratics,"
so I call them. They grew worse for about half an hour until
I told H. if it was the baby, I should'nt mind it so much but
as it was, it did'nt seem as if I could stand it. I got up two or
three times & at last told him he must send for the Dr. So
he spoke to Albert, told me he tho't it *was* the baby & upon
examination of my garments I arrived at the same conclusion
and told H. to get a piece of oil-cloth down stairs. he fixed my
bed. The Dr. came very soon, and said the baby would soon
be here & so it was in about 15 minutes. I did not suffer at all,
scarcely after the first pains that I called "choleratics."

... Hubert gave the Dr. one of my flannel shirts in which the infant was enveloped & laid at my feet.... H. had called the girl & told her to heat water. Everything passed off as nicely as possible.

Emily added, "I wanted a pretty name, and decided some time ago if it were a girl to call it Kate." The baby thus shared the name of Emily's sister, Kate Ketchum Coit, *and* that of her sister Kate's daughter, also named Kate.

Emily wrote another letter labeled "Private" to her sister ten days later, on September 11, 1860. What makes this letter private is her report of a painful boil on her breast and thus the difficulty of getting

Emily Ketchum Bancroft with baby Kate, ca. 1861, courtesy of The Bancroft Library (BANC MSS 73/64 c)

milk from that breast. One hesitates to reveal all the details in a letter labeled "Private," except the passage where she indicated her husband's helpfulness. "The breast pump fitted directly onto the boil when it was applied and it took all Hubert's strength & my own to keep me still during that operation. Taking it all in all, we've had a pretty nice time." Humorous sarcasm duly noted!

Ever optimistic and grateful, Emily then related, "You don't know what a good nurse I've got Kate, how she has worked over me night & day. She has hardly had a chance to rest since she has been here. I feel that money can never repay her for her faithfulness to me." The role of home nurses in those days (and now!) cannot be underestimated, considering that women lacked the option to give birth in a hospital. Following a birth, most women of lesser financial means could depend only on other women in the family or dear friends. Emily even noted, "I believe I never told you who was my physician, a Dr. Whitney, some-one H. knew of. . . . I don't think he knows half as much as my nurse."

Baby Kate became a rich source of epistolary narrative for Emily, who elaborated over time on her child's first smiles, sounds, and sentences; her adorable mischief; the way she doted on her papa; and how her papa doted on her. Soon after Kate's first birthday, Emily described to her sister the presents Kate received, adding, "Hubert thinks she is a <u>real nice little girl</u>! and I think so too. he is becoming quite devoted to her" (Aug. 17, 1861).

When Kate was three-and-a-half years old, Emily reported to her sister, "Hubert has put Kate to bed. She is growing into such a good little girl. . . . She and her father get on splendidly together. She calls him Oobert . . . and they hold very funny conversations together" (Mar. 5, 1863).

With baby in hand, Emily delivered lunch to her husband at his store and then took a trip on the "omnibus" to North Beach when it really *was* a beach (subsequent landfill has made the neighborhood landlocked). Emily observed, "Kate is very fond of watching the waves" (Aug. 23, 1861).

As with every adoring mother, Emily found delight in many details of her child's behavior. On May 5, 1865, Emily recounted,

> This is my husband's birthday, he is 33. I told Kate last night
> to come in this morning & give her father a kiss & wish him
> a great many birthday-days. So she came in on tip toes before

> it was hardly light, climbed up on the bed & did it so nicely.
> She never forgets anything. . . . We had peas off our own vines
> for dinner the night I got home. And I have strawberries
> today for H.'s birth day.

At a time when children were more strictly expected to be seen and
not heard—or not even seen—Emily related how Kate coped with her
banishment.

> I told her last night that I was to have company to dinner &
> didn't want her at table. She must be a good little girl & <u>wait</u>.
> Of course she woke up from her nap just as we sat down to
> table. Such a hanging around the door & eager glances at
> every mouthful we ate, without a word being said, was quite
> comical. (June 23, 1864)

Not all of Kate's mischief was viewed with such forbearance, however. Emily adhered to the dictum "Spare the rod and spoil the child."
Following two previous incidents of Kate eating green apples and being
nearly "whipped" for doing so, on the third infraction, the threat was
made real. To her parents, Emily claimed her "hand was most broken."

> I told her I felt so badly because the only little girl I had was
> naughty. She took it rather more to heart than the whipping.
> As one's children grow older, it makes one feel their own want
> of wisdom to guide them, but there is One who can, & if it
> will only lead us to depend upon Him, it will be right with us
> & with our children. (July 18, 1865)

At times, as with this letter, Emily drew on her religious training—
more so in writing to her parents than to her sister—in speaking of
spiritual inspiration and guidance.

Finally, a letter to her sister in 1865 refers to a painting made of
daughter Kate in a hooded cape, a painting that later belonged to Kate's
great-granddaughter, Ruth Richards Lineaweaver Swisher, in La Jolla,
California:

> We've had a busy day today. Went to town with Kate to have
> her picture taken. A lady is to make a picture of her in crayon

Painting of Kate Bancroft, circa 1865, courtesy of Ruth Swisher

for Mr. Knight. . . . The lady tho't it would be easier for us all
to have an autotype taken first, for her to paint from. So Kate
need not sit but once or twice. I let her take Kate and have
the picture taken to suit herself, tho' I suggested the head &
shoulders to be coming out of a cloud! It seems she tried that
and the red-riding-hood cloak over her head too & liked the
latter the best. . . . I think I shall have some cards taken from
the autotype or from the crayon picture if it is good. (Jan. 10,
1865)

The young Bancrofts would eventually learn that Emily should not
attempt to have more children. Kate would be their only child.

CHAPTER TWO

Managing a Household in the 1860s

Emily and Hubert's Bountiful Social Life

Middle-class Victorian ideals for gender roles emphasized separate spheres for men and women. In playing "angel of the house" and caring for home and children, women enabled men to succeed in their public role.[1] Emily Bancroft provided such a sanctuary of affection, humor, and happiness for her shy and introspective husband, whose public duties were ever increasing and demanding. Hubert's ambitious goals, from running a major bookstore and publishing company to becoming a collector and director of a huge history-writing project, required the company of others. But social engagements could be painful because of his "excessive sensitiveness," as he explained in his memoir: "A simple invitation to a general assemblage oppressed my spirits, yet I would go and endure from a sense of duty." That repulsion from society made him all the more "keenly alive to home happiness and the blessings of every-day life," he reported (*Literary Industries*, 22). Emily's letters illuminate the blessings she helped create in the refuge of their shared home. Her ability to manage the home well and to provide buoyancy for social gatherings offset her husband's melancholy nature.

A river of people rolled through their lives: family members who stayed with the young couple; friends whom Emily and her husband

called on or who called on them—many related to his business interests; and those who shared meals and an infrequent party. In fact, in
recounting a story about a frustrated friend, Emily noted to her parents
how visitors from the rural countryside or from "the States" tended to
impose on city folks for a decent place to stay:

> I went to see Mrs. Davis Tuesday while in town, found her
> most tired out . . . [with] a house full of country cousins all
> the time. You know if any one has a house in this country,
> of any size, it is seen to be full all the time and any body you
> most ever heard of will come to stay with you rather than stop
> at a Hotel. (Sent from Oakland, July 2, 1863)

The Bancrofts entertained a gamut of acquaintances, from clerks in
Hubert's store to luminaries. Emily mentioned that "two young men
from the store who have no home to go to" would spend Thanksgiving
with them, along with a "Professor Wood" (Nov. 30, 1865). Emily had
described the professor from Brooklyn. "H. has asked him here. he
is writing a botany of Cal, wants H. to publish it I believe" (Nov. 14,
1865). Alphonso Wood (1810–1881) had published several botany books
in Boston and New York and apparently grew close to the Bancrofts
during his 1865–66 visit to California.

Emily later wrote to her father about the professor in relation to
Mr. Ketchum's book, *An Authentic and Comprehensive History of Buffalo*,
which had come out a year earlier.

> Prof. Wood came home with H. Saturday & has been here
> every night since but one. He has a room down town, but
> calls this his home. He is a botanist, quite a religious man, for
> which I was glad enough for we meet so few such out here.
> he has been a teacher all his life, but lives now on his botany.
> he got out your book Pa Monday evening and read aloud to
> us all the evening, and praised it up very much. And we all
> became much interested. I've read a good deal in the second
> vol. and am now reading the 1st. Prof. Wood rather laughed
> at me for not having read it all through before this, but finally
> said he knew his own children had never read the book he
> had written, but I'm not going to have it so in this case. Tho'
> I've been a good while getting at it. (Nov. 23, 1865)

H. H. Bancroft, the future historian of California, must also have been impressed by his father-in-law's scholarly historical work. In December 1864, when Ketchum's book was just coming out, Emily wrote to her parents, "I received a prospectus of your book Pa, read it aloud to H. he forthwith subscribed for six books to be sent to Albert when all are printed. We think it reads very nicely indeed."

Various intellectuals interested both Emily and Hubert, but such gatherings were especially important to H.H., given his expanding cultural and business concerns. How painful for a shy man! But these connections became all the more significant as his collecting "malady" led to ever greater research into a web of people and their stories, along with books, maps, newspapers, and pamphlets, for his eventual history of the West.

Emily scoffed at Hubert's antisocial persona. Writing to her parents, she passed along his younger brother Albert's advice.

> He advises H. to mingle in society more, says he will learn to like it. The only way to get him to do so is for me to have company at the house when he will <u>have</u> to meet them. He says so himself but if he was more social, maybe he wouldn't have so many tho'ts to bestow on me. (Sept. 17, 1863)

Once during a party at their house, Emily searched for her husband, only to find him hiding out upstairs after having escaped to his shop for a while.

> The party came off apparently to the satisfaction of all parties. I went down into the dancing room where all the guests seemed to assemble, the parlor being entirely deserted between 10 & 11 pm. . . . Looked on a short time, and came upstairs, when I found H. sitting before the fire. He and Albert had been at the store. (Feb. 13, 1863)

Emily concluded by rejoicing in the good time all (the others!) were having. "It broke up at 4 A.M!"

The Bancrofts' social life also involved various outings, including the new fashion for "pic-nics," "abundant just now—there are some very pretty places around here, hills & brooks quite Connecticut fashion.

Soon the grass will dry up when it will not be so pleasant" (May 13, 1863).

During 1863 and 1864, Hubert's nephew Will (his brother Curtis's son) lived with them intermittently. For Emily, Will offered welcome company, given her interest in socializing. Once when she wanted to attend a party, she said she'd "take Will & leave H. at home. He does'nt enjoy going out & Will is delighted with the idea" (Dec. 17, 1864).

Even if Hubert refused to go out, frolickers came to him. Shortly after Christmas that same year, Emily reported:

> I did'nt tell you what fun we had Christmas night. Monday night. Will was wishing we could have some fun. So we sent him over to the Hudsons. Mr. Hudson never goes anywhere, any more than my husband, but they came over in the rain, bringing their little boy Georgie to play blind man's bluff. We had a great time—played games all the evening & topped off with tea, nuts & raisins. (Dec. 27, 1864)

The relatives who passed through the Bancroft home always came from Hubert's side. His parents and siblings all streamed west, beginning with his father, Azariah Ashley (referred to as Ashley), and older brother Curtis. Hubert reported in *Literary Industries* that Ashley and Curtis had left Ohio in 1850 to work in the gold fields outside of Marysville, where he joined them in 1852. After a stint working as an Indian agent in the Washington territory with the Yakima people, Ashley and his wife, Lucy, moved to California.[2] Over the years they lived in various small towns and in San Francisco, including with their son Hubert and his wife or with other children.

Of the many Bancroft relatives, the most frequent household guests were H.H.'s brothers, Curtis and Albert; Curtis's son Will; Hubert's sister Mary Melissa (or Liss); and his parents, who all played significant roles in their lives, particularly Albert.

Brother Curtis Bancroft

The 1860 California census located Curtis Bancroft (born in Ohio), age 37, in Bidwell Bar on the Feather River in Butte County. With him were his wife, Louisa, 35, and their five sons: William, 13; Curtis, 11; Charles, 9; George, 4; and Harlow, 1. In his memoir, H. H. Bancroft

Ashley and Lucy Bancroft's Children

The seven children of Azariah Ashley Bancroft (1799–1885)
and Lucy Howe (1799–1882):

- Curtis Azariah (1823–1893), married to Louisa
- Celia Marianne (1826–1910), married to George Derby (died 1852), then George Kenny
- Emily Matilda (1829–1907), married to Harlow Palmer (died 1852), then James Pierce
- Hubert Howe (1832–1918), married to Emily Ketchum (died 1869), then Matilda Griffing
- Albert Little, who lived only two years (1835–1837)
- Mary Melissa (1838–1933), married to Theodore Trevett
- Albert Little (1841–1914), married to Frances (Fannie) Watts

The Bancroft Family, 1872
Standing, from left: Albert Little Bancroft, Emily Matilda Bancroft Palmer Pierce,
Celia Marianne Bancroft Derby Kenny, Hubert Howe Bancroft, Mary Melissa
Bancroft Trevett. Seated, from left: Azariah Ashley Bancroft, Lucy Damaris Howe
Bancroft, Curtis Azariah Bancroft. Bancroft Family Reunion, San Francisco, 1872,
courtesy of the Granville Historical Society

described how after mining quartz for gold in 1852, Curtis then ran a hotel in Rich Bar for a while, seventy-five miles upstream from Bidwell Bar, now under Lake Oroville. In fact, his Empire Hotel became a source of depictions of raucous life in gold-mining villages in the letters of "Dame Shirley" (Louise Amelia Knapp Smith Clappe),[3] who commented on the Empire Hotel and its amicable innkeepers, Curtis and Louisa Bancroft. Unfortunately, Curtis took his earnings from the hotel and fared poorly in a real estate scheme.

Curtis appears several times in Emily's reports of visitors to the Bancroft home. In January 1863, when Curtis visited, Emily assessed his personality: "Curtis Bancroft, Will's father, is down. Spent yesterday evening with me. I had a long religious conversation with him . . . I think a change must be going on in his heart. I'm almost sure of it. . . . He is 10 years older than H. a very large man but not very polished" (Jan. 22, 1863).

Emily remarked in 1865 on the visit of "Charlie Bancroft," probably Curtis's son, who would have been fourteen at the time, when Kate (Emily and Hubert's daughter) would have been six. "Friday: . . . Did I tell you that Charlie Bancroft was spending a week's vacation over here? he seems quite a nice boy & has I think enjoyed his visit very much. . . . Charlie is making soap with Kate in the kitchen" (Apr. 5, 1865). Making soap was no crafts project to occupy the children, but a necessary task for the household.

Another glimpse of Curtis's life comes from a note about his family's home burning down again:

> Will Bancroft has heard that his mother's house has burned down with everything in it. She told one of the boys to make a fire in the kitchen stove & he made such a large one, he burned the house up. His father was away. They have been burned out so, once before, and don't seem to mind it much this time. (July 13, 1863)

Nephew Will Bancroft

Curtis's son Will spent quite a bit of time in the Bancroft household. The 1860 census reported that fifteen-year-old William Bancroft was born in Missouri, probably in 1845. From March 1873 on, Will was in the employ of his uncle Hubert in various and often important capacities.

Sadly, twenty years later, in 1893, Will and Hubert would have an acri-
monious falling out that culminated in a lawsuit, with Will charging
his uncle with libel in a case that was found baseless in court.[4] The
conflict seemingly began with Will seeking help from his uncle for his
gambling debts, but ended with Will asking an enormous $200,000 in
damages from his uncle. The case became notorious for its scandalous
accusations against H.H., who was ultimately vindicated.

Given this eventual bitter end to their relationship, Emily's letters
at this earlier stage afford a precious peek into a time of more cordial
rapport. Indeed, she shows how indulgent H.H. was, not only of this
nephew but of the many relations and friends who came to him for
work, housing, and other help.

Apparently, Will often stayed from a Saturday night through Monday morning, sleeping on the sofa. "Will seems to enjoy visiting here
very much," she noted in April 1863. In an earlier letter to her sister that
same year, Emily said of Will that he was "trusty" and will "work just
as faithfully when the master is not there as when he is, which is more
than you can say of everybody" (Jan. 12, 1863).

Hubert and Emily had taken up French lessons because, wrote
Emily, "H. insists he is going to take us to Paris some day." Indeed,
they would go to Europe in August 1866 and spend three months in
Paris. They had even drawn Will and daughter Kate into the lessons,
so Hubert played "as deaf as an adder at table when Kate asks him for
anything in English" (Aug. 13, 1863). Apparently, Hubert learned fast.
"H learns so easily if he will only study, it would be no effort at all
hardly for him to learn, but it is hard work to get him at it" (Feb., no
date, 1864). "H . . . says he will try & study one hour every evening but
nary a word has he studied today. . . . Will Bancroft says he wants to
learn French. . . . H & I took a lesson the other evening & I found he
monopolized all the time and attention" (Feb. 2, no year).

Hubert clearly saw himself as a mentor to his nephew. In several letters, Emily described how Hubert helped provide appropriate clothing
and equipped Will for work and travel.

> Will came over with H. at 3 o'clock with a new set of clothes,
> which made him look so like a man, that even Ashley [his
> grandfather] did'nt know him at first. He is not quite 16 years
> old & is as tall as H. (Sept. 3, 1863)

A year later, Emily reported:

> Will comes over at night until he goes away. He is going on
> a long trip into the country, up into Oregon &c. will be gone
> several months probably. Holds long conversations with his
> uncle. Studies the map, is to wear his uncle's watch, carry a
> pistol, & in a conversation about clothes tonight, I hear H tell
> him to carry one night shirt & no other shirt but the one he
> has on. He is going on business & will assist his parents &
> grand-parents. (Aug 18, 1864)

Will remained an integral part of Emily and Hubert's home for years to come, until the rupture, long after Emily died in 1869. One imagines a softening effect she had on her sometimes headstrong husband and his probably headstrong nephew.

Brother Albert (A.L.) Bancroft

The same pattern of familial collaboration-turned-conflict occurred with Hubert's youngest brother, Albert Little, referred to as both Albert and A.L. Hubert put him to work, and he worked hard indeed. In fact, by 1859, H.H. put the blank book and stationery outlet in the name of A.L. Bancroft and Company and continued to expand the business under Albert's name, giving him a quarter interest in it.

The brothers' falling out occurred much later, after H.H.'s five-story building on Market Street burned to the ground in 1886, ignited by a fire in the furniture store next door. One version has it that A.L. had failed to purchase sufficient insurance on the building, and in a fury, H.H. refused to talk to him ever again, even keeping Albert's very name out of his 1890 memoir.[5]

As with H.H. and his nephew, Hubert's relationship with his brother gains complexity through Emily's letters, showing how warmly regarded and well integrated Albert was in H.H.'s home and business in the 1860s. Emily delighted in Albert's company. One day while she and Hubert ambled in downtown San Francisco, they chanced on Albert. For her sister Kate, Emily created a chummy image of the two brothers, one on each of her arms.

[We] encountered Albert, found him looking in at a few windows at some pictures, "blew him up"! and took him along, Hubert on one side, Albert on the other. We have very nice times. (Mar. 8, no year, probably 1860)

Albert worked with Hubert, and they often came home for lunch together. "Hubert & Albert came in . . ., so I gave H. his lunch . . ., and Albert assisted me in disposing of cake" (Jan. 20, 1863). Emily became close to Albert. In a letter to her father, explaining his trip east, Emily wrote, "Albert left us yesterday. These partings for so long a time and so great a distance are sad, but I believe I could get used to them" (Mar. 3, 1863).

In her fondness for her brother-in-law, Emily appears almost flirtatious. During his long absence, she wrote to Kate, "Had a nice letter from Albert today, quite a 'love letter.' I told H. so & would'nt show it to him because he had a letter from one of his sisters the day before & would'nt show it to me, so I had a good chance to retaliate" (May 6, 1863). A year later, when Albert planned a trip to Buffalo, including a visit with Emily's family, she sent photos of him and Kate to her parents.

I send along a few pictures of Albert for he is a nice boy, and I think "lots" of him. He does'nt "show off" any more than H. does. So I'll not expect you to think as much of him as I do. Kate in the picture has on her little solderino dress, the new one, which you see is white also. I've concluded not to have any more pictures taken of myself for I don't think they are very handsome. (Feb. 28, 1864)

A photo of Kate and her young father shows the little girl, perhaps in her "solderino" dress, a style of the time. No other photos of Emily exist besides the one of her with baby Kate. Meanwhile, the photos of Albert disappeared from the family album after the falling out between the two brothers.

H. H. Bancroft and daughter Kate Bancroft, ca. 1864, courtesy of The Bancroft Library
(BANC MSS 73/64 c)

Sister Melissa Bancroft

For a few months, Emily not only housed Hubert's sister Mary Melissa but also helped stage her wedding in their home in Oakland on January 12, 1865. (Emily wrote her name as both Liz and Liss.) Melissa had met Theodore Brooks Trevett of Portland, Oregon, while accompanying her parents on a trip there. Emily wrote to her parents with news of Liss's beau in October 1863, noting that Hubert had brought home "a very long [letter] to her from her <u>lover</u>. She is engaged to be married to a Mr. Brooks Trevett, and we never suspected such a thing. They seem very much in love and have ever since they first went up to Oregon."

Emily, who only met Mr. Trevett when he arrived for his wedding in late December 1864, reported to her parents, "We all like Mr. Trevett very much. he is quite a gentleman & very social, in other words jolly ... I think Liss is doing very well (only he is not rich)."[6]

With the commotion associated with the coming wedding, Emily addressed what she imagined would be her parents' concern about various family members staying with them.

> You mustn't feel anxious about me. I don't think they will stay long enough to be burdensome to me and tho I do not look forward to their coming with pleasure, still I shall try & treat them well & make it as pleasant as I can God helping me, for I know nothing I can do will raise me more in my husband's estimation. he says it is not personally agreeable to him to have them here, but it is his filial duty to treat them as well as he can & I know he would like me to do the same. (Sept. 23, 1864)

This sense of her duty to her husband and his to his parents illustrate the couple's fortitude and kindness.

Following the wedding, Emily described the simple ceremony and its meaning to her.

> Thursday evening. Well! The wedding is over and the bride and groom are on their way to Sacramento. The day was lovely. Father & Mother B. Will, Ashley & Charley Bancroft, and Mr. Kindig all came over at 12. Liss & Mr. Trevett came into the parlor at 1 pm. We all stood up, and Mr. Kindig

performed the ceremony very handsomely and gracefully, and quite entertained us all, all the time he was here. He is a remarkably agreeable gentleman. . . .

Liss' wedding reminded me so much of my own, and Mr. Kindig reminded me so much of our journey out here just after our marriage, and a letter from Pa coming just after the wedding quite upset me & after they had all gone, I had a good cry. There is something very sad about a wedding to me. It is a great change and no one knows what is before them. Liss has a nice husband I think, only he is'nt rich. . . . He has been rather wild I think . . . he is quite stylish in his appearance, and the only wonder is he took a fancy to so substantial a girl as Liss. . . . Kate insists that it was her wedding & she and Papa are married! (Jan. 10, 1865, to her sister)

Parents Ashley and Lucy Howe Bancroft

When Hubert's father, Ashley Bancroft, came to California in early 1850 to mine gold on the Feather River, his eldest son, Curtis, joined him shortly thereafter. Following his arrival in 1852, Hubert labored painfully alongside them for a few months until a large shipment of books from his brother-in-law George Derby landed in San Francisco after its nine-month journey around Cape Horn. Ashley Bancroft did not succeed in gold mining, but he liked California. His wife, Lucy, eventually joined him. "Father and Mother Bancroft" were often in Hubert and Emily's home and lives.

The potential weight of a mother-in-law's values and expectations is legendary, and Emily experienced some of that tension. However, she expressed genuine affection for her in-laws, as she notes in reporting their move to a home they had built in San Francisco.

I like H's father & mother very much, better than I do Liz, tho' she is very good. They are anxious to go into their own house, expected to get into it next Tuesday, but I hardly think they will, for the plasterers are so slow. The subject of abolitionism seems to have been entirely forgotten in the excitement of a new home & furnishing it. it hasn't been once mentioned. (Dec. 17, 1864)

Emily's letter indicates how much the topic of abolition still motivated the elder Bancrofts, staunch members of the abolition society and even the Underground Railroad in Ohio. In his memoir, Hubert told of spending one night at the age of eleven driving fugitive enslaved people, hidden in the back of his wagon, to the next station north. From Emily's report, we can imagine heated conversations about slavery and the Civil War then raging in the elder Bancrofts' company.

Emily also shared news of charming connections to her mother-in-law.

> I had a very nice note from Mother Bancroft telling me
> how much she loved me! She sent me some cheese of her
> own making. She says I seem like an other daughter!! I like
> her better than any of her daughters, tho' she is as odd &
> old-fashioned. (Jan. 10, 1865)

That Emily in 1865 found her Ohio relations "old-fashioned" reminds us that for each new generation, the prior generation, with its provincial relatives, seems "old-fashioned," whether in the 1860s or the 1960s.

Grandfather Curtis Howe

Hubert's maternal grandfather, Curtis Howe, also became part of the couple's life. He appears as a stalwart old man in Emily's telling. As the young Bancrofts were having a home built, Emily noted both the progress of the construction and Grandfather Howe's progress at age ninety-three as he checked on the house.

> The frame of our house is up & covered. H. goes out every
> day. says he ought to be there all the time. he found his
> grandfather out there yesterday, had walked all the way from
> Mrs. Hillyer's, every bit of two miles. He is over 90–93. (Mar.
> 25, 1865)

This man's sturdy life from his Puritan roots in Granville, Ohio, likely enabled him to traipse up and down the steep hills of San Francisco from downtown to Franklin Street, west of Van Ness Avenue.

A Peripatetic Life: A Family on the Move

H. H. Bancroft in his memoir described his father, Ashley, as seized by "a spirit of unrest" as a younger man. He had moved the family from their comfortable stone house back in Granville to farm in the "ague" ridden swamps of Missouri, a move that Ashley himself later regretted, returning to Granville but no longer having their former solid home. With great self-awareness, H.H. noted: "Call it discontent, ambition, enterprise, or what you will, I find this spirit of my father fastened somewhat upon his son."[7] Emily's letters indicate H.H.'s unceasing pilgrimage. She never wrote an address on her letters, but she did note the city. In the ten years from 1859 until her death in 1869, she and Hubert moved fifteen times, every year or less, for reasons of health, access to H.H.'s business, or connections to family across the country, or for sightseeing purposes.

Presumably, the Bancrofts owned relatively little in the way of furniture or other possessions in order to move quickly into a rented house, hotel, or new home. Emily often described their accommodations with lavish details over the decade of her letter writing, providing some insight into general living and traveling conditions in the 1860s.

Rincon Hill, San Francisco

The June 1860 census noted that H. H. Bancroft (age 28; employment, Bookstore), Emily (age 27), A.L. (age 19; employment Salesman) lived in the same household in San Francisco, along with Mary Sanders (domestic), 35, from Ireland. Baby Kate would arrive on August 21, 1860. The family first lived in the fashionable neighborhood of Rincon Hill in the northeast corner of San Francisco, overlooking the bay. In a letter to her sister Kate (Mar. 26, 1861), Emily expressed joy about her one-year-old baby girl: "Miss Kate is called the belle of Rincon Hill." Although a most prestigious neighborhood in the period following the gold rush, the entire hill was later razed to create better access to the embarcadero. Soon, the wealthy moved into San Francisco's hills to avoid the increasing industrialization of the Rincon area.

The Lick House Hotel in San Francisco

The rising middle and upper-middle classes often took rooms in a hotel that provided in-room or communal dining and other amenities. The Bancrofts did this at least twice at the Lick House Hotel in San Francisco on Montgomery Street between Post and Sutter, only blocks from Hubert's bookstore on Merchant Street. On January 20, 1863, Emily described this arrangement to her parents.

> [We] are on the first floor but have back rooms, but they are quite large and very high, quite nicely furnished, tho' I'm going to have my own furniture soon. I have dinner and tea served in my room, have a girl and we all, Hubert, Kate, the girl & myself board here for $55 per week which is about the same that we could keep a house for.

The Lick House Hotel was one of the beautiful buildings lost in the fire that followed the 1906 earthquake.

In 1868, after Emily and Hubert had traveled in Europe and finally returned to San Francisco, Emily, again writing from the Lick House, Hotel described her joy on returning to its comforts.

> Friday pm Jan 16th Well! Here I am, safely landed after this long dreaded journey which has providentially been the pleasantest & easiest one I ever took. We've escaped storms, the pirates, and all. . . . And I've tho't many times that prayers were doubtless offered for us during our journey, which seem to have been answered. We are at the "Lick House" have a large parlor and large bed room. . . . I should think all San F. had broken up housekeeping and gone to boarding.

To the East Bay and Back

Emily frequently reported to her family about the severe headaches she endured. Hubert also suffered from asthma. His restless quest for a perfect home was thus also motivated by preventing Emily and himself from wrestling with dust, fog, hills, and cold. Hubert's search for warmth led them to drier Alameda and Oakland, which still required daily travel by ferry to San Francisco to work.

In March 1863, Emily wrote to her sister that Hubert was looking for a "farm house on the warmer side of the Bay." On March 5, 1863, she elaborated on her desire to escape from San Francisco:

> I am glad I am going into the country. these winds are so disagreeable. . . . H will leave this hotel & take a room somewhere until I come back in the Fall. I am going across the Bay near here, so he can come every Saturday, or I can come over here. . . . I know it is most sensible for us to go to housekeeping tho' I am contented to board.

Hubert finally rented a house in Oakland for $16 a month. Emily's description of Oakland as quaint and small startles in contrast to the huge, busy, and industrialized Oakland we now know, with its skyscraping downtown. Emily's excitement over an indoor pump for water emphasizes the valuable changes to household technology taking place in the mid- to late-nineteenth century.

> I've just returned from the second trip to Oakland, without my headaches either time & H. says I begin to look better already! The result is we've rented a little cottage over there, a perfect little country house with 5 rooms. front door opening into the parlor, only one story, and a little garden laid out. . . . The house is surrounded by trees and the street consists of green grass with a nice road through the middle of it. Oakland looks as pretty as a picture now. . . . It is so country like that I think we shall enjoy it very much. . . . The next house to us on the left is ½ mile distant, a farm house, where we can get butter, eggs & milk if we prefer. . . . H & I are delighted with the prospect. It will be lonely evenings & nights when he doesn't come over but we will see how it works. . . . [It has] a pump in the sink in the kitchen & another pump just outside the back door . . . Kate has been teasing me all the morning to go to walk with her "across the Bay." (Mar. 28, 1863)

After a month in her new Oakland home, Emily struck a note of ambivalence in a letter to her parents.

Here I am stuck off in the country. I'm sitting in my dining
room window when the afternoon sun comes in, and begin
to feel quite at home. Hubert has been over every night so far
(two) and we are all delighted with country life. (Apr. 4, 1863)

Later, to her sister, Emily noted: "This is my husbands birth-day, he
is 31 years old. He was'nt coming over last night, but I teased him into
it, as I had a pair of suspenders to present to him" (May 5, 1863).

Only three months later in August, Emily spoke of another pending
change:

H. begins again to advocate our going over to the city for the
winter. after he has tried the car arrangement if he still wants
to go, I suppose we will—board somewhere & go into the
country again in the summer. I am quite counting on riding
horseback, hope nothing will happen. (Aug. 17, 1863, to her
parents)

In the same letter, Emily again tried to convince her parents to move
to California, insisting that they could be comfortable living with her
and Hubert.

We are to have a real nice house in Oakland with 11 rooms in
it. I know you would like it there. We passed the new house
yesterday. The situation is delightful. We'll have a pretty
garden, vegetables & flowers. If I could only get you here! H.
says it will probably be two or three years before we go East,
and I mean to live in Oakland until we do. I like it so much
better there than in the city. Then you can go back with us or
stay in the same house while we are gone.

I asked H. how you could get here. He said by all means to
sell the house for all you could get for it, and then come out
here with the money that is left. . . . I don't want you to spend
another winter there.

Nevertheless, Hubert prevailed in moving his family back to San
Francisco, perhaps because commuting across the bay by ferry to his
business in downtown San Francisco was ever more difficult in the

winter. On November 2, 1863, from San Francisco, Emily lamented to her parents:

> You'll see by the date that I've changed my quarters. . . . We came over Saturday p.m. not a good day to make a change, but we had engaged for the first of the month which came on Sunday. . . . I was sick with headache to his great disappointment. . . . We packed away our kitchen things and left our little house looking very nicely. I felt sorry to leave. (This letter is in her sister's volume.)

Then on April 30, 1864, Emily wrote from Oakland again, back in the same house with eleven rooms! "You see I am located in my little cottage again. . . . It seems nice to get back here again, tho' I expect to be lonely." As ever, she adjusted. By July, she explained: "Well, I am stuck up in the new house and feel so grand & have so much room I don't know what to do with myself. . . . H. said the same thing. Coming from the little house we feel as if we were in a castle" (July 6, 1864).

Emily came to love the California spring in "the country," as she wrote from Alameda in 1869:

> This is the loveliest morning and I am sitting before the loveliest window. It is open, the sun is <u>pouring</u> in, and an ivy vine, my favorite, is <u>creeping</u> in. it fairly intrudes, so that when I close the window, which is seldom, I have to push it out. I am more & more pleased with the changes I have made. I ride and ride, & have plenty of fresh air & sunshine. (Apr. 12, 1869)

The Homeowners' Dream Fulfilled —in the Boondocks

With San Francisco rapidly expanding, a "fever" to own their own home grew in the young couple. In August 1861, Emily wrote to her parents about studying house designs:

> H. & I are crazy to own a lot and build on it somewhere, it is quite a sudden fever we've been seized with and will die out

as suddenly. . . . We want our parlor, a dining room, kitchen
& woodshed on the first floor, and maybe a large bedroom
and bathroom. I can arrange all but the closets. There must be
rooms for Albert & the servants upstairs. The house is to be
of wood, and must not exceed $2000 in cost! . . .

[Later in the same letter] <u>Friday</u> H. & I rode out to the
Mission in the new street cars to see Johnny Key's lot. . . .
H. saw a lot yesterday not so far out of town as the Mission,
which he likes better than any other. . . . I tell him not to be
in a hurry but everyone seems to be buying. . . . All the new
houses have water now.

Their unfulfilled plans had to wait for a few years. Finally, Hubert
resumed searching for a lot in late 1864, so reported Emily from Oakland to Kate.

H has bought a lot a little out of San Francisco for his Father
& Mother, expecting to live on it himself some day I suppose. There is a little house on it that his Father proposes to
fix up & live in immediately I believe. I think it was a very
good move & his Father seems very much pleased. It is about
a mile from H.'s store, not too far for a gentleman to walk,
but if ever I live out there expect to have horses & a carriage!
Don't you wonder when that will be? H. says his Father &
Mother may live there as long as they live. When they don't
want it, we'll build a new house & live there ourselves. It will
be very pleasant there in time. I shall like to live there when
we are ready to settle down. (Nov. 10, 1864)

The site for this then-isolated future home in San Francisco was at
the corner of Franklin and California Streets, one block west of Van
Ness Avenue, now centrally located in the city. At the time, Portsmouth
Square, near Hubert's bookstore, was still San Francisco's central area.

H. has had two lots offered him adjoining the one his Father
has & he is cracked to buy them & I don't approve of it. So
we have grand discussions, which H. winds up by saying that
"he will take into consideration all I say, as I am very wise"!

The lots are very pretty, rather inaccessible at present. (Nov. 24, 1864)

Hubert's passion to buy won out. On March 10, 1865, Emily wrote, "Our house is commenced—wish I was more pleased with the prospect of going out there. my only comfort in the matter is the closets."

Closets! Emily's letter hints at a benefit in modern life now taken for granted. In 1865, clothes were generally stored in an armoire or wardrobe. Seeing the value of the new construction, Emily defended closets to all scoffers. "H. took me to see an architect about our new house. they tried hard to talk me out of my closets, but I told them they must'nt take an inch off them. they th't it covered a good deal of ground, but as long as we've got the ground we may as well use it that way" (Feb. 13, 1865). She even laughed to her parents that her mother-in-law wondered what she would put in all that extra space. "I have twenty drawers in closets.... Mother B wonders what I'm going to fill them with" (Oct. 17, 1865). Emily then proceeded to explain in gleeful detail her drawer plan.

With each letter, Emily reported on the home-building process.

We shall go out there tomorrow. it is about a mile from the store, almost in a straight line from it out towards the Ocean. it is more the country than it is to the Missouri. have you a map of San Francisco? We have two lots just alongside of Father Bancroft's. We are building on the back lot, corner of California and Franklin Sts. There are two lines of cars within two or three blocks of us. (Mar. 20, 1865)

By September, they were making plans for moving in, though Hubert wanted their servant, Adelaide, to help with the move and not let Emily do any physical work, for fear of instigating a headache.

H. says he is going into his own house Oct. 1st anyhow. he wants to take me up to Auburn the 27th of Sept. [to stay with his mother's relatives during the move] which comes on a Friday. he will stay thru over Sunday & come home, leaving Kate and myself to stay a week or two. Adelaide says she can move without me, and he wants me to be away, and I'm not sorry. (Sept. 14, 1865)

The new home included a windmill and indoor water use, as Emily rejoiced.

> I came back Saturday to my new home. the house is very nice, tho' the rooms are not large, and the windows are the largest I ever saw. I found everything in nice order & was surprised with a new lounge. it is green & opens for a bed. H. bought it particularly for Kate.
>
> Wednesday evening: Our windmill was finished only tonight and we have the water in our bathroom & throu the house for the first time tonight. . . . We were all delighted with the new acquisition. the ceilings are all high in the lower rooms, making my parlor very nice to sing in. the house seems nicely built and painted, is real convenient, and we are very much pleased with it. (Oct. 17, 1865)

She noted that rooms were set aside for Albert and a library.

At that time, living a mile west of Montgomery Street in San Francisco meant a home in the sand dunes. Emily described Hubert's efforts to conquer the sand. "H. is having soil & manure put on the ground here, worked himself until 10 am & came home with me at 2 pm" (Oct. 17, 1865).

If Emily thought she had lived far away in Oakland, she still contended with living far away in the dunes high above downtown San Francisco. She noted that her friend Mrs. Shipman had such difficulty getting to the Bancrofts' remote house up the hill (and no sidewalks yet either) that Emily invited her to spend the night and go back downtown via coach in the morning.

As ever in San Francisco, access to water presented challenges.

> H. told me to tell you that in digging for the well, they dug through 25 feet sand, 6 ft. clay, & 25 ft. soft rock. & in two or three days after the well was dug had 25 ft water. We've had no winds since I've been here & now the sand is all covered with soil & manure. The men are now at work on Father B's part of the yard. The sand did drift very much in the summer, but it is covered now. (Nov. 14, 1865)

The troubles with the well and the windmill did not let up. "You must rejoice with me that our wind-mill is working for first time in two weeks, and we've had no water at all, hot or cold" (Feb. 1, 1866).

Despite the sand, the couple started a garden. Emily exulted when new sprouts arrived. "H. brought me a trowel & some flower seeds tonight." Later in the week, Hubert sent over many garden "slips," "quantities of roses, geraniums, fushias, honeysuckle, verbenas, australian pea," and "it took me the morning to tell the men where to put them." She added, "in time the grounds will be very handsome" (Feb. 1, 1866).

Years later, Hubert was preparing to build not only another new home for them but also a magnificent building for his store and publishing house. Here follow several of Emily's references to these construction projects from 1868 to 1869. Emily's contributions in meetings with architects, getting advice, and even giving advice are notable.

> H says the city never looked so unattractive to him as now.
> Still we are here. The materials for his house are all ready &
> he will go on & build & remain here four or five years, when
> I think Albert will take the house and business & we will go
> away for good. H. wouldn't build at all if he had'nt purchased
> so many materials. And he is not going to build out where
> Albert is living. He is going to buy a lot nearer town we do
> not want to go out there to live ever again. There are no side-
> walks yet, and so few improvements that it will take ten years
> to make it very accessible. When Albert leaves, H. proposes to
> paint the house & put it in good repair, and have his Father
> and Mother live in it. Until his new house is done, he would
> rather live at this hotel than to keep house anywhere. (From
> the Cosmopolitan Hotel, Nov. 10, no year, but probably 1868,
> as with other letters here)

A month later, Emily accompanied Hubert to the homesite: "We are going to take an architect out to one of the lots tomorrow morning" (Dec. 10, 1868). Days later, she explained her idea for situating the house:

I suggested that the plan should be turned around, to face another street, which little suggestion, tho' involving great deal of trouble, they both declare is being followed out.

Later I was interrupted in my narrative by a man, he came to see H. about some property for a store, for which H. has been negotiating ever since he has been back. I believe they have succeeded. (Dec. 13, 1868)

Emily soon reported, "H. has bought his business property, $91,000. I enclose a notice" (Jan. 10, 1869). This was the site of Bancroft's new building, 733 Market Street, which opened in 1870.

In *Literary Industries*, Hubert also reported on the enormity of his building projects:

In accordance with my purposes, . . . historical and professional, in 1869 I began building. Already I had in contemplation a costly dwelling, parts of which had been constructed in England and at the east, and shipped hither from time to time, till a great mass of material had accumulated. Soon a hundred men or more were at work. (67)

Unfortunately for Hubert, Emily would die at the end of 1869, crushing his delight in the new home that still awaited completion.

"Girl Hunting": Affording, Getting, and Working with the Help

In early San Francisco, managing a modestly well-to-do household, even a small one, included learning how to keep the books and the help. These themes appeared frequently in Emily's letters.

Several months after her arrival in San Francisco, Emily made piquant observations on the comportment of "the ladies" in her new society and the challenges they faced with the city's hills.

I don't know why it is that all the ladies here seem so dragged & tired out. I believe it is the hills (they are very tiresome), poor servants, large families, & lots of children. You can't go anywhere here without toiling up a steep hill somewhere and

> when a lady returns from a trip down town, she is tired most
> to death, and instead of being able to rest, she generally has to
> tend a baby, look after an inefficient girl, with a tremendous
> pile of sewing staring her in the face. So she feels that she has
> no time to rest, and all the married ladies here look as if they
> could last but a day or two longer. All have relatives living
> with them. One of my neighbors Mrs. Flint has two broth-
> ers & a cousin of her husbands living with her, and she has
> 15 or 16 shirts in the wash every week, and her cook does it
> all alone. She has the largest house in the neighborhood and
> 3 children, keeps only two girls. . . . This is quite a harrange,
> but it is really funny to see how much trouble there is in the
> world. (Mar. 21, 1860)

Emily vividly pictured the toil for women lacking help at home, and the toil of the women who did the physical labor. Some of these troubles would also be Emily's, but she rarely showed much frustration.

Common themes in Emily's letters are the cost and supervision of servants. The standard salary seemed to be $25 or $30 a month, with the expectation that the "girls" would live with the family for most of the month, going home only for a couple of days. The work of a servant (or two) in the Bancroft household principally entailed cleaning, shopping, washing, and cooking, with intermittent care of daughter Kate. Women's work at home involved many physically challenging tasks: pumping and carrying water, washing clothes by hand, toting baskets of wet clothes and hanging them to dry, ironing with heavy irons heated from a hot stove, beating rugs, and sweeping the whole house.

Help was crucial when Emily suffered from headaches that forced her to recline for hours until the pain subsided. Some letters indicate that Hubert insisted on Emily having help, precisely because her health could be fragile, while at other times she was fit enough to put in a garden and harvest the family's vegetables. Although independent, Emily knew she must rely on a "girl," which was indeed the norm for a middle-class family. She wrote to her mother, "I was thinking today how dependent we are upon our girls for quiet [and] every day happiness. I know very well that the whole aspect of this pleasant little home would be changed if I had a poor girl" (May 19, 1863).

Emily did complain of the girls' inadequacy every now and then. She exhibited an especially strong prejudice against the Irish, such as in this report to her parents concurring with another woman's criticism: "says she can't have an Irish girl around . . . they do nothing . . . but eat & sleep" (Apr. 7, 1863). Her prejudice against Catholics was even stronger. To her sister, Emily complained, "It is practically impossible to get a Protestant servant in this country" (Aug. 21, 1861).

The 1850s and 1860s saw an influx of European immigrants, particularly the Irish escaping the potato famine of 1845–52, as well as a northern influx of African American freed men and women during and after the Civil War. These migrants and immigrants meant that private households became a testing ground for deeply ingrained notions about race, class, ethnicity, nationality, and religion. Emily was more tolerant of African Americans, though her use of now disparaged terms, such as "darky," and her stereotyped assumptions cause us to cringe today.

Tenuous bonds could form between an employer and a servant, though tested by an imperious personality and rigid value system on the part of a "lady of the house," as Emily shows herself to be here.

Well! I've been and gone and done it! My Annie did'nt like it at all the other day because I asked how long a certain girl had been in the kitchen, and [she] has been rather [sullen] ever since. So this morning I had a talk with her, and told her I did'nt think she had been very respectful to me lately. And she told me that she did'nt like my asking her what [she] did the other morning, tho't I had no right to &c. I told her I should certainly ask any one who lived with me any question I tho't proper, and I had a right to do so. And if she did'nt like it, and could'nt give me civil answers, she must leave. She was rather imp[ish] at first, but improved considerably, is to take until tomorrow morning to decide whether she will go or stay and behave. (Apr. 16, 1860, to her sister)

The extent to which the "served class" depended on the "serving" class is manifest in this excerpt about the various chores of two women who worked for them.

[We have] a great Irish woman, but a protestant, and seems
like quite a nice kind of person. . . . As H & I both liked her
looks, we took her, tho' she insisted on $30 per month. Said
she could earn it. So she does all the work, takes care of Kate.
. . . You know Mrs. King does the washing. So I have nothing
to do but work in the garden. (Apr. 4, 1863)

Emily's religiosity also came into play, for she expected her servants
to abide by the same edicts that governed her own life. Aside from not
putting up with "disrespect," Emily also refused to allow visits from
male friends on the Sabbath, for which she reported having fired "a
girl" in May 1863. A year later and searching again, Emily noted that
she required her servant to pray with them.

A colored woman living in the neighborhood sent me one
this P.M. whom I've engaged. She is a Catholic but will come
in to prayers. I still try to make that a rule. So the old experience of girl hunting has commenced again. I dread it but
cannot be exempt more than the rest of the human race. This
girl is to do all my work & sew besides if she has time. She
seemed glad of the place. (Apr. 17, 1864)

When that employee left a few months later, Emily advertised for
another.

Don't you want to see an advertisement of mine? I wrote it
this morning while H. was finishing his breakfast. It appeared
in tonight's paper. I met a colored man in the st. the other
day. I told him if he heard of a good cook to send her address
to the store and I would come and see her. (Aug. 2, 1864)

The advertisement listed H. H. Bancroft's Montgomery Street store
address.

Protestant Woman (Colored or white) who is a good cook,
washer and ironer—neat, willing and competent to do the
work of a small family—may find a situation by calling at
609 Montgomery street between the hours of 10 and 12 am.
Wages $30. Good references required.

When the Bancrofts lived in "rural" Oakland in 1864, Emily explained that a valued African American woman, Adelaide, worked for them there, though her own family was in San Francisco.

> My colored woman wants to go so much that I've offered her higher wages to stay. don't know but I was foolish, but she is so industrious & efficient & H likes her so much, that I hated to have her go. She does'nt like the country. Says she likes me! & would like to live with me if I was in the city &c. Butter is up to 75¢ a pd. (Sept. 1864)

Adelaide stayed with Emily and Hubert through December 1865, a relatively long period. Emily initially reported in several letters to her parents that she found Adelaide very good looking and hardworking (Aug. 8, 1864). Typical of a relationship between a white middle-class woman and a working-class Black woman, Emily said little about Adelaide's life in her letters home, except how supportive Adelaide was to Emily. Over time, Emily recounted how Adelaide had grown on her, as had her reliance on Adelaide. A month into her stay, Adelaide wanted to go home to her family; Emily did sympathize with her. "She hasn't staid out of the house but once since she came & I don't wonder she is lonely" (Sept. 12, 1864). In this letter, Emily again noted her servant's needs when Hubert returned too late for Adelaide to get off. "Adelaide did'nt get off to town tonight, bore the disappointment better than I did" (Sept. 14, 1865). But Emily's needs prevailed.

When her headaches hit, Adelaide was a ministering angel. "I was sick in bed yesterday with headache. Kate & Adelaide were as good as they could be. Adelaide is quite motherly" (Apr. 5, 1865). Adelaide ran the household when Emily was incapacitated. Emily continued writing that same day.

> Monday pm This is wash day. I've not laid eyes on Adelaide since breakfast. She goes out to the wash house soon as we sit down to breakfast, gets some clothes on to boil before she comes in to do up the work, then I don't see her again till washing is over. & she appears to empty the slops, looking like the "old Scratch" [a reference to the Devil].

In August 1865, Emily shared a story of how Adelaide was getting everything ready in the kitchen, and how capable she was, but then she dropped a teapot with steaming tea in it. "She looked so scared & so mad, I could'nt help laughing" (Aug. 12, 1865).

As Emily relied more on Adelaide, she finally released her from her own religious expectations.

> Adelaide will have been with me a year on Saturday & I've become quite attached to her. I wish I had the least religious influence over her. it makes me feel badly when I think of it. I can't get her to go to Church & very seldom to prayers. (Aug. 14, 1865)

However, a change in the relationship with Adelaide developed when the Bancrofts moved to their new home far away in the San Francisco dunes. Emily conveyed to her parents the moving plan. Hubert would stay in San Francisco to supervise both his business and the building of their home.

> Had two letters from my husband today—he writes me every day. but I told you about the earth-quake—H. says it cracked the plastering badly in our house & knocked down shelves of books at the store.[8] he says Adelaide does'nt like the new location it is so far off. So I shall let her go if she wants to. he says she has not been very efficient cleaning and regulating. they have such nice China boys here that I'm quite disposed to try one. they are not so independent as the servant girls. (Oct. 9, 1865)

Now entered yet another ethnic group, with the derogatory label "China boy," to serve the elite.

Emily hoped to keep Adelaide, even paying her more, but by December, the debate was over.

> Adelaide has finally made up her mind that she must go. her husband wants her at home, he is staying there now all alone, so I've been out today girl-hunting.
> Saw some Irish girls just enough to make me sick, then I tried to find a colored girl & was so much better pleased tho'

I did'nt succeed in finding one, that I think I'll not take any
until I can get a colored girl. (Dec. 11, 1865)

A Mr. Dolan brought over a girl he knew. "She is not very young,
an Irish Catholic, but seems smart and willing" (Dec. 26, 1865). Finally,
a girl named Margaret came into their lives. "I like my new girl very
much, she is not as good a cook as Adelaide, but is more under my
control" (Jan. 11, 1866).

No Idle Hands in This House

Emily Bancroft was privileged to rely on a servant or two, but her letters
indicate she also kept busy with her own tasks. Even with help, Emily
shopped, prepared food, and sewed and mended the family clothes,
among other chores. Early in her marriage, she reported to her sister
what her Monday morning was like, a typically labor-intensive day for
women. "This has been a busy day as usual, gathering up & mending"
(Oct. 16, 1863). She elaborated on her chores—and her tasty reward:

> This is a busy day with us, as with all house keepers I suppose.
> I mended the clothes for the wash this morning . . . and a pair
> of pantaloons for Hubert. Picked up and cleaned up gener-
> ally, changed my clothes, read my chapter and came down
> to lunch. . . . As you like me to be <u>particular</u>, I went into the
> cellar, spread me a slice of bread and butter, brought up some
> dried applesauce, bread cake, and a dough-nut which with a
> glass of water composed my lunch, sat down before the fire, as
> it is a dark windy day to read a paper. (Apr. 16, 1860)

For anyone wishing to discover the palate of a middle-class home
in the 1860s, Emily's letters are rich with gustatory details. She may
have whetted her sister's appetite with this menu: "We had for dinner
boiled lamb & caper sauce . . . peas, new potatoes, broiled kidneys, boild
Indian pudding & coffee & cake" (May 12, 1860). This menu for a "2
pm dinner," the main meal of the day, sounds lavish: "I had steak, duck,
potato, pickles, celery, cranberry pie, nuts, raisins, apples, cake and tea"
(Jan. 20, 1863).

Birthdays were typically celebrated by an especially nice, though not extravagant, dinner at home, without guests. Fresh fruit when available complemented celebrations. Presents were minimized. One year, Hubert received a new pair of suspenders for his birthday, while Emily was given a new parasol.

Emily enjoyed sewing and often reported on outfits she was creating, though sewing was also time consuming. "I'm wishing I had a kind friend (in other words a husband) to take a horseback ride with me, tho' my week's sewing isn't quite finished" (Sept. 19, 1863). Dresses were designated for different occasions, such as her black silk dress. "It seems good as new, and I wear it a good deal. It is my favorite dress, and Hubert's too. I wear my blue delaine at home most of the time & it is a pretty dress. My poplin is serviceable too. It is to be my spring dress" (Mar. 23, 1860).

One valuable item in her wardrobe appeared in a story about a fire that broke out at a hotel in New York City on the family's way back to California in 1862. Emily made fun of the women who had gathered cherished belongings in their arms or in great trunks they tried to drag to safety. One had a greyhound dog in her arms and an ermine around her neck. "H. made me get up and dress while he went down to see. Then told me to carry some small articles of most value down. So I secured my new French corsets, [and] my watch" (Dec. 11, 1862).

While Emily and Hubert both seemed to enjoy keeping her in nice clothes, he was less particular and very thrifty regarding his own clothing. Three years into their marriage, Emily told her sister,

> I went down . . . with my husband to buy a new suit of clothes. You know he chooses my things & I try to return the favor. He wears his clothes until they are threadbare & I've been teasing him to get a new business suit. but he always has some excuse. he is now wearing the coat he was married in! (Jan. 12, 1863)

Home Pastimes

The family shared various pastimes, including music. Emily sang with a talent that Hubert remarked on when he made her acquaintance, noting in his memoir: "Her well trained voice in singing was one of the sweetest I ever heard" (62). Hubert supported her voice training with lessons and eventually a piano at home. In her letters to her parents, though, Emily apologized for the time and money spent on these worldly pleasures—counter to her religious upbringing. "I don't know what you would say to my singing but H. thinks I have already improved so much. he is quite delighted. you mustn't feel badly about it, but I can most make a trill" (June 8, 1863). Later, Emily sought to justify these lessons.

> I don't approve of them myself. tho' if I was young, I should do all I could with my voice. but now I think it foolish & expect to take only a little while. H. admires the style of sing-ing very much, and he is the only one who will ever hear me. I am alone off out here in the country without much to do. (Aug. 3, 1863, to her parents)

Finally, Emily felt she must abandon the lessons. "I think with you that singing lessons do not help me to grow in grace, tho' H. thinks [well of] any improvement or advancement of that kind." She added, "I don't think it would be right to take the time now I'm married. . . . I shall stop as much to please you as anything" (Aug. 13, 1863). Emily's parents continued to influence her from thousands of miles away.

Emily passed the gift of a beautiful voice on to their daughter Kate, who, as a young adult, sang in community musicals.

Reading was, of course, a significant pastime for the couple, from books about gardening and newspapers, some sent from Buffalo, to novels and biographies. Emily reported to her sister that she had read George Eliot's novel *The Mill on the Floss*, a feminist text for its time about the unfair advantages boys had over girls. Emily sent recommen-dations for her parents, such as *Life of Thomas Chalmers* (1780–1847), regarding the conversion of this Scottish minister, thus serving as a conduit between her in-laws, also pious, and her parents for religious reading. "I gave Mueller's 'Life of Trust' to Mother B. to read. She is delighted with it, has read the Chapter on Stewardship three or four times. She is 'carried away' with anything just like you Ma" (Dec. 27, 1864).[9]

Absent other kinds of home entertainment, reading aloud was a general pastime in those days. "We are reading Mrs. Thrale's biography" (May 27, 1861), referring to Hester Thrale Piozzi (1741–1821), a British diarist, supporter of the arts, friend of Samuel Johnson, and fascinating society woman in her time. To her parents in 1866, Emily wrote of another shared tome. "We've commenced reading together a new book 'A Summer in Skye.'" This 1865 book described a journey in Scotland by poet Alexander Smith (1829–1867). The couple enjoyed books about travel, especially in light of their plans to travel to Europe. "[Hubert] has brought over Kallo's travels in Europe & we are all reading them and find them quite entertaining," she mentioned to her sister in October 1864.

Others joined in reading "performances," too, as Emily noted to Kate. "Hubert is reading Napoleon's book about Julius Caesar to his grandfather" (May 19, 1865).[10] And sister-in-law "Liz is reading a story to me 'Emily Chester.' I think H. sent it to me because of its name" (Nov. 10, 1864). Anne Moncure Crane Seemüller's 1864 novel presented a story in "a psychological mode" about "a beautiful and accomplished young woman," her husband, and "a lover."[11] Emily took advantage of such cultural exposure available through these books, despite embedded religious and social strictures.

A key pastime was their "epistolary occupations," as Emily called them. Shortly following her arrival in San Francisco, Emily told her sister that Hubert "has written at home every day this week until today. Yesterday we wrote 89 letters!" (Mar. 8, 1860). She herself had written twenty-six letters two days earlier.

By 1860, H. H. Bancroft had begun collecting materials that would serve as sources for what would become his history of the Pacific West. His inquiries, replies, and regular business all required a plethora of communications.

> It is nearly 10 o'clock. Hubert has been sitting here writing all the evening, while I occupied myself at the piano when I should have been writing, but I'm getting awfully sick of those business letters between you & I. (Mar. 23, 1860, to her sister)

Emily lets us peek into Hubert's relationship to the world while he was incubating his visionary work.

When Hubert's writing at home took precedence over hers, Emily lodged a quiet complaint. "H. uses his writing desk so much lately I'm obliged to write when he is away & my usual time was just after dinner"

(July 12, 1865). This competition for space was repeated months later. "My husband sits here 'respectfully suggesting' that I do my writing in the day time" (Sept. 16, 1865, to her sister). But Emily also goaded Hubert when it got late. "H. is writing in the parlor & I'm in my room before the fire, occasionally reminding him that it is very late & so it is" (Mar. 25, 1865).

Work Comes Home

Emily noted the ebb and flow of Hubert's work, and how his business affected their home life and opportunities to enjoy time together. "H works a great deal harder than he used to, and I think enjoys it more too" (Aug. 23, 1861). In all eras, spouses return home and pour out anecdotes of their day. In Emily's letters, we glimpse what had transpired at her husband's bookstore and publishing house.

Hubert literally brought his work home by inviting employees to share a meal or to join a Bancroft party. Emily mentioned receiving an unidentified present from Mr. Knight, "the young man in the store who makes the Almanac" (Jan. 1, 1864). Hubert himself mentioned William Knight as preparing the Almanac for 1860 and pulling together all the books on the West that were in the store. That event began his collecting mania, for once Bancroft saw that he had "some fifty or seventy-five volumes," he then sought to grow the collection.[12]

Regarding the men in his store, Emily shared her concerns for their well-being:

> Did I tell you one of the young men in the store was sick with a fever? H & I went to see him the other day. he & his mother came out recently from N.Y. She is quite dependent upon him, a nice looking person. . . . H. says tonight the Dr. has given up doing anything for the young man. (Mar. 25, 1865)

In her next letter, Emily mourned the young man's death.

> We've felt quite anxious all the week about "Charlie Hyde" the young man in the store. tonight H. tells me he is dead. it makes us both feel very badly for H. thinks he was

> overworked. they have all been working very hard, moving &
> arranging goods in the new addition & this young man was
> unaccustomed to such labor & probably had the fever in his
> system. (Apr. 5, 1865)

In the same letter a few days later, Emily told her parents that they
had attended Charlie Hyde's funeral, adding, "his poor mother, a uni-
versalist, will be left alone."

The hard work at the store was a recurring theme. The store operated
six days a week, ten hours a day. "H. has a new bookkeeper, a young
man from the country. I asked why he always got that kind. he says
city boys won't work. he thinks he will have more leisure now" (Jan.
22, 1863). Hubert's own farm-boy work ethic might have informed his
hiring practices. The press for good workers was relentless. A year later,
Emily reported: "H. says he has'nt help enough in the store. Wanted to
know if I know of any good boy. . . . He says they are all overworked"
(Jan. 4, 1864).

With a wife his intellectual equal and a very capable manager,
Hubert eventually asked her for a little help with his work. However,
she found the task he assigned her boring. "I've been helping H. read
& correct a catalogue until I wish the book business [were] in France"
(Nov. 14, 1865).

Hubert's business flourished, so he leased more space. "[H.] has succeeded in hiring the whole of the building he is in. Making a very large
addition to his accomodations [*sic*], more than as much again room, but
there are many alterations to be made" (Feb. 27, 1864, to her parents). A
year later, Hubert expanded once again.

> H. is getting very nicely fixed at the store. he has now eight
> large rooms full of goods, some of them very large. the one
> where he keeps his law & scientific books is as large as my
> whole house, has pillars in it & French windows each side,
> South & North, letting in the sun all day. It is very pleasant
> there. I tell him I shall bring over my sewing. (Mar. 25, 1865)

However, unbeknownst to them, in 1865 a two-year-long recession
was just beginning. Hubert soon let Emily know business was suffering. "Kate and I went to town yesterday p.m. bought two table clothes.
. . . H says times are so hard I must'nt buy anything more. Everyone is

complaining. there seems to be a perfect stagnation in business" (June 13, 1865). By then Emily knew how to guard the family coffers.

Innovations Brought Home

Learning about 150-year-old life-changing new things can be fun, especially items we now take for granted. After learning about borax in the *Observer* in November 1863, Emily wrote to her parents about its wonders. Even the word *laundry* was new to Emily; she learned it from a wash lady after Hubert and a helper created "quite a nice wash room, 'laundry' Maria calls it" (July 6, 1864).

Convenient indoor plumbing in their new home thrilled Emily. Yet, as with all new homeowners, the Bancrofts discovered problems, such as a lackluster windmill for pumping the water.

> A strong wind came up to my great joy as we had emptied
> our water tank & there was'nt wind enough to start the mill
> again. someone had to go up and turn it by hand to get a drop
> of water, but it blew all night & the tank which holds 4000
> galls was half full this morning, just in time for the washing.
> (Nov. 6, 1865)

Emily told her parents of various life-improving gadgets. "Our new stoves work beautifully. The arrangement for heating flat irons is a great institution & the oven bakes very nicely" (July 6, 1864). Also, until the 1850s, evening light depended on candles or whale oil. Emily reveled in the 1850s invention of kerosene lamps, more available to middle-class homes by the 1860s. "You don't know what a good light kerosene lamps give" (Apr. 4, 1863). Soon, she literally underlined its magnificence. "H. sits here reading by the <u>kerosene lamp</u> & Kate is in bed talking to herself" (June 8, 1863). By August, she exulted, "My husband and I are sitting by the bookcase desk in the parlor. We indulge in <u>two</u> kerosene lamps now, instead of one, as in the little house."

In 1853, Isaac Merritt Singer created the first mass-produced sewing machine, which dramatically changed the lives of those who had sewn by hand. Emily first noted the machines at the home of a seamstress who owned one. Then Emily borrowed one, telling her parents, "I can make the machine go pretty well. & it is a great institution. I never appreciated one before" (June 28, 1865). Next, she rented one and felt quite ingenious with it. "Did I tell you I had hired a machine? Well, I took it apart, cleaned & oiled it & have sewed myself all up today" (Sept. 18, 1865). Eventually, Hubert got her a sewing machine of her own.

Home-brewed coffee was still uncommon. Emily lauded the enchantment of coffee offered on a visit, which, she added, "is a great inducement to go [visiting]" (Feb. 1864, to her parents). As for home remedies, Emily wrote about the use of opium in medications, to help her get well after being sick all week.

> Our guest Prof. Wood . . . took cold at the same time, and
> as he recommended Dover's Powder, we took them socially.
> You know they have opium in them. I suppose I took hardly
> enough for it made me quite sick, tho' my cold is better. I've
> suffered with headache, sore-throat &c until today. I feel
> much better. (Nov. 23, 1865, to her parents)

A final oddity that Emily commented on was seeing a woman in pants, or "pantaloons," in Mexico on her way back to San Francisco from a trip to Buffalo. On a shore visit at Acapulco, Emily noted that the family "stopped in at Morisse's, a French hotel keeper, whose wife wore pantaloons & a shirt, wears her hair short, has men to wait on her, and she cooks" (Jan. 2, 1868). In the 1850s, some women had taken to wearing the "Turkish dress" or bloomers, named after Amelia Bloomer, who had developed them in order to allow women more freedom of movement, especially as walking and other outdoor recreations were enticing women to exchange voluminous long skirts for ease of mobility. But in 1868, seeing a woman in pants was rare indeed.

The Bancrofts' world was changing, little by little.

CHAPTER THREE

Society around Them

In her own engagements and in sharing meetings and travels with her husband, Emily was exposed to a variety of experiences, some of which challenged her religious and political beliefs. While rarely delving deeply into any single topic given the breadth of news she reported on, Emily's journal does provide a window into the fabric of life in 1860s California. Note her impressions of Californians three months after joining them:

> We are living in changing times seems to me. California
> people make the greatest changes in the shortest time of
> any people on the globe, socially & individually I mean, but
> political & financial revolutions, we feel as little as any indi-
> viduals on the globe, I think. (Mar. 6, 1860, to her sister)

How apt is Emily's surprise at the social changes exploding around her in this frontier land while she was grappling with unconventional nuances of rank and character, as others in the West were doing, adrift from name, family, and background that oriented the East Coast's more tiered society.

As for Californians' relationship to "the globe," Emily remarks how "little" they related to faraway "political and financial revolutions." Major events, such as the looming Civil War, did register on her consciousness and in her letters, yet for California the war was far from actual conflict and the dramas of young Northern men and even women drawn into it.

After five years of adapting to life in the San Francisco area, Emily began to identify as a Western woman in opposition to "you Eastern people." She said of a visit with three acquaintances,

> I enjoyed it very much, excepting Mrs. S. . . . She is so for-
> ward, pushes herself so much, and thinks so much of herself.
> I asked H. why it was that persons who we liked at home <u>we</u>
> found so disagreeable out here. he says it is because we are so
> much more thrown together. I am willing to believe the fault
> is entirely in ourselves, but I think it is partly because strang-
> ers here feel away from home and dependent and disposed
> to make more use of their friends than at home. Some funny
> things transpire sometimes which would make you Eastern
> people stare. (Dec. 11, 1865)

As Hubert suggested, the different people "thrown together" in California could avoid some deeply embedded social strictures from back home, including communication styles, making for the possibility of different kinds of friendships out West. In the Bay Area of the 1860s, Emily may have been more limited in finding women of her class with whom she shared interests. Those thrown together had to be tolerant.

"Christians in California Have a Great Work to Do": Emily, Hubert, and Religion

Given the importance of Protestant faith in the Ketchum family, Emily continued to attend church in California, and Hubert did too, having adopted piety to win Emily's heart. Churches then and now provide community connection, philosophical and cultural contemplation, and spiritual renewal. Emily reveals how the sermons they heard at their church and elsewhere provoked engaging thought, even if Hubert did not adhere to any religious dictates.

The couple joined San Francisco's Calvary Presbyterian Church, led by William Anderson Scott.[1] A dedicated singer, Emily was initially impressed by her new church's spectacular choir.

Dr. Scott preached in the morning & young Mr. Clarke who has started a female Sem. here, in the evening. Our choir was composed of more than 100 singers. . . . H. informed me when we came from church that he wanted to get me a new mantle of some kind. (Mar. 18, 1861, to her sister)

Hubert wished his wife to impress the socially prominent congregation. Two years later, Emily said to her parents of the church choir, "It is rather high filuting as you would call it" (Jan. 20, 1863).

Reverend Scott left the church in 1862 for Europe, reproved for his "Confederate sympathies." He was replaced by the esteemed minister Dr. Charles Wadsworth of Philadelphia (d. 1882), once a special friend of poet Emily Dickinson in the late 1850s. His engaging intellect figures largely in Emily's reports on church services, with indications that H. H. Bancroft himself became enamored of "Dr. W."

Dr. Wadsworth did his best to bring virtue to this still-new land, as Emily recounted of one such sermon. "Christians in Cal have a great work to do & should rouse themselves & make more of their religion. He says we are all too worldly and make our religion too much a matter of convenience" (Jan. 22, 1863, to her parents). Several days later she wrote, "I heard Dr. Wadsworth's Sabbath morning, liked him pretty well. As all say, he is very poetical and what he says is very good. So far, I cannot like him as well as I did Dr. Scott, but there are enough who do" (Jan. 27, 1863, to her sister). By February 1863, Emily noted that her family had "our pew in church all to ourselves," which better fit their budding entourage, for Hubert's employee Mr. Knight and brother Albert now joined them there.

Both Emily and Hubert grew fond of Dr. W. She remarked in March 1863 that he seemed to "lose himself perfectly" while preaching. Soon, she informed her parents, Hubert appeared to like Dr. Wadsworth's sermons better than Emily did (Feb. 16, 1863). Next, Emily declared, "Hubert is becoming quite an admirer of Dr. Wadsworth. I like him too very much tho' to me his chief attraction is his humility and modesty" (Mar. 12, 1863). By April she reported, "H. thinks Dr. W. is about as near perfect as 'men are ever made'" (Apr. 1863). Such devotion appears ironic since Hubert found religious orthodoxy intellectually confining,[2] but the analytical aspects of Dr. Wadsworth's lectures must have translated into authentically meaningful ideas for the doubting Hubert.

Eventually, Dr. W.'s charisma won Emily over, too. After attending a lecture at Calvary Presbyterian, she reported: "I like Dr. W. more & more. He seems to be an exceedingly modest quiet man, but is often very eloquent while preaching" (Mar. 5, 1863, to her sister).

Emily relied on her faith and her religious values to make sense of the world. On receiving news of a young man's death, for example, Emily rationalized with her sister, "No man was ever more generally beloved than John, and he seemed so young to die, but God had need of him or He would not have taken him" (Mar. 5, 1863).

To her mother she decried how after church, Californians treated the Sabbath as a holiday.

> The rest of the day is quite generally spent in visiting and riding. Sunday is rather a holiday in the country throughout California. It is a very unhappy practice ... they say there is a gradual improvement from year to year but it is bad enough. (Apr. 27, 1863)

Emily evinced extra sensitivity to her parents' religious principles in her letters to them. One marked "Private" regarded the dancing school attended by her sister Kate's daughter, Kate Coit. This lengthy grappling with dancing school shows Emily's spiritual struggle over changing values at the time.

> I've had a letter from you this week in which you had just found out that Kate Coit went to dancing school. I ... knew you would feel badly when you found it out. I would gladly then have dissuaded Kate from it, if I had tho't it possible, but it is not.... I know very well it must cause you sorrow. still I wish you might feel that you have at least tried to do your duty by your children and I think you have been enabled to do it well while they were with you, and that now you can leave them in the hands of your God....
>
> I would not say that Kate does a wicked thing in sending her child to dancing school. Still if she granted to bring the child up to God, I should think it not advisable, but her Kate is too young now to be informed much by the ... vanity to be met with in such places.... I think your Kate is a child of God & will be taught her duty by Him in some way. but she

will be guided by her husband now more than by you, and
I would not let it worry me too much. you haven't the help
now. and I feel as if it was your duty to take life as quietly
as possible. If little Kate's soul is to be saved it will be saved
any way, and you must be glad it is no worse. If it will be any
consolation to you I can assure you that I do not think I shall
ever send my Kate to a dancing school. I want to bring her up
for Christ and I should feel as if that was placing a hindrance
in my way. (Mar. 12, no year, probably 1863)

Emily evinces suspicion of other nonconventional religious practices, too. She laughed to her parents about attending a Congregation-
alist Church with its potential influence on her. "So you may expect me
to become a believer in all their 'isms' you ever heard of" (May 15, 1863).
The 1860s were a time of ideological expansion of all kinds, including a
wave of religious revivalism. Novel sects had arisen, such as Mormon-
ism, along with experimentation in practices such as spiritualism, an
attempt to communicate with spirits of the deceased. Emily mentioned
the painful local schisms to her parents. "The Oakland denominations
will have nothing to do with each other. In the City the Unitarians
have been excluded entirely, incurring a great deal of hard feeling of
course in some quarters" (Aug. 8, 1864).

Emily disclosed her confusing and confused thoughts about these
new spiritual developments when she and Hubert were boarding with
a couple in San Francisco, a Mr. and Mrs. Dennis.

I find Mrs. D is partly a spiritualist & has decidedly departed
from the faith. She and her husband have been lately to hear
a Mormon lecture. . . . I told her today I was real sorry to have
her go. It was treading on the devil's ground, begged her not
to go again. . . . I tell H. that those who are led away by spiritualists first leave the old beaten track by becoming homeopotheists [*sic*]; he says it isn't so. I don't think homeopotheists
always become spiritualists but they are hardly ever the latter
without first becoming the former. A person with a sound
orthodox education can become witches so parents cannot be
too careful or too prayerful. (Feb. 16, 1864)

Emily's religious convictions deeply shaped her perceptions, yet we see how the couple's lively conversations promoted their effort to understand religious developments of the day.

Back at Calvary Presbyterian, Dr. Wadsworth aimed to tread carefully through the minefield of proprietary beliefs held by different denominations, and to prevent combustion within his own congregation. Competing cultural edicts were circulating in the new state. How would the church respond? For example, Emily's church took up a collection for the Chinese in San Francisco. Their Calvary Presbyterian Church (founded in 1855 at Bush and Montgomery Streets, close to H.H.'s store) may have been helping San Francisco's Chinatown Presbyterian Church, then two years older and today the oldest Asian American church in North America. Supporting a Chinese church was exemplary in the rough days of early San Francisco, given the often deadly racism directed at the Chinese.

Emily also reported on the role of women in her community. Her church punished women who failed to live up to society's standards: "Did I tell you they excommunicated two individuals last Sunday— females—one for leading a scandalous life, the other for being an habitual drunkard" (Jan. 9, 1864). Widespread alcohol abuse led ten years later to the founding of the Women's Christian Temperance Union and ultimately to Prohibition, which aimed in part to protect women. Emily remarked when women had a strong public presence. One church minister announced that a "Miss Fuller would deliver a lecture here sometime this week, on 'general intellectual progress.'" Women speakers were so rare, in fact, that Emily emphasized in another letter, "My husband has gone to hear a <u>woman</u> lecture," although she neglected to mention the speaker's name (San Francisco, Aug. 5, 1869).

Apparently, "Dr. W." sought control in many realms of his parishioners' spiritual lives. The Bancroft family wished to visit Europe and so were taking French lessons in preparation. They included daughter Kate. How could teaching children French threaten their religion?

> Dr. Wadsworth gave us a very emphatic hint that we were having our children learn French & other accomplishments at the risk of their souls, that we take them from a school where the Bible is read & prayer is offered & send them to an infidel school that they may learn the French accent. French schools for boys and girls are all the rage out here. (Apr. 5, 1865)

Wadsworth struggled to bring virtue to a still "wild West" society without alienating his congregation via politicized or patronizing sermons—a tricky line to draw. Emily noted that Wadsworth rarely alluded to politics, but he often pontificated, and with frustration, on slovenly and sinful California.

> We had a very solemn sermon from Dr. W. The text was from Numbers. . . . He seemed himself filled with sadness at the recklessness and worldliness of all around him, and it is lamentable to see how worldly the church is. it is hard to distinguish any difference between the Church and the world. (Jan. 4, 1866)

Perhaps influenced by the worldliness around her and by the Bancrofts' frequent moves between Oakland and San Francisco, Emily had difficulty connecting to their home church. She lamented to her parents only attending twice-weekly services in San Francisco. "When the cars run to where we live, I can come to Ch. very easily. . . . I feel the influences of going to ch. so little very much" (May 5, 1865). Later that year she wrote from their home in the dunes of San Francisco that her husband arranged for regular rides to church and elsewhere, doubtless out of concern for Emily's fragile health.

> Wednesday evening: We are not at church as we ought to be, we are such a long way from ch. that we both hesitate about walking such a distance in the evening. H has made an arrangement with "Dolan" the hackman to take me out riding by the month, calculating that I will want to go to Church twice on Sunday & down town twice or three times a week. he says it must include Wednesday evening. (Oct. 17, 1865, to her parents)

Although she and Hubert continued to attend Calvary Presbyterian in later years, Emily reported that Dr. Wadsworth's style had become unacceptable. "Dr. W. preached two excellent sermons, but his delivery is certainly execrable and the congregation has fallen off nearly in half. . . . I do not think Dr. W. is at fault at all, but such a man cannot be appreciated in such a community" (Nov. 20, 1868, to her sister).

Other concerns proved more compelling, however.

"We as a Nation Are to Be Terribly Disciplined": The Civil War

Slavery increasingly dominated politics in the United States in the 1850s, and California represented the national divisions. Its admission as a free state in 1850 upset the numerical balance between the sixteen free and fifteen enslaving states. Rep. Henry Clay's Compromise of 1850 retained that imbalance but strengthened the Fugitive Slave Act. The majority of US immigrants to California were from the North, but also present were members of the secessionist or "secesh" Chivalry wing of the Democratic Party, allied with the pro-slavery South. Californians were never drafted to go to the Civil War, given the cost of transportation and other factors, but the state raised thirteen volunteer regiments, most of which served in the state or in the Mountain West (many on Indian-hunting missions). Although the Civil War raged far away from San Francisco, it remained on the minds of many Californians. For those with menfolk eligible to serve—such as Emily's brother George—the war added yet another level of threat to their families.

The purpose of the Civil War was debated everywhere. Most Southerners defended secession as "states' rights." For some Northerners, the war aimed to preserve the Union; others fought to abolish slavery. For H.H.'s parents, who had given much time, energy, and passion to abolition, the antislavery cause was very personal. Back in Ohio, they had held meetings and helped conduct fugitive enslaved people to freedom on the Underground Railroad.

H.H. and Emily avidly read the news regarding developments in the war and awaited reports from her family in Buffalo. "We hear that Vicksburg is <u>really</u> taken," declared Emily to her sister on June 8, 1863, and soon thereafter, "Neither Washington nor Richmond are taken!" (June 23, 1863). In return for news received, she shared her impressions of local responses to the war and its impacts on California.

In the early days of the secessionist conflict, Emily reported to her sister her own conflicting feelings about the brewing crisis, the potential for destruction terrible to contemplate.

> It seems as if all peace, prosperity & happiness for our country were gone. I wish Mr. Lincoln would <u>let</u> the South secede if it wants to. We have quite a number of military ladies &

gentlemen here, and they are in a great state of excitement. they are quite the leaders of society here, and each church has an "Army pew." (Apr. 24, 1861)

We hear rumors of another battle and another defeat of Northern troops. It seems as if the Southerners had so much more heart in the matter than our soldiers who seemed to have gone to the war more for the fame than for serious service.... We as a nation are to be terribly disciplined.... Everything has subsided in the Church, none of [Dr. Scott's] friends blame him for sympathizing with the South. I respect him all the more of it.... how differently we should feel if Pa or George [her brother] or George Coit [her brother-in-law] were in the army. I do hope they never will be, but I believe the best part of Southern citizens are in their army, and it may take our best citizens to match them, don't you think so?

I bought an "Extra" yesterday p.m. of a little boy who was crying it thro' the st. found the battle was rather a small affair in Missouri, supposing I should come home in the Spring and should be taken prisoner by some Southern assault! (Aug. 23, 1861, to her sister)

We were awakened at sunrise this morning by tremendous cannonading. My first thought was, as the news last night was not any encouraging to the North, that the city was being bombarded, but H. happened to remember after I was pretty well scared, that it was the Bunker Hill anniversary. (May 17, 1863, to her parents)

At yet a different Oakland church, a "strange minister" had "prayed that the Confederacy might not be sustained that had as its corner-stone 'negro slavery'" (Aug. 27, 1863, to her parents).

The distant war *did* have a very personal impact on H. H. Bancroft and his business when one shipment of his cargo was lost in an attack.

Every one out here is afraid the Southerners will take Washington. Last night we heard that Lee was on his way to Richmond. This week we hear that he has (to use Pa's expression) turned tail and ran.... It is beginning to look serious for Californians. Two or three ships have been burned off the coast. We have no protections whatever, either for steamers or clipper ships. H. heard yesterday that two ships, with the first of his goods that Albert bought when he went East, is burned. He [Albert] had $11.00 on him. (May 17, 1863, to her parents)

Several weeks later, Emily continued: "We've heard that the Alabama has taken one of the Cal. clipper ships on which H. had goods. He says it is probably only a beginning" (June 8, 1863). She refers to the Confederate sloop-of-war CSS *Alabama*, built in 1862 in England as a commerce raider. The *Alabama* sank twenty-nine ships in the South Atlantic from February to July 1863, including one transporting supplies for Hubert's store. Two months later, Emily added: "We know something about the mischief the Alabama has done as H. always loses some goods by her" (Aug. 8, 1863, to her parents). Those predations ended when the *Alabama* was sunk on June 19, 1864, by the USS *Kearsage* off the coast of England.

News of the New York draft riots, which occurred in July 1863, shook the whole country. With open racial animosity, mostly Irish immigrant and working-class men who resented the draft that sent them to fight for African American slaves in the Civil War took out their resistance by attacking Black Americans in lower Manhattan, leaving 119 dead. In her letter of July 13, 1863, Emily shared with her sister her thoughts about the civil unrest from the perspective of her religious convictions:

We heard last night of the terrible riot in N.Y. Such insubordination is what we might expect to be the fruit & influence of the war. It seems as if we had no general with capacity enough to lead the army to catch Lee when he was on the wrong side of the Potomac, but it is really the Lord permitting all this for some wise end. I am glad George's regiment did not go, even if he did'nt fight. I wouldn't have him take that awful fever for all the Unions in Christendom. . . . tho' I want the Union preserved pretty badly.

As the war dragged on, Emily continued to worry about her brother, George, being drafted. "What is George K going to do about being drafted? Albert says they had his name on the list in N.Y. but it was not drawn. We hear of fighting again, at Chattanooga—drawn battles"

(Sept. 19, 1863). She referred to the early battle between Union and Confederate armies at Chattanooga that forced Confederate general Braxton Bragg to retreat to Georgia, a temporary gain for the Union forces, or a "draw."

Emily noted that Hubert, too, was relieved not to go, though no reason was given why he didn't enlist, nor was drafted. "I am glad Geo. K. has gotten off, but if I had been left to guess how, I should have had time to grow very ancient before. H. says he should have very little heart to fight in this war, & I feel it too" (Sept. 24, 1863).

Emily's ambivalence about the war is clear as she weighed the abolition of slavery with the death of a young man from home. "I was sorry enough to hear of Peter Porter's death. It seems as if all the slaves in Christendom were not worth such lives as his" (July 6, 1864). A heart-and-mind-wrenching musing, given the horrors of slavery and the horrors of war.

Although the cruelest impacts of battles—gruesome death and destruction witnessed throughout the South—were remote from the lands of California, the presence of military ships and men could not be ignored. Describing the bay's beauty and a Spanish frigate at anchor, Emily explained, "All vessels are stopped & examined at Fort Albatross, which is on an island just at the entrance. A British man of war came in yesterday" (Oct. 1, 1863). (Ft. Albatross was on the island later renamed Alcatraz.) A few days later, Emily remarked on a camp of soldiers in Alameda: "The streets are full of soldiers and officers" (Oct. 3, 1863). Rumors spread of sabotage by secessionists, who, it was claimed, damaged several ships in the harbor. In particular, an ironclad "monitor" was destroyed, though ultimately a high wind was found to be the culprit (Nov. 4, 1863).

On a social level, Emily often conveyed the contradictory beliefs she encountered in relation to the war. Emily described how her reading exposed her to varied opinions, including a speech by George McClellan (1826–1885), a complicated political figure. In 1864, McClellan was a major general of the Union Army, former commander-in-chief of the Army of the Potomac, and general-in-chief of all Union armies, while also a Democratic presidential nominee. She said of his speech:

> I liked it very much. It seems to me he takes such a proper
> view of things, but out here, he is called secessionist. Is he

with you? But every one out here who does not fully sympathize in this war is called "secesh." (July 18, 1864)

The Democratic Party platform, while not overtly secessionist, called
for negotiating a settlement with the Confederates. Emily floundered
in regard to the appropriate stance to take, much as McClellan himself
did.

Emily's keen observations of human behavior pinpointed a "secesh"
in other ways. In April 1864, on a trip to San Jose with Emma—the
daughter of her landlady, Mrs. Dennis—she stayed with Mrs. Barnes,
one of Mrs. Dennis's friends. Emily called Mrs. Barnes "secesh" for her
Southern-raised privilege:

> She lives at quite a distance from any one, in an unfinished
> house & does her own work. Of course Em & I helped. This
> lady has of course been accustomed to slaves & knew noth-
> ing about work until she came out here four years ago, so she
> does'nt manage as farmers wives in general. It takes her an
> hour every morning to bathe and dress herself. So sometimes
> it is late before she gets the breakfast. (Apr. 17, 1864, to her
> parents)

By April 1865, the war was winding down. With her parents, Emily
shared the common joy. "Everybody is wild with excitement over the
news of Lee's surrender. It begins to look as if we might have peace once
more, tho it all seems as if we hardly deserved it" (Apr. 5, 1865). Emily's
remark about "deserving peace" foreshadows a bitterness, enduring still
today, engendered by the war.

Throughout Emily's writing come references to the distribution
of divine reward and punishment. On April 18, 1865, she applied the
notion to the news of Lincoln's assassination on April 14.

> We've all been in a state of great excitement as I suppose
> you've been, on hearing of the President's death. Wasn't it
> an awful thing, particularly in this civilized, & we ought to
> be able to say, this <u>Christian</u> age! Secessionists have scarcely
> breathed in S.F. and we have a good many of them. I never
> saw the citizens so worked up in my life. They mobbed a
> Democratic press & were very anxious to do something to

somebody. All business was stopped at noon on Saturday and the churches were all dressed in mourning Sunday and were crowded.... I think we should look upon it as a rebuke from the Lord, that we may not be too boastful & uplifted at the victories we have gained. & I hope we may, as a nation, come out of our difficulties purified, that seems to me to be the Lord's object, don't you think so, to purify & make us better than we've been for many years.

The news of President Lincoln's death touched Emily quite personally. She inquired about reports that a Ketchum family acquaintance had been at Lincoln's side that night. "The papers spoke of a Miss Harris as being with the President at the Theater. Was it Clara Harris of Albany?" A few days later, more eastern newspapers arrived. "We have pictorial papers, with graphic pictures of the assassination of the President. I see it was Clara Harris who was there. She is represented in our picture with her hat on, in another in full dress" (May 12, 1865). The Currier & Ives lithography below, which includes Clara Harris, is likely one that she saw. Emily's letters make the political personal.

THE ASSASSINATION OF PRESIDENT LINCOLN.
AT FORD'S THEATRE WASHINGTON,D.C.APRIL 14TH 1865.

From left to right: Major Henry Rathbone, Clara Harris (Rathbone's fiancée), Mary Todd Lincoln, Abraham Lincoln, and John Wilkes Booth (Currier & Ives, Library of Congress)[3]

Significant People in the Bancrofts' Lives

As the Bancrofts traveled around the city and beyond in pursuit of business and cultural interests, Emily reported on visitors and social activities, representing the wide net relating to their intellectual, political, and academic connections. Some of those people mentioned would reappear in the 1870s and '80s in H.H.'s quest to create a history of the Pacific West. Though lacking education beyond a female seminary, Emily reveals her thoughtfulness regarding certain issues.

For example, Emily wrote to her sister in April 1860 about a bill important to San Francisco merchants, including her husband.

> Mr. Selby, one of the oldest and wealthiest citizens, spent all last evening with us, was very pleasant. There was great rejoicing all over the city yesterday p.m. at the news that the Governor had vetoed the Bulk Head Bill—if it had passed, it would throw all the water approaches to the city into the hands of a few men who have spared no pains and money to bring it about. You will read about it in the papers. (Apr. 16, 1860)

In this brief note on the event, Emily tried to capture a contentious and complicated affair. The Bulkhead Bill aimed to keep San Francisco's waterfront properties in private hands. It was supported by the highest caste of capitalists—to which Hubert did *not* belong. Governor Downey's veto stunned the city's elite. Emily was right that it would make national news. She likely refers to Thomas H. Selby (1820–1875), who owned a shot tower (for making lead bullets) and smelter. He later served as mayor of San Francisco (1869–1871). That Emily and Hubert kept company with illustrious citizens places them in a higher stratum of San Francisco society, though perhaps not the highest.

In June 1860, Emily again wrote of an issue important for property owners, the Peter Smith scandal, and again she reported on connections to a man who would become yet another future mayor. The city government had sold Mission Bay "water lots," assuming that the bay would be filled in. Peter Smith, formerly a doctor serving the city's poor, now sought compensation through the sale of these lots. On their way home one evening, Emily and Hubert found themselves in the

midst of a nighttime outdoor assembly about the scandal—one way
that breaking news was delivered in 1860.

> It was very pleasant last night, no dust and very little wind.
> H. wanted to go down & write, so I went with him, spent
> the time reading the "Mill on the Floss," came home about
> 9 o'clock, encountered a large crowd in front of the "Pavil-
> lion," as they call the large building for the Mechanics Fair.
> They were being addressed on the Peter Smith Swindle. Peter
> Smith drained half the city, his claims have been recently
> in Court, declared null & void. Patriotic citizens pretend to
> consider San Francisco redeemed, don't believe they know
> from what, and made a great time last night. Judge Coon was
> to be the prominent speaker, but I see by the paper he was
> detained at home by sickness in his family. (June 27, 1860, to
> her parents)

The Mechanics Fair Pavilion at the corner of Post and Market
Streets was the site of an annual fair from 1857 to 1899. Judge Henry
Coon (1822–1884), mayor of San Francisco (1863–1867), was a friend
and future neighbor of the Bancrofts. In Emily's account years later,
she described to her parents the mayor's visit to their new home on
Franklin Street, that he might envision his plan to build nearby.

> I had a call this pm from the Mayor, Judge Coon—he is to
> build just above us soon, and wants to know how we like it.
> I showed him the house & he sat himself down in my bed
> room which has the finest view, & staid sometime, to Ade-
> laide's great amusement. she peeped thru the window at him,
> as she had never seen the Mayor. (Oct. 17, 1865)

Though Emily and her husband were not exactly members of the
upper class, she had a penchant for their way of life. In describing to
her sister changes in the Rincon Hill area where she and Hubert had
first lived, Emily lauded the "handsome" architecture of the prominent
homes of the rich.

> It is not as pleasant as it used to tho' they have put up some
> very handsome residences there, Richard Ogden has built

one, and Mr. Giffs another, a beautiful one of a wood French roof, and most of the work he had done at the East and sent out in pieces, it is as pretty a house as I ever saw. (Jan. 27, 1863)

The excesses of the rich also caught Emily's attention on meeting Mr. Fargo, originally from Emily's hometown of Buffalo and its mayor from 1862 to 1866. "[T]hey are having quite a fuss made over them. You know Wells & Fargo's Co. flourishes very largely here. On their way, they had an extra car when they rode the rail and . . . the finest rooms at the Occidental" (May 1863). William Fargo and Henry Wells had an express business that formed a virtual monopoly from New York to San Francisco, via the Isthmus of Panama.

The Bancrofts were also friendly with the Dwinelles, another family of intellectual and political significance. Emily received a formal social call from Mrs. Dwinelle, probably the wife of John W. Dwinelle (1816–1881), who had served on the San Francisco city council and as mayor of Oakland. In 1865 when his wife called on Mrs. Bancroft, Dwinelle was also the state assemblyman from Oakland; he wrote the Organic Act, which transformed the College of California (then located in Oakland) into the University of California, Berkeley, in 1868. He subsequently served on the university's inaugural Board of Regents and is commemorated by a building on the Berkeley campus. Ever aware of social propriety, Emily laughed with her parents at herself as she reported the faux pas she had made. "Mrs. Dwinelle called today. When she rang the bell, I thought it was Kate playing at making calls, so I called out to 'come in' rather unceremoniously—for Mrs. D!" (Mar. 25, 1865).

Emily frequented the salons of many of those making Bay Area history. Soon after her arrival in San Francisco, on March 8, 1860, Emily told her parents, "I called on the Haights." It's not clear which members of that family she was referring to, but several of them were eminent: Henry H. Haight (1824–1878), the tenth governor of California, who signed the Organic Act creating the University of California; his nephew, banker Henry Haight (1820–1869); or Fletcher Haight, a judge who died in 1866. Later, Emily told of attending the marriage of Mrs. Fletcher Haight's niece, and on other occasions wrote of "calling on Mrs. Haight." Years later in 1869, Emily reported on the tragic death of Henry Haight:

> Do you remember Miss Flora Haight who took tea at Pa's
> one morning last winter, and whose mother was visiting in
> Rochester? Her Father was buried this p.m. He was a very
> wealthy banker here in early times, but lost everything some
> time ago, which led him to drink, tho' he has kept his family
> very comfortably. His wife has been devoted to him & exerted
> a good influence over him. He has been sick for the last two
> months, but was better & able to be out two weeks ago &
> finally died quite suddenly, leaving his family destitute.
> (Mar. 22, 1869, to her sister)[4]

Then there is the "Mrs. Dr." with whom Emily socialized. Emily wrote, "Mrs. Dr. Tuthill, whose husband is an editor of the Bulletin, called today" (Feb. 3, 1863). Franklin Tuthill (1822–1865) was a physician who took up history writing and journalism as editor of the *San Francisco Evening Bulletin*. H. H. Bancroft published Tuthill's well-regarded *History of California* in 1866.[5] One would like a taste of the conversation between these cultured women, but we only know that they visited. Two years later, Emily recounted calling on "Mrs. Dr. Tuthill whose husband died in Brooklyn [a neighborhood of Oakland] a few months ago & whose last work was to correct proofs of a history of Cal. he had been writing for my husband. he was a very interesting man" (Nov. 30, 1865, to her parents).

These interactions manifest the social network that Hubert was developing, vital in his later efforts to build his collection and his history—and eventually a site for his library. "H has just come in (8 ½ pm) the first I've seen of him since breakfast. Has been attending a meeting of the trustees of the college" (Jan. 12, 1863, to her sister). Emily refers to the College of California, then located in Oakland, where the Bancrofts were living. She noted in May of that year that the college would be leaving Oakland. "Soon as the College moves out, we might go too" (May 22, 1863).

The Ketchums evidently shared an interest in higher education in California, for a newspaper clipping from the *New York Observer* dated May 11, 1863, was tucked among Emily's letters, regarding a "University in California, San Francisco," one with a religious foundation. The article relates efforts to "establish a first class University under Presbyterian auspices" in San Francisco, under Dr. Burrowes, a Presbyterian minister. This University College of San Francisco was founded in 1860 under the auspices of and in the basement of the Bancrofts' own Calvary Presbyterian Church.[6]

The Bancrofts were thus both connected to various stellar men then establishing these academic institutions during the 1860s. In 1863, Emily said that she had "made a long call on Dr. and Mrs Burrows in their College building" in San Francisco. "Their College is quite large now, and the building is delightfully situated, tho' two years ago I could hardly get to the house, thro' the sand. The sand hills have all been cut away" (Mar. 19, 1863, to her parents). The college was then on Haight Street between Octavia and Laguna. A month later, Emily reported:

> H. informed me that his sojourn in the city Friday night cost him just $2006! On inquiry it seems he has bought a lot about 4 miles out of the city. Dr. Burrows College [*sic*] had a track [*sic*] of land that they are selling for $2000 per block, $1000 of the money goes to the original possessor of the land, the other $1000 to the College. Mr. Selby, M[ess]rs. Roberts, Haight, Ralston and others of the best men here have taken lots, all at that price, some simply to help the college, some with a view of living there some day. H. was persuaded into it, but says whether he ever lives on it or not, it will be doing good to somebody. (Apr. 7, 1863)

H. H. Bancroft made sure to contribute to this new foundational institution in his community.

As for the nascent College of California, Emily reported from Oakland in 1864:

> They had a grand time over here at the college yesterday. All the graduates on this coast of all the colleges at the East were invited to the Alumni meeting and they had quite a large gathering, an Oration in the Church and a collation on the college grounds, speeches, etc. They said they had a very nice time, the first meeting of the kind ever held on this coast. (June 1, 1864)

Though H. H. Bancroft never served on the college's board of trustees or as a regent of the University of California, his connections with the scholars and administrators were crucial to his literary industries from the 1870s on and to the eventual sale of his library to the University of California in 1905.

A distinguished military acquaintance of the Bancrofts was "Major Kirkham," who sometimes visited their home—probably Ralph W. Kirkham, who commanded the San Francisco military post from 1861 until 1870, rising in rank to brigadier general in 1865.

Their visitors also included Messrs. King and Gardner, soon starting on a trip to Yosemite: "I'm afraid their roaming lives will unfit them for everything else" (Sept. 23, 1864, to her parents). How wrong Emily was about that! Their roaming *was* their livelihood. Geologist Clarence King (1842–1901) became the first director of the US Geological Survey from 1879 to 1881. James Gardner (1842–1921), who later spelled his name Gardiner, accompanied King to California from New York in 1863. In September 1864, they went off to Yosemite under the orders of President Lincoln to survey the rim of Yosemite Valley. For the rest of his life, King roamed the wilderness while writing books on geology and mountaineering.

Frequently, Emily was invited to "smart talking" ladies' luncheons with the wives of prominent men. In her description to her parents of one elegant event, she puts "lunch" in quotation marks, perhaps to denote the new nickname for luncheon.

> I went to the "lunch" [with] about seven ladies all dressed
> in silk and point lace, excepting Mrs. "Ross Browne" whose
> husband has been writing very amusing letters from Germany
> in Harpers magazine[7] . . . <u>she</u> was plain as a pipe stem, a niece
> of Senator Latham's was there (very pretty) and we had quite
> a distinguished assembly. All Episcopalians . . . but me. They
> are smart at talking, if nothing else. We had a very handsome
> lunch table. (Aug. 19, 1863, located in her sister's volume)

Another example of a wife whose husband would be important to her own husband was "Mrs. General Bidwell":

> Made a <u>very</u> pleasant acquaintance in the house last evening,
> a Mrs. Gen. Bidwell. She is from Washington, was married
> last Spring, Gen B. is a very nice man, an early settler here. . . .
> I don't know that I have met a more interesting person. One

of the gentlemen who knew him well said I must call upon her. (Nov. 20, 1868, to her sister)

What made Annie Kennedy Bidwell (1839–1918) so interesting? She was both the daughter of Joseph C. G. Kennedy, a high-ranking Washington official in the US Census Bureau, and the wife of John Bidwell (1819–1900), who had come to California in 1841 on the first wagon train to cross the Sierra Nevada into Mexican Alta California. Bidwell received a Mexican land grant of twenty-two thousand acres, now encompassing the city of Chico, and he served as a congressman (1865–66). "Mrs. Gen. Bidwell" was committed to many social causes, suffrage and prohibition among them. Her deeply religious values may also have appealed to Emily. A meeting between these minds would have been lively, one imagines.

Incidentally, Emily added: "I've also made a pleasant acquaintance from the Sandwich Islands," referring to what were later known as the Hawaiian Islands, a note that indicates the geographical diversity of some of her contacts on the Pacific crest of the world. Mark Twain had visited those islands in 1866, writing a series of letters for the *Sacramento Union*, and then gave lectures about his visit, starting with one in San Francisco on October 2, 1866.

Significant Events That Touched Their Lives

Emily's journal demonstrates how the Bancrofts responded to memorable events in Bay Area history and beyond. She noted a lively day spent with Hubert at the laying of the cornerstone of the David Broderick monument by Governor Leland Stanford on February 22, 1863. Broderick had arrived in San Francisco in 1849 and eventually worked his way up from the smelting business into a seat in the State Senate. In a drama rife with corruption and betrayal, Broderick was killed in a duel in September 1859 by a former friend, David Terry (1823–1889), a chief justice of the California Supreme Court.

Emily was also thrilled to learn that the governor was staying in the same luxurious Lick House Hotel as the Bancrofts. "The governor and family are at this hotel & Owen my waiter also waits on the Stanfords" (Feb. 23, 1863). This young woman, brought up in a somewhat sheltered household, had come a long way, brushing elbows with the governor of California.

News regarding commerce naturally interested Hubert and Emily, such as developments in relation to the gold standard: "H. has had his supper [and] sits here discussing the attempts being made at Sacramento to change the currency, which attempts are creating quite a frustration" (Jan. 18, 1864).

The Comstock Lode discovery was hugely compelling when silver ore was discovered in 1859 near Virginia City in Nevada (which became a state in 1864). In 1863, Emily discussed developments in the Washoe Valley that generated eager news of "discoveries."

California people are feeling very proud of their State these days, say that speculators from the East arrive [on] every str [steamer]. on an average more than one new mining company is formed each day. a great deal of money is made at Washoe and new discoveries of something are made constantly. . . . I saw Lillie Clifford's two brothers walking up & down Montgomery St. the other day, dressed "to kill" and appearing like gentlemen of leisure. if they have nothing to do, as living is expensive, I'm afraid their money won't last. they evidently like it out here, judging from appearances. (Feb. 18, 1863, to her parents)

The awful drought of 1864 led Emily to report on the unseasonably warm weather and news of starving cattle in Southern California.

It is as warm as summer tonight. they say it is terrible in the country, cattle dying & crops . . . all dried up. the warm dry weather seems to induce earthquakes too. we will really be a distressed country if it does not rain soon. think of our being nearly a year with almost no rain at all. (Feb. 22, 1864, to her parents)

That disaster caused the loss of thousands and thousands of cattle. Subsequently many ranchers and farmers lost their land, including many Mexican *Californios*—land rich and cash poor—who could not pay their mortgages, most of them held by "Yankee" banks.

Emily also reported on the impeachment trial of President Andrew Johnson, under way when she and Hubert visited Washington, DC, in 1868.[8] She wrote to her sister about the notable senators they had seen and the drama of two of them brought in on sickbeds to cast their votes.

> An acquaintance from SF whom Hubert met on Friday … went with us to call on our Senator, Mr. Cole, we procured tickets from Mrs. Cole to the "Impeachment" Saturday morning which was said to be the final day but many prophesied that it would not. We went about 10 am with everybody else & his cousin. The galleries were full, but we were quite comfortably seated. Saw some senatorial business disposed of until 12 when Chief Justice Chase entered & the business of the Court of Impeachment began. … The President was acquitted on the 11th article. (May 18, 1868)

Another event that caught Emily's attention was a scandal regarding the famed composer and singer Louis Moreau Gottschalk (1829–1869). She reported to her parents that a San Francisco newspaper in May 1865 said he had "travelled 95,000 miles by rail and given 1,000 concerts."

> Some ladies have been in today and each one told me of an affair that took place out on Temple College the other night. Gottschalk and a friend of his enticed two of the young ladies away with them the other night. The young ladies returned towards morning & were discovered. Gottschalk left very unexpectedly on the Str. today. (Sept. 18, 1865)

Gottschalk was forced to leave not only the Bay Area but the United States because of his affair with a student at the Oakland Female Seminary.

An incident that deeply moved Emily and much of San Francisco and the nation was the death of Dr. Thomas Starr King, the minister of the First Unitarian Church, at age thirty-nine. King became a prominent intellectual in the new state, reaching not only his congregation with his sermons but the larger community and country through his lectures. Already renowned, Starr King had come to California in 1860 to help strengthen the infidel city. His praise of Yosemite contributed to its preservation as a state park in 1864. An ardent abolitionist and Unionist, his lectures during the Civil War had great influence on keeping California in the Union despite the "Chiv" sentiments of many of its citizens (referring to the pro-Southern Chivalry party).

Emily told her parents how impressed she was by his virtues, including an inspiring lecture she heard him give on charity, and how his death shocked her.

> We've heard this morning that Starr King is dead. I could not believe it at first, for he was on the street Saturday & didn't know he was sick. He was a healthy looking man too. I believe his disease was dypsteria [*sic*]. It was a very sudden death & much felt in the community, as he was very popular. he has been very prominent in the Mirror & has given many lectures for charitable purposes . . . & he always drew a full house. His last lecture was to help pay the debt of one of our Congregational churches. he leaves a wife (a remarkably handsome woman, tho' he was remarkably homely) and two children, one a baby boy born out here, the other a girl 12 or 14 years old. I hope he has left some money. . . . The flags all over the city are at half mast for him. (Mar. 4, no year, but Starr King died in 1864)

Three days later, Emily described his funeral procession.

> Tuesday evening: Starr King was buried with great pomp on Sunday, the Free Masons performed the ceremony. the crowd extended across the street it was impossible to pass the church—his body was brought to the Church Saturday morning when he lay in state, guarded by "Masons" during the day, by soldiers during the evening & night. thousands went to see him. of course he was beautifully laid out in a casket & such flowers. I never saw anything like this. The whole church was trimmed with them. . . . Colored people were conspicuous at the funeral. . . . They buried him under the pulpit.

Emily, like the rest of the city, was shocked by the loss of a talented man so young and suddenly taken. Indeed, lethal illnesses and deadly perils abounded in early California, as elsewhere in the 1860s.

Finally, on a lighter note, Emily delighted in gossip about Miss Lillie Hitchcock (1843–1929), who secretly married Benjamin Howard Coit (1824–1885) of the San Francisco Stock Exchange.

> A clandestine marriage has recently taken place here, between Dr. Coit's son and a notorious young lady of this place, a Miss Lillie Hitchcock. She is very fast. Even for Paris, where she spends a great part of her time. She with her father & mother left overland for the East. A few days after we came home and previous to going, she and the young man went to a church & were married, unbeknownst to anybody. It has created quite a buzz in the house. <u>he</u> has been taking his meals at this house for a few days. Looks a little like the Coits, but has quite light hair & eyes, is large & looks manly but has the reputation of being quite licentious. I do not think he drinks, it seems it was an old love match, opposed by the parent on both sides. (Nov. 30, 1868, to her father)

Fascinated by San Francisco firefighters, eccentric Lillie Coit became the mascot for Knickerbocker Engine No. 5, wearing its medallion proudly. Emily scoffed at this unconventional love match, but it would eventually deliver Coit Tower to San Francisco's skyline from Mrs. Coit's bequest to the city.

Emily's enjoyment of the stories of those around her likely made for interesting conversation. She was a keen observer, and willing to take the time to share a few choice tidbits on a multitude of topics.

CHAPTER FOUR

The World of Travel

The young Bancrofts often traveled for local sightseeing pleasure and to reconnect with friends and family near and far. The transcontinental railroad would not be completed until 1869, so steamships were required if one wanted to end up across the country. Travel along the coast of California also required steamships, and inland travelers tolerated uncomfortable stagecoaches and carriages, if not going by horseback. Emily's letters reported on the nature of her travels with and without Hubert, including their nine-month grand tour of Europe from 1866 to 1867. Her observations remind us of the privileges we enjoy in traveling today.

Dangers and Pleasures

Shipboard travel all too often meant discomfort if not danger. Emily's letters described common travelers' woes, from typical inconveniences to spectacular disasters.

> Two steamers came in today. The *Golden Age* towed up the *Uncle Sam*, which had broken her shaft near Acapulco. . . . Some of the passengers & all the freight have been waiting at Acapulco this month or more. If you asked for anything

at the stores, they all said they were waiting for the steamer.
(Mar. 18, 1861, to her sister)

Setting to sea under such threats had to be daunting. After three
years in San Francisco, Emily finally returned home to Buffalo in 1862
for several months. In August she wrote to Kate in Albany that she
was awaiting Hubert to join her in Buffalo from London, where he
was collecting books.[1] She hoped to avoid a rough winter voyage to
California later that year.

> My husband writes that he expects to sail next Wednesday
> on the Scotia. It will make it the middle or the last of Nov
> and maybe even later before we can leave for Cal. I am not
> sorry to have my stay prolonged, but do not like to take that
> journey so late in the season. (Aug. 23, 1862)

Then in December 1862, Emily and daughter Kate sailed on the
Champion from New York to return to San Francisco. They would
arrive at the east coast of Panama's Isthmus, disembark, take a short
railroad trip to the west coast, then embark there on a steamer heading
north. Said Emily of the journey,

> I see very little drinking or card playing so far, but plenty of
> seasickness, as this ship rolls terribly. I should hate to be on
> her in a storm. She is small and dirty, but everyone seems to
> take it philosophically. Wednesday morning yesterday was so
> rough that all we could do was to hold onto something all day
> to keep from rolling over. Today it is not much better. Kate
> has just pitched over, chain & all. I managed to save her.
>   There is a very pretty woman on board going out to her
> husband who is in S.F. She has not seen him in 3 years. (Dec.
> 27, 1862, to her parents)

As ever, Emily is sparing in words with so much to tell in each letter.
How laconically she reports on saving her small daughter from "pitch-
ing" overboard! Her mention of another passenger soon to reunite with
her husband after *three years* of separation shows the typical hardship
of many marriages lived apart in the pioneer years of California and

the West. Emily and her fellow passengers were lucky on that trip. That same ship, the *Champion*, sank in November 1879, with many lives lost.

Another tragedy struck the paddle steamer *Brother Jonathan* off Crescent City on July 30, 1865, as Emily explained to her sister on August 5. "We've had a terrible accident on our Northern Coast. Several very prominent men were lost." On August 10 she elaborated:

> We've all been made very sad lately by the loss of the Str. "Brother Jonathan" on the upper coast. it struck a rock & sank in half an hour with 200 passengers, only 15 ever found. Every boat they got out & filled was either tipped over or swamped by the waves & the Str. it was in a terrible storm and on a very rough coast, 12 miles from land & it was impossible to get nearer than 6 miles of the wreck for 3 days. Moreover it was entirely out of sight. You will see accounts of it in the papers. those who survived spoke in the highest terms of the Capt. & his officers. it seems that all was done that was in human power. if the tide had been a little lower they would have seen the rock or a little higher & they would have passed over it without knowing of its proximity, reminding us strongly that every event is ordered.

The ship had a load of gold on it and 244 passengers. Only nineteen were saved.

Another ship, the *Golden Age*, also sank, as Emily reported in June 1864. And in a letter to her sister dated April 5, 1865, Emily noted that a shipwreck led to the freight loss of her newlywed sister-in-law Melissa Trevett. "Had a letter from Liss. She had not gone up to Umatilla yet, tho' her husband had. All the furniture they bought here was lost by ship-wreck, but was mostly insured."

A final example entails a near miss for Emily, who planned to take a Sacramento River steamboat from Auburn, above Sacramento on the American River, to San Francisco. "I was intending to go home Thursday, but Aunt said stay until Saturday, & the boat that went down Thursday night was blown up, 40 or 50 lives lost, and a great number hurt. Was'nt it a narrow escape!"

Regardless of problems and dangers, the Bancrofts journeyed far and often. For those of us hopping into a car and quickly traveling dozens of miles over asphalt-covered roads and highways in a mere hour, we rarely consider the difficulty of getting from one place to another 150 years ago. However, some old-time inconveniences remain today: Emily noted the "commuter" traffic that Hubert faced by steamer to and from Sacramento in February 1863.

> Monday PM My husband came home about 11 o'clock last night. had to sit up all night on his way up—so many members of the Legislature come down to S.F. to spend the Sabbath that Monday night's steamer is always crowded. H. went to collect money from the State Library—writing did no good.

Travel by ferry to San Francisco also meant taking account of the tides. "H went off at 5 ½ yesterday morning on account of the tide & at 6 ½ this morning" (May 5, 1863).

Nature unblemished by cityscapes was often their reward. Emily praised remarkable scenery on a beautiful horseback ride "with the Bay on one side and the hills on the other," and on a longer trip to San Jose: "Went through the lovely countryside of San Mateo and Redwood City" with "trees large & abundant" (Apr. 17, 1864). She reminds us of the time when Redwood City was so named for its "abundant" red-woods that subsequently supplied lumber for the construction of San Francisco.

Another scenic journey was a horseback trip planned around the bay with friends.

> Mr & Mrs. Kittle came in a few moments last night and pro-posed to us to go "around the Bay" with them next week. It is quite a journey, but a beautiful ride they say. It takes four days to go and come. We ride the first day to San Mateo, 30 miles, about as far the next day and so on. They propose to have fast horses, leave here at 2 pm either Monday or Tuesday, get to SM at 7 or 8 pm &c. Think we will go Monday and get back Thursday night. . . . I expect to have the headache all the way but as H. has talked a great deal about that ride, and seems rather disposed to go, and as I won't be in the fashion until I've taken that trip, suppose I must. (May 28, 1860)

Emily was clearly eager to please her husband and to be "in fashion," even at the expense of her health. The headaches that plagued Emily could be brought on by physical duress or by eating sugar or for no reason at all. Though she may have had to take to her bed, she continued an active life overall.

At times Hubert's business involvements curtailed the family's leisure time. On June 26, 1864, Emily forlornly told her sister, "He can spend a day with me so seldom."

Emily wrote to her parents about an invitation to travel that seemed to please her.

> H. came home & said I had an invitation to Napa. That is, to Suscol Ranch to visit Mrs. Thompson who was Mary Gluyas. . . . Suscol Ranch is the most famous farm in the State. it is in the highest state of cultivation. they raise the nicest fruit that is sent into market. have a nice house, plenty of money, servants & houses. moreover, they are inclined to be religious & keep the Sabbath, which is a rare thing in the country in Cal. (May 5, 1865)

Suscol Ranch became the object of a tremendous legal battle. The ranch was originally part of a Mexican land grant of 18 square leagues (approximately 84,000 acres in Napa and Solano Counties) to the then commandant of Alta California, General Mariano Vallejo, who sold it to his Yankee son-in-law, John Frisbie. But like Mexican *Californios* in the crush of squatters and homesteaders, Frisbie had trouble holding on to his land. A Supreme Court act ruled in his favor and evicted occupiers on the ranch.

A letter about a journey to the South Bay in August 1869 conveys the beauty of Santa Clara, in now Silicon Valley. Emily described the trip from her lodging at Auzerais House in San Jose.

> We came down very comfortably Saturday [riding] all day for thirty miles, stopping several times in the middle of the day to rest man, woman and beast. We rode thro' some beautiful country, particularly after leaving Redwood city, and the road between here and Santa Clara, three miles, is lined on each side with large willow trees, set out a hundred years ago by monks, and was a lovely drive as we came through.

Emily stayed at the hotel for the week. She continued,

> My husband returned to the city early this morning. Will
> not come down again until Friday morning, when I expect to
> be at Congress Springs [Saratoga], ten miles from here. He
> will come over by stage & we will go next day to Santa Cruz.
> (Aug. 16, 1869)

A few days later, she reported on her travels from Santa Cruz.

> This is a lovely place on Monterey Bay, there are so many
> beautiful indentations in the shore, but it is past "the season",
> and I am too far away from my husband to enjoy myself very
> much. So I am going back over the mountain to San Jose.
> (Aug. 25, 1869)

A place that enchanted Emily vicariously, as it did many people
around the country once illustrations were published, was Yosemite. Between 1856 and 1861, James M. Hutchings, later proprietor of
a Yosemite Valley hotel, published *Hutchings' Illustrated California
Review*, which publicized sublime views of the Valley's granite forma-
tions, its gorgeous waterfalls, and giant sequoia trees nearby. In 1864
Emily had mentioned geologist Clarence King's visit on his way to
Yosemite. By 1869 the valley had become a popular tourist destination,
albeit for only rugged travelers (which did not include Emily), entail-
ing a stagecoach ride of 130 miles from Oakland to Merced and then
another 70 miles on horseback. She wrote to her sister, "I have just
come up from lunching with Mr. Harper. He leaves this P.M. for the
famous trip to the Yosemite" (July 12, probably 1869).

Emily envisioned such a trip, repeatedly mentioned in her letters, as
a goal for when her health should improve. "If it wasn't for the fatigue,
I would go. Hope to do so in a year from now, when travelling will be
easier and Pa will be with me" (June 14, 1869). As noted here, Emily
never gave up hope—nor relented in sending reminders—that her
family would visit one day. Less than six months before her death in
December 1869, she told her sister about her desire to see Yosemite
in the company of her family and to share California's wonders with
them:

We took an early dinner & as the evening was fine, I walked down to the store with my husband, as he was going down and staid until nearly dark. Found a very interesting book there, which I wish you and George would read. It gives a very good description of some of the trips to be made in this country, it is entitled "The New West" by Charles Brace.[2] I was interested in his account of the Yosemite. That is a trip I very much want to take, but do not feel adequate to it yet, but the facilities for going there are improving every year. I gave up going to the Geysers on that account. I hope to visit all these places, perhaps, in your company. (June 30, 1869)

A Grand Tour in Europe

Emily and Hubert's greatest journey took them to Europe from August 1866 to April 1867, leaving behind in Buffalo both daughter Kate, in the care of her sister-in-law, and Emily's ailing mother. Those separations might have been troubling enough, but Emily's precarious health also threatened to spoil the trip. As they set out on a long and arduous voyage, even for the joy of experiencing European culture, Emily felt querulous. Arriving in London, she wrote to her sister that Emily had found letters from her. She complained,

I have been quite homesick since I left, and most inclined to think travelling in Europe a "great humbug" but since my letters, which I gave a second perusal this morning, I feel quite "continuing on" & as if travelling wasn't so bad after all but it is tiresome work. The time to take such a trip is when one is young, just out of school or with all one's family. I've wished many a time you Kate & George C. were with us, as you spoke of, when our two Kate's are older, we'll leave our younger children at home, and make a party of six & come over. (Sept. 14, 1866)

Although Emily intermittently expressed wistfulness for her child, her family, and the familiar routines of home, she did appear engaged in her European experiences. She provided reports on and critiques of all they experienced, from the quality of churches, museums, and landscapes to that of hotels, restaurants, concerts, and theaters. After traveling to Ireland and Scotland, she and Hubert spent nearly two months in London and a month in Paris, then traveled through Spain and Italy and back to Paris and London again, where they departed for home.

H.H. had already been to Europe once. In his memoir he noted how that prior trip fanned the flames of his passion for educating himself in the creative cultural cauldrons of Europe.

> In January, 1862, my wife made a visit to her friends at home, and the following summer I took a hurried trip to London, Paris, New York, and Buffalo, bringing her back with me. This knocking about the world, with the time which it forced from business devoted to observation and thought under new conditions, was a great educator. It was then that ambition became fired, and ideas came rushing in on me faster than I could handle them. Notwithstanding I had read and studied somewhat, yet the old world, with its antique works and ways, seen by the eye of inexperience, was at once a romance and a revelation. In 1866-7 I spent a year in Europe with my wife, made the tour of Great Britain and the continent, came back to Buffalo. There we remained the following winter, visited Washington in the spring, and returned to San Francisco in the autumn of 1868.[3]

During their 1866–67 journey, H.H. was surely browsing in European bookstores and markets to bolster his collection, but such shopping sprees never made it into Emily's letters.

Whether describing lofty or drafty accommodations, an arduous but stunning journey to an illustrious or overly glorified site, the melodious or pitiable music emanating from a cathedral, and relentless rain or exuberant blue skies, Emily shared the details of her adventures with her family back home. With humor, perspicacity, and curiosity, Emily's observant eye and well-tuned ear captured stories to entertain and inform her family.

Emily found Glasgow "a pleasant city with fine squares and streets." There she also met someone with a name familiar to seamstresses of her time and ours: a Mr. Coats at his thread factory, possibly Peter

Coats, partner in the J & P Coats company, where "Mr. Coats made us a present of a package of thread" (Sept. 7, 1866).

In Paris by November, she marveled at the newfangled streets, whose old cobblestones had been paved over. "Many of the [streets] are made of cement so carriages make no noise in rolling over them, which is delightful after the noisy, narrow, smoky streets of London" (Nov. 13, 1866).

On January 2, 1867, Emily explained a Paris New Year's custom that piqued her curiosity.

> The streets were full that night & all yesterday and all last night. Such a hubbub! The beggars were permitted to come into town & beg. The streets were full of them. They are kept outside the city walls and are not permitted to beg excepting Jan. 1st & August 15th, when they get plenty. The Emperor held a [hearing] yesterday. All the officers of State called upon him. Some of our [group] saw the carriages drawn up at the Tuileries.

Seeing the begging poor in contrast to the pomposity of the royal palace of Emperor Napoleon III made Emily wonder at this strange custom.

A Mother Gone, "So Ripe for Heaven"

Halfway through her trip, a terrible loss left Emily bereft. While in Spain in January 1867, the couple learned that her mother, Lamira Callendar Ketchum, had passed away (the cause never stated in Emily's letters). Anyone who has lost a cherished mother can identify with Emily's sorrow, especially if that loss is multiplied by insuperable separation from the beloved. When Emily left Buffalo, her mother (not quite sixty-three) had been ill, though seemingly not deathly so. Perhaps Lamira did not let her daughter know how sick she was so that Emily would still embark on her rare and wonderful European tour.

In her first letter to her father upon learning of her mother's passing, Emily expressed great guilt at having abandoned her mother. Writing now to her father alone, Emily called on her faith to cope with her own grief, while hoping to support her remaining parent (age sixty-nine).

My dear Pa,

To think I can never say Pa & Ma any more. Your letters reached us this morning. My husband who saw them first & found they were both from you, was afraid they contained bad news & with his usual thoughtfulness gave me the earliest date which you told me of Ma's sickness, first, but it came to me as you said it did to you, as suddenly as if she had not been sick.

It seems as if I never could forgive myself for coming over here, to recover from the disappointment of not seeing her again. I've looked forward for several years to being with her during her last sickness, felt it would be such a privilege and she seemed so ripe for Heaven last Summer, I might have known I would never see her again. . . . I believed too readily what the Dr. said, "that she might live two or three years yet, but they would be years of great suffering." We should rejoice that she was spared that, that her sufferings were of no longer duration, but I feel that I have lost my best friend, we can have but one mother, and every day I lived, I have appreciated more & more what a mother I have had. My visit with her last summer is of infinite comfort to me tho' I fear I was not much comfort to her. If I had only staid and been with her these last six months, it seems as if I would not so regret her death for we know how well prepared she was, and how she must have suffered if she had lived, with her disease.

I have no doubt but the Lord took her in answer to what has been her prayer for years, that she might not live to be helpless and a burden. I cannot realize it at all. She looked so well & strong last Summer that I have felt since I've been away that she might quite recover.

You belong to me now, wherever I have a home, you have one with me. My husband has always said this, ever since Ma's sickness. I want to come straight home, but do not suppose I will. I came away with reluctance and I've really not enjoyed myself at all, have had a yearning for Buffalo. I wanted to spend the remainder of Ma's days with her, but it has seemed to be ordered otherwise. . . .

> If you do not dispose of your house, I would like to come
> and keep it for you a year or so, and when we return to Cal.
> I want you to go with us. I think you will enjoy the change,
> the country and the climate. And it would add greatly to my
> happiness to have you there. (Jan. 12, 1867)

In her first letter from Madrid to her sister and brother (George K.)
after hearing of her mother's death, Emily poured out her anguished
attempts to endure this tragedy so far from home.

> To think you were all passing through such trials at Christ-
> mas time! And I not know it. And I am never to see that
> dear face again! It seems as if it would break my heart to
> think I came away when I might have been with her all this
> time. Not that I could have <u>done</u> anything for her more than
> I know was done, but it would have been such a comfort to
> me. She has sent me so few messages since I've been away.
> She wrote me once on a little slip of paper. Do you think she
> felt that she would never see me again? <u>You</u> have nothing to
> <u>reproach</u> yourselves for my dear sister tried. . . . You did so
> much to make her last days happy. She told me so often last
> summer of your devotion and attention. She spoke partic-
> ularly George of you, that few sons could be as kind as you.
> How I envy you both this consolation.
>   I rejoice she was so soon taken from suffering, and that
> she was so well prepared. My only regret is that I was away.
> I have'nt enjoyed Europe at all. I've felt in such a hurry to
> get through and go home. I wanted to go back from London
> when I heard of her first sickness. I consulted a physician, told
> him all I could about her, and he said she would not die sud-
> denly, but would probably linger two or three years in great
> suffering, but the Lord has spared her that. If I had <u>only</u> staid.
> You will miss her more than I and how <u>Pa</u> must miss her.
> Won't you try to tell me what she said? did not she leave me
> any message. H. is waiting to mail this. God bless you both.
> (Jan. 12, 1867)

Emily wrestled with her guilt over the next month or so, nearly
unable to enjoy herself while thinking of the suffering of her family.

Yet the grand Old World around her provided distractions, especially because, in her very sensible mind, Emily knew that nothing could be done now but grieve and travel on.

Finding Entertainment and Edification in Sites, Songs, and Studies

Emily still took delight in her remaining European tour. She often noted to her sister the singing lessons Hubert had provided for her and the musical pieces she was singing or hearing in concerts. In Paris, Emily even found an opportunity to perform.

> H. wrote you a letter last week. I mislaid it & forgot to send it. It was prompted, I think, by my appearance in the choir at the American Chapel. I was prima donna for ½ day. . . . I proposed to contribute my voice, & it was accepted with apparent pleasure. I sang one P.M. with the choir. (Nov. 28, 1866)

In this same letter, Emily reported: "Did I tell you we went to hear Patti.[4] We were rather disappointed in her. She sang in Crispino. I had my second singing lesson today. My teacher is rather airy. I don't know whether he amounts to much or not. He gives me very different exercises to sing, makes them up as he goes along. . . . I tell H. it is a waste of money, but he says I had better take lessons while I'm here." Frequently Emily named the songs she was singing, assuming her cultured sister would also appreciate that Emily was tackling pieces such as "Montechichi Capuletti" and "Il Crocciato" [*sic*].[5]

But the hectic rhythm of their European travels also wore on her, even early in their voyage. "We are living very quietly here. I don't feel as if I want to go sight seeing any more for a long time. I would rather leave it until spring. it seems quite homelike here." Her added note from Paris indicates the ever-determined focus of her autodidact husband: "H. studies nearly all the time" (Nov. 28, 1866).

Hubert and Emily both enjoyed learning from books as they absorbed the sights. In Rome she recounted travels to excavation sites, ancient Roman monuments, and museums. "It is so entirely different here from anything we have ever seen before that we find a great deal to interest us. H. too has just finished reading a history of ancient

Rome. We have a book telling of the little things we encounter every day, called 'Roba di Roma,' by W.W. Story.[6] You would be interested in it" (Feb. 5, 1867).

Back in Paris again in April, Emily reiterated what H.H. had said about enjoying the freedom in Europe to ingest voraciously all that the world might offer him. "Hubert is reading as much as ever. He never had an opportunity before.... It is 11 pm & time we were in bed.... He sits here with his feet as high as his head & will read until tomorrow morning if I do not make him go to bed" (Apr. 8, 1867).

A last item in Emily's commentary from Paris elucidates the busy education they received at the International Exposition that had opened on April 1 that year.

> We've commenced the "exposition" and found that if we had
> 12 hours per day to devote to it for a month, we could not see
> it all. as it is we go out directly after breakfast and stay until
> 3 or 4 pm which is the most the strongest can do, for there
> are no seats, excepting outside, near the cafés ... there are
> so many beautiful things to see, that one is quite exhausted
> before they know it.... All the articles are arranged in circles,
> the different nationalities radiating from the inner to the
> outer circle. This way, we take a circle visiting all the apart-
> ments on each side. yesterday we did two. [She enclosed a
> diagram to illustrate the design.] On the outside are plenty
> of cafés with all kinds of refreshments. Most of the Amer-
> ican articles are still unpacked. I noticed yesterday a glass
> case containing very handsome silver, from Tiffany's N.Y.
> by its side stood a Yankee cook stove and in the distance any
> quantity of kitchen clocks. The show in our department is
> not particularly brilliant.... The Swiss & German clocks are
> <u>beautiful</u>, a great many are cuckoo clocks of wood. Vienna has
> the most beautiful fancy articles, particularly in leather—bags,
> purses, cigar cases, writing desks, etc. but the laces! Particu-
> larly from Brussels. such shawls & lace dresses & flounces I
> never dreamed of. We've seen only a few pictures, but they
> were very fine, and those from America as good as any.

With her European tour soon ending, Emily's letter concluded with thoughts about returning to California, seeking, as ever, to entice her sister and brother-in-law, George, to join them there eventually.

> We've seen no climate yet as fine as Cal. particularly in the Winter. And I'm beginning to feel with my husband that there is the place to live. if George Coit could go there, I would be quite willing to go back. As it is, I quite dread it. I believe you would all enjoy living there better than anywhere else. You would miss old associations but new ones are more easily found there than anywhere else. My husband wants to go out before I do, & build a house, where we will all go maybe. I think it would be very nice, but man proposes! (Apr. 16, 1867)

Thus Emily closed her letter by repeating a statement made earlier, an acquiescence to forces far greater than her own wishes: "Man proposes; God disposes." As with all her letters, she signed off: "Affctly Em."

In a last letter from Europe, written in London (date uncertain), Emily informed her sister about Hubert's association with another publisher. "Perhaps you remember the Bohn library books. Mr. Bohn is very wealthy and has a handsome place out at R[ichmond], and insists upon H.'s coming out & bringing us. I've not laid eyes on him, but H. has seen a good deal of him." The Henry Bohn Bookstore, named for the publisher (1792–1884) who popularized mass-market books on academic and literary topics, still exists in Liverpool. Bancroft's many visits to Mr. Bohn may have influenced his own publications.

Emily emphasized her readiness to return home. "We are counting the weeks, and almost the days before we will be in B. We are tired of travelling, and I am very tired of London. It is the gloomiest filthiest place I ever was in. I do not think America will look at all like a wilderness to us after Europe. On the contrary, I think it will look very pleasant to us."

A "wilderness" indeed!

CHAPTER FIVE

Emily's Demise

"Thinner Than Ever": Forebodings from Europe

While reporting on fabulous places she and her husband, H. H. Bancroft, were enjoying during their European tour (August 1866 to April 1867), Emily Bancroft's letters also warned of her failing health. Writing to her sister from Geneva in March 1867, Emily confided how she grappled with both her absence from their mother's deathbed the prior December and her own physical frailty and lethargy.

> I think as you say we always reproach ourselves for some-
> thing when we lose our friends and no doubt it was best I
> was not with Ma. I've tho't lately that perhaps I would have
> been more care & worry to her than help for I'm not good
> for anything. I've felt it more lately than ever. Mary Ketchum
> [her sister-in-law] says I'm lazy. I've tho't maybe it was so
> and hoped travelling and an opportunity to see so much that
> was new would rouse my energies, but I seem to get worse
> and worse. Finally took to my bed in Rome & Naples from
> sheer laziness or exhaustion I don't know which, & felt as if
> I would'nt go outside the door to see anything, and I cannot
> get up any interest in what I see. . . . When I return you must
> expect to see me thinner . . . than ever. I feel that the money

has been almost thrown away on my travelling. Still I <u>live</u> & <u>eat</u> as much as any body. maybe I'll turn about one of these days & make a strong woman. (Mar. 9, 1867)

What *was* wrong with Emily? She would die two-and-a-half years later, in December 1869, reportedly of kidney disease. This last chapter in Emily's life portrays her advancing ailment through letters that record a long decline until her death.

Emily's most frequent comment was about her "sick headache," which today we might call a migraine, when the head throbs so violently —exacerbated by any light or sound—that one can only lie prostrate in a dark room, nauseated and incapacitated. Emily explored what might have instigated these headaches and their effects. Most often she pinpointed sweet foods. Her letters also hint at the possibility that she may have developed diabetes, an illness not yet commonly identified as such in the 1860s, but one that confirms the "kidney disease" stated as her cause of death. Diabetes may also explain problems with her pregnancies and the death of a newborn daughter, as well as her gradual wasting and blindness. Even without a specific diagnosis, Emily's letters provide a poignant picture of the struggles with such diseases in a time when little appropriate medical help was available.

Emily's Sleuthing about the "Sick Headache"

In the hundreds of letters Emily wrote during more than eight years of absences from her family in Buffalo, she mentioned her headaches at least eighty times. Often Emily simply announced their presence, as in a letter to her sister and brother-in-law soon after arriving in San Francisco: "Yesterday I had two sick head-aches" (Dec. 4, 1860). Other times she conveyed the news with humor.

I was sick in bed with headache, tho' I managed to appear in the kitchen after noon . . . frightening the carpenter most out of his sense as I was without hoops & my garments rather scant anyway. . . . I was quite sick yesterday with headache tho' I was up nearly all the P.M. & quite revived by evening. (July 21, 1864)

Emily often suggested possible causes. In writing about an upcoming horseback tour around the bay with her husband, traveling thirty miles a day, she anticipated future suffering. "I expect to have the headache all the way" (May 28, 1860, to her sister). Imagine such a ride, the horse pounding beneath and the head pounding within! A day of strenuous exercise could bring on the headache. "H took us to ride in the pm, beautiful day, but I came home very sick, had a good old fashioned headache" (Mar. 25, 1863). Yet on other occasions, Emily reported that after riding, she did *not* suffer a headache.

In Emily's analysis, the most obvious cause of the headache was sweet foods, such as when she'd made and eaten mint jelly and then ended up with "the sick headache" (May 13, 1864). Emily also noted the consequences of eating fruit and anything made with sugar.

> [Hubert] brought home some elegant straw-berries enough for dinner & breakfast the next day, at which time I partook of them, very foolishly, and a sick headache ensued. I went over into the city in the pm (this is Thursday) at 1 o'clock & staid until 5 pm & such a head-ache as I had before I got home! (May 5, 1863)

> Adelaide is to set doughnuts tonight so you may expect to hear of a series of headaches from me, expected to have it today as she made more molasses candy yesterday. She makes it as nicely as the confectioners. (Mar. 7, 1865)

> Adelaide met me as I was coming in & said I'd have the headache tomorrow she knew. Mrs. Hudson sent us a basket of plums last night, Mrs. Taylor sent peaches this morning, & Mr. Hyer some elegant blackberries—haven't we kind neighbors. (Aug. 1, 1865)

Just as many of us struggle with junk food today, Emily had a problem with "trash" food in the 1860s. "I'm most sick again today with head ache, so can't write much. I ate candy and trash yesterday. I'll never learn to be careful about what I eat" (Sept. 20, no year). Emily seemingly could not reject forbidden food. A friend brought over candy, "and we are revelling. You'll say in head-aches but I do really wish they would'nt bring over candy" (Sept. 9, 1864, to her parents).

At one point, when Emily had been particularly unwell, she recognized the link between eating candy and fatigue, as well as the headache.

> I really think my health is improving. H. says it is because I take life quietly and don't get tired. I go out twice a day, have no hills to climb, know just how far I can go without fatigue, and am careful not to eat candy and I've not felt better in a long time. never lived so quietly before in my life. (San Francisco, Feb. 18, no year, likely 1863, to her parents)

Yet on a later date in this same letter, Emily wrote: "Sick with headaches all day."

The Fourth of July festivities brought with them a slew of headache inducers: "H. is going to bring over some peanuts & candy & some fire crackers. You may expect to hear of the headache on Wednesday. but I eat candy very seldom. I suppose if it was you you wouldn't eat it at all" (June 28, 1865). She followed up:

> As I expected, I was quite sick yesterday with headache. think I'll not eat pea-nuts & candy again until next 4th July. I'll be with you then probably & you can keep me from it. isn't it funny! my husband never says one word against it, & when I have the headache, never reproaches me for indulging in things that I know will hurt me, as I think I should him if he did so. (July 6, 1865)

On her European trip, Emily reported several bouts of suffering from headaches. Of a day sightseeing in London she wrote, "We did'nt get home until nearly 11 p.m. & I was about used up. Had a headache, and did'nt get up until late this morning." However, by the next morning, she reported, "feel quite recovered. I've been quite well generally. We manage to keep out in the open air all day most of the time" (Sept. 14, 1866). Emily often felt better after getting fresh air without strenuous exercise.

Regardless of her best efforts to discover a pattern to the problem and address it, Emily had to resign herself to frustrated ignorance. "I got up this morn from a two days' headache. I cannot account for my headaches, so often. I seem to have them any way, do what I will" (Sept. 26, 1865). Bravely, she even sought a silver lining to her cloud: "I try to be careful & am generally very well, but in spite of all I can do, I <u>will</u> have the headache about so often. There is one consolation, people that have the headache never have anything else" ("Thanksgiving morning," 1863).

How the Headache Wreaked Havoc

Anyone who has suffered a migraine's invading army will know that the unfortunate effects are not limited to pain but also include plans derailed and energy depleted. Emily did not belabor the impact of her headaches, but did indicate the difficulties they caused.

At a basic level, on account of a headache, a day or more would go by without writing. "Yesterday I had the head-ache & couldn't write" (May 31, 1861). Years later, Emily wrote to her sister from a hotel in New York, "I've wanted all day to gossip with you, but have had a miserable head-ache, and have done nothing at all, but lean out the window watching the crowd pass to & fro" (Apr. 30, 1867).

Emily's social life involved a stream of visiting and visitors, to which a headache put a halt. One day when visitors arrived, Emily persevered. She explained to her sister, "I had the head-ache all day, but did'nt want to give up to it, so I have it again today, am most down sick" (Mar. 21, probably 1861).

Sometimes, a migraine forced Emily to miss events she had greatly anticipated, from church to concerts. "[Went to] the German rehearsal at 12 pm. They are to give a grand concert this evening. I'm most sick with the headache. Don't know as I shall be able to go, at which I shall be quite disappointed" (Aug. 1861, no date).

More important, Emily's headaches affected her life with Hubert. She did not want her illness to dissatisfy him. He proved to be sympathetic and supportive, though she knew he too suffered when she was incapacitated. "I was sick with headache to [Hubert's] great disappointment" (Nov. 2, 1863). Hubert often came to the rescue of his wife and child.

> Kate & I went over yesterday to spend the day with Grandmother Bancroft—by afternoon I had such a headache I was too sick to come home, as Kate was with me & Mother so pleased to have us there, I resigned myself quite willingly

> to staying all night & when my husband found I was not
> coming home by my not being there, he turned about & came
> back to town & out there too, was'nt he good? (Aug. 5, 1865)

As ever with Emily, a sense of humor could lighten the load. She
wrote about a practical joke she played on her husband, who had left
her ill in the morning.

> By the time he reached the house I was spread on the bed
> with a wet towel over my head & only faint groans now audi-
> ble in reply to his sympathizing inquiries if I had been sick all
> day. Of course I laughed before a very great while, for I was
> perfectly well before noon. Made some gingerbread this P.M.
> (June 8, 1864)

On another occasion, Emily was not joking with her husband but
deeply depended on his help—and felt chagrined not to help *him* at
his midday meal.

> Since writing the first of this, I've had two days siege of
> headache. Consequence of making & tasting preserves &
> pickles. I was really quite sick & feel rather slim today tho I
> was glad enough to get to work. Such a pile of stockings and
> socks to say nothing of the white shirts to be starched....
> I was just sick enough that I did not want any waiting on,
> & to want the house quiet, so I let them go to have a good
> time. My husband came home in the 11 am boat to stay with
> me because I was sick & it was fortunate he did for my head
> ached so he had to apply laudanum & vinegar. I had quite a
> time but there was no one home to get him anything to eat
> for which I was sorry tho' he said he did'nt mind it. (Oakland,
> July 25, 1864)

A Search for Remedies

One effort to cope with the headache included applying vinegar
and laudanum. A tincture of opium, laudanum was widely used in

combination with other substances in Emily's day for pain relief. Presumably she was applying it topically, although it was also ingested.

But Emily's accounts of attempted remedies were as infrequent as the headache descriptions were prolific. One time she wrote that a good friend, Mrs. Rud, merely sat with her during a terrible headache (Jan. 12, 1863). Intermittently, her husband came to her aid, as mentioned earlier and here: "Instead of going to town & spending money yesterday I was flat on my bed with sick headache. H came home at 5 ½ and most cured me in a little while" (Oakland, Aug. 10, 1864).

In correlating diet, exercise, and the headache, Emily wrote about experiments to improve her health. "I've had the headache since I last wrote, on the 22nd but not nearly so hard as usual, enough to keep me from writing or sewing. I've been taking more exercise lately, which with the bran I eat, keeps me feeling very well, and my headaches are not nearly so severe lately" (Jan. 22, 1866, to her parents).

A year after speaking of laudanum, Emily explained that a doctor gave her another unidentified medication, which she presumed would do little good.

> I was sick in bed yesterday with headache. Kate & Adelaide were as good as they could be. Adelaide is quite motherly. the Dr. thinks he can cure my headaches & has left a medicine for me to take three times a day, but I've no faith in it. my headaches are hereditary I think. besides I hate to be dosing. He says if I will [continue] in taking it for three months, he knows it will cure me. what do you think? (Apr. 5, 1865, to her parents)

A Baby Lost

As noted in chapter 2, Emily's letters about being "sick" when expecting baby Kate illustrate contemporary attitudes toward pregnancy and birth. Both brought worry over the vulnerability of mother and baby. Even aside from the deadly threats in the birth process, the pain of the ordeal without drugs to facilitate labor or ease discomfort made giving birth a "trial," as Emily called it. When Emily's sister Kate was to give birth in early 1865, Emily shared her anxious, prayerful anticipation, writing, "By this time you have passed through your trial or are near it. May your Heavenly Father sustain you my dear sister & give you a living perfect child & may it prove a comfort to you" (Jan. 10, 1865).

Her remark was especially poignant because Emily had lost her own newborn daughter just two months earlier. She had been pregnant during the same summer and fall of 1864 as had her sister. In an October letter to her parents, Emily had disclosed news of a pending November birth.

I am getting rather dilatory about writing, I think—there are two reasons for it. One is that I have so much interesting work on hand that I allow myself to become altogether too much absorbed, then it is rather hard work just at present to write.

I hope by the time you receive this letter you will have a telegraph from H. conveying some <u>news</u>. Maybe you've had intimations of the news before this but I hope not for I want to be the first to tell you that I expect to be sick [in labor] early in Nov.

You must not blame me for not telling you sooner for it was entirely for your sake. I knew you would worry about me constantly and as I was very well and am in the kindest and best of hands, I felt that it would be foolish to cause you needless anxiety. H. will telegraph you soon as I am sick—it is superfluous to add that he is delighted at the prospect before us, with the great happiness. . . . I am very far from feeling badly. I was never so pleasantly situated since I've been married. . . . My girl is a real comfort. She is quiet and does everything without waiting to be looked after. My husband is all devotion (& so is Kate). My friends are all kind and helpful & every earthly wish is gratified & you must be grateful with me that it is so. Lizzie White is with me & makes herself very useful. . . .

My husband made me a present last summer of a very elegant cradle, the handsomest thing I ever saw. It is a large basket of blue netted cord tied with blue satin, edged outside with a deep blue fringe. The basket is hung on a gilt frame to rock or be stationary. (Oct. 13, 1864)

The couple's happy anticipation of filling that cradle with a new baby would be crushed.

Surprisingly, among the letters to her parents bound in the leather volume that Emily's husband had created are two letters from Hubert himself (signed "H.H.") explaining the mysterious circumstances of that baby's death and reporting on his wife's condition, both quoted in full (Oct. 20, 1864, Oakland).

My dear Mr & Mrs. Ketchum

A little girl was born in our house this morning but it only lived two hours. It was a beautiful child, nicely formed, seemed perfect in every respect. The doctor said something was wrong inside. It came about two weeks before we expected it.

At first we were a little disappointed it was not a boy—but as soon as we thought there was danger of its not living I felt as though I would give anything if it only might live. We both of us wanted a baby. Emily was well and we counted upon telegraphing to you the arrival of a fine boy but we would have been only too well satisfied if it had lived. It seems as though God's hand was upon us—still it might be worse. Emily is well & I sincerely hope will get up well.

I do not think it best for her to try to have any more children for a long time to come.

Kate has not been very well lately—nothing serious, but it makes me feel as though we were not deserving of children & that God is taking them to himself.

Truly yours
HH Bancroft

Hubert's letter to his parents-in-law reveals a bald honesty. First, he states his preference for having a boy, perhaps to balance out a daughter. In later years he comes across as a male chauvinist, providing better educational and financial opportunities to his sons than to his daughters. But Hubert also shows here his yearning for *any* child, and for this child to have lived. His despair is real.

His last comment about God taking their children—"them," plural—points to another miscarriage or infant death suffered in the intervening years between Kate's birth in August 1860 and the loss of this child in October 1864. Emily's letters do not report the prior loss, but she may have been at home with her family in Buffalo. In a letter dated September 27, 1861, Emily's parents encouraged her to come home to be "sick," and there are no letters from her between August 1861 and August 1862 in the archived volumes. Probably during that period, Emily lost another baby.

Further attesting to that earlier infant death is a penciled in comment on the back of the long letter from H.H. above, noted as from Mary Ketchum, possibly Emily's sister-in-law, married to her brother George Ketchum. She apologized for keeping H.H.'s letter for so long and said, "Emily seems very unfortunate in her children. I hardly realize she has had three children." The writer might be referring to a baby that died in 1862.

Returning to Hubert's letter, it is worth noting how forthright he was in asserting that Emily should not have any more children "for a long time to come." This determination had to be devastating for the young couple, who anticipated a large family (as Hubert later had with his second wife, Matilda).

In a later letter from Hubert to his mother-in-law on October 26, 1864, he expressly offered comfort to "Ma" Ketchum during Emily's recuperation. Oddly, he lapsed into discussion of dramatic political events in San Francisco, as if it were too awkward for him to focus on the female nature of Emily's "sickness" and aftermath.

> My dear Ma
>
> Emily was going to write today but she had a little headache & thought she had better save her eyes and wait a few days. She never was so well before. Has permission to get up ... but her room is so pleasant she is in no hurry—it is the pleasantest room she ever was sick in. She can lie and look out of the window ... her neighbor Mrs. Taylor and Mrs Hudson are sending her something nearly all of the time.... Tomorrow is the anniversary of our wedding day....
>
> She wishes to know if I cannot write a little on my own responsibility....
>
> My father mother & sister came down from Washington two or three days ago. They leave for Auburn CA to visit some friends there tomorrow—that is my Father & Mother.

My sister remains here & expects to be married here in about a month & then go to Umatilla Oregon to live for awhile.

Politics are running very high with us. I today joined a home protective association to act under the Police authorities for the prevention of outbreaks until after election. San Francisco is easily worked up into an excitement but there is a strong element in the most respectable portion of the community as manifested in Vigilance Committee times, determined that mobs shall not rule.

I have read your letters to Emily with much interest. I hope we shall see you all again in time.

Truly yours, HH Bancroft

A week after the baby's death, Emily herself wrote to her "Ma" a letter labeled "<u>Private</u>." Had she wished it to be destroyed, she might have given such instructions, but didn't. She narrated a heartrending, courageous, and even somewhat humorous account of what had befallen them.

This is the 5th anniversary of our wedding. I feel so well today that I must write to tell you about it & have you rejoice with me, that the Lord has spared my life though He saw fit to take that of my child. It was an unscrutable providence, and a great disappointment to us both. I never saw H. so overcome. There seemed to be no cause for death, that is, as far as we could see. It was a larger child than Kate was, just as fat as it could be & so pretty, looked just as Kate did. One thing was against it—it was come feet first. My labor was so quick the Doctor had no time to right it and I suppose the reason that I did not go my full term was because I had so much water. I grew rather suddenly to an immense size & told H. on going to bed that night that I felt as if I could'nt go another day. about 3 o'clock in the morning I was wakened by the water breaking & I must have lost two pails full. It was such a relief! my pain, what little I had, soon came on. H sent the man who lives back of us ... for the Dr. & a nurse whom I had partially engaged for fear of such an emergency & who lives over here. H. fixed my bed soon as possible but in spite of everything he could put under me, the water filled the bed, soaked through the mattress paillasse [a straw mattress] & made a pool on the floor. The baby was born at 4 o'clock in one hour. I never supposed so little & never was so well after. It does'nt seem as if I had been sick at all.

My nurse got me a little dog the same day, a cunning little thing, no larger than a kitten. He drew my breasts until the milk came, when my nurse had to help him but it came so hard she blistered her tongue, and then could not get it all out. So we set Mr. Hayes out for a larger puppy & we brought a bouncer—it was like a young bear, but he cleaned two breasts out nicely so the nurse could draw them. Between him and the little dog, I got along very nicely. I had a great abundance of milk for the first few days but it is beginning to fall off rapidly, so the little dog takes about all. Now he comes tumbling out of his basket.

Saturday: I sat up again yesterday & today. Was up an hour today & did'nt want to go back to bed at all, but the nurse said I must. I have fire in my grate, and I can lie in my bed & look out of the window. I don't believe any one ever had a pleasanter room to be sick in, or kinder friends—my neighbors come in every day to see how I am, & are all the time sending me something. Mrs. Rud came over day before yesterday. Mrs. Glenyas yesterday. Mr. & Mrs. Bancroft & Liz came Sunday night & left Thursday for Auburn where the Grandfather is & [will] stay until time for the wedding. Liz is here, has improved a good deal & is good company for me, takes all the care of Kate, & Kate seems to like her very much. Even as I am quite well, H. wants me to go to town and board with him a while at the new hotel the Cosmopolitan. Liz says she will keep house here & take care of Kate. they think the change will do me good. I can come over here every day if I like & H. wants to be in town. (Oct. 27, 1864)

Emily's letter to her sister three weeks later shows Emily still trying to make sense of losing what seemed like a perfectly healthy baby.

It is a long time since I've written to you. Three weeks this morning since I was sick. Yesterday, Nov. 9th, was the time I expected to be sick. I do not know whether you were

surprised to hear of it or not. . . . My only object in keeping it
from you all was that you need not worry about me, as I knew
you would & you must not feel anxious now, for I'm doing
splendidly. Could not have better care if I had been home tho'
I sometimes feel it might have been different with the baby.
Still I cannot tell. There was no one here for nearly an hour
to wash & dress it, & it seemed to me that in that time it
became chilled. The reason for its death that the Dr. gave was
a very unsatisfactory one to both Hubert & I, that the proper
circulation after birth had never commenced but he seemed
as much astonished as any one when it died. It was such a
large splendid looking child, so nicely developed & so fat. I
could not understand its dying, but as I said before I cannot
tell how it was and it was permitted for some wise reason. H
& I had looked forward to its arrival with the greatest pleasure. I had never felt that way before. It was a great disappointment. I never saw H. so overcome. I hope good may
grow out of it.

I've had a very comfortable sickness, many things have
been pleasant. My room, the weather and the company. The
latter I've enjoyed. Liz Bancroft & her father are here now.
She is real kind & thoughtful & I enjoy having her here very
much. She will be married I suppose in Dec. or Jan. She is
almost ready & we are both engaged in various kinds of fancy
work.

Friday morning. My nurse goes today, has been with me
three weeks. If my baby was living I should dread to have
her go, as it is, I can get along very well without her. She has
taken very nice care of me, is good & motherly.

You don't know how cunning my little dog is. he is black &
white, and no larger than a little kitten, fat as butter. H. makes
all manner of fun with it, dandles it like a baby & talks to it just
as I do, & pulls its tail when I don't behave. (Nov. 10, 1864)

The reference to the puppy is puzzling until one understands that
sometimes women used a puppy to draw off their milk so the mother's
breasts would not ache so painfully if the baby had died or she was
separated from it. Emily mentioned that her sister-in-law also used a
puppy to help with the postnatal milk burden.

Melissa Bancroft Trevett (Liss) was married in Hubert and Emily's home in January 1865. She and her husband, Theodore, then moved to Portland, but Liss had returned to stay with the Bancrofts in San Francisco in order to have her baby in their house. (Emily disapproved of this, saying that "the proper place for a woman to have her baby is in her husband's home, but where they live, there was neither physician nor nurse" [Oct. 24, 1865].) Liss's baby was born on New Year's Day, 1866. On January 4, Emily wrote, "Liss seems to feel very well, the baby takes hold as if it would nurse, tho' at first she made a fuss. they got a little dog, which is quite a help, both to the baby & Liss."

The Mysterious Illness and Its Impacts on Pregnancy

Other aspects of Emily's letters following the death of her baby provide more evidence of what might have been diabetes, noting that the baby was fat, even fatter than Kate. In the one available picture of Emily with baby Kate (no date indicated), Kate appears to have a very large head. When Kate was eight months old, Emily noted in a letter to her sister that Kate had a "large face." Oddly, Emily added: "You don't know what a nice baby she is Kate, the healthiest looking baby in the neighborhood, and I never expected her to live to this time." (Apr. 2, 1861).

Contemporary medical research indicates what Emily and her newborn may have been undergoing. Typically, infants of diabetic mothers tend to be larger and fatter than normal babies. Their bodies undergo "macrosomia" to compensate for the excess sugar in their mother's blood. Emily had noted the large amount of amniotic fluid associated with the birth, a condition occurring in about 10 percent of births to diabetic mothers.

To answer Hubert's plaintive question about what was "wrong inside" with this baby he called "nicely formed" and "perfect in every respect," the doctor suggested that the baby died because "proper circulation had never commenced." Today we know that diabetic mothers' newborns have birth defects more often, which may have affected Emily's infant.

Despite the loss of her baby, Emily continued with her positive attitude. To her parents on November 24, a month after the baby's birth and death, she reported,

I seem to have plenty of milk—for the little <u>dog</u>. Don't know how it would answer for a baby. H. wants me to keep it as long as I can for he thinks it will do me good & I think that is something else that does me good, for I never felt better than I do now, and I assure you I enjoy my health.

With the six weeks between mailing and receipt of a letter, Emily's family would only hear of the baby's death long afterwards; nor would Emily receive a letter of support from her family until mid-December, two months after she lost her baby. On December 17, 1864, Emily wrote: "Monday evening: Steamer came in yesterday and brought a nice long

Emily Ketchum Bancroft with baby Kate, ca. 1861, courtesy of The Bancroft Library
(BANC MSS 73/64 c)

letter from both of you. You had just heard of my sickness." How hard to experience this delay in receiving loving care from our closest family members after such a trial.

Her December 4 letter to her mother, quoted in full, weaves together the many facets of Emily's ordeal.

> I suspect your heart has been full of anxiety for me my dear mother, but you must not let it be so. I trust that this late dispensation may be sanctified to us both. I am in the hands of a kind God & a kind kind husband. His Father & Mother are so kind and considerate & seem to think so much of us both that I cannot help loving them. And I hope I am a little different from what I used to be that I am more kindly disposed. Liz seems determined to make herself useful & agreeable, so if we do not get along it will be my fault. She expects to be married in December. Her mother is coming down then & going directly back to Auburn, unless something turns up. They soon hope to go back to Ft. Lincor, their heart is evidently in the work, and I wish they might be gratified.
>
> I am sorry to hear you are [ill] again. it makes me feel in a hurry to go East. and I should'nt wonder if we came sooner... the baby [would have] lived. After our lease is out, next July, I think H. will want to leave Oakland. We only staid here this winter for that but we must leave all these things to Him to order who doeth all things well. for my part I feel more and more that here we have no continuing city, and must call no place upon earth our "home."
>
> My nurse is an old maternity body. English. has had 14 children. she takes the best of care of me & seems to enjoy seeing me eat, and I do considerable in that way. my appetite is tremendous. Kate has gone visiting. One of the neighbors came for her. she is to bring me some flowers. she is better than she has been all summer. enjoys the company we've had very much. But I must stop for this time. afftly, Em

It took Emily a long time to regain her health fully. In March 1865, five months after the birth and loss, she told her sister: "Last week I undertook to have a lunch party, and made myself quite sick. think I shan't try it again. It takes me just about a year to get my strength after a confinement."

One wonders how Emily and Hubert coped with the recommendation not to have more children. She did not often convey her darker feelings, perhaps to avoid worrying her parents or sister. But signs of her mourned opportunities for a larger brood did crop up. In an August 1865 letter to her parents, Emily mentioned plans to travel east "to go home" early the next year, in March 1866. Meanwhile, Emily was buying new clothing for their servant, Adelaide, who might have accompanied Emily and Kate, had there been another baby to take care of.

> I bought her a very pretty street sacque yesterday for $10.
> You know last week I bought a poplin & a silk dress. She is
> getting quite fixed up. I think she means to go home in the
> spring as well as myself. She wishes I had a baby for her to
> take care of on the way home. From present prospects I'm
> afraid I cannot accommodate her.... I want to send Kate's
> baby a blue plaid cloak I cut out for my baby last summer.
> (Aug. 10, 1865)

Sending the "baby cloak" to her sister, made for her own child, signals that Emily was resigned to not having any more of her own babies.

"Nothing but a Skeleton": Trying the Granville Cure

A major effort to remedy Emily's ailments took place in July 1868. A year earlier, while still in Europe, Emily wrote to her father that she and Hubert were planning to go to Granville, Ohio, Hubert's hometown, to consult with his uncle, Dr. William Wilson (known as W.W.) Bancroft, who practiced the "water cure." Developed in the 1850s in Europe, the water cure soon became popular in certain areas of the United States as well. W. W. Bancroft established his water cure at the Granville Infirmary in 1851 or 1852, later establishing a partnership with Dr. Edwin Sinnet. The theory was that immersion in water would force toxic substances to flow out of pores and tiny bodily crevices, even resulting in pustules and causing a "crisis" that would be ultimately healing.

GRANVILLE WATER-CURE.

THIS Institution has now been in successful operation nearly six years, during which time, the results of our treatment of disease in its various forms, warrant us in laying our claims before the public, in the form of an Annual Report.

For a long time, the treatment of diseases Hydropathically, was regarded as an experiment in the West, which must depend upon the results of practice for its favor with an ever-jealous public. In the following pages, we propose to present to our patrons, friends, and the public generally, our claims and the results of our treatment, and leave them to judge of our merits.

It is the experience of every physician, that a great number of chronic diseases will be found which cannot be treated successfully at home, but which could be cured or greatly benefited, by treatment in an establishment of this kind. The obstacles to success in these cases do not consist so much in a correct diagnosis and medication of them, as in the judicious exercise of that dietetic, mental, and moral management, which are absolutely necessary and contribute so largely to a happy result. Old morbid associations must be broken up—new habits of thought and action established—new and harmonious actions in the secreting and excreting organs induced—the blood purified, and its circulation equalized—weak organs sustained and strengthened—impaired ones corrected and subdued. The nervous system so strengthened and freed from the action of disease, that the vital powers can go on and renovate the system, and restore its proper functions.

Stationery for the Granville Infirmary, ca. 1855,
courtesy of the Granville Historical Society

Following the Bancrofts' return from Europe in 1867, they waited a year before going to Granville, even though Emily's 1867 description from London of her dire health conveys a sense that she was "coming home to die." They were desperate for a cure.

> I want to go to Ohio & let Hubert's uncle put me thro' "a course of treatment". My travelling over here has done me very little good and I am so thin, I'm really ashamed to come home. I am nothing but a skeleton. I think there is a difficulty with my stomach and bowels, which if not attended to before long will carry me off. I have felt for sometime that I was only coming home to die, but I think it is worth while to try something effectual first. (Date uncertain, 1867)

From mid-July 1868 to the end of August, the good doctor had Emily cleanse her body of almost all foods in order to isolate those that might be problematic for her digestion. To her sister, she wrote:

> I suspect you've had a good laugh over my present situation, but you had better cry, for I assure you I am having an <u>awful</u> time, as you can imagine. You know what my habits of eating and drinking have been & it is <u>such</u> a coming down to a slice or two of brown bread, a few berries & a little piece of meat! I don't mind the tea & coffee if they would only give me a little more to <u>eat</u>. I am . . . starved, but I'm going to give the "treatment" a fair trial. I shall come out <u>better</u> or <u>worse</u>. (July 23, 1868)

Later the same day: "The Dr. has been in to see me today, and increased my allowance of food a little, and says I am better. . . . He says I must do nothing besides my regular exercise, but sleep and rest."

A week later, Emily's sense of humor sparkled as she replied to her sister's comment that she had become as thin as a "split match."

> Your remark that I would resemble a split match after the water curing process afforded much merriment to all to whom I repeated it (& I repeated it to all) and they evidently thought I had a very facetious sister. I think you are about right, but the Dr. says I will grow fat on my diet if I will

persevere in it. I really am better. Everyone says I look so and
am satisfied with my present quantity and quality—brown
bread, berries & meat compose my diet. (July 30, 1868)

Three weeks later, Emily wrote, "This is my birth-day. I'm 34 or 35,
don't know which. . . . My health continues to improve. I think if I
could stay here six months, the improvements would be visible to the
naked eye. I now have all I want to eat of plain food" (Aug. 19, 1868).
    The couple left at the end of August, with Emily fattened up, but
with no cure for her disease.

Wasting and Blindness

Calling herself "skeletal" was perhaps hyperbole, but Emily, who hoped
to go home to Buffalo in 1869, joked to her sister in May, "You must
certainly have a horse and go-cart by the time I come, to carry my
bones around in" (May 25, 1869).
    In another attempt at humor in her report on a diagnosis and rem-
edy, Emily wrote to her sister that her friends, Mrs. Gaviss and Mrs.
Rud, disguised an intervention as a shopping trip.

And where do you think they persuaded me to go, but to a
worm doctor. they made up their minds that I had a tape
worm! So to satisfy them, I went. He told me I had no tape
worm, but animalcular [referring to microscopic organisms],
which were constantly gnawing the coat of my stomach and
the mucus membrane, which he could destroy by medicine
& heal my stomach by dieting. Don't say a word about it, for
if I put myself under his charge, I don't think I shall let my
husband know about it. (June 30, 1869)

An additional degeneration in Emily's last year of life was her eyesight, perhaps a sign of diabetic retinopathy. She believed that her close
sewing work was weakening her eyes. "My eyes are troubling me so
much, I cannot use them at all evenings. I think embroidery affects
them, and I am going to stop it tho' I must finish my sofa cushion
& Mother's afghan" (Mar. 30, 1869). Two months later, she reported:
"My eyes are failing me so that I cannot see anything in the morning,

and I am only feeling my way along" (June 30, 1869). By July Emily's deteriorating eyesight seemed dire.

Furthermore, Emily found herself dropping off to sleep even when she wanted to stay awake, a condition that her sister apparently also experienced, though it is not clear to what extent.

> I have your <u>complaint</u>, badly, <u>sleepiness</u>. I cannot keep my eyes open, when there is <u>gas</u>. I attended a concert Monday evening with my husband and daughter, and just dosed thro' the whole of the first part, when I came home. I have been asleep this morning, since dinner, until 9½. . . . Everything is so blurred before my eyes that I can scarcely see at all, cannot sew & can read but very little. I think it is owing more to the debilitated state of my system, than to anything else. (July 12, 1869)

What did Emily sense about her debilitated body? Did she sense her kidneys shutting down?

Emily sought persistently to understand what *was* happening to her. In August, she told her sister: "I think I have the dyspepsia decidedly fastened upon me. I am constantly making some effort to overcome it, . . . and I hope gradually to get better. Hotel life is very bad for me I know, and I mean to give it up soon as possible" (Aug. 5, 1869).

A Modern Doctor's Retroactive Evaluation

What plagued Emily and robbed her and her husband of more children? Endocrinologist Dr. Rayhan A. Lal (Stanford University) agreed to read Emily's story at my request and provide an analysis based on the limited information available in her letters. Interestingly, Dr. Lal's enthusiasm was kindled by the fact that he had spent a good many hours as a Berkeley undergraduate doing research in The Bancroft Library's Heller Reading Room.[1]

Lal's diagnosis of Emily's ailments began with his observation of a goiter on her neck (see the close-up photo on p. 117). Emily may have suffered from an iodine deficiency (typical of the time when salt was not iodized), or she may have developed an autoimmune thyroid disease. Having one such disease puts a person at risk of other similar diseases. Lal hypothesized that Emily may have developed a latent autoimmune diabetes in adulthood with some minimal "preserved insulin secretion" that may have prevented her from undergoing an even earlier death from starvation, tuberculosis, or diabetic coma, which can occur within one to two years of type 1 diabetes onset and "absolute" insulin deficiency.

Thyroid abnormalities can adversely affect pregnancy and off-spring. Hypothyroidism is associated with increased risk of gestational diabetes mellitus, which in turn may have contributed to the death of Emily's newborn baby in 1864, as well as her putative miscarriage in 1862. Baby Kate's unusually large skull in infancy points to macrocephaly, often seen in offspring delivered from mothers with gestational diabetes.

Little understanding about hypothyroidism or diabetes existed in Emily's time. With no treatment available, the ultimate impact on the kidneys was the same in 1869 as in the twenty-first century: death.

In 1869, Emily's debilitated body had to undergo one more significant challenge—yet another pregnancy and hoped-for birth.

Emily's Final Months

In April 1864, Emily wrote to her parents with a curiously contradictory and prophetic assessment: "I don't see why you think I look thin and sober. I never am anything else but thin & believe I was never less sober than now. I think sometimes my life is too smooth & easy to last long."

Emily's life was, indeed, filled with comforts provided by a doting and prosperous husband. Yet her unstable health imposed tremendous discomforts, compounded by the busy life she and her husband led. With her propensity for migraine headaches while caring for a young child and managing her peripatetic household, she might very well have felt that her family's itinerant life was undermining her strength.

However, Emily benefited from her husband's business success, which allowed the family to stay in luxurious hotels and rent or build comfortable homes. She had servants to help with her daughter and house duties. Hubert provided opportunities for her to travel east to see her family in Buffalo, and even take a tour of Europe. Nevertheless, Emily was correct about her life not lasting long. Despite Hubert's accomplishment as an entrepreneur, and despite his efforts to give Emily a "smooth and easy" life, he was not successful enough to prevent her death.

In late September 1869, Emily revealed to her sister and father that she was pregnant again, her baby due in mid-February 1870. She probably had known that she was pregnant by June, perhaps even in May. However, she did not notify them that she would be "sick" until September.

Emily repeatedly implored her father and sister to come visit. In May she wrote to Kate,

> Hubert asked me the other day if I could'nt persuade you to leave your family for a while next winter, and come out by railway & make a visit. Tell George he and <u>Miss Lockwood</u> could keep house, and let us have you for a little while. We both want you to come <u>so</u> much. We will take the best care of you. And send you back when George says. Tell us if you can both make up your minds to it & we will make all the arrangements. I think we would go as far as Salt Lake City or Omaha & meet you. You had better think seriously of it, for I think we shall leave here next year & be gone sometime.... but I do not suppose any amount of talking will induce you to come. (May 21, 1869)

In August 1869, Emily wrote to her sister from Santa Cruz, describing their sea bathing and presents from Hubert for her birthday on August 19th and for Kate's two days later.

> Here I am at last and almost wish I had'nt come for it is'nt as pleasant as I expected to find it and the ride over the mountains, tho' beautiful beyond description, tired me very much, so that Hubert was very anxious about me. I staid in bed one day, and just begin to feel a little like myself this morning.... This place is on the sea-shore, it is rather a quaint little village, and must be very pretty indeed when everything is fresh and green, but now it is so intolerably dusty, and everything is so dry and brown that it is anything but agreeable.
>
> ...I have felt so unwell since I've been here, that some days I've done nothing but lie down. I begin to feel like myself

again, and want to get back to my husband and Alameda—it seems more like home to me there than anywhere. (Aug. 25, 1869)

Back in Alameda, where the Bancrofts lived until Emily died in December, she attempted to recover. The family stayed with a Mrs. Bissett while their house was being completed in San Francisco.

I have been here nearly a week, confined to my bed most of the time. You know it always uses me up to go about, and I was glad enough to take the cars at San Jose and come to Mrs. Bissetts. It seems like "home" here. I have my old rooms, and three beds, so we manage to sleep comfortably. You asked me in your last letter if I would like you to come out for four weeks—yes! for two or one. And in view of your coming, I've been looking for a furnished house, and have heard of a dozen, right away. I think I could entertain you more pleasantly if I was housekeeping. We have commenced building our house, and when it is finished, we shall want very much to have you see it. . . . Mrs. B mothers me. . . . My health is better here. I think hotel life is killing me and it seems as if I never wanted to see the inside of another, at least for a long time. . . . We would either go to the Occidental [hotel] or take a furnished house. I found a very pretty one in Oakland last week, new, hot and cold water, gas. . . .

. . . Katy has commenced her school again, crosses the Bay every other day, then alternate days, she goes to her Grandmother's with her father. I imagine I shall be there about every other night too. It is necessary for Hubert to be there a good deal, and I find the change quite pleasant. (Sept. 10, 1869, to her sister)

In writing to her sister again ten days later, Emily dreamed about her future.

This is a lovely afternoon tho' not as beautiful as with you, I know, for your trees are turning red & our oaks do no such thing. It makes me real homesick every time I think of your place. It rather worries Hubert to have me say so, and I am not

going to think about it. He will go away from here he says,
just as soon as he can. In the meantime he will build just as
pleasant a house as he can for me to live in while I am here. . . .
. . . Here it is a whole week since I commenced this letter.
. . . Our home is progressing so rapidly that I want you to
wait until it is finished, and all our pretty things in it. . . . I
think it will be done so you can come in <u>March</u>. The weather
and country here will be lovely then. . . . I hope Pa will come
right away. He will spend the Winter, and see our country at
its best. (Sept. 20, 1869)

In the same letter, Emily finally revealed that she was pregnant,
probably four months by this time—hence the push for Hubert to get
the house finished for a February birth. Emily's good cheer and optimism at the news are poignant.

I've been intending some days past to tell you that I think
something <u>is</u> the matter with me, and I am the most
delighted woman you ever saw. I didn't want to tell you until
I was sure, and I haven't allowed myself to think anything
about it but I'm pretty sure I think, and that is why I am staying here in the country. I cannot think of a better place than
this to be sick in. It is almost like being with my own mother.
Mrs. Bissett is so good to me. I have such nice large rooms,
every comfort, and the surroundings are the pleasantest I
know of. I am thoroughly rested from my journeying, and
begin to feel <u>very</u> well, as I usually do when I am in a family way, and I think by taking good care of myself, I will go
through with it. About the middle of February is the time if
anything does occur. This will be a splendid place for me to be
sick in, & to get well in. . . . You must'nt feel anxious. I shall
have the best of care. We have an excellent physician close by.
I can get a real good nurse, there are a dozen about the house
ready to do anything for me. Everything is so cheerful and
comfortable about me. (Sept. 20, 1869)

A week later, Emily adamantly reassured her sister, asking her to
wait to visit until after the birth.

> You mustn't feel badly that I do not want you to come out now. It is only within a few days that I have decided that anything was really the matter with me and that I want to stay here quietly until the matter is over. When I was over the Bay last, and saw how rapidly our house was progressing, I felt as if you must wait. (Sept. 28, 1869)

In the same letter a few days later, she admitted that she was "quite unwell." However, "Dr. Trevor the physician I've engaged is very agreeable." Tellingly, Emily complained: "Did you ever see such horrid writing, my hand trembles, and I cannot see as it is evening now" (Sept. 28, 1869).

Emily's penultimate letter to her sister, dated October 6, was marked "Private." She explained that she had "engaged" another room for their father in the same house where she was staying, when it seemed he *would* indeed arrive for his visit that autumn. However, Hubert's cousin Frederick was then recuperating in that same room from a broken leg, which could possibly prevent Mr. Ketchum from arriving or at least from staying with his daughter and son-in-law. Emily had noted in an earlier letter (Aug. 25) that "Hubert's cousin, the Dr.s son, who has recently come out here, has broken his leg, and is at Mrs. Bissett's in Alameda." In October his leg had still not healed:

> F'rck Bancroft is in [Pa's room] now, has been lying there eight weeks, and his limb hasn't commenced to knit together yet they say that he has to lie there several weeks yet—isn't it discouraging! He is rather a delicate person which somewhat accounts for the delay, and it is a compound fracture. (Oct. 6, 1869)

A few days later, in the same letter, she mentioned that one doctor believed she had kidney disease.

> Oct. 11th Since writing the first of this letter, I've been quite unwell again—the mere physical effort of writing always was very fatiguing to me, and when I'm not well, it seems quite impossible. I'm in the hands of two physicians, to say nothing of Mrs. Bissett. She is better than any of them. One of the physicians, the one in town, thinks I may have a disease of

the kidneys, is making an examination of the urine today, of which I sent him a small phial this morning! I made a desperate effort and went to town yesterday to see Mrs. Gaviss.

Emily expressed how "delighted" she was that her father planned to visit, though we do not know whether he arrived in time to see Emily alive. She begged her sister not to worry. "You mustn't think it strange if I do not write much just now. It is such hard work for me. I'll try to get H. to write for me." How could Emily have tolerated the severity of childbirth if merely writing was too laborious?

Emily carried on with optimism, as if to convince herself and her sister that all was well.

It is a lovely afternoon and I must go and walk in the sun & see if I cannot get warmed up a little. We are to have a grand race near here this week. H & I think of attending! [Kate's] father presented her with a locket the other day, and it produces more satisfaction than anything I ever saw.

F'rck Bancroft seems to be improving fast the last few days, so I hope Pa's room will be ready for him. If not, we'll have another. I'm sorry to send so short & unsatisfactory a letter but you will think it better than none. Don't let any one see this. My Kate has a letter all ready for your Kate I see. Farewell for the present, afftly Em

In her last letter to her sister, started on October 19, 1869, and labeled "<u>Private</u>," Emily sounds intrepid. She reported on her health and told of getting ready for her father's pending visit. She wrote that the hired man was preparing Emily to go riding again, as she desired.

I am feeling so much better that I improve my first strength in writing you. I have really been very unwell, so much so that Hubert has been very anxious, tho' I have not felt so much so about myself. We find I yield readily to the Dr's treatment and tho' I may even be very robustius [*sic*], still I think I'll drag along through life like old Mrs. Palmer!

We are expecting Pa <u>daily</u>. I only wish he would telegraph us. Hubert would meet him somewhere on the road.

If his arrival was expected daily in October, "Pa" may well have made it to Emily's bedside before she died in December.

> Mrs. Bissett is going to give him her front parlor until Fred Bancroft is ready to vacate the room I had engaged. . . .
>
> I think we shall go to town somewhere when the rainy season finally sets in. I'm afraid to trust myself at the Hotel. I am thinking seriously of going into our own little house & sending Father & Mother B over here to board. I wish I was housekeeping on Pa's account, & that we had a regular church to go to. . . .
>
> Oct. 22nd You cannot imagine anything more lovely than our weather now. We've had a heavy rain of three days, and now the sun is out. . . . I do wish Pa would come just now before it dries again as I am afraid it will for you know our rainy season does not set in until November. I wish too you could see my beautiful flowers. My room is filled with them. My friends are so kind to keep me well supplied with them. And I am making such decided improvement in health that my husband is the happiest mortal living I believe. . . . We got a buggy this week for Pa to drive . . . which we think he will enjoy very much. . . . I will send this, as it is all I feel able to write at present, & I want it to go. Mrs. B is nursing me up so nicely. I believe I'm going to be better than I have been for years. I am <u>not</u> in _____ the physicians say.

Emily left a blank space, perhaps not wishing to write, let us say, "deathly danger."

Why is this the last of Emily's letters preserved? Did she no longer have enough energy to write to her sister again? If her father visited, perhaps he wrote to Emily's sister instead. We do not know.

Emily Ketchum Bancroft died in December, date unknown, the cause given as kidney failure.

We have no information about her last months and passing. We can imagine that she was well and sorrowfully tended by her husband; their kind landlady, Mrs. Bissett; and—we hope—her father. Her nine-year-old daughter, Kate, would not have been in the room at Emily's death. A family friend might have kept the little girl elsewhere, not allowing the child to witness this tragic scene.

Death from kidney disease would at least mean a gentle passing into sleep and coma, so for Emily herself there was surely little pain. Not so for her loving husband and bereft young daughter.

Hubert Howe Bancroft's Lament

The loss of his wife was one of H. H. Bancroft's most cruel ordeals. While we have no letters from H.H. referring to Emily's death, he wrote poignantly about her death in *Literary Industries*.

> And now began a series of the severest trials of my life, trials which I gladly would have escaped in death, thanking the merciless monster had he finished the work which was half done. In December, 1869, my wife died. Other men's wives had died before, and left them, I suppose, as crushed as I was; but mine had never died, and I knew not what it was to disjoin and bury that part of myself. . . . True, I had my little daughter; God bless her! but when night after night she sobbed herself to sleep upon my breast, it only made me angry that I could not help her. . . .
>
> She is gone, and who cares? Neither deities or men. The world laughs, and swears, and cheats as hitherto. . . .
>
> The burden of my loss was laid upon me gradually; it was not felt in its fullest force at first; it was only as the years passed by that I could fully realize it. Occupation is the antidote to grief; give me work or I die, work which shall be to me a nepenthe to obliterate all sorrows. And work enough I had, but it was of the exasperating and not of the soothing kind. . . . It was building and business, grown doubly hateful now that she for whom I chiefly labored had gone. I stayed the workmen on the house, and let it stand, a ghastly spectacle to the neighborhood for over a year; then I finished it, thinking it well enough to save the material. The carpenters still hammered away on the store building, and completed it in April, 1870. (67–69)

Postscript: Life after Emily

That nine-year-old daughter of Emily who sobbed herself to sleep following her mother's death? Kate continued in her father's direct care until 1874, when she left home to attend the same boarding school in Farmington, Connecticut, Miss Porter's, that her mother had attended. In 1876, Hubert finally remarried, taking to wife Matilda Griffing, from that same state of Connecticut.

Kate's prominence in her father's life is evident in small ways, such as his mention of the journal that she kept when they toured the Spanish missions throughout California in 1874.[2] Kate's love for her father is evident in yet another thick, bound volume of letters, from Kate to him, also held by the Special Collections & Archives at UC San Diego, surely compiled by her father, the collector nonpareil.

When Matilda came into Kate's life seven years after the death of her mother, the girl seemingly became close to her stepmother in time, as evidenced by Kate's letters addressed to "Mama and Papa." References to "sister Kate" filled the memory books that Matilda wrote for her own children.

In 1887, a year after her father's marriage, Kate, at the age of twenty-seven, married Charles O. Richards. Their two daughters, Ruth and Katherine Richards, lived in the San Diego and Baltimore areas respectively, with further descendants spread around the country. Thanks to them and other relatives, the letters of Emily and Kate have been preserved, so that the story of this one intrepid letter writer from the 1860s can be shared with the world.

PART II

Matilda Coley Griffing Bancroft: A Writer in Her Own Right

CHAPTER SIX

A Meeting of Minds

Six years after Emily's death in 1869, H.H. met his new bride-to-be in New Haven, Connecticut, Matilda's hometown. Precisely how they met is unknown, but Bancroft was spending time there to gain critical academic support from Yale professors for *Native Races*, the first five books in his history of the American West.[1] His daughter Kate was attending her mother's alma mater, Miss Porter's school in Farmington, Connecticut. After school let out for the summer in June 1876, H.H. took Kate and her friend to the Centennial Exhibition at Philadelphia for two weeks in July, "the great world's show," he called it.

> Thence we all returned to New Haven. During a previous visit east I had met Miss Griffing, and I now determined to meet her oftener. After a few weeks in New Haven I proceeded to Buffalo; and thence, after a time, to the White mountains, whither Miss Griffing had migrated for the summer.[2]

There, finding a meaningful bond between them, H.H. and Matilda declared their love.

He had met his match. In a chapter called "Home" in *Literary Industries*, H.H. described what he had hoped for in a future wife. Matilda fit his expectations perfectly in her intellectual ability and desire to join in her husband's work. In the intervening years since Emily's death, he had become more devoted to historical studies than to his business enterprises. He did not want a conventional wife who might distract him from his scholarly endeavors. Bancroft's wry introspection is worth quoting at length in order to illuminate both Matilda's character as his chosen mate and the general conundrums of companionship for any writer or creative person.

> I almost despaired of ever having a home again. I was growing somewhat old for a young wife, and I had no fancy for taking an old one. The risk on both sides I felt to be great. A Buffalo lady once wrote me: "All this time you might be making some one person happy." I replied: "All this time I might be making two persons miserable." . . .
>
> There were certain qualities I felt to be essential not only to my happiness, but to my continued literary success. . . . To write well, to do anything well, a right-intentioned humane man must be at peace with the one nearest him. . . .
>
> I had sold my dwelling on California street for several reasons. It was large and burdensome to one situated as I was. Much of my time I wished to spend out of the city, where I would be removed from constant interruption. As long as I had a house I must entertain company. This I enjoyed when time was at my disposal; but drives, and dinners, and late hours dissipated literary effort, and with so much before me to be done, and a score of men at my back whom I must keep employed, I could take little pleasure in pastime which called me long from the library.
>
> My great fear of marrying was I should fasten to my side a person who would hurry me off the stage before my task was done, or otherwise so confound me that I never should be able to complete my labors. This an inconsiderate woman could accomplish in a variety of ways—as, for instance, by lack of sympathy in my labors; by inordinate love of pleasure, which finds in society gossip its highest gratification; by love of display, which leads to expensive living, and the like.
>
> Naturally shrinking from general society, and preferring books and solitude to noisy assemblies, . . . I was undoubtedly regarded by some as sulky and morose. . . .

Often I had been counselled to marry; but whom should I marry? I must have one competent, mentally, to be a companion—one in whom my mind might rest while out of harness. Then the affect must have something to feed on, if one would not see the book-writer become a monstrosity and turn all into head. As the healthy body seeks food, so the healthy mind faints for friendship, and the healthy heart for love. Nor will love of friends and relatives alone suffice. The solitary being sighs for its mate, its other self.

Whom should I marry, then? The question oft repeated itself. Do not all women delight in the fopperies of fashionable life more than in what might seem to them dry, fruitless toil? Where should love be found of such transforming strength as to metamorphose into a female mind of fair intelligence, and endow its possessor with the same extravagant enthusiasm of which I was possessed?

No; better a thousand times no wife at all than one who should prove unwilling to add her sacrifice to mine for the accomplishment of a high purpose; who should fail to see things as I saw them, or to make my interest hers; who should not believe in me and in my work with her whole soul; who should not be content to make my heart her home, and go with me wherever duty seemed to call, or who could not find in intellectual progress the highest pleasure.

. . . It had been intimated by certain critics that I had allowed love of literature to rival love of woman. But this was not true. I was ready at any time to marry the woman who should appear to me in the form of a dispensation. (145–48)

In Matilda he did find a woman "of fair intelligence" and "extravagant enthusiasm," the mate who would "make my interest hers" and "believe in me and in my work with her whole soul." And she was far from a woman motivated by "fopperies of fashionable life."

H.H. described how they committed themselves to each other:

Walking down the dusty road, we turned aside into a rocky field, crossing into a lane which led us to a tangled wood, where seated on a fallen tree, each spoke the words to speak for which we were there. It was the 12th of October, 1876,

Matilda Coley Griffing Bancroft, wedding portrait, courtesy of The Bancroft Library
(BANC MSS 73/64 c)

that I married Matilda Coley Griffing; and from the day
that she was mine, wherever her sweet presence, there was
my home. (149)

As for Matilda, H.H. noted, "There was no little risk on her part, in
thus committing the new wine of her love to an old bottle; but that risk
she took" (150).

Perhaps so, but Matilda was no fool. By then twenty-eight years old,
she was already an "old maid" by the standards of the time. How grand,
then, for this mature woman to marry a relatively wealthy entrepreneur
and intellectual, live in a still-nascent city and state on the Pacific Coast,
and join her husband in his travels across the West and beyond, while
contributing to his scholarly work. How could these opportunities *not*
appeal to a smart woman desirous of putting her life to good use?

Neither Matilda nor H.H. refer anywhere to the early meetings
between Matilda and her new sixteen-year-old stepdaughter, Kate,
only nine years old when her mother died. In the intervening years she
had become her father's frequent companion. The announcement of
the Bancroft-Griffing wedding included Miss Kate Bancroft as one of
the bridesmaids.[3]

Matilda en Famille

Matilda Coley Griffing was seemingly destined to be the perfect partner for Hubert Howe Bancroft. Born on May 10, 1848, to John Starr
Griffing (1815–69) and Mary Matilda Coley (1820–1898), she was sixteen years younger than Hubert. Her father owned various businesses
and also participated in business-related organizations in New Haven.
Of Matilda's family her husband later said, "New Haven had been her
home, and of the families of that old university town, hers was among
the most respected."[4]

In the detailed genealogical record Matilda created for her children,
she celebrated her father's accomplishments.

After a few years he entered into mercantile life and for many
years conducted in partnership with a brother Jasper Griffing
the hardware and iron business. He has filled many places of
trust in the community. He was a director in the Merchants

Bank from its commencement, and vice president for many
years, which position he held at the time of his death....
His perfect method in mercantile affairs, his promptness in
financial matters, his genial disposition and agreeable manner
all secured him a large circle of friends.[5]

Sadly, seven years before Hubert and his daughter would marry,
John Griffing got "sunstroke" in Ogden, Utah, in July 1869, and died
in Chicago ten days later while traveling with his wife back from San
Francisco to Connecticut. Clearly intrepid, he and his wife were among
the first to take the brand-new transcontinental railroad, which had
only been completed that April.

The father of Matilda's mother, Mary Coley Griffing, was also a
merchant, and from her own writing about her travels, we can guess
that Matilda's mother had some education. Mary Griffing wrote a
travelogue during a long 1882 journey with Matilda's older sister, also
named Mary. Her mother's description of one site implies that Matilda
might have inherited a great sensitivity to the hardships of others, for
Mary Griffing often lamented the poverty she encountered on her
European tour. In Glasgow she wrote of seeing a parade of three thousand ship carpenters on strike: "The streets are full of poor women and
children, wretched creatures who look with their bare heads and naked
limbs as if a little increase of wages would do them no harm" (21).[6]
Later, in Murren, Switzerland, she described child lace makers in an
impoverished village.

The poor little children not over nine or ten years of age sit by
the road side from morning until night with their cushions
making their lace and offer it to you as you pass by. We went
into some of the chalets where they live and the interior was
so devoid of all comfort that it makes me even now uncomfortable to think of it. (226)

The majority of Mary Griffing's comments deal with visits to operas,
historical sites, churches, museums, and more, common on European
tours, also indicating that Matilda grew up in a family that cared as
deeply about "high" culture as they did about the fate of the poor.

The young Matilda shared her mother's cultural interests as well as
her compassion, according to the announcement of her marriage to

H. H. Bancroft in one Hartford newspaper. "Actively interested in the various benevolent and charitable enterprises instituted by the ladies of this city, she will be greatly missed, not only by her companions, but also by the poor, from whom, in their hour of need, no storm was severe enough to keep her."[7]

The second of seven children, Matilda had one older sister, Mary, followed by three younger brothers, Jasper, Frederick, and John, then another sister, Josephine, and finally a brother, Willie, who died at the age of seven. Her family was very close, traveling with and living in proximity of one another whenever possible. Mother and sister Mary traveled to visit Matilda in California several times, and eventually her sister Josephine (1856–1940) settled in Santa Barbara. Visits to Aunt Jo appear repeatedly in later family letters.

Two of Matilda's other brothers also died relatively young. For her children's memory books, Matilda reported the death of her brother Jasper, age twenty-seven, from cholera in 1877 in Shanghai, and wrote poignantly in 1883 of John's death in Portland at age twenty-nine. Matilda saw her stories of John as a bulwark against forgetting him: "In the memorial I shall prepare will be preserved a record of his life and he will never be entirely forgotten by these children. He was very fond of them and they were of him. It was very hard for me to lose so dear a brother" (Griffing, 141).[8]

Apparently neither Matilda nor her family preserved letters or documents about her early life. She writes later of having been raised in the Episcopal Church, but churchgoing had not taken a deep hold on her. In an 1889 letter to Mary Coley, her mother's more devout sister-in-law, Matilda confessed,

> As a child the Episcopal forms seemed meaningless and
> hollow to me; as I grew up I saw so much in it of mockery
> and fashion, and so few who seemed at heart to care for its
> truths and to revere its forms, that your sweet example and
> consistent life has been to me its sanctification, hallowing and
> blessing its teachings as only personal character can do.[9]

As for Matilda's character, she portrays herself as extroverted and talkative in youth: "The family said of me that I didn't talk until I was three years old and have never stopped since" (Lucy, 47). And finally, we know that she was pint-size, only five feet four inches tall. On an 1888 voyage "en famille," Matilda reported that she weighed 107 pounds, exactly 100 pounds less than her husband (Griffing, 318).

Short and slim, especially in comparison to H.H.'s six-foot-tall frame, talkative and bright and with a self-assured worldliness, Matilda could surely hold her own against this author and dreamer who joined his life to hers in 1876.

The Honeymoon

On her honeymoon, Matilda jumped into her husband's research on visits to important figures who had settled the Pacific West but now lived in the East. The couple also toured Philadelphia's Centennial Exposition. H.H. described Matilda's response to the exhibits—and the initiation of her writing.

> With new interest Mrs Bancroft now regarded everything pertaining to the Pacific coast. "The Indian trappings in the government building," she writes in her journal begun at this time, "the photographs of the Mound-builders and the Cave-dwellers, the stone utensils and curiously decorated pottery of the Pueblos, the glass photographs of views in Colorado and Arizona, so vividly displaying, with its wild fascinations, the scenery of the west, all seemed suddenly clothed in new charms."[10]

Undoubtedly, H.H. enjoyed his new wife's attentive study of items pertaining to her future in the West. Given H.H.'s drive to preserve information, one may surmise that *he* encouraged her to keep a journal. And he ultimately benefited from it because he copied some of her accounts of their shared experience at the exposition into his memoir. Over the coming years, H.H. would continue to make use of some of Matilda's research and writing in his own histories—although she was never credited.

One of the newlyweds' first visits was to General and Mrs. John C. Frémont in New York.[11] Mrs. Frémont may have inspired Matilda as a model of a wifely editorial assistant. In her inaugural journal, Matilda commented that Mrs. Frémont was "thoroughly engrossed in her husband's literary work and reputation; assisting him now as she has done for years writing and arranging in notes, where she is satisfied she says, if one word out of her twenty answers his purpose" (5).[12]

In Litiz, Pennsylvania, the couple interviewed General John Sutter (1803–1880) and his wife. In *Literary Industries*, H.H. described at length his interview with Sutter, from whose land in Coloma the gold rush had sprung, which eventually led to Sutter's ruination as squatters overran his rich land holdings. H.H. also described the role Matilda had begun playing as his unofficial assistant. He noted her patience during the five days while H.H. took Sutter's dictation—what we now call an oral history—recording the interviewee's stories.

> Ten hours a day for the next five days resulted in two hundred pages of manuscript, which was subsequently bound and placed in the library. Forty pages a day kept me very busy, and at night I was tired enough. Meanwhile my devoted bride sat patiently by, sometimes sewing, always lending an attentive ear, with occasional questions addressed to the general. (156)

In her diary, Matilda reported on this meeting as well, providing her sympathetic view of Sutter's situation.

> A mogul for a time in California among the miners and first-settlers, there seems something sad and incongruous in the resignation of himself to the quiet retirement; a fact which he himself seems now to regret on account of the many inconveniences attending a life in the country. (8)

Matilda noted with concern that they "had come none too soon" to interview Sutter, given the old man's fragile state of health. Sutter complained that "his memory is weakened by age, but we could see no indication of that in our further interviews with him." In her journal, Matilda writes insightfully of her husband's "patient" strategy for securing archives and dictations.

> [General Sutter] received us very graciously, and listened with deep attention and interest to the account Mr Bancroft gave of the effort he is making to collect materials for his history of California. We had heard that the old gentleman felt hurt at his treatment by the Gov't, and the people, and for

this reason was chary of giving his experience to those who sought it. He has been besieged by newspaper reporters, petty local historians, and by the curiousity [*sic*] of others, until it is necessary for him to see the importance due the work, before securing his interest and confidence. Mr Bancroft patiently and kindly explained it all; then speaking of the General's experience, said "I hear of you very often, and frequently come across some of your experience, but I have never yet heard any but the kindest feelings expressed toward you, and know that only the kindest sentiments are entertained for you. I want to place you in your true light, and have your life history from yourself."

The old gentleman's eyes filled with tears, at this expression of kindly feeling, his voice choked, and he with difficulty recovered himself to speak, and promised to dictate whatever Mr Bancroft wished to take down. (11–12)

Matilda also explained her own metamorphosis: "It was opening a new field to me, and one in which I had every reason to enter with keen enjoyment" (12).

The newlyweds surely engaged in fascinated analyses with each other following their visits with significant historical people. Matilda reported briefly on other such meetings in Washington, DC.

[We] met Major Powell of Western territory survey fame.... The Major has but one arm; he seemed specially interested in the Indian languages, and said he had found Mr Bancroft's work and references a great assistance in his studies.[13] From there we called upon Mr Geo. Bancroft.[14] I remained in the carriage, but the old gentleman came out and insisted that I should come into the house. (6)

In Baltimore they called on Daniel Coit Gilman, former president of the still new University of California, Berkeley, but then president of Johns Hopkins, also a new university.[15] Matilda transcribed as best she could Gilman's comments regarding personalities East and West. He said,

"The hospitality of the Californians is owing in a great measure to Eastern ties. They have so many relatives and friends in the Eastern states, that any stranger coming from there is welcomed into many families where they have personally or known by reputation mutual acquaintances and friends. . . . Elsewhere, it would take years to establish the hospitable treatment gained in a few months in California.

"In the East there are hidden causes, always governing society, motive springs that can hardly be explained or accounted for, such as family reputation and ancestry. In California everything is on the surface—everyone feels himself as good as everybody else, and everything about himself is known to everybody. Their buoyancy of character is very striking, nothing seems to dishearten or keep down a man. His buoyancy makes him rise above every discouragement and is inexhaustible." (6)

Perhaps Matilda took heart in knowing that she too could find such "buoyancy," which might help her "rise above every discouragement."

Matilda's First Winter in San Francisco

The Bancrofts arrived in San Francisco via train on November 28, 1876, and lived in the elegant Palace Hotel on Market Street until the middle of March. In his own memoir, H. H. Bancroft sang the praises of his inquisitive and sociable new bride, whom he was perhaps showing off to all those friends who had despaired of his ever marrying again. Here H.H. recalled Matilda's arrival.

[From Pennsylvania] we proceeded to New Haven, and shortly afterward to San Francisco, stopping at Stockbridge, Buffalo, Granville, Chicago, and Omaha, at all of which places we had friends to visit, before settling finally to work again.

With kind and womanly philosophy Mrs Bancroft on reaching San Francisco did not look about her with that captious criticism so common among newly made California wives, to see if she did not dislike the country. There were some things about the city unique and interesting; others struck her strangely, and some disagreeably. But it seemed never to occur to her to be dissatisfied or homesick. When she married a man, she married him, and there was the end of it, so far as shipping her happiness upon the accidents of his surroundings was concerned. Sweet subtleties! Happier would be the world if there were more of them.

The Palace hotel for a short time was as curious as a menagerie; then it became as distasteful as a prison. We had many pleasant little dinner parties the winter we were there, made up of widely different characters. First there were our nearest and dearest friends, those who had always been to me more than relatives. Then there were the intellectually social; and a third class were Spanish-speaking Californians and Mexicans, among whom were Pio Pico,[16] General Vallejo,[17] Governor Alvarado,[18] Governor Pacheco,[19] and the Mexican refugees, President Iglesias, and Senores Prieto and Palacio of his cabinet.[20] Mrs Bancroft began the study of Spanish, and made progress; Kate was already quite at home in that language. (156–57)

Matilda would maintain a positive, enthusiastic attitude no matter the discomforts, challenges, and even chaos that life with Hubert might impose. She noted how intriguing her new city was.

San Francisco is indeed a wonderful city. It's age and mine the same, a city of but twenty-eight years growth, numbering already about three hundred thousand inhabitants. The ocean and the Bay give it fine natural advantages, and lines of continuous peaks and hills on every side add to its picturesqueness. The city is built up with wooden buildings, of endless variety of architecture, and many private residences are very large and imposing in appearance, built regardless of expense on elevated sites, which the general hilly nature of the country readily affords. The people prefer wood to stone or brick on account of it being an earthquake country, and they think there is less dampness in wooden houses. The Palace Hotel is the most remarkable building in the city. It was completed in the fall of '75; occupies a whole block, bounded by Market, Jessie & Montgomery sts. . . .

Gathered from every part of the country, there is a freedom from the observance of any particular fashion that is remarkable. In mid winter one is not surprised to see black grenadines on the street; straw hats and fur cloaks are not at all unusual—a child dressed in white marselles throughout, even to the white sun bonnet, I have seen walking on the streets, while the next one was dressed in fur. So the people in character show the distinctive differences of the localities from when they came; and all feel independent of the restraints of formal society rules.

In speaking of the society of San Francisco, Bishop Kip[21] said to me: twenty years ago, in early times, the tone of society was very different from now. All were on an equality; if a man fell, there were twenty hands outstretched to raise him. All were in sympathy with one another. Now, there are many rich nabobs, who separate themselves from their fellows; they are high feeling "cockey" and feel altogether superior to those of low degree. There are very many educated people, but in society they form a small proportion; they are quiet and secluded.

Others speak of society here as being in a crude condition; so many incongruous elements brought together, that there has n't been time enough yet for them to assimilate. I feel as tho' it will take me a long time to know understandingly the true character of the people and of society. (13–16)

Matilda also commented on her introduction into her husband's society of influential leaders:

We have had several dinner companies—some of the people are identified with the history of California. . . . Gen'l Vallejo, a man of seventy perhaps, rather stout, hair but slightly grey, bright black eyes, smiling and sparkling. He speaks good English, tho with some difficulty, and is the more entertaining for that reason. He evidently is proud of his position in California's history, and has considerable dignity in his bearing. He is a handsome man, and very agreeable in conversation. (16–17)

> We have also entertained the Mexican exiles, Señor
> Iglesias, Minister Prieto & Palacio. They have been in San
> Francisco for a month or six weeks. Immediately after their
> arrival, Mr Bancroft, Kate and I called upon them, taking
> Mr Savage with us, whose Spanish was of great assistance.[22]
> Mr Iglesias is a middle-aged man, iron-grey hair, whiskers
> and moustache trimmed close, bright-black eyes, always
> wears glasses, has a little choking sound that he frequently
> makes.... He is very sanguine that his pretensions to the
> Presidency in Mexico will be recognized. He escorted us
> down stairs, giving me his arm. Afterwards, they all dined
> with us, and spent one morning in the Library, where all
> found some works of their own in the collection. (17–18)

Matilda, perhaps a little starstruck at meeting these significant
figures of old California and contemporary Mexico, knew she must
gain fluency in Spanish, as Kate already had. Matilda reported that she
later traveled twice a week by ferry to San Francisco from Oakland for
Spanish lessons (28).

Her hopes for her own role as wife and writer were likely reflected in
Governor Pacheco's wife, Mary McIntire, who was a playwright. "His
wife is quite talented, as an artist, and as a writer and is successfully
dramatizing several works. Some pieces have already been put on the
stage" (16). Did McIntire inspire Matilda, as Mrs. Frémont may have
done, to step out onto her own writing path?

Writing and Editing Together

In early April 1877, on their way to create a writing retreat for themselves north of San Francisco, the couple stopped in Oakville, near St.
Helena, to visit H.H.'s parents, Azariah Ashley and Lucy Howe Bancroft. Matilda's admiration of her new in-laws reflects her estimation
of their son.

> On the first day there we drove to Oakville, seven miles dis-
> tant and saw for the first time the home of my husband's par-
> ents. A cozy little home they have built, and cozily they live,
> enjoying a peaceful old age. Nearly eighty years of age, they

still retain youthful vigor of thought and action. Energetic to
a remarkable degree, they find employment enough to fully
occupy their time and minds. Mother Bancroft was engrossed
with the making of a large mat for the parlor floor, working in
brightly colored pieces of woolen cloth, and so all important
to her was the completion of her work that she seemed to feel
that her house could not be considered in readiness for our
unexpected call until that was finished. The same spirit which
impelled her to persevere with her work, considering it <u>the</u>
one thing needful to which all else must succumb, animates
her son and makes of his undertaking a success. The old gentleman came in from his garden and impressed me as a man
of remarkable intellectual powers for his age, though hidden
beneath a quiet demeanor and expressed in few words. (18–19)

In her own way, Matilda would become vital to H.H.'s enterprise.
Although he had strong feelings against women as scholarly writers,
he clearly valued Matilda's responses to and support of his work. H.H.
described the two months they spent working together in the relative
quiet of resorts north and south of San Francisco in the late spring and
early summer of 1877, prefacing those remarks by acknowledging how
Matilda increasingly contributed editing help over time.

There was little lack of sympathy between us, my wife and me,
little lack of heart, and help. After the journeying incident
to this new relationship was over, and I once more settled at
work, all along down the days and years of future ploddings,
patiently by my side she sat, her face the picture of happy
contentment, assisting me with her quick application and
sound discrimination, making notes, studying my manuscript,
and erasing or altering such repetitions and solecisms as crept
into my work.

At White Sulphur springs [near St. Helena], and Santa
Cruz, where we spent the following spring and summer, on
the hotel porches used to sit the feathery-brained women of
fashion from the city—used there to sit and cackle all the
morning and all the evening, while we were at our work; and I
never before so realized the advantage to woman of ennobling
occupation. Why should she be the vain and trifling thing

intellectually that she generally is? But little cared we for any
of them. We were content; nay, more, we were very happy.
Rising early and breakfasting at eight o'clock, we devoted
the forenoon to work. After luncheon we walked, or rode, or
drove, usually until dinner, after which my wife and daughter
mingled with the company, while I wrote often until ten or
eleven o'clock. In this way I could average ten hours a day;
which, but for the extraordinary strength of my constitution,
must be regarded twice as much as I should have done.

Never in my life did I work harder or accomplish more
than during the years immediately succeeding my marriage,
while at the same time body and mind grew stronger under
the fortifying influences of home.[23]

This passage underlines H.H.'s determination to complete his grand
scheme. No matter that he deemed women to be "frail." Now his new
wife could fortify him for any pressures he would face. What a boon to
have Matilda's strength beside him wherever he went, for "home" was
a relative term, given H.H.'s restless nature and the need to travel for
his collecting work.

In her own writing, Matilda also referred to editing her husband's
work (though she rarely spoke of specific volumes). For example, in her
1876–78 journal, she explained how H.H. taught her to help him as a
sharp-eyed critic of his work. She also noted the copying work contributed by Kate. Everywhere he went, H.H. created a literary workshop.
Her account echoes his.

At White Sulphur Springs two months were spent between
working, walking and riding. The long walks of five or six
miles that my husband and I would take frequently together
are full of pleasant remembrance. The library or working
room was filled with books pertaining to our subject, and
together we would be engaged every morning writing. Kate
in a room adjoining was as busily employed in copying for
her father. Mr Bancroft was then writing about the Vigilance
Committee, and I was engaged in sorting incidents, rewriting
and arranging them. Always after writing them, I would hand
them to my husband who would criticize and correct, thus

teaching me how to criticize the better his productions, which is also a part of my occupation.

We were at the Springs too early in the season to see the fashionable life usually represented there, but which now interest has [been] made less attractive than ever. One lady, Mrs Dr Toland[24] pleased me very much by her finely cultivated mind and rare talent as a poetess. Her choice of words and beauties of thought were wonderful, as she repeated in our rooms verses of her own composition. Her fear that a publication of her poems would possibly receive severe criticism and expose her to unpleasant notoriety have hindered her from any such undertaking. (19–20)

Again, Matilda remarked on a kindred wife with a "finely cultivated mind" who used her talents as a writer. But she also implied that for women to bear "unpleasant notoriety" would be harsher than for men, a pity if her writing gifts truly merited positive public renown and appreciation.

A Mother on the Move

In August 1877, Matilda and Hubert's first son, Paul, was born. Nevertheless, Matilda's zest for travel and for sharing in her husband's endeavors meant she would still take every opportunity for social engagement and even adventure.

Fortunately, like her predecessor Emily, Matilda could rely on various nurses and eventually governesses and tutors to help take care of her children, along with family members willing and able to keep them while Matilda and H.H. traveled on business. Matilda's diaries report on a multitude of social engagements in her life with Hubert, meeting enthralling characters in her husband's world of historical scholarship. For example, in December 1877, she reported on inviting to dinner one of the early linguists of Native American languages, Alphonse Pinart.[25]

On Sunday the 17th of December, we had to dine with us Mr Alphonse Pinart from Paris. He has been in this country for the greater part of the last ten years, studying languages, the Indian dialects are his specialty. He has studied at least fifty

> languages, as he admitted with extreme modesty, but says that although he acquires a language very quickly, he forgets it remarkably soon. . . . He was extremely reticent in replying to my questions about himself, and tho' I felt that there was an inexhaustible resource of interesting experiences at his command, I could not draw him into telling them. (23)

Matilda continued as an editor for her husband that winter, working on his memoir, which would not be published until 1890, the last volume of his great history of western North America.

> Through the week we have been engaged on *Literary Industries*. I say we because I do a certain amount, enough to take the most of every morning. My chore is to take the chapters as Mr. Bancroft completes them, read them carefully and critically, finding places for loose papers relevant to his subject.
> Gen'l Vallejo and Cerruti, the two Generals as Mr Bancroft entitles the chapter, have claimed my attention and others of that type. The Chapter "Home" has made me blush; with pride that my husband could find it in his heart to speak of me as he does; with shame, that I fall as far short of what I would be to him and his work. And of the baby! what can I do? He gives such a description of things before and after his birth, and while I must admit they are truthfully portrayed, I shrink from such a description being preserved in print for other than my own family. But the matter rests for the present; I doubt whether it will ever be published. (24)

Many a writer can identify with pride in one's work shadowed by fear of its faults. Since her writing would not be published, Matilda could hide behind that proscription. But she knew her husband would value her work, and his approbation might have been accomplishment enough, although in later years, as we shall see, she did indeed try to publish some of her essays.

Matilda then elaborated on the family's Christmas celebration and the anticipation of the new year, seeming to enjoy using her writing as a source of pleasurable memories.

And now as I write on Christmas Day 1877, the early morning scene comes up vividly before me. In the back parlor on a big arm chair, were hung our stockings, well filled they were, as was the seat of the chair which was crowded with packages. Between the Bancrofts' stocking and mine, was hung a tiny little sock of Paul's, and next her father's, hung Kate's stocking with a little mitten for Josephus (Kate's dog). . . . On Thanksgiving Day, about a month ago, baby was baptized at home. We have not connected ourselves with any church here, on account of our short sojourn in Oakland. We called upon Dr. Benton of the Seminary to officiate. The two grandmothers were here, and as Dr Benton had performed Mother Bancroft's golden wedding ceremony, we asked him to baptize our dear boy. It was done in the parlor with our family circle. . . . To me, such a service seems far more impressive than baptism in church. . . . The New Year has been ushered in, and the strange feeling each New Year brings, when you look upon the blank leaves of a journal of the unrecorded events that none can foretell. I tremble with apprehension. (24–25)

Historical Mysteries Solved in the Archives

A brief remark in a diary or letter can resonate with greater significance when triangulated with other references. In 2010, I traveled with my father, Paul Bancroft III, to the graves of H.H.'s parents, Ashley Azariah and Lucy Bancroft, in Napa Valley's Yountville. There we found beside our ancestors' gravestones an undated one inscribed, "Susan, Our Adopted and Redeemed Apache, Age 16." Who was Susan? We'd never heard or read any stories about her.

The mystery was somewhat revealed upon reading Matilda's remarks about the elderly Bancrofts' fifty-fifth wedding anniversary in February 1878:[26]

Father and Mother Bancroft with their little Apache, have spent a few days with us, celebrating their wedding anniversary, the fifty-fifth, by a family gathering, when we seated twenty of the family at dinner. The old people are in their eightieth year, robust and vigorous, mentally and physically.

They keep up sympathy with younger people, and although strong-minded are liberal in their opinions. (27)

While lauding the octogenarians, Matilda did not provide any information about "their little Apache." Matilda's attachment of the possessive pronoun to the child without otherwise identifying her speaks

SUSAN,
OUR
Adopted and Redeemed
APACHE,
From Arizona.
Aged 16 Years.

I have found redemption
through the precious
merits of Christ.

Susan's grave at a Yountville cemetery, courtesy of Kim Bancroft both to a kind of invisibility of people of color in the world of whites and to their subordinate relationship.

More historical sleuthing brought to light the tragic story of this Apache girl. In 2016, Patricia Prestinary, university archivist at California State University, Fullerton, alerted The Bancroft Library to the recent discovery among the university's holdings of an original 1884 diary from Azariah Ashley Bancroft.[27] In it, Ashley explained,

> About 1870, in the providence of God there was a little
> Apache captive girl captured by Ge. Crooks command, near
> Prescott Arizona, aged about 4 years, & two years later she
> providentially fell into our hands at Oakville & we had her
> legally bound to us. She had been in bad hands in Prescott for
> a while, so there was much to unlearn. (37)

Ashley also noted that "she thought she saw both her parents killed by Gen Crooks soldiers."

The "Indian fighter" George Crook (1828–1890) waged battles for decades against Native people in his military career in the western United States, before and after his service in the Union Army. He was assigned to the Arizona territory in 1871 with orders to "subdue" the Indians and relocate them onto reservations. Though we can't know, it may be that the girl later named Susan lost her family in the December 1872 Battle of Salt River Canyon, in which Crook's soldiers massacred over seventy-five Yavapai Indians and their Tonto Apache allies. Many women and children survivors were captured. If Susan had survived that battle, she might have been three or four at the time. Ashley indicates that she came to them around 1872 at about age six. This scenario of one girl's family destroyed in a massacre can only be tentative, though it was all too common for Indian children across the eventual United States.

Ashley claimed, "My wife taught her to read and I gave her religious instruction." They were as dedicated to her, he claimed, as to their own children. However, Susan contracted consumption (tuberculosis), and "no power that we could avail ourselves of" could save her. "Her death was peaceful, at the age of 15 years" (though her gravestone appears to have the number 16 there). Ashley declared that Susan was so well loved that she remained a "star" to Mother Bancroft.

This incident reveals the senior Bancrofts' lifelong commitment to the oppressed of other races. In the 1840s in Ohio, they had actively worked to end slavery. In the 1870s, this elderly white Christian couple presumed they were providing "Susan" with a better life. However, the adoption of Native children into white families has a nefarious history in California's 1850 Act for the Government and Protection of Indians that did exactly the opposite, mandating ways to force the indenture of Native peoples and remove children from families as a means of "cleansing" them of their language and culture. Though the act was repealed in 1868, the practices ordained therein continued into the twentieth century, including continued adoption of Native children into families that sought to "civilize" them. As for so many Native peoples in this country, Susan embodies the tragedy of losing her family, community, and identity. To a visitor like Matilda Bancroft, this girl's history had already been erased.

"Impelled to Work"

Meeting people of all kinds and learning their stories would become Matilda's fate in her relationship with her history-gathering husband. In the late spring of 1878, the couple would depart on a collecting journey to the great Northwest.

> We feel, if possible, more strongly impelled than ever to work and complete as much as possible before leaving here the 1st of May. Mr Bancroft has written a chapter on California's Biography which he intends for separate publication from his works. . . . The style of the chapter surprises me; most of what he has written, that I have read, has admitted of the sentiment and beauty of expression with which, I think, this is characterized. It seems to me I can read his writings in a somewhat unbiased manner, for often I strongly condemn, and often praise, as though written by some one else. We have had a large collection of notes to arrange and rearrange, and we have gone over them together, trying to classify them, so as to make them available. . . . [26–27]

Our home life in Oakland has been most delightful. The
winter has been a rainy one, but plenty of congenial employment with my husband, and baby for recreation, has made
indoor life simply fascinating. . . . We have lived quietly, with
but little society, our work has been absorbing. Mr Bancroft
has been engaged during this month, in writing a chapter
on China, with Mr Nemos, from the library assisting. He
is able to continue his writing, even during our breaking up
house-keeping, for with men from the store to assist in pack-
ing, he is exempt from that duty. (28)

Over the next eighty-seven pages of her journal, Matilda described
their two months of travels throughout the Northwest, up the coast
by steamer, on sometimes terrifying wagon rides over steep mountain
passes, and by train through gorgeous valleys. Matilda had caught a
passion for writing and gave herself to it completely.

Free School, a fine brick building accoma-
dating two hundred children; then we walked
some distance to the Nursery where I
learned something of their difficulties
in raising flowers. The lily of the valley
is poorly grown here, and all the plants we
saw had been imported from Germany. Their
garden flowers seem coarse and hardy;
slow of growth, and early frosts discourage
the efforts made in raising them. I appreciated, as I never have done before the
beauties of E.T. flowers. The pansies however,
are great in variety and wonderfully large.
     When I returned, I found a Mr Good
giving a dictation. He is a minister and
his early life and labors here, he relates
with minuteness and in fine style. He
says he has often contemplated writing his
experiences, and is glad of this opportunity.
I have enjoyed listening to him and even
acting as Amanuensis for a short time. I
craved as a favor that I might take down some
dictations, and so have begun with Mr Good. He
has worked at it with wonderful assiduity; for
five days or parts of days, I have written as fast
as he would dictate. Some morning we wrote before
breakfast at five or six o'clock as it happened, and
so have, now that it is completed 120 Mss pages
to show for our work. His descriptions of scenery
and interior life, are remarkable for vividness

Page from Matilda Bancroft's 1876 diary,
courtesy of The Bancroft Library (BANC MSS 83/22c).

Becoming a Writer

From 1876 to 1878, Matilda Bancroft underwent an apprenticeship as a writer and as an oral historian, all the while becoming the mother of two boys. H.H. had essentially given her the task of keeping a journal. None of Matilda's writing before her marriage has been preserved, so it is impossible to know how accomplished she had been before marrying Hubert. Matilda began her first journal immediately following her wedding. She then continued writing as a means of capturing their explorations of the great Northwest on a two-month journey from late April to late June, 1878.[1] This diary is full of gorgeous and insightful descriptions of people, places, and sociological phenomena, exactly the kinds of observations that H. H. Bancroft would want to include in his histories.

The next diary Matilda would write was a memory book for her first child, Paul, born August 22, 1877. Less than a year after his birth, Matilda put her role as adventurer ahead of motherhood, leaving her baby behind in Napa Valley with relatives there while she embarked on the rigorous Northwest excursion. Since the primary purpose of the voyage was for H.H. to collect archival material, information, and dictations on the history of the Pacific Northwest, this working trip would not permit an infant. Matilda often indicated in her diary that separation from her baby pained her. Weeks passed without news of how Paul was faring. However, Matilda was resilient. In fact, she endured part of the first trimester of pregnancy while coping with seasickness and riding in badly sprung wagons along rugged mountain roads. Griffing would be born the following January 21, 1879. Tough indeed!

This expedition exposed Matilda to a wholly different world than the one back East. With stimulating new vistas and stories of more recent American pioneer life, her writing developed and deepened. Just months earlier, her descriptions of people and places tended toward the superficial. Now she captured the beauty of specific locations, nuances of interpersonal dynamics, and the historical relevance of social changes. She also revealed a subtle sense of humor.

In her diary, Matilda always referred to her husband as "Mr Bancroft." Although formality was more typical of their era, this nomenclature reinforces the semipublic nature of Matilda's journal. It was not a place for her to share her feelings as Emily had in more personal letters to her family, referring to her husband as H. or Hubert. Matilda was "performing" for her husband and later for her children in their memory books or for the eventual readers of *Bancroft's Works*. Her audience was small, but she had a job to do, and she did it well.[2]

Setting out on the Great Northwest Adventure

April 25th We are just about to leave our pleasant Oakland home for a journey up the Coast as far as Victoria [the capital of British Columbia]. Kate is to be with her Aunt Fannie, and my dear baby, too, will be left behind. He is going to Oakville to stay with my sister, Mrs. Kenny,[3] and his grandparents. The necessity seems forced upon me, and feeling sure he will have the best of care, I accept the opportunity for travelling. Kate had her choice and preferred remaining in San Fran. where she can continue her music.... (27)

On Tuesday the 30th we sailed from S.F. on the *City of Panama*, Captain Seabury; Mr Holmes from the store introduced us to his friend the Captain, who promised, and gave us, every attention. He reserved for us seats at the table beside him, which we never used, as we were obliged to take all our meals in our stateroom. The *City of Panama* is one belonging to the P.M.S.S. Co. [Pacific Mail Steam Ship Co.] and is considered one of the safest on this route, which is pronounced the roughest on this coast. The usual story of sea-sickness I might tell, for though old to others, it was all new to me, being my first experience of the ocean. The very thought is sickening, now. . . . (28)

We followed the coast closely for the entire distance, 720 miles, following the Oregon coast line nearly 300 miles and Washington Territory some 150 miles. On Thursday at six o'clock we rounded Cape Flattery, passing from the Pacific Ocean, treasonable name, into the straits of Juan de Fuca, where we enjoyed seven or eight hours of smooth sailing. Just before reaching the Oregon line we saw Mount Shasta, with its snowy peak proudly displayed. I was obliged to be satisfied with a glance. As we neared Cape Flattery, the coast was beautified with pines and hemlocks growing to the water's edge, a thick deep green growth which the soft azure of the sky made still more beautiful. On a little island just off the cape was the light house which we sailed round into the sound. These straits are the mythological straits of Anian . . . believed to connect the two oceans. Seven or eight hours of smooth sailing brought us to Esquimalt, a fine harbor where we anchored at midnight or early Sunday morning. At eight o'clock we left the steamer, for a cab ride of four miles to Victoria, the baggage being taken on a raft to [the Driad House]. . . . Our first call after breakfast was for a bath; we were directed to a bathhouse nearby, which was remarkable for its cleanliness, commodiousness and warmth. (29–30)

Social and Geographical Observations

Everywhere, Matilda explored how people got along, including those serving and those served.

Though the Victoria papers cry down the Chinese, they seem indispensable for servants. My landlady said in reply to some inquiries, we can not get along without the Chinese. She says that the white women refuse to do menial work, feel so superior to the Chinese that they will not consider themselves servants, and want to receive their friends in the parlor. Further than this . . . they want a reception day, [and] they demand the privileges of picnics, . . . which are continued out of doors sometimes until two o'clock in the morning. . . .

The Bishop brought out here from the old country two relays of young women to do housework. All came with an expectation of getting speedily married and living at ease. In their portmanteaux, you could find plenty of fine dresses, but no plaid aprons for housemaids. Those that went into service were ill-fitted to their place. Many went into families where they excited the jealousy and hatred of their mistresses, because the latter had risen from the laboring class, ignorant and illiterate, and the young women whom they employed were superior intellectually. The experiment was a failure and never has been repeated. So the class of white servants is now working Irish women. Tho' they command high wages, there are few comparatively able to pay them. A Chinaman in a family of even two will obtain twenty-five dollars, without doing the washing, while a white woman would not take less than thirty-five dollars. (30–31)

Matilda noted that Victoria's population at the time was "6000 whites, and about 1000 Indians & Chinese, the latter predominating" (32). Sixteen years earlier, she noted, forty thousand Indians lived in the region.

Surely meeting women of her class who were Métis (half-Indian) was unusual for Matilda. The Métis are still considered a distinct culture in Canada, one of many recognized Indigenous groups. Some early trappers who succeeded in business and society had married Native women. So it was with Lady Amelia Douglas (1812–1890), the Métis widow of Sir James Douglas (1803–1877), the former governor of British Columbia. Douglas himself was of mixed race, born to a Creole woman of Barbados and a Scottish merchant. His wife, Amelia, sought to instill in their thirteen children some Native traditions learned from her Cree mother, and she supported other Métis women facing prejudice in Victoria.

In describing Lady Douglas and her son, Matilda echoes contemporary prejudices on race mixing.

The old lady is a half-breed, as all the wives of the Hudson Bay Co. are. They do not appear in society, except at rare intervals, and do not receive at their own homes but seldom. They have large families, but intermarriage is generally unfortunate for posterity. The sons are morally and physically weak, everybody says; and in this case all speak slightingly of young Douglas. He is of delicate physique, and can not live long; intellectually, he is not strong and never could make a speech without his father prepared it for him; this is what is said of him to me. Is he dissipated? I ask, and they reply he hasn't money enough to be dissipated, for the property was all left in the mother's hands. The truth is, that it is the fashion to speak deprecatingly of young Douglas, and at his wedding ... whenever I mentioned his name, it met with the same response. (39)

The Collecting Begins

On Monday morning Mr Bancroft commenced a tour of investigation into the resources of the place for material for his purpose. The people enter into his plans for collecting material with great enthusiasm. An old gentleman, a pioneer forty-six years ago, came to the house in the evening with his wife, a daughter of a Mr Ogden, formerly a commander of this district for the Hudson's Bay Co. He was very peculiar; evidently had had a rich experience but seemed crazed at the thought of relating it. His name was Archibald McKinlay.[4]

"If it's statisticals you want, I'll give 'em to you," he reiterated from the time he came in till he left; but he objected to "personalities"; and when Mr. Bancroft, who was trying to take his dictation, would ask historical questions, he would object, telling him that all that had been written up better than he (McKinlay) could tell it. When he reached the "statisticals," he had none to furnish. He was a *rara avis*; but the discouraging feature didn't discourage Mr Bancroft. The old man promises to write up incidents by himself. I think his mind must be broken. (33)

Here in Victoria began Matilda's first opportunity to take a dictation. She spent days taking down Reverend John Good's very detailed
story of his early years.[5]

> When I returned, I found a Mr Good giving a dictation. He
> is a minister, and his early life and labors here he relates with
> minuteness and in fine style. He says he has often contem-
> plated writing his experiences, and is glad of this opportunity.
> I have enjoyed listening to him and even acting as amanuen-
> sis for a short time. I craved as a favor that I might take down
> dictations, so have begun with Mr. Good. He has worked at it
> with wonderful assiduity; for five days or parts of days, I have
> written as fast as he would dictate. Four mornings we wrote
> before breakfast at five or six o'clock as it happened, and so
> have, now that it is completed 120 mss [manuscript] pages to
> show for our work.[6] His descriptions of scenery and interior
> life are remarkable for vividness and beauty of expression. The
> graphic descriptions have so fascinated me that I have had no
> feeling of weariness, but have been almost unconscious of my
> own effort.
>
> In the meantime, dictations are being taken from many
> others, from Mr Anderson, Dr Tolmie,[7] Mr Todd, an octo-
> genarian, Mr Deans[8] and others. . . . The old man [Mr Todd]
> walks up and down the room, leaning on his cane, and tells
> his story with great enthusiasm; sitting down and rising as
> he pleases, but he mustn't be interrupted nor questioned; it
> makes him angry for it breaks the thread of what he was say-
> ing and he can not take it up easily again. (34–35)

Matilda's dictation from Reverend Good was, indeed, remarkable.
He told moving stories about the shrewd leadership of James Douglas
and of his own attempts to provide ethical guidance during a period
stained by the atrocious treatment of and wars against Pacific Northwest Native peoples. Good's tales make riveting reading. Matilda's
skills as an "amanuensis" were clearly equal to the task of capturing his
descriptions of life in the early colonization period. In the first of these
two brief examples from the dictation Matilda took, Reverend Good
described the suffering he had witnessed of British Columbia's First
Nations, including;[9]

fearful scenes of small pox which so decimated the ranks of the natives and had to be stamped out with fire and sword, which led to the ultimate expulsion of the Indians from Victoria, carrying with them contagion and destruction wherever they went, leaving the dying and the dead and the wreck of their ill gotten property for a thousand miles along the whole track of their hurried flight. (6)

Good described a landscape to Matilda that illustrated the "beauty of expression" that so captivated her:

A very charming and favorite ride was out to South and North Sannich, which at that time contained but a few old, chiefly Hudson Bay settlers, very much in the condition which nature had adorned it, the glorious Sannich arm with its sparkling sun lit waters and shaded sandy shores, the long avenue of oaks, [and] sequestered lakes reminding us forcibly of some of the more picturesque scenes of eastern climes, the freshness of nature, with the constant currents of the native deer crossing the path and the beauty of the natural flowers, large open tracts, carpeted with luxurious floral growths, make the whole a wilderness of sweets; the magnificent vista of mountain and forest, clothed with richest verdure, all impart a charm and relish which has to be felt thoroughly to be appreciated. (8–9)

Matilda's diary also noted many others who provided their stories, including Judge Matthew Begbie, whom she described as a "man of mark."[10]

It was his admirable judicial power exercised with discrimination and stern promptitude, that more than anything else preserved Victoria from scenes of violence and crime in '59 and later, when the gold excitement drew hither hordes of miners, and thus the elements, that in lawless California could only be subdued by Vigilance Committees. (37)

Some settlers promised to send their accounts to Mr. Bancroft. Matilda noted how Mr. Pemberton, a gentleman farmer with an "intellectual face," showed "keen sympathy with Mr Bancroft's work" (38).

A Journey up the Fraser River

On Friday, May 17, the small Bancroft party traveled up the Fraser River to New Westminster, now part of metropolitan Vancouver, on the stern-wheeler *Enterprise*. Matilda waxed enthusiastic.

> The Olympian mountains extend in a range, their summits in perpetual snow. Their snow covering was penetrated ever and anon by purple lines, like the pencillings on a frosted window, the sun-light softening though not dazzling in effect, sometimes blending sky and mountain top, sometimes giving the effect of heaps of fleecy clouds against the horizon while the lower part was shut out from view. (32)

She described the Strait of Georgia at the mouth of the river, using the present tense to capture the momentous beauty there and her first view of a First Nations village.

> The trees all along the shores and islands are very beautiful, everywhere growing down to the water's edge. Eagles flow about in large numbers, and we even saw several fine specimens of the bald eagle. There are just as present an abundance of fish which attract an unusual number of eagles. We enter at last the Fraser River which all along its course affords most picturesque and varied views . . . displaying an Indian village, and canoes, or here an isolated house, while beyond is a salmon canning post.
>
> At last we reach a bend in the river which we round, when suddenly is revealed to us the royal city of New Westminster, so designated by the Queen. . . . The trees, which should form a handsome background to the pictures are withered and blackened by fire, and stand like mammoth fingers pointing with scorn and derision toward the approaching stranger. (41)

Fascinated, Matilda saw how the Indians were catching *oulahans* [euchalon], "a small and delicate fish," from canoes with a kind of rake, lit by gum torches, providing an eerie reflection. Their guide, Mrs. Bushby, another Douglas daughter, knew everyone; "she conversed in the Chinook language, and in fact she had a pleasant word for all" (45).

Nevertheless, H.H. cut the idyll short:

> We had only been out an hour or two when a spirit of unrest seized Mr Bancroft.... He thought of all that was left undone in Victoria, of the short time left to us there, and that if we went to Yale,[11] we should just reach the point of greatest interest in scenery, just peek into the magnificence of the Cascade Range, when we should have to turn our back on it and return. It would take us four more days, and little comparatively to enjoy for the valuable time sacrificed, and so we decided to return the following day which brought us here on Saturday afternoon. (40–41)

Return to Work and Study in Victoria

Having returned to Victoria, H.H. was determined to collect government papers. He had also paid locally hired clerks to copy, but they were "slow and poor writers," so "there is not as much accomplished with these assistants as one would suppose," said Matilda (45). Further, her husband had "some delay and difficulty in obtaining access to Government papers; but at least procures about all he wants thro' printed documents and blue books" (53). He endured—and she with him—ever-present "red tape" in his attempts to gain access to key documents.

Meanwhile, Matilda made a return visit to Lady Douglas in Victoria. She found herself charmed and even surprised by the devotion of her daughters, noting "their superior education." Nevertheless, her underlying prejudice again showed when Matilda questioned how Lady Douglas's daughters, who could pass for white, should be "as proud of her as any <u>Lady</u> or mother could wish. In their manner you would never suspect Indian blood. The male members seem to suffer most from amalgamation" (44).

Later, Matilda's sense of propriety likely chafed upon meeting another woman of mixed race, Mrs. Josette Work, the wife of John

Work, the "Chief Factor" (merchant working on commissions) of Hudson's Bay Company and a prolific journal writer himself.

> We called upon [Mrs. Work] one evening and felt that there was a study of character. Mrs Work is a half breed sixty-five years of age probably—she followed her husband thro' all his journeyings and tells with graphic intenseness of expression how she saved his life and that of her two little girls, now Mrs. Tolmie and Mrs Finlayson, by burying a hatchet in the neck of an Indian; otherwise she said she would have been left a widow and her little daughters taken as slaves. She speaks Canadian French, Indian language, and broken English so it is hard to understand her, but her gestures and changing expressions and tone convey wonderful information and are fascinating.
>
> Their old log house was curious and interesting and is preserved as an heirloom, but they live in a new and large one nearby. Mrs Work showed me the cradle in which she used to tend David, her youngest, which was strapped on her back true Indian fashion, and in which the baby is kept all day. It was of wood, oiled, well polished and finely carved with a penknife by her husband. There was an oval frame extending along the lower portion and half way up to confine the feet and legs; and over all a handsomely bead embroidered covering which laces thro' the center. (51)

Yet Matilda found commonality with her hosts. One evening, Lady Douglas's daughter Mrs. Harris spoke of her "filial love" for her father and how dear he had been with her, having "superintended" her studies and "all the difficulties he smoothed out of her way." Matilda reported Mrs. Harris as saying, "I miss him more and more everyday." Matilda then noted, "After all, how alike we are in our loss, for though father died ten years ago, the mourning for his death and the longing for his sympathy has never disappeared" (48).

The Bancrofts' visit to Victoria concluded with the "Victoria style" celebration of the Queen's birthday, including Indian races in bark canoes and amusing attempts to walk on a greased pole. Matilda rode and then trekked with "Mrs Dr Jones" up Cedar Hill, now Mt. Douglas, a steep slope. But "when we reached the summit, the view was recompense enough for the hard climb.... This view surpassed anything I ever saw. Mt. Baker stood out alone in its grandeur," presenting the appearance of "two magnificent icebergs, as the setting sun illuminated and glorified its two peaks." Then she looked to the Olympian range beyond, "clothed in deepest purple," the bluish-white streaks of snow amid its rocks "like tracings by some inimitable artist." Matilda lauded the beauty of the islands in the bay and the setting sun's display. "While admiring the scenery and congratulating myself that I had enjoyed it, I couldn't but feel how much I should have lost without knowing it, if I hadn't taken that climb" (49–50).

If Matilda felt that her husband lost out by not enjoying the experience himself, her detailed depiction allowed him vicarious joys. Matilda's story also underscores her spirit of adventure, how some people grasp every opportunity to pursue whatever life throws before them.

On departing from Victoria on May 30, H.H. was satisfied with his accomplishment. He sent to San Francisco two large boxes of documents, both printed and manuscript, loaned or presented to him.

As for Matilda, after one month of their journey, she was "impatient to return to baby, who I learn by a telegraphic dispatch is and has been perfectly well ever since I left." Her motherly curiosity sufficiently quenched, she focused again on the voyage: "We leave Victoria with regret, for the country is so beautiful and the people so hospitable." She also expressed the feeling of so many travelers who leave behind heartfelt connections, the "many friends that we shall probably never meet again" (53).

Onward to Port Townsend in the Washington Territory

On the steamer heading south, the small group stopped at Port Townsend on the northeast tip of the Olympic Peninsula. Matilda described the beauty of the sound with its islands and inlets, the town itself perched on an open plain at the water's edge. "We learned afterward that it was its natural open character that decided the pioneers to locate a town here" (54).

Her husband, starting out at once on his hunt for material, soon met people who "furnished him reminiscences." Among those were "Mr Pettygrove,[12] Mr Plummer, Mr Van Bokkelen,[13] Mr Hill, Mr Bradshaw and Mr Swan or Judge Swan." Matilda noted, "I assisted, also, at some of these dictations," but she did not elaborate on her role.

Intrigued by "Indian curiosities," Matilda collected a few items during this trip. In Victoria, Mr. Work had given her a handsomely carved box. Here in Port Townsend, "I have been most fortunate. Judge Swan has a fine collection and all for sale. He has been employed by the Smithsonian Ins. and is a writer and quite an ethnologist."[14] The Bancrofts bought several items amounting to "$20 or $25." Then,

> To my astonishment and delight Major Van Bokkelen made me a present of his collection which he made twenty years ago. It is very interesting and exceedingly valuable. He wanted to give it to someone who would value it and preserve [it] and so presented it to me. I shall arrange the articles in some room at the Library, and what we can spare shall take home, or <u>east</u>, for that I have always had in mind. (55)[15]

When the couple toured the fort at Port Townsend, they met many military men.

> They were all greatly excited at the prospect of being called into the field, as an Indian war has broken out in Idaho, and they have had orders from Gen'l Howard to be in readiness if needed. The ladies seemed perfectly disheartened at the prospect and I felt sorry enough for them. (56)[16]

Notably, as typical of her class and race, Matilda's concern was only for the soldiers' wives, not for the Natives then being forced from their ancestral lands.

Seattle

The next leg of the Bancrofts' trip took them on the side-wheel steamer *Dakota* to Seattle. Always on the lookout for majestic mountain vistas, Matilda wrote of merely glimpsing Mt. Baker, which "has coquettishly kept itself veiled, admitting only the faintest outline to our eye" (57).

The city itself disenchanted her. "Seattle presents an attractive appearance as you approach it, but you are disappointed upon closer acquaintance. It is built up on a slope . . . plenty of ugly stumps are visible and everything about the place appears as if its initial step alone was taken. . . . The people seem rather lethargic and uninteresting" (57). She learned about the commercial "springs" that drove Seattle, the coal mines and sawmills, the owner of one mill being a prominent citizen, Mr. Yesler.[17] Matilda took special note of his wife, who "impressed us as a remarkable, energetic and able woman" (58).

Meanwhile, H.H. was collecting dictations, "though none of special significance."

> Mr. Bowman, whom we met at Pt. Townsend, has made an arrangement to travel with us to Portland to take dictations in short hand. He is quite a scientific man and living on Hidalgo Islands, feels greatly interested in the subject Mr Bancroft is engaged upon. The consequence of this arrangement is that I am thrown out of employment, and so am devoting myself to reading *Daniel Deronda*, and walking more. (57)[18]

What disappointment Matilda must have undergone! She had been thrilled to take dictations and surely was doing a good job, as evident in Reverend Good's long and well-told story. However, Matilda could not dispute her husband's work plan.

Still, her efforts as an unofficial "journalist" continued unabated. On a carriage drive to Lake Washington, Matilda marveled: "This was the most genuine frontier road I have ever seen—very narrow and very rough; trees hewn or burned down to make a clearing, and alongside the road trees were burning as we passed" (58). The work of pioneer clearing and building was continuing before their very eyes.

Olympia Bound

Days later, they were bound for Olympia, the capital of Washington, at the southern end of Puget Sound, on the stern-wheeler *Messenger*. For Matilda this portion of the trip was most delightful, though "I was obliged to lie down much of the time." On this voyage, too, H.H. was working. "Mr Bancroft obtained dictations from the Captain and from Capt. Ellicott[19] of the Coast Survey," another passenger.

At Tacoma, Matilda exulted:

> Mt. Ranier [*sic*] stood exposed in its full glory. It is 14,444
> feet high (Mt. Shasta 14,400) and has never been ascended by
> scientific men. Two adventurers, without taking any observa-
> tions, once reached its summit. . . . There is something ethe-
> real in its fleecy whiteness, piled against the sky, seemingly
> ready to evaporate before your very eye, and yet impressing
> you with its grandeur, for you know that under all that fairy
> lightness is solid rock that testifies to what eternity means.
> (58–59)

Captain Ellicott and his wife invited the Bancrofts to visit their
camp on their way to Olympia.

> This camp is about ten miles from Olympia. There are six
> or eight tents, and is as perfect a way of camping for sev-
> eral months as can be devised. There was pretty furniture, a
> complete set in the Cap's bedroom, and carpets spread on all
> the floors. . . . The meals were nicely cooked by Chinamen, for
> our few hours stay turned into overnight. Mrs Ellicott says
> she does not meet a lady from one months end to another,
> and seems to find this kind of life rather dispiriting, but with
> true devotion to her husband tries to make the best of it,
> preferring it to living on a schooner. This little insight into the
> home life of the coast survey, and Capt Ellicot's enthusiastic
> devotion to his work, which he would not relinquish for a
> fortune, is a charming little episode in our travels. (60–61)

Mr. Bancroft was furnished with "considerable information," the
gold *he* was digging for on this trip, but Matilda received a gift as well.
Perhaps intrigued by Mr. Bancroft's intelligent wife, the Captain paid
Matilda a compliment that reveals her qualities rarely found in that
region.

> Capt. Ellicott questioned me enough to understand my inter-
> est & share in my husband's work, and said he did not know
> another lady on the Pacific Coast who had such an opportu-
> nity for culture, education, and for obtaining general infor-
> mation as I have. A conclusion which is very gratifying, and

which I think might naturally be made. I only hope I shall be able to take advantage of my opportunities. (61–62)

Traveling down Puget Sound and winding along its inlets, Matilda noted: "After making a final turn you discover a city." She liked Olympia, which seemed more refined than other coastal cities they'd visited. "It seems like an Eastern city, like some New England village with its broad streets and thickly planted maples. We have been told that the society is superior to any other in the Territory" (62).

In Olympia they met Mr. Elwood Evans, known as the historian of that region.[20] He generously gave all his papers to Mr. Bancroft. Ever curious about social roles, Matilda wrote her impressions of the matron of the hotel where they stayed, again revealing her own sense of racial differences.

While at Olympia we stopped at the Pacific Hotel which is kept by a colored woman, a Mrs Howard. There is much that was peculiar about her. She resents it if her guests appear to recognize any difference between herself and a white woman. . . . Capt. Ellicott . . . informed us of Mrs. Howard's aspirations. She is worth about $100,000 and is entitled to all the respect she demands. (64)

Indeed, Rebecca Howard (ca. 1827–1881) made history as the first African American businesswoman in Olympia, running the best hotel and restaurant in the city with her husband.[21] However, H. H. Bancroft did *not* take her dictation. Mrs. Howard had adopted two "halfbreeds," half Indian and half white, yet who now had "colored" parents by adoption, a mix of family that clearly confounded Matilda.

Matilda noted the pluck of the people of Olympia in bringing the railroad to the city, after it had ended in Tacoma. "They used to have field days when all would turn out and work; money was raised to pay for labor, but where they could not give money they gave their own labor. This is in character with the enterprise of the people of this country" (64–65).

Their Own Oregon Trail: Portland and Salem

From Olympia, Bancroft and company traveled to Portland, staying at the Clarendon House, where they received numerous people who participated in H.H.'s historical work. Matilda wrote that Governor Stephen Chadwick came to meet the historian at the hotel and "listened with interest to Mr Bancroft's explanation of his plans and expressed readiness to cooperate with him in every way. He sent messages on ahead of us to Salem which have secured for us the best assistance" (67).[22]

They traveled to Salem with tickets provided by one of the railroad men. There they took a "bus" (a many-seated horse-drawn wagon) to the Chemeketa Hotel. On the Friday morning after their arrival, they went to the fairgrounds for a meeting of the Oregon Pioneer Society, where many of Oregon's "celebrities" met to retell pioneer stories. Matilda reported at length.

> This was fascinating, as one after another told incidents of hardship and exposure, or more often related humorous experiences in which those about them had participated. After, the speaker's statement would be verified by an excited "that's so," "I was there," "I remember him," etc. Among other speakers was Mrs. Minto, who told of how they all went barefoot in those days and of her receiving from a shoemaker, a young friend, a pair of shoes as a present, hearing afterwards that he had taken her measure from her foot-print in the mud. This was all told with such earnestness and simplicity that it was most effective.
>
> Through all these speeches, which were limited to fifteen minutes each, Mr Bowman was taking them down in shorthand. Then Mr Bancroft was standing either listening or suggesting to the president or other officers that this one or that should be called upon to make remarks. Thro' the morning & afternoon he was engaged the whole time in interviewing pioneers, for the opportunity was a rare one, and all were enthusiastic, as the object of the gathering had created unusual interest in early days. (69)[23]

Later, Matilda and H.H. danced a "pioneers' quadrille" at the ball. "We left the ballroom at midnight, quite tired. This was the first time either Mr Bancroft or I had seen each other dance" (70). Dancing was not encouraged in H.H.'s Puritan home. One wonders if he and Matilda enjoyed this frivolity.

H.H. was relentless, but Matilda kept pace. "Every day and evening the time has been spent in collecting material. On Sunday after church we went to Mrs Clarke's to dinner, then after dinner received from her an interesting account of her experiences, for she crossed the plains in '57 when she was nineteen."[24] Matilda was present for this interview, but Mr. Bowman was the writer.

Matilda's friendship with Mrs. Clarke led to an offer to join her on a rugged walk whose finale would be a vista of four snowy peaked mountains from a single vantage point—Mts. Rainier, Hood, Baker, and Jefferson—together presenting "a grand appearance." On leaving the very helpful Clarkes, H.H. presented the couple with a copy of his new *Native Races*.

Oregon City

The small Bancroft party left Salem on June 18, riding "the cars" through the beautiful Willamette Valley to Oregon City, where they stayed at the Cliff House. Matilda keenly appreciated the riverside views of waterfalls and bluffs, the homes of the well-to-do perched along the river, and what they learned of the woolen and paper mills. Most captivating were stories about Dr. John McLoughlin,

> endeared to the people for his kind-hearted treatment of the suffering emigrants who had arrived at Vancouver [Washington state] in starving condition. This humanity and noble devotion to the alleviation of the distress of Americans, was censured by the English and lead [sic] to Dr McLoughlin's final resignation of his position, and to his taking up his residence in Oregon City where he died and is buried. (72)[25]

At the hotel, H.H. received several pioneers who provided their stories. Most of them fascinated Matilda, such as Mr. Crawford, "ready with incidents that strongly illustrated character."[26] Going out one evening to the home of another settler provided Mr. and Mrs. Bancroft with a lovely riverside stroll.

> In the evening we started out to see Mr Lovejoy, who with Mr Pettygrove, now of Port Townsend, founded Portland. Mr Lovejoy lives a mile and a half or more from the hotel, a walk we all needed and enjoyed with a zest. As we went out, we walked over the trestle work of the R.R. The country was alive with its wealth-producing vegetation. The fields were every shade of green, and the hills on the one side, and the river on the other made the scene one of exquisite beauty. The coloring of sunset, the fresh coolness after a heated day and the peculiar stillness completed the effect.
>
> When we reached Mr Lovejoy's house, we found a large farmhouse, far back from the street, with immense fruit trees, and a pebbled walk to the door. A nicely painted white fence, showed us that our friend was owner of a place that was neatly cared for in all respects. (75)

At the Lovejoys, Matilda once again helped her husband hear the stories he so ardently desired, in this case by intercepting an interrupting wife.[27]

> He met with an accident five years ago, which somewhat impaired his physical & mental strength, his wife says, and which she made her excuse for acting in a most ridiculous manner. To us he appeared vigorous and his memory keen and reliable. Mr Bowman had scarcely commenced to take down his narrative before Mrs Lovejoy interrupted with, "Mr Bancroft, I prefer that Mr Lovejoy should not give you any account this evening of his early experiences. I wish to have him have two or three days to think about it, so that his accounts may be strictly correct."
>
> Mr Bancroft explained what he required, and that he was satisfied that Mr Lovejoy could furnish it all. Also that we had come expressly for this purpose and that our time was limited; then they proceeded notwithstanding the continued demurring of the lady.

I endeavored to interest her in conversation, which more than anything else prevented the breaking up of the evening, I think. That would make her forget her objections for a while. Several times came these threatening objections. An hour after the narration had commenced, just at a most important point, came suddenly the stern command form the lady of the house, "Mr Lovejoy, stop! You could go on in that way all night, while I could tell what you are saying in ten minutes. You must wait a few days. You can go to Portland and meet Mr Bancroft, but don't say another thing to-night."

We were dumbfounded for a moment. Mr Bancroft's manner was that of dogged determination, utterly ignoring the woman. Mr Lovejoy's manliness asserted itself, and he replied he was all right; and could do no better six years hence; Mr Bancroft put another question to him, the lady grumbled. I asked her about her baby and in her reply she forgot herself again for a while.

This baby, four months old, she has just adopted, as her daughter died at its birth; her love for it, makes it an absorbing subject. We remained until half past ten, and left satisfied with the interview. I am afraid that Mr Bancroft would have said something he would have regretted if Mr Lovejoy had yielded to his wife's suggestions. Evidently she is accustomed to his obedience, and her manner undoubtedly is what gives the impression that he is feeble mentally, as we were told in Salem. (76–77)

Return to Portland and Travels on the Columbia River

The traveling history troupe returned to Portland the next day, where they met the mayor, along with Judges Deady[28] and Strong[29] again. Matilda remarked on the importance of their influence on Oregon's history and how their "strong minds" significantly improved their narratives because they had "keen remembrance" and were able "to trace cause and effect with discriminating analysis" (78).

They also called on Mrs. Hervey, the daughter of Dr. McLoughlin and his wife, Marguerite, who was part Native American. Matilda commented, "She is a lady of intelligence, tho' she shows in her appearance her Indian ancestry." Mrs. Hervey offered not only her dictation but also documents. "Mr Bancroft felt his valuables increased by the loan of journals and other papers of Dr McLoughlin's, owned by his daughter" (78).

Meanwhile, Matilda attempted a collecting task of her own, to little avail. "I am trying to collect the pictures of all of these most important founders of this coast, at least of those who narrate to us their experiences. Necessarily, the collection will be most incomplete for most have no photographs and a promise of one, even, is not always secured" (79). She also alluded to another purpose of her journal writing: Matilda, like a filmmaker trailing another to document the making of a film, strove to recount the making of her husband's collection. "While in Portland Mr Bancroft was busy every moment, but as I did not go out with him nor hear any of the dictations, I am unable to describe our work here, in detail." Note *our* work."

One of their meetings allowed Matilda to connect with an old friend of hers at the home of Anna Bancroft, the widow of a Dr. Bancroft, presumably Dr. William Wilson Bancroft of Granville.[30]

> On Friday evening we took dinner at Mrs Dr. Bancroft's on Fourth St cor Jefferson. This Mrs Bancroft is a widow, Aunt Anna, and her daughter and son-in-law Mr & Mrs Suskedorf are living with her. We met there Judge & Mrs. Strong, & Mr & Mrs Corbett.[31] The latter was an old schoolmate of mine, nee Emma Ruggles, and I was much gratified at the renewance, after eleven years, of our acquaintance. Her husband is an ex-senator. From Aunt Anna's we went down to the boat, the *Wide West*, where we spent the night preparatory to a five o'clock start in the morning for the Dalles. (79)

Matilda remarked that the Dalles had a population of fifteen hundred people and twenty saloons, typical of Western towns, and explained that the name "Dalles" came from the French for "trough," to represent the depth and narrowness of the river there, with "fearful" currents and rapids.

Their stateroom on the side-wheel steamer *Mountain Queen* was pleasing, as was the delightful trip up the Columbia River, "the high mountains so close in together that you almost wonder did you pass through." She added that one "could see from the appearance of the water that the navigation must be difficult. It is not impossible, for we have been told of Indian canoes making the passage in olden times, but probably not at all seasons of the year" (80). The snowy heights of Mt. Hood and the picturesque hotel at the confluence of the Hood and Columbia Rivers charmed her.

On Mrs. Clarke's recommendation in Portland, they met Mrs. Elizabeth Wilson at the Dalles. Now a widow, she had arrived twenty-seven years earlier as a schoolteacher, and then married Joseph Wilson.[32] She told a story about "Indian troubles" in the early days and a dramatic attack on a fortified block house. "Mrs Wilson entertained us with many incidents and afterwards gave Mr Bancroft a dictation" (83). Mrs. Wilson continued on their trip with them further up the river and by wagon.

The history of the Dalles was also full of lore about Dr. McLoughlin and the "succor" he provided to famished pioneers, such as Jesse Applegate, who had led a large company of emigrants along the Oregon Trail.[33] Mrs. Wilson also related the terrible fate of Applegate's son, age eighteen, who capsized and drowned in those rapids, along with five other men. "The last sight he ever had of boat or its passengers," wrote Matilda, "was the face of his boy upturned on the foaming waters for an instant" (85).

These stories humbled Matilda, despite her own relative hardship traveling by wagon.

> While I think of the hardships of the poor emigrants twenty or thirty years ago, I hesitate to write complainingly of our ride out here. As we started, the driver remarked to me that we would go down a pass that was as bad as any in the Rocky Mts. That it was, going down into the bowels of the earth.

She drolly noted how the driver enjoyed making the voyage more frightening by remarking that his horse would easily shy—it was "awful scarey"—and its collar did not fit correctly, so it might slip off.

> "But your brake will be your dependence," I mildly suggested.
> "No," he replied, "that's no good; I told them to-day 'twouldn't hold and ought to be fixed before we started."

> Now that the ride is safely over, I think our driver wanted
> to impress us with his skill in conquering great difficulties.
> (85–86)

On reaching the pass, they chose to walk down the steep and rocky road on the other side to the bottom, perhaps not to test those brakes.

When they returned to the Dalles, Mr. Bancroft met with Judge McArthur. Finally, on June 23 the group reboarded the *Mountain Queen* to travel back down the Columbia to Portland, all the while collecting stories, including one about several other men who had recently been swept away on the river's fast spring flows. "Life is constantly risked and lost here," Matilda stated pithily (88).

From the Upper Cascades, the party learned how the unnamed Native people fished; they may have been a group of the Chinook people: "The Indians have little platforms built out on a triangular foundation, and catch the fish in nets, striking them with a club on the head. I have clubs they have used for this purpose farther north, given me by Major Van Bokkelin of Port Townsend" (88). Fish so caught had a cord run through their gills and were then tied to a barrel and floated down to the cannery two miles below, Matilda reported.

Once back in Portland, they planned to stay at the Clarendon Hotel until June 26.

> While here were very busy. Mr Bancroft is driven every
> moment. Mrs Corbett drove me about in the morning, show-
> ing me some very handsome residences, and in the afternoon
> at Dr. Hawthorne's invitation we went out to the Insane
> Asylum, of which he has charge. . . . It is a beautifully situated,
> and is large, airy and kept remarkably clean and neat. (90)[34]

Next, they took a ferry and then a "car" for Roseburg in southern Oregon. For Matilda's comfort, H.H. purchased a rubber pillow for the ride.

In Southern Oregon

At Yoncalla in southern Oregon, H.H. hoped to meet with pioneer Jesse Applegate. Apparently, however, Mr. Bancroft's telegram had gone astray, so they knew not where to meet him. They asked the railroad conductor, who abruptly informed them that to speak with Applegate, they'd have to get off the train at the small town of Drain.

> Drain is a very small place; no stores scarcely—saloons,
> of course, there were, and a P.O. But it is a good farming
> country and on the R.R. He [Mr. Applegate] is living up
> on a mountain, the Yoncalla Mt., three miles away from the
> town. Mr Bancroft hesitated between riding alone, or taking
> a team, and taking me up there. The first I urged, because
> these mountain roads, with which we are unfamiliar may be
> too rough for me to ride safely over. I want to be benefitted
> by this trip and so am cautious. After supper Mr Bancroft
> mounted a horse and rode alone up the mountain; at its
> summit, he tells me the view was very fine. Mr Applegate
> lives in a rough hermitage, away from everybody but his wife
> and children, with a commanding view of the beautiful valleys
> surrounding him, which he once owned, but which he was
> obliged to surrender in payment of an official bond which
> he once signed for the Secty of State who proved a defaulter.
> (92–93)

The next day, Applegate met them at the hotel and related his stories, including how he had led a party of seventy-two along the Oregon Trail. "He seems the most important man in Oregon, and has promised to write out fully all he can, at his leisure. His memory is perfectly reliable, he thinks" (93).

Applegate preferred H.H. to delay his trip and take down his story, but Matilda's baby's picture induced him not to detain them further. "Oh to think I had to leave Portland without any word from Oakville for three weeks past! I only hope and expect good news, however, when we reach baby" (94).

In fact, Matilda ultimately wrote quite a bit about Jesse Applegate herself, submitting twenty-two pages of a biography to her husband's collection.[35]

The Journey Home

The party reached Roseburg, Oregon, on Thursday evening, June 2, but still faced an arduous road trip, three days and two nights, to Redding, California, where they could take a train again. The regular stagecoach, however, was a "lumbering concern, and one which I am very glad we are not obliged to patronize. . . . Our plan is to take a private conveyance," which they acquired by "going shares" with two other passengers to Jacksonville (95).

While in Roseburg, H.H. continued his work, meeting "several old residents, the most important of whom is General [Joseph] Lane, who has had a most eventful history from boyhood" (96).

General Lane's son, Lafayette, would also serve as his "amanuensis," while the General himself gave Matilda his photograph.[36] She savored the scene of the dictation: "He talked for hours with us in the parlor, collecting quite a crowd of interested listeners, not one of whom would he let leave the room. They themselves had been present in many of the scenes he described" (96).

Finally, Matilda and H.H. set off for California an hour before dawn.

> At four o'clock the following morning Sat. June 29th we were
> ready to start on our ride. We had made some provision for
> cooking our own dinner as we might not be able to reach any
> house at dinner hour. At half past four we were en route in
> a large easy wagon but with horses that we feared could not
> make the journey, 90 miles in two days as agreed. (97)

Along the road she spied a man dressing a cougar skin in his front yard. She relished the rolling hills and beautiful valleys along the first stretch of their voyage. After eight miles they enjoyed breakfast at the Mountain House: fresh bread, butter, milk, delicious coffee, ham, and eggs, all for "only two bits."

> We ate with a relish. . . . At six o'clock we were again on our
> way . . . now on a more mountainous road, making curves
> sometimes that were short and perilous with a precipitous
> descent from the brow of the ridge to the river below, and yet
> the stages whirl over this road in the day and in the night,
> with their six horses and in perfect safety. (98)

They stopped at Myrtle Creek for an hour to cook dinner and rest the horses. Matilda declared the meal delicious, with steak cooked on an open fire, "nicer than cooked any other way."

As they feared, however, the horses began to give out: "One of the poor animals had to be goaded at the point of a bayonet" with "the whip constantly applied" in order to arrive at a hotel for the night after making forty-five miles that day. The freshly painted hotel outside belied the poor accommodations inside. With wry humor, Matilda wrote, "My bed, called double, was so narrow and short that Mr Bancroft decided to occupy one of the four in the large room. These, as I was afterward told, had but one sheet each, and so full of life that the wonder was there was any bedding left" (99).

The next morning they passed Grave Creek, thus called because a woman had died on the trail and was buried there, but so desperate were the emigrants that they disinterred her corpse, robbed it of her belongings, and threw it back in the grave.

> Again we stopped for lunch in the woods—and again made our camp fire and broiled pork . . . . The next thing of interest was the mining that had been done, leaving the ground . . . most unsightly infringing on the road, so as to make careful driving imperative to safety.

Now Matilda wrote more about General Joseph Lane's battles against the Cayuse, Takelma, Tolowa, and other "Rogue River" tribes at "table rock" and Mt. Pitt, during the Rogue River Wars of 1855–56. Until this outbreak of violence, the Tolowa people had engaged in many skirmishes to remove settlers and miners from their lands. Matilda had heard that the war had ended with "the red braves jumping off the cliff to their deaths rather than surrender to whites" (102). By 1856, General Lane marched the surviving Native people onto various reservations.

Having wended their way along the forty miles of the Rogue River Valley, Matilda described its splendor as well as its formation, where the Coast and Cascade Ranges united to create the Siskiyou Mountains. In such lessons as this, one imagines Matilda unconsciously preparing herself to be the teacher of her children in coming years.

Changing horses twelve miles north of Jacksonville, they reached the town on Sunday evening and spent the night at Mrs. Vining's hotel. As ever, H.H. relentlessly hunted for and collected stories. In Jacksonville they met Judge Prim,[37] as well as the nephew of Judge Strong, and Mr. B. F. Dowell. "Mr. Dowell gave his dictation to me and as usual I became much interested in the account."[38] He also proffered his journal, which Matilda agreed to copy, "and with other copying will find enough to occupy my time for a while in Oakville" upon returning (104). Matilda was undoubtedly inspired by her husband's "indefatigable" dedication to his cause, even at the cost of a sleepless night.

> There was a Col Ross who took supper with us. He commenced about 8 o'clock to give Mr Bancroft his dictation. When I re-entered they were still at work. In the morning at four o'clock, Mr Bancroft called me, as we were to start in half an hour. The Colonel was still there, and then I learned that these indefatigable workers had written all night long. The way it happened was that at mid-night, they had got only partly thro'; neither seemed tired nor said anything about stopping. Mr Bancroft thought the two or three hours only that he could sleep before starting would scarcely amount to anything, and so they continued with the narration until daylight. Mr Bancroft has worked under high pressure the whole time, and so is not as much benefitted by this trip as he otherwise would be. Still he always considers the accumulation of material as the ultimatum of his daily life, and so the satisfaction of the trip will be in proportion to this accumulation. (104–5)[39]

When H.H. himself referred in his memoir to this all-nighter with Ross, he expressed his revulsion at the tales he had heard from "the Indian fighter," or rather "Indian butcher": "At Jacksonville I sat through the entire night, until my carriage called for me at break of day, taking a most disgusting dictation from the old Indian-butcher John E. Ross. This piece of folly I do not record with pleasure" (173).

The next day, their small company paid $90 to engage a driver, a pair of strong horses, and a good "rockaway," a light carriage. They were still almost two hundred miles from Redding. Upon leaving the region, Matilda commented that she and her husband had both "enjoyed the beauties of the Rogue River valley, which are thought compared favorably with Napa, which for Mr Bancroft to say is highest possible praise" (105).

Their seventeen-mile ride had encouraged a large appetite, so they enjoyed a hearty breakfast of venison steak in Ashland, "a little village of some 700 inhabitants." By chance, "Mr Bancroft found in the proprietor an old acquaintance of Crescent City, twenty years ago, a Mr Hauck" (105). H.H. had lived in Crescent City, in California's far north, where he operated his bookstore for nearly three years, from 1853 to 1855. The old companions enjoyed renewing their acquaintance.

At Last, Northern California— and More Stories to Collect

They continued by stage up the mountains. Her driver apprised Matilda of dangers in those parts.

> The driver pointed out the spot where a few weeks ago two robbers had attacked the stage at mid-night and rifled the Treasure box of Wells & Fargo of its contents. This occurs about once a year. The highwaymen always obtain what they demand, but are generally caught as there is a standing reward of $900 offered for their capture. These mountains are always crossed by the stage at night as are the Klamath Mountains; the passengers losing the finest scenery of the trip in consequence; beside taking the most dangerous part in the dark where light is most needed. We came down quickly and crossing the boundary were in California. (106)

Northern California's mountains captivated Matilda as the most stunning of all, "the finest scenery of the whole trip; in fact the grandest I have ever seen or imagined" (106–7). Matilda then explained how they crossed the Klamath River via a ferry contraption, "guided by ropes and pulleys, and moved by the current of the river," for the cost of $1. Of that dramatic journey and the eventful information collected in following days, Matilda wrote:

> Now the ascent of the mountains began; winding in and out over a fine road so well graded as to have its ascent scarcely

perceptible, the Klamath River flowing proudly on as it bathed the feet of these gigantic hills; now you find yourself shut in the canyon, now whirling around a curve until you close your eyes from dizziness, until finally after the sun has gone down, and darkness enveloped the mountain tops and the gorge below, we look way up to the highest point . . . and are told that we have to round that before we have reached the summit. The clouds break a little and the moon and stars come out. We had not anticipated such a trip by moonlight, . . . tho' familiar to our driver is all new to us. At eight o'clock the summit is reached and in an hour and a quarter we have been whirled down into the town of Yreka, where we spend the night. . . .

At Yreka, Mr Bancroft met Judge Roseborough [*sic*] . . . of all men in northern Cal. the one of the greatest importance, most conversant with the history of that section, and most interested in collecting and writing it. He has been for 27 years in Cal, and on the bench for 22 years, longer than any other judge in the state. . . . His interest in Mr Bancroft's work is substantially manifested by his offer to write a ream of paper on the history of this part of the state. Mr Bancroft at once telegraphed to SF for the paper.[40]

Dr. Hearn, a dentist, commenced his dictation, which I took, but he could not complete it, and promises to write it up at his leisure. He had once owned a complete file of the Yreka paper from its first publication, but a short time ago, they were all sold to a Chinaman by mistake, for old papers. His regret is enhanced now, when he sees the practical value they would be to-day to history.

Leaving so soon after dinner there was but little time to gather material; however the interview with Judge Roseborough amply paid for stopping over.

Soon after leaving Yreka, rounding the base of a hill, we came into full view of Mt. Shasta, which we had seen for the first time day before yesterday tho' less distinctly. Now it rises before us in all its broad and silvery magnificence. There, too, are Shasta Buttes, a succession of hills of peculiar appearance. Originally Yreka was named Shasta Butte City, but the Indian name Ieka was preferred on account of confusion arising from the multiplicity of Shastas. Ieka was anglicized unintentionally, if Yreka can be called English. For two years the sign <u>Yreka Bakery</u> swung in the air before it was discovered that the name spells backwards and forwards the same. (107–9)

Their route took them to Sisson's hotel in Strawberry Valley.[41] "Here is the finest view obtained of Mt. Shasta and from where people start to make their ascent." There the Bancrofts encountered Mrs. John Swett, a San Francisco acquaintance and wife of the prominent educator. Matilda noted that many people from San Francisco "patronized" the hotel in the summer season—a long voyage to make in those days, but well worth the travel to rest in that beauty.

Off they went again, on a rough and jolting road through the forest. "The dust has at times been blinding, but never worse than here," Matilda lamented. Finally they enjoyed their first view of the Sacramento River, "a pure, clean, gurgling stream, and we follow it the rest of our journey, as far as Sacramento at least" (110).

On the way, Matilda noted, a private toll road exacted a high price, $5, on individual conveyances and $40,000 a year to stage companies, but the good condition of the road made the tax worthwhile.

Meanwhile, the ride was enhanced by the companionship of the Sacramento River frequently flowing alongside them. "It springs from the bosom of Mt. Shasta, it dances in sunlight and moonlight through dales, forming cascades rivalling those of the Columbia until gaining volume with its progress, it throws itself into the lap of the great ocean" (111).

Matilda also observed the "Chinamen" and others mining along the river, "altho' not destroying the purity of its waters as where mining is carried on below to great extent" (111).

They spent one more night on their "carriage trip" at Dog Creek. On July 5, Matilda and H.H. reached Redding at four in the afternoon, though they had to wait until one in the morning to finally enter "the cars bound for Sacramento, Napa Valley, and our darling baby" (111).

Their journey was not quite over. The railroad trip brought them into Sacramento at 10:30 a.m., "hot, tired, and dusty." Then they had to wait until 4 p.m. for the train to Vallejo. Of course, this wait was "time wisely spent," for H.H. took them to the library in Sacramento. There,

Mr Bancroft obtained information and memorandum about books and engaged the librarian ... to write the life of her father for presentation in the Bancroft Library. We met Mr Mills of the Record Union and furnished him information of our trip which he embodied in a full column article the following Tuesday. Then at last we were ready for our home trip but our hearts would have been lighter had we heard recently from baby. As it was we could not know whether we should find our boy sick or well, living or dead. (113)

Their pent-up desire for their child in the absence of communication had reached a crescendo of emotion.

Returning Home to Her Baby ... and More Travels Ahead

After over two months of very rugged travel, Matilda intensely anticipated arriving at the home of her parents- and sister-in-law to embrace her baby, Paul. However, the homecoming was bittersweet, she wrote, having "lost place in his love."

The reaction was almost painful in its intensity when our little one was in our arms, strong in health, with never one day's illness since we left him. We came as strangers to him, and it was long before I regained the lost place in his love.
The Oakville home was very pleasant for the following three months. Mrs. Kenny's house was new and pleasantly arranged. She was in charge of the house, but we had all the privileges of home. Father & Mother Bancroft took their meals with us, and Mr Bancroft had his library in the parlor of his mother's house. There he worked hard throughout the summer; often I would spend several hours, copying or otherwise assisting, tho' my summer has little to show. Baby was my recreation and often my occupation. Then we rode considerably, and I read some, including a little Spanish. Mr Bancroft indulged in one or two little illnesses of about a week's duration, in which time I enjoyed reading aloud to him and in having him more to myself than ordinarily was possible. (114)

This last sentence hints at Matilda's quiet longing for the company of her husband, a man so driven by his studies and his business responsibilities that he may often have seemed elsewhere, even in her presence.

This respite at home in California with her husband and baby would not last long. Matilda would leave in early October for New Haven, this time taking Paul with her. The following January, she would give birth there to her second child, ensconced in the care of her mother and sister. She would never write overtly in her journal of her pregnant state, perhaps too unbecoming for a "lady" to announce in a semipublic diary. However, she said of those three quiet months in 1878 in Oakville,

> Such opportunities were the more highly valued as we knew the time was at hand for a long separation, for it had been decided that about the first of October I should go East with baby to visit my New Haven home for the first time since my marriage. Mr Bancroft could not leave his library and work this winter, and so with nurse and baby I started on Monday Oct 7th. (115)

Matilda was six months pregnant, traveling across country by rail in the early autumn with her baby and, fortunately, a nurse. She claimed that "the trip was very comfortably made." Still, as the Bancrofts knew too well, not only from the death of his first wife, Emily, but from many other women at the time who did not survive childbirth, such a separation could be forever.

Once in the East with her family again, relentless Matilda wrote about the work she hoped to accomplish, including reading her husband's writing. One senses she found rationales for connecting to Hubert in these ways. She even took up the study of "phonography," hoping it would be useful to her husband. She may be referring to spelling by phonemes, recognizable syllables used for interpreting Native languages that appeared in her husband's work, *Native Races*.

> Everyday brings me a letter from my good husband. He is working harder than ever this winter, he says and is doing the heaviest work of his life, so I cannot regret that he decided for me the impossibility of his being here this winter.

. . . I have received a great many calls since returning, and have been delighted with the cordiality of my friends. Over eighty calls I find from my list, and the most of them I've returned, altho' that necessity was limited to a smaller number by deducting the gentlemen callers. On New Years Day, tho' not very well, I saw many who called, tho' not including them in the above number. I have read 4 volumes of *Native Races* this winter, and have taken up the study of phonography so that my time has not been wholly lost to work in our direct line. Phonography would be a great benefit to me if I could obtain a practical knowledge of it, and that I shall do when I can study and practice it every day for several consecutive months. But I was obliged to drop it now with the beginning of the New Year and its expected new responsibilities with the new year, responsibilities to which I look forward with great delight and proud anticipations.

She did not say so, but by new "responsibilities," she was referring to her pregnancy. Her second son, Griffing, would be born January 21, 1879.

She closed this diary of her early marriage and travels by recounting how sadly H.H. bid farewell to his baby boy. "It was a terrible trial to his father, this parting with his baby. The child seems to be idolized by him; he enjoys him for what he is without daring to hope what he may become. And yet he gave us up most unselfishly" (115).

CHAPTER EIGHT

"Lovingly, Mamma":
Matilda as Mother

In the fall of 1878, Matilda Bancroft and baby Paul returned to the home of her mother, Mary Matilda Coley Griffing, in New Haven, Connecticut. Pregnant with her second child, Matilda would give birth in January to Griffing, giving him her maiden name. She was nursed in the nest of the woman who exemplified motherly love, as Matilda wrote in her 1878 journal:

> If I could write what is in my heart, my home life would be
> pictured in warmest colors—Mother's love and consistent
> attention seem almost a marvel to me, and I wonder, often,
> if ever in my own home and motherhood I can be such a
> woman as she is. So patient, forbearing and gentle, anticipat-
> ing all our wants as if we were still children, never irritating
> us by word or look, such an influence must be felt and burned
> into our characters, and I truly believe my children will have
> much to bless my mother. (119)

How Matilda lived out her dreams of motherhood is captured in her extensive records about her children's lives and her role in them. As mentioned earlier, over fifteen years, Matilda kept a "Childhood Memory Book" for each of her four children up to the age of ten. These books also reveal Matilda's character as a mother and as helpmeet to her husband.

Most parents hope to preserve memories of their children's first words, early antics, and developing personalities, but today we rely on photos and videos, soon buried in our digital archives. How many parents could put pen to paper for ten years to capture conversations, illnesses, playtime pranks, punishments, educational developments, sibling rivalries and bonding, travels, and more?

Matilda committed herself to this careful recording of her children's experiences, from the birth of her eldest child, Paul, in 1877 to the tenth birthday of her youngest, Lucy, in 1892. She juggled four handwritten books, which ranged from almost 400 pages for Griffing, her second son, to Lucy's 211 pages, in the midst of other family duties and her work with H.H.

The Bancroft children: Lucy, Griffing, Paul, and Philip, ca. 1883, courtesy of The Bancroft Library (BANC MSS 73/64 c)

Just as Matilda's diary from 1876 to 1878 provides a personal perspective on H. H. Bancroft's collecting journey to the Pacific Northwest, these memory books also open a window onto other aspects of his career. Matilda wove stories that preserved her family's memory of itself.[1]

How did this grand commitment to write about her children begin? Home from her travels with her husband to the Northwest in early July 1878, Matilda wrote in her first journal, "Of baby I shall write but little in this journal, for at his father's suggestion I am keeping a journal for baby in which I write fully of his little life" (116). Unfortunately, that book for her eldest child, Paul (my own great-grandfather), has been lost, but Matilda wrote so fully about all the children's activities and sibling relationships that much of Paul's story and childhood character can be found in the other three books.

Keeping these books was not easy. While both mother and writer, Matilda also oversaw a small staff, joined her husband on travels, maintained their shared intellectual interests, and kept vigil on family business interests. Matilda often regretted long periods passing without recording specific events. In Griffing's book, she bemoaned:

> The children's journals are a poor excuse for what is attempted. It is but a fragmentary account, at the best, of their sayings and doings, . . . when once a break occurs it is difficult to fill in the breach. I specially desire, however, to continue these journals till each child is ten years old, and so I will start in with another good resolution and hastily tell a little of Griffing's life for many months past. (234)[2]

She noted especially of Lucy's book that "Lucy's journal being the last is sadly neglected" (85).

Despite Matilda's self-criticism over her lapses, we can thank H. H. Bancroft for recognizing his wife's talent and asking her to write these books. In their later lives, did the children read from their books to remember and reflect on their childhood and family? Matilda herself did, reporting in Griffing's book, "I have lately been reading aloud to the children from Paul's Journal, and they have enjoyed it immensely. It recalls many things which they can now remember with great distinctness, and which shows how imperfectly I have recorded daily events" (292). She also let the children dictate stories about their experiences, surely enabling them to feel valued as subjects of their own oral histories.

Sister Kate

Matilda did not keep a journal for her stepdaughter Kate, already sixteen when Matilda married H.H. in 1876. However, she often spoke of "sister Kate" in the children's journals. Though the texture of Kate's relationship with her stepmother is not fully clear, in many letters home from the two years she spent in Europe and elsewhere, her salutations read, "Dear Papa and Mama." She often sent warm greetings to "Mama" in particular. In this letter to her father, dated May 19, 1878, when she was eighteen, Kate closed with, "Love to Mama & keep lots for your dear old self. I <u>do</u> want to see you & Mama & the baby . . . dreadfully. Good-bye write soon. Your loving Kate."[3]

Taking up the role of stepparent is not easy, especially after the child's loss of a beloved biological parent. In Kate, Matilda faced a young woman who adored her father (as Kate's letters indicate) and may have felt replaced as the focus of her father's affections. But Matilda seems to have incorporated her stepdaughter into as much of the Bancroft family travels and activities as possible.

Certainly, Kate was integral in Matilda's narratives. In the spring of 1878 in her first journal, Matilda reported, "Kate stays with her Aunt Fannie [H.H.'s brother A.L.'s wife], where she is having a good time, enjoying company and making a place for herself in S.F. society. She is following up a course of reading and devoting much time to music" (116). Like her mother, Emily, Kate had a beautiful singing voice, and H.H. ensured that she received vocal training. Years later in 1886 in San Diego, Matilda noted, "Sister Kate is going to take part in the Mikado" (Griffing, 250), "an entertainment that was then gotten up for the benefit of the Episcopal Church" (Philip, 142). Descendants shared family lore about that performance, and a family photo of Kate in Japanese costume attests to it.

Kate spent two years in Germany and Italy from December 1880 to October 1882 in the company of Bancroft family aunts. In early January 1883, Matilda wrote:

> Sister Kate now returned from Europe where she had been
> for a little over two years. I gave for her a large party as a wel-
> come home, inviting over two hundred. This was on the 9th of
> January. The house was prettily dressed with Christmas greens
> and papa asked that the tree should be dressed again, as the

children had utterly demolished the other. All this involved
much work and thought. It was a welcome from her friends
that brought much pleasure I am sure. (Lucy, 19)

In Griffing's book, Matilda elaborated on the invitations, presents for
all, lace stockings filled with candy, and the Punch and Judy show.
Toy canaries all sang at the right moment. Matilda recalled her "lively
work": she had laid out "over a hundred little cakes frosted and candied
and little cookie birds, all done in one week" (87). She spared no effort
for Kate's return.

Along with some babysitting, Kate's talents with singing and languages were occasionally put to use in tutoring the children. Said
Matilda of her work with Paul and Griffing, at the time ages seven and
six, in German, "Sister Kate has grown very fond of them and they of
her; she has always shown a partiality for Griffing and pronounces him
the better scholar, too" (Griffing, 178).

Kate apparently enjoyed a relatively free life, as on a family trip
to Denver in December 1884, when Kate stayed behind. "Sister Kate
located herself for the winter at Mrs. Dr. Edson's, where she has prospects of a gay winter, while ours will be of a very different character.
She will join us in the Ojai [east of Santa Barbara], whenever she feels
so inclined" (Philip, 96).

Nevertheless, Kate also contributed to her father's history project,
at times copying manuscripts and accompanying him on his travels.
When H. H. Bancroft's Market Street store in San Francisco went up
in flames in April 1886 while the whole family was in San Diego, it was
Kate who accompanied her father to help him cope with the disaster.
H.H. wrote on May 5 to Matilda that Kate "has been very attentive and
has done all any body could do."

Matilda chronicled the events leading to Kate's engagement and
wedding in 1887. Sometime in 1886, Charles Olcott Richards, a San
Diego engineer and rancher, visited the Bancrofts, who had both a
home in that city and a farm in Spring Valley ten miles east. Then,
over Christmas and New Year's 1887, when the family returned to their
Walnut Creek farm east of Oakland, Mr. Richards visited them there.[4]

The children will probably have no remembrance of the very
pretty German party that sister Kate had New Years Eve.
The company all came over to our house at midnight, to take

supper. . . . On Christmas Day . . . we grown up people went on a paper hunt with about twenty in the party, some on horseback. We went to the Mussel Beds.[5] Sister Kate & Mr Chas. Richards led the party. (Griffing, 254–55)

In a January letter, H.H. thanks his wife for being an "angel about Kate," perhaps referring to that party.

In May 1887, Kate embarked on a trip to Alaska in the company of Mr. Richards, among others. "While she was on her Alaska trip she became engaged to Mr. Charles Richards, who has a ranch in El Cajon [just east of the Bancroft's Spring Valley ranch]. They were married

Kate Bancroft on her wedding day, courtesy of The Bancroft Library
(BANC MSS 73/64 c)

in San Francisco in September and all the children went to the wedding which was in St. Luke's Church" (Philip, 165). In Griffing's book she noted the date, September 21, and, "After the wedding there was a lunch, or wedding breakfast at the Renton. Immediately after the wedding was over Sister Kate went to Lake Tahoe" (288).

Matilda briefly described H.H.'s hopes for his prospective son-in-law: "Papa wants Mr Richards to go into the store, particularly as he has given Sister Kate a half interest in the business" (Griffing, 280). Soon she added, "Sister Kate & Mr Richards have come up from San Diego, to live in SF. Mr Richards is going into the store as Vice President" (Griffing, 297–98). That arrangement did not last long, for an unknown reason, and the Richards family returned to San Diego, where Kate remained for the rest of her life, except for return visits to Europe. Circumspect, Matilda never revealed unpleasantries.

Kate raised her two daughters in San Diego. Matilda announced the arrival first of Ruth: "While this journal should close with Griffing's tenth birthday, I will carry it over a little. Almost on his birthday he had a little niece, Ruth, for Sister Kate's baby was born on the 22nd of January 1890. Now indeed is he Uncle Griffing, and papa is truly Grandpapa" (Griffing, 386).

On a later family trip to San Diego, they received Kate and both daughters, Katherine having been born in October 1892. "Sister Kate has spent a month with us and was here over Thanksgiving. Lucy has now two little nieces as baby Katherine was only a month old when she came here" (Lucy, 210).

Even though Kate lacked her own book written by Matilda, her stepmother did preserve many of her memories in these stories.

"Perfectly Self-Possessed" Paul

Matilda's memory book about her first child, Paul, born August 22, 1877, has been lost. Unfortunately, she committed some fuller family stories to that book, as she noted in Griffing's: "I find in writing these journals, Paul's always comes first, for being the oldest there is much more now to say about his ways and ideas. Then the two are so inseparably connected that baby's life comes into his. So Griffing I refer you to Paul's journal for what I omit here" (27). And "In regard to our trip from Santa Barbara that was a very successful experiment . . . the account of it is fully given in Paul's journal" (Griffing, 205). Similarly, she wrote to Philip in his book, "If you want more particulars you must ask Paul to let you look at his journal" (107).

However, Paul's character and stories about his childhood *were* saved in Matilda's other books. She actually first referred to Paul when he was in utero, but obliquely, as she never explicitly mentioned any pregnancy. In her 1876–78 diary, Matilda reported on her activities in June 1877, while camping with H.H.'s brother A.L. near Cloverdale. "This to me was a novel experience, but my health prevented me any active participation in the hunting or climbing; so that camp life meant little more to me than lolling in a hammock and a sense of ennui" (20–21). Since Paul was born two months later, Matilda's "health" problem was likely her advancing pregnancy. Upper-class women were expected to rest, while working-class women often labored right up to their "labor." We also gain a sense of Matilda's natural energy; the requirement to "loll" in a hammock only bored her.

Matilda probably had not started Paul's journal yet, for in the diary of her first two years of marriage, she reported on Paul's birth in their house at 566 11th Street in Oakland.

> On the morning of the 22nd of August 1877, our little boy
> first saw the light and cried out lustily. From that time our
> happiness seemed complete. His father named him Paul, and
> the name pleased me. I grieved for some time at the necessity
> of employing a wet nurse, but the experiment has proved a
> great success as far as the prosperity of the child is concerned.
> (21–22)

Oddly, though Matilda never spoke of pregnancy, she openly intimated a wish to breast-feed her baby, noting her unhappiness when a "wet nurse," or lactating mother, would have to serve instead.

That disappointment was overshadowed by a greater disaster just weeks after Paul's birth: the death of her younger brother, Jasper, age twenty-seven, which she reported in her 1876–78 journal.

> I had scarcely regained my strength [after having given birth
> to Paul], when the terrible news of my brother Jasper's death
> in Shanghai China, on the 10th of September, reached us.
> The letter containing the news was the first intimation of his

sickness. In his consideration for me, he would not permit any telegram to be sent. His nature was a most loving one; never was a boy more loyally devoted to his mother and sister's [*sic*]. ... He had just received an important advancement, when he was taken ill and died at the Hospital. This is no place for expression of my bereavement. Mother was an inexpressible comfort to me in her sorrow and sympathy. Her lovely character shone forth more beautiful than ever, for bereavement followed by bereavement of the severest kind, have chastened and sanctified one of the sweetest dispositions God ever made. Through all my sickness and slow convalescence, she has been like an angel of light, and though her visit here has been limited to Oakland, she has enjoyed the baby and being with me thoroughly. The trial of parting is over with, and now we look forward to my home visit next Fall. (22–23)

Her mother's "bereavement followed by bereavement," may refer to Matilda's father's death eight years earlier in July 1869, while traveling by train with his wife from San Francisco back home to Connecticut.

Matilda never professed any religious sentiment (compared to her more pious predecessor, Emily), but a near-death experience in 1878 led her to speak of her destiny in relation to one-year-old Paul.

I had a very narrow escape from being killed or injured for life, by a horse we bought on Christmas. It fell with me, and in struggling, beat its hoofs against me so that it broke my corset bones, but miraculously almost, left me unhurt. It also dashed down the street with my riding skirt attached to the saddle, but fortunately tore it in shreds from me. It was the narrowest possible escape. I was alone; a countryman brought me home, who said that he shut his eyes for fear of seeing me kicked to death. He asked what saved you, and I told him I thought it must have been that my baby could not spare me. (25–26)

Though modern-day feminists decry the corset and its discomforts (if not disfigurements), Matilda's whalebone corset, along with her own determination to live for her baby, may have saved her life.

In his brothers' books, young Paul's steadfast character shines through. A toddler's personality presages that of the teenager and even the adult. From boyhood, Paul was described as "serious & earnest" (Griffing, 56). Matilda often remarked on her first sons' very different characters: Griffing neglected his homework assignments while Paul "is my goodie-goodie boy, and . . . was carefully tracing his copy in his writing book" (Griffing, 95). Matilda further noted, "Grif [is] always intent on the moment, on spontaneity. Paul's quiet, manly way is a restful contrast" (Griffing, 118–19). Paul's early "manliness" manifested itself during a frightening forest fire in the Ojai Valley in the late fall of 1883.

> There was a solid column of flame a mile distant. . . . Paul awakened and after looking at the fire, crossed himself without any excitement, and was perfectly self-possessed all the time. I told him he could go out and watch it with Uncle James; "no," he said, "I must help Grif"; he wasn't getting dressed quick enough alone, and "you know mama, we must save the children before we do the clothes," as he saw me packing things in shawls which could be removed more easily than trunks. (138)

Paul's early talent for drawing foreshadowed his later engineering career: "Mrs Burbeck gave them a little attention in their studies and particularly in drawing. Paul's teachers, Mrs Rice and Mrs Burbeck, are very much pleased with his aptitude. Griffing does very well, but hasn't as much talent nor application as Paul" (Griffing, 268).

Finally, Matilda trained her keen eye on her children's interactions, how they played and competed. The eldest, Paul assumed responsibility, a lifetime role, as it would turn out. Their work in the garden was a case in point.

> Paul is a real help but Grif's chief thought is how to escape as much work as possible and so bring in as much play as possible. Philip turns to Paul if he wants to work, and to Grif if he wants to play. Griffing depends on Paul to plan out & support him in his work, for "Paul is boss of this work, you know"— and he has to supply the backbone. (Griffing, 305)

Paul sometimes took his role too seriously: "Paul inclines to tyrannize a little which to Philip's sensitive nature is most painful, but we are on our guard and papa applies the check in time; we mean to be watchful and avoid the consequences of such a disposition" (Philip, 250).

Griffing: "Crazy Headed and Quixotic"

Matilda began Griffing's 395-page book with a beautiful account of his birth on January 21, 1879, at five o'clock in the morning.

> Once upon a time, for this is the beginning of a story of a life just opened, the continuation and end of which is known only to its Maker; once upon a time, on a clear, cold midwinter night when the ice-crusted snow creaked beneath the sleigh that occasionally passed over it, a little soul, pure as the snow without, crossed the portal and was welcomed into our family.

Months later, in June 1879, Matilda returned to California via a seven-day train trip with both children. She greatly anticipated greeting her husband with the new son he had not yet met. The family spent part of the summer in Oakville, Napa Valley, with H.H.'s parents.

> Both father and mother Bancroft are vigorous in mind and body, altho' 80 years of age. They are energetic people to whom idleness is sin, conscientious from sound religious principle, liberal in their sympathies, and with strikingly intelligent minds. They live in a comfortable home of their own and through the summer their children spend more or less time with them in an adjoining house built by their daughter Mrs. Kenny. (14–15)

That summer, baby Griffing fell ill with dysentery. "We were obliged to give brandy every half hour and concentrated beef juice to keep up vitality . . .; we felt his chances of living were very slight" (16–17). He recovered with the spunkiness that characterized him throughout his childhood: "The little fellow astonishes us with his activity and spirit" (18).

Ever comparing her sons, Matilda wrote that Griffing was often more overtly mischievous and disobedient than Paul, but she would not spare the rod and spoil the child. "I have to use the hair-brush" (30). Griffing typically played the Pied Piper, leading his siblings into trouble. Once when the Bancrofts were visiting others, Matilda noted that this "wild colt" of a child immediately caused mayhem:

> In a moment he had snapped off a rose, filled the rain gauge with gravel, scattered sand over the front steps, and all before I knew he was doing any mischief. The old doctor looked at them through his glasses and shook his head, and said, "If the children are too destructive, I can't keep them; that's all." Papa was disgusted with [Griffing's] behavior, but I own I was a little amused withal. (72–73).

At least this Victorian lady retained her sense of humor in the midst of her child's hurricane force.

However, Griffing's pranks were sometimes dangerous, once nearly getting Philip killed.

> Grif had been playing horse with Philip . . . and forgot to unharness him. The cord was tied to his arms as well as to Phil's. Philip was first placed in a high chair; when Grif cantered off, poor little Phil landed heavily on the back of his head. He escaped serious consequences, but I could scarcely tell how. I have always been afraid that Griffing's carelessness would sometime bring some dreadful accident on somebody else, if not on himself. It is a marvel how children escape, with their constant exposures to danger. (236–37)

And what of playing with dynamite, as the boys did at the family's Walnut Creek farm?

> Our next alarm, a few days later, was when we found the boys with lighted paper, out of doors, undertaking to explode some blasting powder under a small box. . . . They had got three or four ounces or more, and all that prevented an explosion was the wind blowing on the fire. The powder being about the place is easily explained. When papa bought the land it was

all covered with grand old oaks, and to make it valuable for
a fruit farm all those grand trees have been cut down except
on 30 or 40 acres which form the homesite. These trees have
been cut down and the roots blasted and dug up so that we
may plough deep enough in subsoil. We have had companies
. . . engaged at the work for months, and they had this blast-
ing powder in cans. An empty can was lying about which
contained . . . enough in it to reward the boys' efforts . . . with
about half a cup full, and it was this they had in readiness
to ignite when they were discovered at their experiment.
Griffing as usual was the ringleader and his papa afterwards
frightened him nearly out of his wits by setting him on the
box and threatening to light the powder and blow him up.
(222)

The penances Griffing repeatedly endured did not much reduce his
penchant for mischief. In fact, he readily submitted to the inevitable
punishments. Once he even offered to go get the water for his retribu-
tory cold bath, but his governess told him that she had no time to give
him one; however, she would instead tie him up. Griffing consented,
"All right, Jennie, you can tie me up for all night." Added Matilda, "He
seems to acknowledge the justice of punishment" (82).

Griffing's book is rife with stories of his impropriety toward elders,
acts of destruction (including breaking his mother's precious watch),
and "hair-breadth" escapes, such as being tossed from a horse. "He can't
keep his hands off anything," Matilda complained (151). When trouble
erupted, "as usual Grif was responsible for the venture" (111). One mis-
adventure ended with Griffing receiving four stitches above one eye,
having been kicked by a donkey after pricking it with a sharp stick! No
anesthesia was used while he was being sewn up in his mother's lap,
but he did not flinch. "The doctor told him that he didn't know of any
man who would bear that as bravely, and Griffing specially requested
I should write that down in his journal" (197). Thus Matilda also reinforced this child's best qualities. She knew "his disposition . . . will enable
him to push his way through life without suffering from sensitiveness
and from rebuffs" (118). After all, Griffing never acted maliciously. He
claimed he was "as good as God would let him be" (318).

Matilda viewed the children's pranks with good humor and applied a rational approach toward crime and punishment, as in the case of the egg battle:

> One Sunday afternoon the three younger children were off by themselves for two or three hours; when they appeared they were covered with egg; they had been having an egg battle. Griffing began it, of course, with Phil, and Lucy was supplying them with eggs as their ammunition. . . . I couldn't but laugh to myself at their appearance and their excited story on their return. We had a trial, judge and jury to prove who was most guilty. I wish I had made notes of the proceedings, they were so amusing. We never had any reoccurrence of that kind. (116–17)

Griffing could also be loving, loyal, and helpful. When Matilda teased Papa, who said he'd spill hot tea on her hand, Griffing protected her: "Take care you don't hurt my mamma or I'll order your coffin" (159). Another time, Griffing "said with his arms wound around my neck, 'Mamma I love you so much, I'll do anything for you; I'll help you write History, just the same as you help papa.'"

This tidbit shows how Papa's "History" was "an ever present subject in their minds" (90). Matilda sought to inspire her children with their father's achievements. In Griffing's book, she described H.H.'s travels to his office in San Francisco from Piedmont during the late spring of 1883.

> Papa has been working very hard even here. The Alaska volume has been the most absorbing, although he flits from one subject to another rather than be for one hour without work. He has spent a day or two of every week with us, but usually he goes over to SF every day, breakfasting at 6.30 and returning on the 3 o'clock boat. Shall you, my boy, work as hard and to as good a purpose at his age?" (97)

Griffing's book foretells future vexations between himself and his father. On an 1884 family camping trip to Napa's Soda Springs, Papa had put up a tent. Griffing was then age five, Paul six.

The boys made a path leading to it and over the hill; that is, Paul made it and Grif looked on approvingly. I am afraid, Griffing my boy, that you are inclined to be lazy for you will stretch yourself across a stump and <u>rest</u> while Paul is tugging away as for dear life. It won't do my son; papa has discovered your proclivity and says you must be set to work. (164)

A last example of Grif's impudence: "Papa got very angry with Griffing for his impertinence. Grif hasn't the least reverence; he is so daring the only wonder is he doesn't oftener get into trouble." Apparently, H.H. grew tired of hearing Phil say "papa dear," and Papa joked that Phil should call him anything else. So that night Grif answered his father by saying, "'You crazy donkey, you wild bear, what do you want?'... Griffing got well jerked about by his ears and was sent off in disgrace." Matilda sought to intervene on her son's behalf, but noted, "papa was vexed with my interference." She concluded, "I imagined then scenes in after life, of more serious import, when I should be trying to shield and excuse my boy, perhaps through that very weakness and indulgence harming him" (172–73).

Matilda's chronicles proved prescient. In later years, Matilda and H.H. inundated Griffing with letters exhorting him to meet their expectations. H.H. verbally boxed his son's ears while Matilda tried to cajole him into more responsible behavior. The trail between Griffing's childhood and adulthood is so evident because his second wife, Margaret Wood Bancroft, preserved the letters Griffing received from his parents from 1901 until Hubert's death in 1918.[6] The impudent child retained his defiance of the patriarch and matriarch and their expectations that their sons should dedicate themselves to hard work for society's benefit. Griffing did not seek to follow in his father's big footsteps. Instead, he became a writer of middling success rather than the lawyer and public speaker his father had hoped for. Griffing lived in Southern California, as far from his father as possible, where he capably managed family properties, but with little ambition to be a legal or literary magnate or a leader in real estate or business. Nevertheless, other family tales suggest that Griffing ended up happy in his own way of life.

Delicate and Devoted Philip

In the 271 pages devoted to her youngest son, Philip, Matilda portrayed a child with often grave health troubles, as well as a child supremely dedicated to his father. The health problems dissipated over time, though Philip himself in his oral history done seven decades later said he was "always in poor health when I was a child" (6).[7] But Philip turned out to be the son who most took after his father, not only in his ambitions but also in taking over the family farm.

As with the other children, Matilda initiated Philip's book by recounting his birth: "Your birthplace was in the home we have owned for the past two years in San Francisco, 1298 Van Ness Ave., S.E. cor Sutter St., the room the large bed room. . . . It was on Thursday night, at half past eleven, on the 30th of June '81 that you gladdened our hearts by your welcome presence" (2).[8]

Within months, Philip exhibited great love for his father.

> Baby Philip is wild about his father; he demonstrates it as plainly as if he could speak and papa is delighted with his preference of him to anyone else. . . . Papa must keep out of his sight unless he is ready to give him attention, or else Philip will make a terrible ado. (18)

In the summer of 1883, when Philip was two, the family spent two weeks at Lake Tahoe. Heading for Tallac House (South Lake Tahoe) across the lake aboard a steamer, Philip was terrified by the boat's loud horn; "only papa would comfort him." Then, one afternoon,

> Phil made a slave of his papa; at the sound of Phil's voice he was ready to yield to his slightest whim. Once as he started with him to the beach, he picked up his ms [manuscript], but Phil said, "No, no, me no like," and it was left behind; Phil wanted all the attention. Papa remained only a week. It was pitiful to see how the little fellow missed him. He would go all around for days . . . saying "I 'ant papa." (40)

H.H. was known for having a good singing voice and for love of song, which he used to the advantage of his children, especially Philip.

Here in Philip's book, Matilda shows how H.H. referred to Phil by the nickname of Joe.

> In Alameda, as at Lake Tahoe, papa would take little Phil into his bed and sing to him; which was the happier of the two, it is difficult to say. Phil would say, if I approached the bed, "Mamma go away; Phil's papa's baby boy," and then would settle down with such complacency, and his papa would grind out all the old Mother Hubbard songs the child would demand. All this warm devotion of the child touched the father-heart deeply, and he would sometimes say, "I shall lose my little Joe [Phil] when I go away; he never will be the same again." In a letter from Mexico some weeks later, he said, "Alas! My little Joe. His love for me was one of the most pleasing episodes of my life." (47)

Knowing that he would miss out on his toddler's growth during his trip to Mexico, H.H. offered his philosophy on life. "So all things must die, or change, which is the same; and I think it is best to live more in the present, than in the past and future as I always have for the present is all that we have" (48).

In reading Matilda's descriptions of Philip's early love of riding with his father, one can see how he ended up with the family farm in Walnut Creek.

> Every time papa starts out for any place on the farm, his first thought is for Phil. He saddles old Bayard with the little saddle and Philip rides like a veteran; he no longer holds on, and even whips up the old fellow into a gallop without holding on. . . . He seems as contented to be with his papa as his father seems to have him with him. Philip has the monopoly now. He helps with the painting of the little cottage or lodge that is being built for one of our men; and how he busies himself with papa at the artesian well, on the ploughed ground, with the surveyors, etc. . . . He seems to have come back from some Paradise every time he comes back from these trips. (115)

Though H.H. was devoted to all of his children, one more comment, from 1887, when Philip was six, underscores the mutual nature of this father–son love affair:

> Papa was here [at the Farm] all the time I was away [in San Diego]. He takes so much pleasure in being with the children on the farm, and wrote me of the comfort they were to him all the time. He often speaks of the peculiar pleasure Phil gives him; that there is something quieting to him in his very touch; he feels it as he holds his hand. (Philip, 165)

Perhaps Philip's early and repeated health crises contributed to his father's sense of special care for him. Philip had weak lungs, first reported in September 1883 when he was two while in San Diego. Matilda worried that Phil had bronchitis. A doctor prescribed iron for tonic and bromide of potassium for sleep. When the prescribed medicines proved ineffective, Matilda feared he had whooping cough, given a recent epidemic. She finally moved the family to drier air in Ojai. "Phil reveled in that ride. We had 50 miles in a large wagon, plenty of room. . . . It was the beginning of decided improvement in the little fellow" (52). The 105 degree heat dried up his cough.

However, respiratory ailments repeatedly plagued him. Griffing called him "delicate" (Griffing, 209). Shrouded in San Francisco's fog in May 1884, Phil took ill again with a severe cough, such that "he is our great anxiety now," Matilda wrote in Philip's book (79). Seeking to escape the cold, the family went to Napa Soda Springs. There Phil soon took violently ill with convulsions and delirium. "He did not know me at all," wrote Matilda, shaken. They "were prepared for all emergencies" (80). Finally, his fever broke.

They made copious attempts to diagnose the lad's sicknesses, including "albuminuria" (albumen in the urine). Matilda reported, "The severest suffering Philip experienced was with ear-ache one evening, but a few drops of a preparation of Laudanum & cocaine prescribed by Dr. McNutt gave him immediate relief, and he slept it all away" (171). Cocaine and laudanum! Matilda always listed the remedies prescribed: fresh air and sea-bathing, electricity, iron, brandy, wine, "Roche's Embrocation on the chest and burned Cresoline as a vapor" (153), even arsenic.

Finally, early in 1889, when Philip was eight, his health crisis drove his parents to a new doctor. Matilda's analysis of the doctor's assessment combines perspective on late-nineteenth-century medicine, the dawning of twentieth-century farming, and a mother's dedication to chronicling her child's illnesses.

> Philip began to run down again about the last of January. He had so much headache I took him out of school. . . . He came in . . . and said he had the worst headache he had ever had. "Soothe me, soothe me, mamma," he exclaimed in a tone of excitement and command he had never assumed. He was laying on the sofa and I was trying to keep him quiet; "confound it" he shrieked, "I can't stand it, darn it," and he rattled off any number of such expletives that I thought were all unknown to our quiet, innocent little boy. I was almost frightened at his condition, but finally quieted the pain and his excitement with Bromide of Potassium and a menthol pencil. . . .
>
> I took him to Dr. Edwards for treatment, as at this time he began to cough again, and his breath for the first time was very bad. The Dr. has just come from Philadelphia where he has had an extensive practice, and has been associated with the famous Dr. Weir-Mitchell.[9] He has rented our house, intending it as a health resort or sanitarium. He was very much interested in the sketch I was able to give him of Philip's condition from his babyhood; I made it out from this journal, which he said was a remarkable diagnosis from a "layman". Who would keep such a record but a mother? (Philip, 199)

In Philip's book, Matilda detailed the doctor's summary of his tests and examination, and then his treatment.

> Dr. Edwards commenced with a treatment of the nostrils which was very painful, inserting a tube from the mouth through the back passage of the nose; Philip bore it manfully; then he used iodine with a bellows, if that is what smells so horribly. We had to use an atomizer regularly and salt water baths and the rubbing with alcohol. The offensive breath developed later and was from his stomach, for that was

> quickly relieved with proper medicine. He was sent out to the
> farm in April, I think. . . .
>   Phil improved from the start. Fraulein [the children's
> nanny] took charge of his food and kept up the rubbing. Dr.
> told me that his trouble was one of the mucous membrane,
> and that he thought, as we have always thought, that it was in
> consequence of Bright's disease . . . but . . . farm life, the open
> air, and special care of his diet may turn the current and he
> may grow into a healthy man. (197–203)

Matilda then explained to the doctor Phil's nervous temperament,
how upset he became over memorizing a piece for a school recital,
working himself into a frenzy of sleeplessness the night before.

> As Dr. Edwards said, "Don't you see with his nervous tem-
> perament how he would brood over business anxieties? Never
> put him in an office; make a farm his life work; let him grow
> there and develop mentally and physically, until he is strong
> enough to resist his weakness."
>   I wrote papa that Dr. Edwards thought Philip's life should
> be spent on a farm. Papa said in reply to this, "all right; if
> the farm will be his salvation he may take his choice of San
> Diego or Contra Costa [Walnut Creek]; either shall be his."
> I added (myself) that we should make him a scientific farmer.
> My idea was that study and education should apply here as
> well as anywhere else. Papa's reply was most characteristic:
> "I don't know what Dr. Edwards means by being a 'scientific
> farmer'; the only science in farming I know is to take off your
> coat and go to work." (204–5)

Matilda's assertion that Philip would make an excellent "scientific"
farmer highlights her foresight. Both H.H. and Matilda saw the promise of intellect in their youngest son, which she illustrated in story after
story, such as her tale of H.H.'s remarks when Philip was still quite
young: "'It seems to me as if Philip had the most intelligence in his eye
of any child I ever saw'" (33).

Matilda once posed a trick question to her sons that evinces Philip's
innate intelligence.

I said, "Boys, which is the heavier, a pound of lead or a pound of feathers." Griffing said at once, "lead." "No," says Paul, "feathers," thinking probably that was the answer expected. . . . Phil chipped in, "Why! They are the same . . .; o'course a pound is the same whatever it is." The older ones looked quite sheepish at his reply—but Philip, as we've always said, has the clearest mind of the three. (Philip, 218–19)

Matilda's characterization of her three boys was reinforced by Griffing's future second wife, Margaret Wood Bancroft, who used a metaphor of the brothers approaching a fence: "Paul just stopped this side of the fence and Phil behind him, and Griff went over the fence and got into trouble" (36).[10]

Self-Reliant Lucy

"Into the midst of a lovely trio of brothers stepped our Rosalind on Thursday morning the 28th of September 1882." Or so Lucy was initially named, and then Daisy, until her parents finally had her baptized in January 1885, settling on the name of Lucy after H.H.'s mother, Lucy Howe.

As ever, Matilda's comments on her children's characters were prescient, including the role that Lucy would play in her family:

While each boy was gladly welcomed, at heart I was not satisfied till la petite filled my cup to overflowing. I think papa perhaps places undue appreciation on boys, and our little one must grow into his heart and so wind herself into his love that he will wonder how he ever could think slightingly of girls. He accepts the gift without expression of pleasure or disappointment, merely saying "I am satisfied if you are," but with the announcement "it's a boy," there is no concealing his satisfaction. (Lucy, 2–3)

Like her siblings, Lucy was smart, later picking up German quickly and learning the game of whist merely by watching her siblings play. She was also smart enough to realize at the age of five that her father preferred boys, so she decided to become one.

> In the fall I had Lucy's hair cut short, as tight to her head
> as was possible without shaving it. She had complained that
> "the sun was so wet" she wished she could have her curls cut
> off. . . . She was so anxious to be a boy; the transformation
> was complete when she put on Philip's outgrown Jerseys.
> She called herself Tommy at once; just as we left the barber's
> someone asked her name, and she answered unhesitatingly:
> "Tommy—I'm a boy now, and my name is Tommy." When
> papa came she met him on the road in her new guise, jersey
> suit, white straw hat & cropped hair, of course he didn't know
> her for a moment, much to her delight. (Lucy, 102–3)

Lucy already understood the very different expectations for boys and girls not only in her family but in society. In fact, three generations later when I was a girl growing up in the Bancroft family, Lucy's name had been almost wiped from family consciousness, whereas the three boys—Paul, Griffing, and Philip—played extraordinary roles in perpetuating their father's legacy.

As the little sister of rambunctious brothers, Lucy learned gumption, and Matilda admired her for it. "You are a spunky little piece, but some spunk is necessary to carry you through life" (Lucy, 40). Matilda always looked out for her older girl, stepdaughter Kate, and her "petite" to insure that the girls would not lose out to the boys, clear beneficiaries of their father's attention, patriarchal views on gender roles, and financial largesse.

When Lucy arrived, Matilda already had a very young brood to contend with: Paul, age five; Griffing, three; and Philip, one. Phil in later years asked his mother to include in his memory book a story about Lucy's arrival, one very telling in terms of gender roles in the Bancroft household. On his birthday in 1886, Philip described how his parents arrived home one day and found a little baby boy crying upstairs in their bed. That was his own arrival. The lad added what must have been a legendary conversation.

> Mamma said "wouldn't it be nice if it was a little girl"? but
> papa said "boys are good enough for me, you may have the
> girls." And then mamma went and got a little girl for five
> cents and that's Lucy. (Philip, 147–48)

Matilda's description highlights the quandary of many parents in explaining where babies come from.

> Philip was still so much a baby that it came as a great surprise
> when they found another baby was sent us; . . . a little sister
> baby, and it is warmly welcomed. The children have so many
> questions to ask and our old nurse Mrs. McGowan told them
> the usual story in regard to her bringing the baby in a basket,
> all of which papa so heartily disapproves that I tell them all .
> I can; that God sent our little sister for us to love and take
> care of and that the first I saw of her she was lying on my bed
> without any clothes on her." (Griffing, 84–85)

Throughout Philip and Lucy's books, Matilda noted their special relationship, since they literally shared the same baby carriage. But "the poor little fellow is the greatest sufferer by this event" of Lucy's arrival. "He does enjoy petting so much, and exacts so much attention that . . . it seems a pity his babyhood is so severely threatened, his kingdom . . . invaded most assuredly" (Philip, 23).

Although Philip might have wished to push his baby sister from the carriage, he actually became protective of her, a relationship that endured throughout their lives. "Sometimes Phil will hear her cry and says, 'I'll make baby happy, mamma,' and brings her her bottle or any-thing at hand to quiet her" (Philip, 57).

Despite such sibling love, Lucy, "an inveterate tease," early pestered her brothers, from pulling her brothers' hair to imposing destructive "catastrophes." As she recalled these events in Lucy's book, Matilda found them "amusing" at times.

> Philip is building a tower with his blocks, while Lucy is
> keenly watching him; Phil is in nervous dread of Lucy's
> knocking the structure down. "I can tell you is going to knock
> over my blocks," he exclaims, "cause your eyes say so"; her eyes
> are just dancing with the tempting thought; "then my eyes tell
> lies", she answers demurely. But soon the dreaded catastrophe
> happens; the temptation was too strong; the tower topples
> over and Philip indignantly exclaims, "there I was right; I
> knew you'd spoil all my fun"—Lucy complacently explains,

> "well, I've got good eyes; they wouldn't tell lies o'course."
> (Lucy, 97)

By age three, Lucy's spunk had mutated into impudence, like that of brother Griffing.

> I had my first encounter with her obstinacy. . . . She would not come to me as I called her; I talked with her, tried persuasion of every kind but she grew more and more determined, until I had to whip her to make her yield. She understood the lesson perfectly and kissed me over and over again. I've had to repeat occasionally since, but not often. (52)

For Matilda, there would be no spoiling the child.

Yet Lucy remained unyielding in her headstrong attitude. Once she played rough with a child at a hotel dining room: "As she passed him at the table, she struck his hand roughly to attract attention. I afterward reproved her and told her it made me feel like crying that my little girl should act so like a little hoodlum. She braved it out at first but finally burst into tears" (170).

Lucy's spunk meant she was often the first among her siblings to try something new and reckless—perhaps to get her brothers' approval or simply because it was in her nature, as it was in Griffing's, to be daring. For example, H.H. wanted the children to harden their feet in the summer by going barefoot,

> so he offered them $6.00 a month for doing it, with the understanding that they should put their shoes on whenever they had any occasion to do so. Griffing and Lucy were first and foremost in it. Lucy is anxious to do whatever the boys do, and in fact to go a little ahead. (121)

Matilda also reported that

> the boys were in the habit of calling on Lucy to help them when they killed the chickens. They would get her to hold the head while they chopped it off, until I heard of it and put a stop to it. Lucy said when I called for her one evening,

> "I'm watching that rooster take his last walk, clucking for his
> head." It is astonishing how she can do such a thing. (164)

When her brothers were learning to shoot a rifle, she wanted to do
the same.

> Lucy was most anxious for a little rifle and so exchanged
> old Dan for the rifle "cause the horse was old and would die,
> while the rifle would last always." She is learning to fire at a
> mark; the boys are excellent aims. It is amusing to see her do
> everything they do. (182)

Most impressive were Lucy's skills with horses, stemming from her
great tenderness for them.

> When I was reading "Black Beauty" which is the "Uncle
> Tom's Cabin" of the horse she had a sudden "pain in her
> stomach" which accounted for her tears, not the story, oh no![11]
>   Poor child, her sympathies with horses is so great that this
> autobiography of a horse has entered her very soul with its
> account of hard treatment; she has felt every rough touch and
> enjoyed every stroke of tenderness Black Beauty experienced;
> and she never will forget its lessons. The book has had an
> immense sale and general distribution, and was introduced
> into public schools as a benefit to humanity or rather to the
> brute creation. (192–93)

Lucy's love of horses was equaled by her lack of fear. "Lucy's fear-
lessness with horses is remarkable," wrote her mother, describing an
incident when the horses in the corral were stampeding for a gate that
the workmen had left open. The men ran to drive the horses back. "But
before they got there, Lucy had darted toward [the horses], turned
them back and closed the gate; the men were terrified to see her do it,
but it was done in a moment before they could prevent her" (103–4).

Lucy suffered several riding accidents that might have dissuaded
another child from ever climbing back on a horse. In the summer of
1888, Matilda described several such incidents while Lucy, age five, was
learning to ride her beloved Chiquita.

Lucy and Chiquita, courtesy of The Bancroft Library (BANC MSS 73/64 c)

Chiquita was almost unmanageable for, though of gentle disposition, she was not used at all and was headstrong, determined to circle about home as soon as anyone started to ride her. Papa said the children must ride her; I was anxious to exchange her for some old horse, well broken. Lucy was anxious to try, and for several days papa went out with Lucy, leading her horse while he rode Bob. The men were hauling sand, so Lucy soon rode along by the wagon without difficulty, and Chiquita became as manageable as a kitten.

One day while they were in the Creek, the boys in the wagon and Lucy on horseback, she rode under an overhanging branch and her head got caught in the fork of a tree; it held her neck like a vise. She screamed, the horse stopped instantly, Paul at once ran to her rescue and the danger was over. Jim [Griffing] said if the horse had not stopped immediately, it would have broken her neck.

A few days after she was riding bareback near the house when she slipped and screamed, grasping the reins and hanging on the side barely. Again Chiquita stopped. Papa ran out, took her off, and said she needn't ride any more. "Can't I ride

> Chiquita to the stable?" she asked sobbing, and she was again on her back as happy as ever. I showed some nervousness and she said reassuringly, "don't be afraid, mamma, whenever I scream, Chiquita stops." (118–20)

Little comfort to the mother of a daredevil child!

As much as Matilda permitted her hoodlum of a daughter the same freedoms as Lucy's brothers, she also instilled messages about Lucy's future role as mother and keeper of a home and family. She wrote at length in Lucy's book about some of the problems she faced finding competent and reliable help with her children on travels with her ever-moving husband. "I write this fully expecting, Rosalind [Lucy], that in future years, when you yourself are experiencing some of these perplexities, you will be interested in these present perplexities" (15–16). Matilda assumed that Lucy would have her own brood of children and would face the same kinds of problems.

Presciently, however, at the dinner table one night,

> Lucy remarked, "I'm going to be an old maid, 'cause it's too much trouble to find a husband." "Oh, no, Lucy," said Philip, "girls ought to get married, 'cause they get money from their husbands, but I won't ever marry, 'cause I'd have to give my money to my wife and I'd rather give it all to mamma." "Well," I chimed in, "what did I get married for, Phil? I had money enough, and didn't care for any more." "Oh, you got married to get children o'course," was his quick reply. (Philip, 178)

Lucy never did marry.[12] Her private life remains a mystery. She was as independent in her adulthood as she had been in her childhood.

The Challenges of Mothering

Matilda could be contradictory in her mothering—who is not? On the one hand, she adhered to some Victorian notions of child-rearing, such as the principle of her sons (but not her daughter) "hardening" themselves.

> This morning as I was talking with the boys I told them there
> was one thing they were now doing, I wanted them to do
> through life; continue with their cold baths, just as papa does;
> the boys for some time have taken them regularly and have
> bathed themselves, standing on an oil cloth, and throwing the
> water about freely; and with never a complaint of the tem-
> perature of the room or the water. They are delighted with the
> idea of hardening themselves. (Griffing, 189–90)

On the other hand, Matilda read voraciously and absorbed new
ideas with an impulse to experiment. She described sending Griffing to
the dentist at age seven, "his first experience with a dentist, for it is the
modern theory that children's teeth should be filled so as to preserve
the first teeth as long as possible" (Griffing, 244). Her experimentation
included various medical remedies for childhood illnesses or for her
own health issues. She revealed problems with breast-feeding Griffing,
for instance, so she had tried "lager, broma, gruels, and the frantic use
of fomentations of castor-oil leaves and the internal use of the bitter extract" (Griffing, 11), but finally hired a wet nurse and eventually
resorted to condensed milk: "Baby thrived."

Like every mother called to her children's bedsides, Matilda frequently had nursing duties. Matilda catalogued earaches, bouts with
the measles and chicken pox, croup, whooping cough, and Asiatic
flu, and she included the diverse treatments that she and/or a doctor
applied. Fortunately, all her children survived, whether because of or in
spite of her remedies. Many children in the 1870s did die.

Of course, Matilda was also fortunate to have a nanny or "nurse"
always on hand. Coping with her brood alone in Tahoe on one occasion—with H.H. not yet arrived—Matilda lamented that "all my babies
were on my hands alone for two or three days, with the nurse sick in
bed and no one to lift a finger that we could get for love or money. That
so far has been my hardest experience" (Griffing, 96). She likened her
entourage to "moving a caravan" or having a "delegation" with all four
children, two nurses, and one husband.

> We had quite a baby show . . . each required a nurse either to
> wheel or carry them. Both nurses wore caps and aprons, and
> when papa took us all out riding together, it appeared like
> a delegation from some institution. Paul was but five, and

Griffing three and a half; all babies in fact. The boys would
take their velocipedes [tricycles], Phil in his buggy and baby
in [our] arms. (Lucy, 13)

Keeping her boisterous herd in check at a "fashionable" hotel in San
Diego was impossible.

After great difficulty in finding a boarding house where they
would take such a family of children, we succeeded in being
accommodated by Mrs Giddings ... but within twenty four
hours was satisfied that it was not feasible to stop at any hotel
unless I had two nurses for the children. (Lucy, 34)

H.H. must have had utter faith in his wife's ability to move this
pack—or was he insensitive to her need for help? Once she had to herd
her entourage onto a stagecoach (place unspecified, perhaps Walnut
Creek), and then meet "papa and sister Kate" at the train station in
Oakland. "The stage was late which necessitated the hustling of bag and
baggage and babies most unceremoniously into the cars. Everything
was tumbled on to the platform and the baggage was checked while
the whistle was blowing" (Philip, 34). Could H.H. not have reduced
this havoc for Matilda with all those babies and baggage?

Wherever the family landed, Matilda understood that getting her
brash bunch outdoors as much as possible would keep them out of her
nicely pinned hair. She claimed, "We are all advocates of country living,
and think ourselves and little ones will be the stronger for it in years to
come" (Griffing, 65).

Perhaps the most unsettling example of dangerous play was a fire
that the boys inadvertently set in the carriage house at the Walnut
Creek farm in 1889. Their father was in San Diego, but on learning
of the fire, he wrote a sardonic letter, which Matilda also included in
Philip's memory book. Her narrative, abounding in tension and pathos,
merits quoting in full.

We had a fine 4th of July celebration. I got a good supply of
firecrackers, rockets, etc. ... which Paul [age eleven] enjoyed
"bossing." He is so careful it seems safe to leave such things
in his hands. We were so afraid of fire, particularly as papa
is still away, that while in San Francisco I tried to get fire

extinguishers, hand-grenades, etc. but none were sent to me until further order, as they were looked on as useless.

On the Monday following the 4th, the dreaded fire made its appearance. At noon, Paul came with a fire-cracker in a tin spice box, a hole through the cover and the bottom of the can, and asked if he could fire off the cracker at the monkey's cage, as it was such fun to see Yum Yum jump. . . . I consented. All of the children enjoyed the fun; Philip and Lucy ran in afterwards and got the can. Yum Yum had become so tame that she grew more interesting every day. . . . She had gradually grown so gentle but we were accustomed to drive her off when she jumped on us; now she in turn sprang on to Griffing and Lucy and Philip, cuddling down into their arms in happy content; all of which has left happy remembrances of her and sincere regrets at her loss, for the poor monkey perished in the fire which suddenly broke out in her cage at 4 o'clock.

Paul and Griffing were at Walnut Creek in the buggy; Philip and Lucy were at their music with Fraulein in the parlor; the rest of us were scattered about. Rover, our little collie, barked furiously and looking for the cause of it, we saw the carriage house in flames. Not a man was within call; we rang the large bell furiously; we ran to the burning building; we tried to get out the wagons; all care for Yum Yum was lost in the thought of saving what we could of the carriages. Mrs. Carpenter . . . tried with me to move the rockaway; the flames then were burning through the partition. We left it in dismay, and the other woman took out the lighter wagons, while I rang out the alarm. Phil and Lucy in obedience to Fraulein's orders stood on the porch, though afterward I was sorry I did not have the children ring the bell, or let them pull out some of their toys themselves before the fire reached that wing of the carriage house.

Soon one man appeared who with Mrs. Mitchell's help removed the rockaway from the blazing building; everything was saved including harnesses, with the exception of a new lumber wagon which was too heavy to move. Men now rushed in from right about us. The threshers were at work in the Randalls' field; they blew their whistle for an alarm and

rushed over, ten or twenty of them, to our help. The wind at
the start was blowing directly toward the barn which was
just filled with new hay. The men worked incessantly trying
to save it; a great oak supplied powerful aid; it shielded the
men from the intense heat; & while it was all in a blaze it
was too green to burn well; now tree choppers ascended and
cut off some of the burning limbs; the manure pile spread at
the base of the barn took fire repeatedly, but it was as quickly
extinguished with the buckets of water poured on it; the roof
was in a blaze at intervals, but the water applied at the right
moment averted the danger, and most important of all, the
wind suddenly changed (it was blowing a gale) and wrapped
the hen house in its embrace.

All night men watched for a possible breaking out of the
fire, and all night long there was a furious wind but with our
fortunate escape from a greater loss, we won't complain of
what happened. Papa must have felt so, for this is his reply to
the information. (Philip, 220–27)

Their father's letter:

My dear children:
I congratulate you upon your glorious Fourth! I hope you
will never be lacking a carriage house for a bonfire and a
monkey for a sacrifice to be offered on the altar of liberty. Our
glorious institutions must be preserved and the star-spangled
banner long may it wave. Next time if you have not a carriage
house and a monkey, you may set fire to the farm mansion
and burn your mother. Children must be amused and the
American Union must be preserved, regardless of fathers,
barns, or monkey.
Well, while you are burning there, I am building here, and
whenever I come here to build, somebody burns there.
                                    Your aff. father HHB
                                    July 12th, 1889

Their own shame, along with their father's cutting words, may have
been punishment enough.

Matilda's good humor helped her withstand the trials of raising this wild bunch, along with her many other tasks, but she was not invulnerable to the strain it placed on her. She ultimately died at the relatively young age of sixty-two in 1910.

Matilda's strong character is emphasized by the fact that the children saw her cry only once, when Griffing seemed mortally ill. She broke into tears when telling Lucy, "'I'm afraid Griffing may have meningitis and then he will die like my little brother Willie.' The children it seems had never seen me cry before and it made a profound impression of which they often speak" (Lucy, 184).

Although Matilda suffered from terrible headaches, she did not allow them to prevent her from letting the show go on. When she had planned an elaborate "fit-a-tail-on-the-donkey party" for thirty children, she refused to let her headache ruin the extravaganza. She explained the new game.

> We had tables spread with sandwiches, cake, ice cream &
> chocolate for all. Then they adjourned to the cottage where
> candy bags & other games, with the special attraction of
> fitting a tail on the donkey, blindfolded, amused them for an
> hour or two. This game came into vogue a year or two ago; a
> tailless donkey is cut out of a dark cloth or painted on a white
> background; a dozen or more tails, each numbered is distrib-
> uted to the company; each in turn is blindfolded and after
> turning around three times, attempts to place the tail where
> it belongs. The one most successful has the best prize; the one
> who is the most unsuccessful has the booby prize, or some-
> thing ridiculous. In this case, we gave a toy donkey bobbing
> its head as it was drawn on the ground as the booby prize.
>
> I had a very severe headache all that day, but from the
> moment the children appeared at five o'clock, the excitement
> drove it away. These headaches are peculiar in yielding to any
> excitement, or being created in an instant by worry or anxiety.
> Aunt Josie [her sister] helped all day, while I lay on the bed.
> (Philip, 210–11)

Regardless of her personal problem, Matilda persisted.

These memory books show Matilda's indulgence as a mother paired with her willingness to impose discipline, her imaginative experimentation, and her fierce commitment to keeping her children strong in body and spunky in spirit. Matilda's letters were typically signed, "Lovingly, Mamma," displaying the essence of her relationship with her children.

Fitting now to end by circling back to the woman from whom Matilda learned the art of good mothering. In Griffing's book, Matilda opened by describing her own mother, Mary Griffing, as "always remarkable for her equanimity, ability, and patient and unselfish thoughtfulness. If I can be so to my children and to my husband such a mother and wife as she has been to her family, my highest ambition will be gratified" (2). Matilda's children left remarkably little information about her, but her own stories show that she had learned her mother's lessons well.

CHAPTER NINE

Matilda as Teacher

Elementary education was free and compulsory by 1874 in California, but Matilda and H.H. rarely pursued formal schooling for their young children. Matilda never states why they preferred home-schooling. One reason may be that at the time, many schools were poorly organized and understaffed, especially in rural areas. The family's peregrinations also made regular school attendance difficult. In her children's journals, Matilda reported when they were sometimes sent to one school or another, but rarely gave names or noted whether the schools were private or public.

Apparently, H.H. preferred that his children be tutored at home until ready to attend a boarding school and college—the boys, that is, who ultimately went to the elite preparatory school Philips Exeter Academy in Massachusetts, and then Harvard, their father's college choice for them. Lucy seemingly attended neither high school nor college. However, she became a well-read woman, as later generations of her family claimed, continuing as an autodidact throughout her life, especially in the humanities.

The drive toward being well educated is clear in Matilda's copious descriptions of the children's lessons as part of "our plan of study at home." Also clear is that Matilda herself was the principal and head teacher in her very own home school—with excursions elsewhere. She sought to balance the children's academic and social development.

Of one of Philip's stints in a school around the fall of 1888 she wrote, "Everybody likes Philip, but he doesn't seem to make any special friendship; rather a consequence, perhaps, of our plan of study at home. It has its disadvantages, but seems the best in a general way for the children. To go to school occasionally will help them out" (196).

Matilda's Pedagogical Methods

Matilda kept meticulous notes on how her children were instructed, and recorded their progress in the subjects they studied. She applied some experimental methods for the time. Her children practiced the rote memorization and recitation conventional for the time, but they also learned in holistic ways. For instance, Matilda created a trial by jury for a lesson on ethics.

> We had one trial in which all participated. The children are allowed five cents for finding the other's things lying around and putting them in place. Griffing found Lucy's paint-brush on the ground and started to put it in its place for the usual reward; however, he lost it instead. Then Lucy said he must pay her for it; they agreed upon an exchange. Later Griffing said he had found Lucy's paintbrush and exacted the five cents; to this she demurred; there were certainly two sides to the question. As usual Philip stood up for Lucy. I proposed a court and trial by jury; Lucy employed Philip for her lawyer for ten cents; Griffing had Paul for his lawyer. The jury decided in Lucy's favor, or as Griffing expressed it, he "got licked." (Griffing, 382–83)

She encouraged active learning, "hands-on" methods that allowed children to engage physically with materials, such as by making a map of the United States in the sand. The children also helped teach each other—not a new method, but Matilda saw its value: "I exercised them with their multiplication tables, and papa sets Paul at teaching Grif immediately he has mastered a little that is new. It's quite amusing to watch them; Paul is impressing it upon his own mind at the same time he is teaching" (Griffing, 174–75). Sometimes, however, using one child to teach another backfired.

> Paul was teaching Philip to draw and having ten cents a
> lesson; Griffing had the same offer for teaching Lucy to read.
> The scholar and teacher were too much alike to harmonize
> well, and after the first lesson, Griffing said he should save
> all the money he earned for teaching Lucy to buy a cowhide
> with, for he couldn't do anything with her without one. (Lucy,
> 109)

Introducing play surely made lessons pleasant for Matilda as well. In
early 1885, she wrote:

> The past week the boys have been to me regularly for two
> hours each morning. They are intensely interested and excel-
> lent scholars; it's play rather than work, and not the least
> wearisome to me, as yet, on account of the interest they take.
> I have a box of letters with which they spell, and have ordered
> a blackboard; their multiplication table makes the learning of
> arithmetic lessons very easy and easily varied. (Griffing, 193)

She delights in learning, too. As many teachers know, in teaching,
we learn and grow.

> An intelligent family of children, the Cronyns, near neigh-
> bors, . . . first interested the children and myself in the devel-
> opment of tadpoles into frogs. It has resulted in my making a
> study of frogs and writing up their story in the language that
> children can understand; possibly, as I am now thinking of
> doing, I will write up all I can pertaining to animal life about
> us, and keep it in ms. [manuscript] for the children or make
> more public use of it. It would be a most profitable study for
> me and for them. (Griffing, 160)

As systematic as she was spontaneous, Matilda hired others for
specific studies. She reported that the children "have begun taking
lessons in elocution and in singing, alternate days, and in dancing and
writing twice a week" (Griffing, 299). Sometimes the homeschooling
was combined with two hours or more at a local school when possible.
Here Matilda refers to the children being "in the school" in fall 1889

in Walnut Creek. The first grammar school, Walnut Creek Central School, had opened in 1871, but with a town population of only 447 in 1890, surely the school pickings were slim.

> Every afternoon the little ones begin at half past two with English writing, while Griffing is taking a half hour lesson on the piano. They sing together half an hour with Fraulein, German songs; Philip has half an hour's practice and then together they read for half an hour. In the morning they are in the school from 8 till 10, the older boys remaining an hour longer. (Philip, 216–17)

A Panoply of Teachers

As "principal" of her school, Matilda was charged with finding and hiring an array of instructors who could fill in what she could not teach herself. Relatives, teachers, tutors, governesses, and schools all helped complete her children's education. "Their sister Kate ... is giving them German lessons" (Griffing, 165). Later, on a trip to Oregon in the summer of 1888, Matilda reported how she made geography lessons relevant while on the road and then roped in "Cousin Millie"—the daughter of H.H.'s sister Melissa Bancroft Trevett—in Portland, along with lessons from the governess, Fraulein Sigrist, who accompanied the family.

> I am trying to have Grif and Paul draw a map of Oregon, and am writing up a simple description of the state for them to study. I intend they shall learn all about the geographical points they visit as well as something of its history. I haven't half time for all I would like to do for the children. Fraulein continued their lessons more or less as it happened. They also took drawing lessons of Cousin Millie, drawing from casts. (Griffing, 321–22)

Hubert played a role, too, paying the children when they learned.[1] In 1890 Matilda wrote that "Papa started the boys learning Spanish, giving them five cents for every word; they got quite a fine start. Sometime we hope to go to Mexico and this will help them out" (Philip, 255). (They did go to Mexico a year later, in October 1891.) H.H.'s financial incentives also helped when Griffing, age six, and Paul, age seven, "attacked the multiplication tables, and have learned two and three—with hard plodding—though Grif easily keeps up with Paul in everything except writing. Papa promises them a valuable present to keep always when they have learned the whole table" (Griffing, 165).

With his great love of literature, H.H. encouraged his children to memorize passages from works of all kinds. "The boys have learned the 23rd Psalm quite easily and even Phil has picked up considerable of it. Papa wants them to learn passages from the Bible and from Shakespeare, and has marked several which I have promised to teach them" (Griffing, 154).

Qualifications for governesses and tutors often emphasized foreign languages. A governess was expected to know a foreign language as well as to have other talents.[2]

> On the 27th of March 1888, Fraulein Dartsch left us as she was to be to be married, and Clara Sigrist, from Biene, Switzerland has come to take her place. I advertised for a nursery governess competent to teach music, and had several applications. One young woman engaged with me, before I went to San Diego, but she became engaged to be married while I was away. Then I advertised again and was very much pleased with this Fraulein. She will instruct in French also. We now have a piano, and the children are taking lessons in instrumental and vocal music. (Griffing, 307–08)

Formal Education

One attempt of the Bancrofts to put their children in an actual school occurred in Walnut Creek and sheds light on the paucity of early schooling opportunities for country children. "The last day of the year, 1883, Monday, they began attending a little school here. The Perkins and Bancrofts made four of the five original scholars. The terms are $1.50 a week; they are to be kept in two or three hours with two or more recesses" (Griffing, 148). But this plan quickly went bust. "The school lasted but four weeks as Mr Bliss had a call to Oakland. Still they have made some little progress and I shall sometime or other continue their lessons" (Griffing, 151).

Getting to school sometimes required that the Bancroft scholars ride a horse, as noted in this passage from the fall of 1887. "The boys, as a regular thing, ride Chiquita bareback, carrying their books and lunch bucket to school. Paul is in the front. Griffing occasionally manages to drop his cover to his bucket & then they manage as best they can in mounting" (Griffing, 291). Children's safety on the way to school was rarely a problem. While in Denver for three months in 1884, they sent Paul (seven) and Griffing (five) to a school half a mile away and soon let them get there on their own.

> We enjoyed life here very much. The children went into a
> little kindergarten kept by Miss Stafford and Miss Chase; it
> was next to Brinker's Institute[3] nearly half a mile from the
> house, and not very direct, but they found their way alone
> quickly. . . . They made a little progress there; caught the idea
> of numeration and some new ideas of reading, writing and
> spelling. They are so interested in all these developments,
> that I know they would be good scholars if they but had the
> chance. (Griffing, 174)

A San Diego school the children attended in September 1886 had been founded by Emily Pierce, H.H.'s sister. "Aunt Emily has built, or is building, a fine school building called 'The Southwest Institute,' a name papa gave it as being in the most Southwestern part of the state" (Philip, 140). Their cousin Emma Derby was in charge. "Mrs. Cronyn for a time had charge of the Primary department. She is a very intelligent woman and an excellent teacher. Her husband is the Unitarian minister here, and they are near neighbors" (Griffing, 250).[4]

A new school might present challenges, as in this 1890 recounting from San Francisco.

> [Lucy] commenced at Miss West's new building on Van Ness
> near Jackson. She rode every day on her tricycle; but she was
> not at all happy and Paul was miserable at the Urban Acad-
> emy; both would come home every day with headache and
> complaints; they were not suitably graded to drop into place
> in a large school. Lucy always says of it "that she doesn't like

Miss West's school and never will go there again if she can help it." As soon as papa returned with the boys the arrangement ended and as usual they were placed under private tuition. (Lucy, 198–99)

Because of their idiosyncratic education, the children's skill levels compared to other pupils also made joining regular schools problematic. And perhaps the children preferred being home together "under private tuition" and with the undivided attention of handpicked teachers.

Matilda described an incident in which Griffing was severely disciplined for his misspellings. At the time Griffing was eight and Paul eleven. Hubert found that the punishment did not fit the crime.

Toward the last of July we moved over to the farm, and on the 1st of August (1887), the children began school. . . . Mrs Cox is an excellent teacher but rather too strict a disciplinarian. The boys ride their new pony, Chiquita, to school every day.
. . . One day when they both returned as usual on her back, Paul said: "We had a disaster today"; and I supposed it was some trouble with the pony. It seems, however, that Griffing had received a whipping with a ruler, for misspelling. It seems the omission of a dot over the i, the crossing of the t, or a period, or the rewriting or correcting of a word or letter, is included in the mistakes, and in that way Griffing's mistakes counted 20, and the punishment followed in consequence. We were very much excited over it, though the boys took it quietly enough. I doubt if Paul would have been willing ever to have gone back to school, he would have been so mortified, but Griffing seemed to look upon it as deserved. The method in spelling in the public schools is this—There are four or five grades writing words at once, and just as fast as the teacher can speak the words she gives them out, raising each finger successively as she calls out the words. Our boys were wholly unaccustomed to such attention & alacrity and it's not surprising they should make mistakes, particularly as they are still very deficient in spelling, on account of studying English so little. Papa told the boys he wished them to understand one thing: that they must look upon being struck or whipped by any one but their parents, as a disgrace, and that they must

always strike back, and if anybody undertook anything of that kind again to fight as well as they were able.

It made quite an excitement with the trustees and Mrs Cox at the time. She explained that she had been instructed not to show any partiality and probably she was more severe with our boys for that very reason. There are twenty-two children in the school. (Griffing, 280–82)

Matilda's reference to the teacher having been "instructed not to show any partiality" toward the Bancroft children indicates that someone—perhaps H.H. himself—may have had her not go easy on them just because they were the offspring of a wealthy man. What can we make of H.H.'s odd advice to his son to "strike back" at a teacher? In cultures that venerate elders, the idea would be outrageous.

Matilda swept through various pedagogical endeavors in early 1891 while in San Francisco.

I started the children at school under protest; their papa is always opposed to it. Paul [twelve] comes home every day with headache and so does Lucy [eight] from the excitement of being with other children and the competition, I suppose. So, after a heated discussion papa has engaged his old library assistant, Mr. Peafield to come three hours a day and have the children recite to him, preparing their lessons out of school. This worked pretty well for a month, when the old habit of drinking occasionally overcame him and he had to absent himself. Immediately, March 1, 1891, I went to the Educational Agency, and we engaged a Dr. Kelly, who is here from 8–11 and 1–3. This has proved a long engagement and the boys have become very fond of their tutor.

The first day Dr. Kelly was here the children all remarked with surprise that he said, "German grammar I think is a delightful study." They have learned German conversationally, without study really, and now it seems a good deal like work to have to delve and study into its construction. This is the only way they can do it in the future.

. . . Philip is taking up the violin with Mr. Austin as his teacher. He is very much interested in his work though he is nervous and Mr. Austin has to favor him a little as all his teachers do. He satisfied them that he does to the best of his ability and has no desire to shirk though his physical strength is not equal to his ambition.

Dr. Kelly is fond of music and helps the children with it. This will be of benefit to them in the country particularly.

Philip has enjoyed many good matinee performances. The Twelfth Night and Henry the VIII. Robin Hood he particularly enjoyed, an opera by the Bostonians, the story he is so familiar with. But the opera of Mignon failed to interest him and he said he wouldn't go to another opera unless he had to.[5] (Philip, 264–66)

Unsurprisingly, Lucy's memory book gives far less information about her education than do those of the boys. Like her brothers' books, it breaks off when Lucy turned ten, in 1892, still in grammar school. Matilda explained, "This journal is sadly neglected—I think I must be growing lazy as I'm growing older for I don't do as well by the two younger children as I did by the older ones in the matter of their record of their daily life" (100). She then excused herself with "I will skip over a year" (101).

Subjects of Study

LANGUAGES

The children's education covered a fair variety of subjects, but foremost in Matilda's reports were the foreign languages taught. German was a high priority, perhaps because H.H. himself drew from many German sources throughout his histories or on German literature for inspiration. The stories of the *Ankunft* (arrival) and *Abfahrt* (departure) of various German-speaking governesses weave their way into Matilda's tales. She expressed the joy of learning languages in natural ways.

Their first exercises were object teaching, and singing German songs. And four hours of a day, two in the morning and two in the afternoon, the two older boys were drilled. Then, too, they went to dancing school, Philip also, and made some progress, though it was pretty slow. . . . Grammar was too hard and so they were taught simple things in a

conversational way and to spell in German and to write. Their
first songs were: "Kam ein Voglein geflogen" [a little bird
flew] and "ich hat einen Kamieraden [I have a friend]." The
first verses were "Zwei Augen hab ish clar und hell," and the
first four verses of Schiller's "Taucher": "Wer wagt es Kitters-
man a der Knapp." It was easy progress after they had learned
the alphabet and could read and write; "to build words and
sentences," as Fraulein said, "was easy enough." It was a great
surprise to us to see how much they accomplished in the first
three months. . . . For four hours they would work over their
German and evenings we would bring out their magic lantern
and show pictures on the screen; Paul used his printing press
also. (Griffing, 233–35)

Two years later, the new Fraulein Sigrist applied the "immersion"
method.

In Fraulein Dartsch's place, we got an excellent Swiss, Clara
Sigrist, who was better educated and instructed them admi-
rably in German, French, and music. Throughout the time
we were here, some eight months, they never spoke a word of
English with her. I remember at the time we were going to
the vineyard gathering grapes, Lucy was telling the Fraulein
Sigrist the story of the three bears without the least hesitancy,
and every word was in German. (Lucy, 109–10)

A year later in 1889, Miss Sigrist left, and along came "Miss Schulz
of Heidelberg, who is the best teacher we have yet had. She is very
thorough; a little severe perhaps but the children will certainly make
good progress. She came about the 1st of June" (Griffing, 364). In Philip's book, Matilda embroidered on that comment.

Fraulein Shultz . . . is a German, born and educated at
Heidelberg, has taught two years in France, and several years
in Germany; and one year in New York. She teaches the
children German, English, and music; and Paul and Griffing French. As she is to be married in December, we feel as
though we must make the most of the opportunity. Lucy

and Philip sing together every afternoon for half an hour,
and Philip practices on the piano with his teacher, half an
hour. (215)

By December, Fraulein Schulz had departed.

Mrs Schulz' lessons are now over. She has been the most
thorough teacher they have ever had. She has made them
study very hard; commit a great deal to memory and has been
very exacting; a little too severe I know, but it has done them
no harm. They have made a thorough study of the French
verbs; her pronunciation was not good, but she had a thorough knowledge of French and taught the verbs and grammar
thoroughly. I will have them take it up later with a native.
(384–85)

As a result of this homeschooling, "Lucy chatters away in German
more easily than Philip; they lost considerable during the winter in
talking, tho' they seem to understand it just as well. I have got to keep
it up uninterruptedly for many years to have it of any benefit" (Philip,
216). Matilda put the burden on herself to maintain the children's fluency by having the children memorize and recite publicly. "Paul and
Griffing recited some German pieces at a German Church entertainment" (Griffing, 273).

The children also studied Spanish. Unfortunately, a trip to Mexico
planned for 1887 was foiled.

Papa is intending to go to Mexico again, and writes that he
will take us all along with him; but although I was delighted
with the proposition, I had no idea it could be carried out
because the whooping cough would probably interfere.
However as the boys could n't go to school, I got Martin, a
Spanish teacher from the school, to come in every morning
and teach them Spanish. It all ended by papa going without
us, and as soon as it was decided, the children stopped their
Spanish studies, which had continued perhaps a month.
(Griffing, 262–63)

With a trip to Mexico in the winter of 1891–92 planned, however, their Spanish studies recommenced. Matilda was envious of how quickly her children learned.

> Lucy and Philip spend considerable time with Isabel talking Spanish. She tells them stories and they talk with her. They acquire Spanish much more readily than I do. I don't like to admit it, but I know that I have very little aptitude for languages. I think my musical ear being deficient makes a difference in the observation in language, but I don't want any one else to say so. Foolish isn't it. (Lucy, 201)

HISTORY

In the home of a historian, the study of history was naturally a high priority. The children took well to this subject through Matilda's story-telling methods.

> Our reading evenings are about Egypt and the pyramids. It never seems to matter what is the subject, my audience is always sure to be interested; that is my children. I'm afraid I could n't say as much of others. On Sunday afternoons we have Sunday school, the children in the neighborhood often coming in. (Griffing, 244)

Matilda read aloud British history, and they sang to memorize some dates. H.H. had bigger plans.

> I am reading to the children Dickens' Child's History of England, a good book for a beginning.[6] Papa and I have been preparing dates for them to learn. I made a jingle on English dates, but his plan was much more comprehensive. It is to fix clearly in their minds some fifty dates of the most import-ant in the history of the world, and to have them learn them perfectly, so they cannot be confused; he thinks they can be so learned that they never will be forgotten, and that will link together events in history that will be of incalculable impor-tance to them throughout their lives. (Griffing, 379–80)

Another course in history was also suggested by H.H., which Matilda took up enthusiastically.

I have all along been reading aloud . . . to the children in a desultory sort of way, and now suggested to papa that I thought it would be well to take up United States history in a systematic way. Papa's ideas are so much broader than mine as this will show. "Why not begin at the beginning?" he says, "and reach that subject in order of time." Then he suggested the commencing with the geological history; to tell how the world was first all chaos; how it gradually, after many ages, because habitable; how savagism preceded civilization; what the distinction is; how animals at first were so immense and all vegetation so luxurious and gigantic; how gradually civilization grew enlightened; of the progress in explorations, early adventures by sea and land, the earliest history recorded of the Chaldeans and Phoenicians etc. of the Persians, Grecians and Romans and so on, calculating upon following up such a course of reading for many years.

Upon the first suggestion I remonstrated; they were too young, I was too ignorant; but these objections their papa quickly over-ruled. Then as he thought longer over it, the idea grew upon him; he said that I could not calculate the benefit such a course of reading would be to them; while they could not understand but little at first they would remember something, and it would lay the foundations of a taste for study and classical reading, that they would carry through life. To test the matter a little papa called the boys into his room and told them the story in an hours talk, of the creation of the world and in chronological order many of its great events. I was delighted with the interest he excited; they asked many questions which he told them we would answer later, and would read to them a little about every day if they would like to have us do so.

And so our course of reading began. It seemed to matter little to them what it was as long as I read to them; and I began by taking books on geology, studying them sometimes for two or three hours at a time and taking down notes and simplifying it for an hour's reading in the evening. From the

beginning they never wearied or seemed to find it dull. I have
noticed for some time that they much prefer I should take the
Bible stories directly from the Bible to any children's versions,
and Shakespeare to any tales simplified. They liked the text
with my explanations. It is certainly a good idea to always be
a little beyond your audience, to stimulate their understanding. (Griffing, 224–27)

WRITING, SPELLING, AND PUBLIC SPEAKING

Matilda and H.H. both admired the ability to speak with comfort and
even distinction, whether one was interviewing for a job or speaking
before the public. Their youngest son, Philip, would develop this skill to
the point of seeking public office. Beginning in 1888, the children were
instructed to use their writing—and refine their spelling—in conjunc-
tion with weekly recitations.

> While in San Francisco, Mrs. Dr. McKensie suggested to
> us an idea that they put in practice for their children, which
> we have carried out ever since. It is to give them confidence
> in speaking. Once a week each one makes a speech of a few
> minutes about some familiar object. One evening, after I had
> been in S.F. several days, Griffing said he had "some original
> poetry he had written himself," and he read off some exploits
> of the Argonauts in rhyme, and then made his speech. . . . We
> hope he will make a good speaker. He has the best command
> of language of them all. (Griffing, 312–13)

These exercises continued on various topics. "Sometimes it's about
mythology, natural history, or any subject in which they have taken an
interest" (Griffing, 338).

Writing exercises could take the form of letter-writing campaigns
when Mamma or Papa were traveling. In Walnut Creek in September
1877,

> Mamma had to go down again to San Diego for about three
> weeks. Aunt Mary went with her. While we were away, papa
> was most of the time at the farm, and the boys wrote me
> graphic accounts of their good times, hauling lumber from
> the old place and making themselves generally useful. The

windmill was put up while I was gone. The boys have a great
fancy for letter writing and for compositions—making stories
and reading them aloud. They are getting ready for examination at school. (Griffing, 288–89)

Writing lessons included keeping their own diaries—with Matilda's
strict attention to spelling.

The boys spelling is so bad that I am taking them in hand
now. I think I have lately hit on the best expedient of all; to
make them look in the dictionary for every doubtful word
when they are writing in their diaries, and I have promised
Griffing a present, when he writes for one week without a
misspelled word—he has tried it two weeks but has n't won
his prize yet. (Griffing, 316)

READING

The children's first formal reading instruction came via "readers," and of
course the Bancroft children were assigned *Bancroft's First Reader.*[7] Of
Philip in 1889 (age eight), Matilda wrote:

In June when he began his lessons with Miss Schulz, he
couldn't read or write in English; now in the middle of
December he is writing a Christmas letter to his Grandma,
he has just finished Bancroft's First Reader and has entered
the fascinating domain of story reading. He picked up a little
book of fairy tales that I had given my little brother Willie
twenty years ago, when he was seven years old and it came
to Philip as a revelation that he could read it for himself.
That finished we must find more for this greedy appetite.
Papa selected for him the Bible in words of one syllable and
Pilgrims Progress; the latter I had been reading aloud of late
to all the children. It was very interesting to the boys but
specially so to Philip. (Philip, 239–40)

Their reading regime included Shakespeare, but also popular
children's books of the time. "At Aunt Fannie's suggestion, I started
reading the Swiss Family Robinson to the boys. I was surprised to see

how intensely they were in it, for I thought it was too old for them"
(Griffing, 160).

> Philip enjoys my readings as much as ever; we have inter-
> rupted the ancient history and have read some Shakespeare,
> Hans Brinker or the Silver Skates[8] for its description of
> Holland; and just now I am reading a general history of the
> discoverers of the Americas; it is called "Children's Stories of
> American History" by Henrietta Christian Wright.[9] So many
> charming books are now written for children that one is del-
> uged by them, and I find it is impossible to confine myself to
> ancient history without neglecting much other useful reading.
> The main thing however is secured; it has given the children
> a healthy taste in reading, and books of information are as
> greedily read as the stories for children. (Philip, 217–18)

> I should mention one book I have read to the boys which
> they have enjoyed very much—Robin Hood, written and
> illustrated by Howard Pyle.[10] Papa wants me to read the clas-
> sics for children. . . . These I am reading, and hold their inter-
> est easily. In fact, they are delighted to have me read anything,
> and I enjoy their flattering appreciation. (Griffing, 298–99)

> At the beginning of the New Year 1887 Aunt Mary com-
> menced reading to the children Dana's "Two Years before the
> Mast".[11] She read to them, played games evenings and oth-
> erwise relieved me very much, for my time began to be very
> much occupied with building and business matters. (Griffing,
> 254)

THE ARTS

Music was supremely important in the Bancroft home, going back to
H.H.'s love of singing, the beautiful voice of his first wife Emily, and
his daughter Kate's singing accomplishments. Drawing lessons were
also arranged. Matilda reported on her offspring's developing talents—
or lack thereof.

> The boys have commenced taking singing lessons with Mrs
> Dr Derkey. Poor Griffing is lamentably deficient; it seems

almost impossible to make him distinguish the notes or strike one not right in the scale. But we are going to persevere. The boys are also taking writing lessons. (Griffing, 298)

The boys began drawing lessons with Mrs. Curtis. Paul has the most talent and perseverance, but Griffing does much better than I should have supposed possible. He is gaining a little, too, in music. Mrs Dr Derkey says that she has never but once met with a person who could not be taught distinctions of sound; with Griffing that it is impossible is the case, like color-blindness; by degrees however he is gaining a note or two in the scale. His papa is very fond of music, and has a sweet voice, but I have no voice and no ear, nor had my father, nor any of my family. (Griffing, 301)

While we were in the city we heard the Denman Thompson troupe in the Old Homestead sing "Rocka bye Baby," a very sweet arrangement of the cradle song.[12] Papa wanted the children to learn it and after many efforts they have succeeded pretty well. We struggle with them to give them some love for music and some idea of it, but it is under difficulties, as I can neither sing or play. Griffing is the most deficient in musical ear of them all, but we tug away at it all the same. (Griffing, 340–41)

Interestingly, in later years, Griffing became deaf, so perhaps these early reports of his inability to distinguish notes on the scale indicated a preliminary loss of hearing.

Considering that both Paul and Philip studied engineering in college, the early focus on drawing lessons at home surely helped. Paul at least had talent and application: "Mrs. Rice . . . gives the boys drawing lessons. She has the old fashioned cards for them to copy. It is quite surprising to see how well Paul succeeds, and even Griffing does much better than I supposed possible" (Griffing, 256).

PHYSICAL RECREATION
In letters later in life, H.H. forcefully promoted the health effects of regular exercise. Even some of Matilda's earlier reports on their days spent at writing noted afternoon breaks for walking or other recreation.

She too believed that physical exertion helps children develop mental acuity.

One source of exercise was gymnastics, through classes at the Olympic Club in San Francisco, "a practice their papa intends shall be kept up every season we are in town!" (Philip, 246).[13] They also paid for a few lessons at home on the farm in the spring of 1890.

> We have a gymnastic teacher, Prof. Smyth from the Olympic
> Club, and various apparatus arranged for exercise. Lucy is
> wild about it and wears a gymnasium suit of boys clothes and
> turns the bar as easily as any of them. In this suit she rides the
> velocipede in the yard, jumps the fences and plays "robber"
> with the boys, being the quickest to thieve and escape arrest.
> As yet they want no other playmates. (Lucy, 179–80)

MATH AND SCIENCE? ANYONE?

In the many pages Matilda devoted to various subjects, mathematics was remarked on very little, except for memorizing multiplication tables and the rare mention of arithmetic. She said of Philip, "He is a natural arithmetician and so has always been ahead of Lucy in that study" (Lucy, 187).

Science was discussed even less. No systematic discussion of science appears in her children's journals. Matilda reported attending two astronomy lectures. "Prof. James, from Oakland, the Englishman who visited us once before, spent several days here, and delivered two illustrated lectures on Astronomy, which I took the children to hear" (Griffing, 315).[14] Such neglect may speak to the parents' own orientation toward history and the humanities.

Learning through Play and Travel

Asking children in primary school to name their favorite subject, you may hear, "Recess!" Matilda herself appreciated the value of playtime and enjoyed her children's inventive play, even without fancy toys. "I asked papa to send them some boats. They soon preferred rafts of their own manufacture. Money doesn't give the pleasure to children that it does to older ones; that is they can invent greater pleasures from stones and sticks and paper than all the toy stores can give them" (Griffing, 114).

Matilda also recognized that the children's play made them more adaptable. Griffing invited another boy to come and play with him some afternoon:

> "We've got some string and a dog, and we'll have lots of fun."
> This is an excellent illustration of the adaptability of both
> Griffing and Paul; wherever we are in our travelling, they find
> something to amuse themselves with, without any care on
> any part. That is one of the many advantages of being one of
> several, and having to push for themselves a little. (Griffing,
> 176–77).

Nowadays we are relearning that "free play"—offering opportunities to be creative and interact socially—is a value worth returning to, after years of play becoming more individual and technology dependent.

Travel also provides learning opportunities. Matilda made up lessons on the go, as when the family was in Oregon and she taught them the geography of that region. On a trip East in May 1885 to visit her family, with Griffing in tow, Matilda had him studying maps.

> Griffing has traced the whole route on his maps and arranged
> his dissected map of the U.S. until he has grown very familiar
> with the location of all the states and principal rivers. It was
> a happy thought on my part and he has enjoyed it as well as
> been helped by it. (Griffing, 212)

The children received a grand educational journey to Mexico from November 1891 to February 1892, of which Matilda wrote extensively in another diary called *Our Winter in Mexico*.[15] Matilda detailed the many places and encounters her family experienced on their three-month excursion through parts of northern and eastern Mexico. Her often stunning descriptions and reflections are accompanied by dozens of photos taken by her oldest son, Paul, then fourteen years old, capturing everything from bedraggled street children to soaring cathedral pinnacles.

An appropriate concluding note on Matilda as teacher comes from Matilda herself. Ever observant of how her children fared in the world, she ultimately judged her pack of energetic kids in terms of how they were developing *with each other* in positive ways.

> It is really amusing to play with them, or to see them play together. They play better, more understandingly than many grown people. . . . People from the hotel sometimes had one or two of the children join in a game, as they called of an evening, and it interested and amused them very much to see how intelligently the children played. (Philip, 212–13)

Such would be every parent's wish: that their children should grow up to interact with others in understanding and intelligent ways.

CHAPTER TEN

A Craving to Take Dictations: Matilda as Oral Historian

In 1884, Matilda Bancroft spoke in her son Griffing's memory book of her work with his father in Utah and Colorado:

> I took several dictations from the Mormon women, and
> assisted papa in making extracts from the journals in the
> Historian's office; later while in Denver, I worked on all the
> material we together collected into chapters. . . . This is the
> most writing and re-writing I have ever done; papa afterward
> revised the whole, but left a good deal just as I had prepared
> it. I enjoyed the work immensely. (Griffing, 169)

In this depiction of her contributions to her husband's historical epic, Matilda reveals her pleasure in this intellectual work. H.H. likely did not introduce her as "my wife, a capable historian *herself*, for she collects important dictations wherever we go." Yet Matilda took more than twenty-five dictations for her husband's history of the Pacific West, some quite remarkable for their penetrating social reporting.

Gathering "Reminiscences"

H. H. Bancroft developed the art of interviewing for what today we call oral history, then called "taking dictations." He or his assistants would sit with a subject for hours, days, weeks, or months, to learn how that person experienced life in the early West. He aimed to acquire "reminiscences" from early inhabitants and pioneers, especially those who helped establish settlements, enterprises, government, and culture. In *Literary Industries*, Bancroft inserted an 1877 letter he would send to potential interviewees.

> California is still a new country; her annals date back but
> little more than a century; most of her sister states are still
> younger; therefore personal reminiscences of men and women
> yet living form an element by no means to be disregarded by
> the historian. . . . There are to be found—though year by year
> death is reducing their number—men of good intelligence
> and memory who have seen California pass from Spain to
> Mexico, and from Mexico to the United States. Many of this
> class will leave manuscript histories which will be found only
> in the Bancroft Library.

He included here recognition of the *Californios*, the early Spanish and Mexican colonizers of the late eighteenth and early nineteenth centuries. Although his first sentence mentioned both men and women, he then focuses on men only. Bancroft continued, referring to the stories of later pioneers.

> The personal memoirs of pioneers not native to the soil are
> not regarded as in any respect less desirable than those of
> *hijos del pais*, although their acts and the events of their time
> are much more fully recorded in print. Hundreds of pioneer
> sketches are to be found in book and pamphlet, and especially
> in the newspaper; yet great efforts are made to obtain original
> statements.[1]

Bancroft's memoir refers to the dictations taken on his honeymoon with his wife in 1876, when they spent ten days with General John Sutter, and Matilda sat patiently absorbed in Sutter's tales, asking questions from time to time.[2] This oral history *cum* storytelling session was Matilda's first. It sparked her enthusiasm, perhaps born of an atavistic experience of storytelling as the original form of entertainment known to humankind. Whether beside a fire or in a cave or hut, a master bard or griot could captivate attention and convey cultural mores, history, and traditions, using myth, poetry, song, and dance.

The questions interviewers asked are not known since they were generally not transcribed. In reading the dictations, however, one can deduce questions about specific topics when a transition in the narrative indicates a new topic. Some interviewees had little to say and needed prodding; others clearly delighted in talking and might "run at the mouth" on a topic for twenty pages.

Matilda's stories about her 1878 Northwest trip with H.H. (discussed in chapter 7) show the private side of how H.H. arranged these opportunities, from prior appointments to happenstance, such as meeting someone interesting on a ship. When taking a dictation was impossible, H.H. would exact a promise from the informant to send his written story later. H.H. took many dictations himself; others were written by assistants, such as Amos Bowman, who replaced Matilda for part of the 1878 Northwest trip. Ultimately, Matilda did take numerous dictations herself over time, including in San Francisco and during an 1884 trip to Utah and Colorado.

Matilda's work transcribing the stories of early settlers shows yet another fascinating side of her versatility and indicates all that she must have learned about early history of the West in this direct way. Here we focus on her more unusual work with the women of the Latter-day Saints.

In Pursuit of the Saints

Of the many changes in nineteenth-century US society, grievances against members of the Church of Jesus Christ of Latter-day Saints, then referred to as Mormons by outsiders and as Saints within the Church, led to tremendous conflicts.[3] Matilda's oral histories take us right to the core of problems that the LDS community faced in the world of "gentiles" (meaning people outside the Church).

The 1820s had been a time of religious revivals during the "Second Great Awakening" in upstate New York. Young Joseph Smith (1805–1844) claimed to have had several visits starting in 1820 from an angel, Moroni, who gave him the location of golden plates that revealed a history of and prophecy for a restored Christian church. By 1830, Smith had transcribed the plates and published the divinely inspired texts as the *Book of Mormon,* borrowing stories from the Old and New Testaments, along with stories based on Smith's visions and the tablets. The revealed stories claimed that ancient peoples of the Middle East traveled to the Americas and became the ancestors of contemporary Native Americans. Most important, Smith believed that *his* Church of Jesus Christ would restore Jesus's teachings to their original and true state, lost after the apostasy of subsequent Christian leaders.

The charismatic Smith quickly gained scores of followers, sending some out to spread the word. In 1831, land for their own community was found in Kirtland, Ohio, east of Cleveland. By 1838, Smith had renamed his religion the Church of Jesus Christ of Latter-day Saints, incorporating his prophesy that church members would enter into a millennial kingdom after an imminent apocalypse.

Some church leaders determined to follow only the law of God, not the law of the American government, a stance that conflicted with local communities. Provoking further disputes was Smith's later revelation that elders of the faith should take more than one wife—but only with the first wife's agreement. Smith based this notion in part on Old Testament culture when men had many wives, but he also claimed that this "celestial marriage" would both increase the seed of the Saints and provide for widows. Following his own first plural marriage in 1841, Smith quietly introduced the idea among his closest apostles.

Conflicts with non-Mormons occurred in New York, Ohio, Missouri, and Illinois, often leading to death and destruction. The persecuted Mormons repeatedly migrated in search of a safe place to practice their religion. Smith himself was taken from jail and killed by a mob in Nauvoo, Illinois, in 1844. Brigham Young then succeeded Smith in leading the church. In 1846, Young guided a trek to the Utah territory, which still belonged to Mexico and was thus beyond the control of the US government.

In the 808 pages of his 1889 *History of Utah,* H. H. Bancroft intended to tell the complex story of the Mormons from their own perspective as much as possible and to counter what he saw as unmerited "calumny" against them.[4] Bancroft claimed, "Those who wax the hottest against the latter-day saints and their polygamous practices are not as a rule among the purest of our people" (361). Bancroft devoted a chapter of sixty-four pages, with seventy-one source-packed footnotes, to a recounting of the history of polygamy in the LDS community, hoping to provide an objective context for its practice.

However, Bancroft walked a fine line between supporting the indus-triousness and courage of LDS believers on the one hand and echoing criticism of their embrace of polygamy on the other. He noted the hypocrisy of those gentile men who took mistresses or practiced big-amy, whereas Mormons sought to justify the practice of plural marriage through sacred religious ceremony and in community-sanctioned, legal terms. "Christian sects hold up the patriarchs as examples in their sacred instruction, and yet condemn in these personages a practice which Christ nowhere condemns" (370). At the same time, Bancroft himself found monogamy to be more ethical and a better social system for women, for families, and for society. He doubted that one man could adequately care for many families and serve many women. He also questioned a community in which a few older men could monopolize several women and wondered how that affected the marriage prospects of younger men.

Nevertheless, Bancroft's effort to let the LDS faithful speak for themselves is extraordinary, and many Mormons supported Bancroft's attempt to collect their history. Church members also kept their own personal, family, and historical records. To this day, writing one's own diary and researching and preserving family history are central to the Church's services and practices.[5]

The Saints were buoyed by the endorsements of women who sup-ported plural marriage, such as those recorded by Matilda Bancroft. These oral histories reveal the intricacies of arguments about the treat-ment of women within the religion. Matilda's interviewees defended polygamy even while acknowledging its difficulties. Whatever ques-tions Matilda asked, the answers help flesh out the reality of what it meant for women to accept their husbands' other wives.

A GENTILE WOMAN'S PERSPECTIVE

We gain context for the Mormon women's stories from a dictation taken in 1878, "A Young Woman's Sights on the Emigrant Trail," in which Matilda had participated.[6] A non-Mormon, Harriet Clarke spoke of the struggles among Mormon women she encountered. (The original spelling has been retained.)

On her 1851 journey from Ohio to Oregon, Clarke reported having had an uneventful journey in a relatively small group of emigrants. "The trip accross the plains for me was a pleasure trip and a perfect delight the whole way. There was so many wonderful things to be seen. There was a good waggon road all the way. And there was no discomforts on the trip" (3).

However, she came upon others for whom the journey had been excruciating. Some of the most disgruntled emigrants whom Clarke met in Salt Lake City were Mormon women, who had begun their own migration five years before, in the late 1840s. Clarke reported sadder tales of plural marriage than those recounted later to Matilda in 1884 by LDS women who affirmed strong belief in the faith. Clarke said, "At Salt Lake we found the women feeling very much disatisfied with that sort of life as far as they dare tell it." Clarke described a conversation with an LDS woman from England.

> She said if I had known of this two wife business I would never have come here. She said if her husband got a second wife that she would go home. But when a woman once got there it was impossible for her to get away. An old woman told me they would drown her in the lake if she knew she talked against them. . . .
>
> An old Mormon woman came to our tent to sell potatoes and peas. She said she had left her children in Illinois and followed her old man; they were married and she did not want to leave the old man; she wanted to die with him.
>
> We had a rocking chair; she sat in it and rocked herself and cried. She said her husband had gone that morning to be sealed to a girl 16 years old. She said they lived in a adobe house with a mud floor and that young girl was to go in and take her place and her heart was nearly broken. She wanted us to take her away with us but Mr Smith [Harriet's uncle] did not dare to take her.
>
> We had many other applications from women that wanted to get away. We did not dare take them. The Mormons would have followed us and scattered our cattle. We found places where whole trains had been destroyed, nothing but waggon ties left. We supposed they were murdered on account of interfering with the Mormons.
>
> I did not see a single Mormon woman that was satisfied with her lot. The women would be very free to unburden themselves if we would promise not to tell. I used to go around visiting to the houses. (7–10)

One can ruminate on why the LDS women whom Clarke met were so negative—most obviously because they were the ones who *wanted* to leave, and thus sought pity and support from outsiders. And like many gentiles, Clarke may have borne a prejudice that led her to exaggerate these stories. Or memory may have rested heavily on the negative impacts of Mormon life for the women she encountered. We can't know for sure, but those stories contrast sharply with oral histories from faith-driven LDS women whom Matilda heard and recorded years later in San Francisco and Salt Lake City.

STORIES FROM LDS WOMEN

We can only imagine why H.H. chose Matilda as an interviewer of LDS women, perhaps because a woman interviewer stood a better chance of getting these oral histories than a gentile man, especially in relation to very personal aspects of the LDS women's experiences with plural marriage—asking questions that only a woman could pose.[7]

Matilda took two LDS dictations with Jane Richards, the wife of church elder F. D. Richards, in San Francisco in 1880. In 1842 in Nauvoo, Illinois, Jane Snyder Richards (1823–1912) became the first wife of Franklin D. Richards (1821–1899), one of the church's senior leaders as the fourth member of the Quorum of the Twelve Apostles. When Matilda interviewed her, she produced one manuscript called *Reminiscences*.[8] Also in 1880, Matilda collaborated with Jane on an essay called "The Inner Facts of Social Life in Utah."[9] In this latter document, Matilda speaks of Jane Richards in the third person, though the stories are directly from Jane herself.

A few years later in the summer of 1884, Matilda took down the stories of three Mormon women in Salt Lake City: Sarah Cooke, Clara Young, and Mary Isabella Horne. She also received a lengthy letter from Mary J. Tanner, while another from Martha Brown went to H.H. All of these women described the trajectories of their lives in the Church and specifically discussed their experiences with plural marriage, which they supported, despite the difficulty of sharing their husbands with other wives.

One focus here is to understand Matilda's experience as a scribe in taking these dictations. Listening with her to these women's voices, we can develop insight into their spiritual experience of Church doctrine and practice, in particular how their faith shaped their commitment to polygamy. We also see the strength of these women in their pioneer experiences as they underwent persecution and travails on their way west.

WHY PLURAL MARRIAGE?

These LDS women seemingly wanted Matilda and the larger world to understand plural marriage, which for those outside the Church was a confounding practice. They speak of their faith and the circumstances that made plural marriage a sensible choice, regardless of its hardships. Jane Richards defended polygamy as a religious duty for men but a duty that women actively chose as well. She emphasized the positive nature of legally arranged and divinely inspired plural marriage among Mormons, in contrast to how gentile men indiscriminately took women outside marriage.

> Now what sin is there against the government in this prac-
> tice? It is simply a religious persecution. The difference
> between right and wrong in the matter of a man's having two
> wives is this: In bigamy, a man sets aside his lawful wife and
> unbeknown to her marries another woman; and it is all done
> wickedly and from the basest motives. In polygamy, a man
> marries again from a sense of religious duty; he consults with
> his wife and with her consent and perhaps recommendation,
> takes to himself another wife. His religion demands it, and
> all three enter polygamy with earnest convictions of it being
> done in the sight of God at his command; . . . at least the
> relation is openly acknowledged, and before God and man it
> is lawful and holy. At the time Polygamy was revealed to us as
> a sacred duty. (*Reminiscences*, 56)

Richards deftly turned the "sin" back on the US government, which sought to outlaw the practice: "What a sin it would be not only to deprive wives of what they consider their lawful husbands, but to brand their children as illegitimate. . . . The Government has no right to deprive our women and children of their husbands and fathers" (*Reminiscences*, 57).

One of the stated purposes of plural marriage at the time was to provide a husband to women who had been widowed or were otherwise seen as vulnerable and lacking support. Jane Richards, in fact, "gave" her sister to her husband as a wife after her brother-in-law's death. "So I gave her to my husband as a wife . . . now we were able to do much more for her comfort" (*Reminiscences*, 38).

Jane's husband, Franklin Richards, reinforced her justification of selfless service. In the early 1840s when Joseph Smith revealed the necessity of taking plural wives, many men in the church initially did not wish to do so, but came to believe Smith's revelation, that plural marriage was necessary for the salvation of all. Eventually they saw themselves as serving a higher purpose. Matilda reported part of her conversation with Mr. Richards in that light: "Mr Richards said to me that as Elders in the church they did not dwell much upon their personal difficulties, that their mission was to give consolation and comfort to their poor brethren and afflicted sisters when they came to them in trouble" ("Inner Facts," 12).

This declaration of noble purpose fits with modern stories of the LDS community still dedicated to social service, such as feeding the hungry or providing for the homeless. They continue to abide by Joseph Smith's 1842 Mormon Article of Faith: "We believe in being honest, true, chaste, benevolent, virtuous, and in doing good to all men."

SPIRITUAL CALLINGS

Jane Richards's stories of spiritual motivation to accept plural marriage were echoed by other Mormon women whom Matilda recorded. Sarah Cooke (1808–1885) was an Englishwoman who had immigrated to the United States with her husband.[10] Eventually they continued westward, stopping over in Salt Lake City in July 1852. While her husband continued on to California for business, Cooke stayed behind and was converted. When her husband returned, she convinced him to join the LDS Church, too.

Cooke's dictation reiterates how faith guided these women, led by the divinely inspired and absolute authority of church leaders. Cooke explained how she had gone for advice to a leading Mormon woman, Mrs. Cobb, who cited the words of Orson Hyde (1805–1878), one of the church leaders:

> "You must accept everything from the Priesthood; it is given of God; don't oppose it, if it perplexes you, lay it away; sometime it will be made plain to you, then you will understand

and receive it; but don't resist." This was probably referring to the revelation of polygamy. (4–5)

Cooke described to Matilda the "martyr's" role for women in undertaking plural marriage, a role that other leading church women, Eliza Snow and Mrs. Heber Kimball, reinforced.

> One of the women who came to Eliza Snow told her that she suffered so from the distress polygamy brought upon her, she thought she should die. Eliza Snow replied "What if you should? What if it kills the body, then yours is the martyr's crown; . . . it is a martyrdom that has its reward in heaven."
>
> Mrs Heber C. Kimball was a noble woman and was pointed out as an example to other wives to follow. One woman asked Mrs Kimball after her first year of polygamy when she had striven in vain to yield herself to the situation that it might be for her husband's exaltation, what should she do? She had been married many years and had encouraged him to take an other wife thinking she could stand the test; she said many a time she would go into the cellar and pray in agony asking if it was really God's will that polygamy exist.
>
> Mrs Kimball told her that she, too, had suffered as she did until she had learned, as this woman must learn, that her comfort must be wholly in her children; that she must lay aside wholly all interest or thought in what her husband was doing when he way [*sic*] away from her; she said she was pleased to see him when he came in as she was pleased to see any friend, "and thus she counselled me," says she to Mrs Cooke, "to simply be indifferent to my husband if I would be happy." Mrs Kimball interested herself very much in the welfare of other's [*sic*] wives and their children to see that there was plenty of homespun clothing etc for all; and set a noble example to others situated as she was. (5–6)

Another reason, then, for women to accept polygamy was to be *seen* as virtuous. They deeply valued virtue in others, as their religion dictated. In sharing her husband with three other wives, including her own sister, Jane Richards said that her situation was ameliorated by knowing the other wives' virtues: "They were all good women who entered into marriage with good intent and tried to live just and honest lives in the sight of God" (*Reminiscences*, 39).

This aspiration for a righteous life motivated women living in polygamy, which, ironically, the outside world condemned as sinful. In an 1880 letter to Matilda, Mary Jane Mount Tanner (1837–1890) shared her "testimony," reinforcing this point.[11]

> I have been personally acquainted with Brigham Young, Heber C. Kimball, Geo. H Smith, Jedediah M. Grant and more or less with Pres. Taylor and all the leading men and their families. Also with Eliza R. Snow, Zina D. Young, Emeline B. Wells, Rasheba Smith, M.T. Smoot, Jane S. Richards and many others, and I can testify that they are women of intelligence, holding pure and upright principles and worthy of the highest respect from any community. I also know that the lives of many of those who have left the Church are not free from reproach. Many of those who are most bitter in the denunciations, and loudest in their accusations against the people were never pure and upright in their own principles. (7–8)

In exploring the doctrine of plural marriage with her interlocutors, Matilda learned that, contrary to public opinion of these women as captives, they defended the practice as completely voluntary and felt unharmed by it. "As Mrs Richards said, she felt she must renounce her earthly covenant or her religion, [but] she had faith enough left to accept these conditions, that she should leave her husband or the church when she felt she had a reason, [yet] she never had had a reason yet" ("Inner Facts," 8).

The duty to follow their wifely obligation was divinely ordained. In her 1880 letter to Matilda, Martha Brown expands on the theme (with her original spelling and punctuation transcribed here):

> Being born in the Church I naturally believed the Gospel and after arriving to the years of accountability and complying with its ordinances I have received a knowledge of its truths for myself and I have a living testimony that it is from Heaven and of God there has been no compulsion or coertion on the part of any one (As those who do not believe

as we do think or try to persuade them selves to believe) to
compel me to comply with any of its ordinancies but I have
willingly yielded obedience to its doctrines through an honest
conviction of its truths No secret underhanded course was
taken by my Husband to obtain my hand and heart neither
was the fact kept from his wife for our courtship was all in
the presence of his wife and with her full consent and approbation We have lived together in the same house and we have
lived in seperate houses and never have had a quarrell or any
difficulty from the time I united with the family up to the
present time I am the Mother of eight children six of which
are living and we are comfortable and happy and I would not
exchange my situation with the Queens of the earth I did not
take up with Poligamy because I could not obtain a young
man for a companion for I refused many offers but I adopted
it because I was convinced and satisfied that it was a divine
institution and eminated from God and I know it will prove
the exaltation of everyone who receives it with a pure and
honest heart.[12] (5–6)

For those skeptical of the power of religious fervor, stories of the
faithful giving themselves over to a higher authority may seem strange,
even implausible. But Joseph Smith's Church of Jesus Christ arose
during a time of general religious revivalism; many aspects of their
practices were redolent of such fervor.

In her dictation with Matilda, Mary Isabella Horne (1818–1905)
spoke of the ceremony of healing by laying on of hands: "Bro. [Par-
ley] Pratt [1807–1857] stepped forward and laying his hand upon her
commanded the evil spirit to come out of her. She was healed instantly
and never was troubled in that way again" (3).[13] Horne also witnessed
parishioners speaking in tongues.

At a weekly meeting at her home soon after her conversion,
one of the church elders, Brother John Taylor [1808–1887],
looking intently upon her, said "Sister Horne you have the
spirit of tongues; speak." She immediately arose and spoke
by the gift and power of God; at the same time the gift of
interpretation was given to a young Scotchman McKensie,
who rose and [said] "I have the gift of interpretation." The

very things then prophesied have been and are being realized in these valleys of Utah. (3)

Baptism itself was seen as having magical force. Jane Richards reported that her brother, Elder Robert Snyder, was consumptive and on the verge of death, yet after being baptized by Elder John Page (1799–1867), he lived five more years and baptized many hundreds more. Jane, too, had had a transformative baptismal experience. While on her way to Missouri with other Mormons, she fell gravely ill and was paralyzed, ready to die. However, her brother prayed with her and asked to lay oil on her. In her delirium, she said she saw the need of baptism. This very realization turned the tide, and her recovery began. "At that moment all pain left me, the paralysis was gone; I was only weak" (*Reminiscences*, 7).

Begging for baptism, she convinced her family to take her to the lake, where they broke ice one to two feet thick and immersed her. Richards said that her brother might have been arrested for threatening her life, given her grave condition. "But she was well after that" (*Reminiscences*, 7). Such miracle healings reinforced the power of faith.

FACING HARDSHIPS WITHIN PLURAL MARRIAGE

Of course, the assertions that plural marriage was righteous did not mean it was easy. Mary J. Tanner told Matilda how she coped with adversity within her own plural marriage, just as single wives had to learn to cope with marriage troubles.

Our religion is founded on the Bible and on Revelation; and holds in itself nothing that is corrupt or offensive. Poligamy [*sic*] I know to be a sacred principle. Like all sacred principles it is capable of being abused as marriage itself frequently is: but every safeguard is thrown around it that can be brought to bear as on any religious service, lest any should enter it unworthily. There is no accounting for or directing the dispositions of men and women, and many live unhappily together where there is but one wife. I believe it is given for the regeneration of mankind. There are no healthier or better developed children than those born in polygamy. I cannot recall a single instance, as far as my observation extends of idiocy, malformation, or deformity among those born in pologamic [*sic*] relations. . . . It is thought to promote jealousy, but I believe it allays it; for our ladies certainly have unbounded faith in their husbands, which I am told by those having opportunities for observation, the Gentile ladies who visit among us have not. (5–6)

Some women also revealed to Matilda how repugnant the concept was to them initially:

Mrs Richards in private conversation with me related the following in regard to her personal experience. A few months previous to her marriage the idea of more than one wife was generally spoken of, tho' the practice of polygamy was of later growth. It was repugnant to her ideas of virtue and it was not until she saw Joseph Smith in a vision, who told her in time all would be explained, that she was satisfied to abide by Mormon teachings whatever they were. About eight months after her marriage, Elder Richards told her he felt he should like to have another wife. It was crushing at first, but she said that as he was an elder and if it was necessary to her salvation that she should let another share her pleasures, she would do so. . . . He wanted to know . . . if she thought she could not be happy in such a relation, he would not enter into it. She said if she found they could not live without quarrelling she should leave him. At last two or three years later he told her that in three or four days he should bring such a one home as his wife. It was a surprise to her that he should select as he did; she knew the young woman very well; she was amiable and all lived happily together. ("Inner Facts," 1–2)

A specific issue was how polygamy would affect Jane as a mother or affect the children. She was very honest about her scruples.

When the subject of polygamy was first talked of between Mr Richards and herself, she used to say that she could yield herself to everything but the children; but that she should feel like wringing the neck of any other child than hers that should call him papa. That they were poor and could not see their way clear to provide for their own easily; what could they do with more. Before his marriage her mind was satisfied on every other point. She saw clearly that it was in accordance with Mormon teachings, and it was not such a trial as she had feared, when she was tested. ("Inner Facts," 2–3)

Jane was to be sorely tested in relation to sharing children as well as her husband:

When the first child was born in polygamy [to the second wife], she thinks it was fortunate perhaps that her husband was in England. She had lost a daughter, Wealthy, and her heart yearned for another little girl. When she found this child was a girl, her heart failed her. But she said she soon recovered herself and dressed the baby and took care of it a great deal—she kept a nurse for the mother for two or three weeks. For these children she has always felt an interest, though it is not at all the same feeling she has for her own flesh and blood. If his child and hers were drowning and but one could be saved, she should save her own. In reply to the question, she thought her husband would be in a dilemma, and would have to take the first that came along. ("Inner Facts," 3)

Mary Isabella Horne also conveyed "the trial of feelings" she underwent, but explained a liberating experience she had within polygamy. Note the initial sentence; whether it is Matilda's value judgment or Mrs. Horne's is not clear.

Plural marriage destroys the oneness of course. Mrs Horne had lived for 28 years with her husband, before he entered into polygamy; she said and re-iterated "no one can ever feel the full weight of the curse till she enters into polygamy; it is a great trial of feelings, but not of faith." It is a great trial, no one would deny that; but she was willing because it was a duty her religion demanded. For years she says, she was so bound and so united to her husband that she could do nothing without him; "and that unitedness I should enjoy to this day", she added, "if God had willed it so". But since his plural marriage she could see some advantages, now she feels better;

she is freer and can do herself individually things she never
could have attempted before; and work out her individual
character as separate from her husband. (34–35)

This last sentence provides an important revelation about female
independence. Did Horne's understanding of her independence affect
Matilda's thoughts about her relationship with her own husband? We
cannot know, except to see hints of her own freedom and individuality,
perhaps inspired by these women who had to learn to take care of their
own families while their husbands were gone, sometimes for years on
faraway missions, or for nights with other wives.

Jane Richards herself offered an example of amazing fortitude.
Matilda wrote, "She said that in a woman's accepting the position of
a plural wife, she knew she must submit to some such privations and
if she felt inclined to complain she would remember she entered that
state voluntarily and that would act as a sort of curb" ("Inner Facts," 17).
No self-pity there!

HOW THEY MADE PLURAL MARRIAGE WORK
Matilda delved into how plural wives lived with each other in an
extended family unit. Jane Richards explained an agreement with her
husband regarding the need to maintain privacy with each wife.

Previous to Mr Richards taking a plural wife, she had made
him promise that any matter that concerned any one of them
individually should be always talked over with him in private,
and that had been lived up to. He told her that he would not
marry if he did not think she would love his wives as much
as he himself, which she says to me, shows his love was not
lustful; that he married simply because his religion demanded
it. ("Inner Facts," 7)

Jane also spoke of the dangers of gossip:

As far as the Mormon people are concerned they are an
industrious, peaceable and conscientious people. They do not
run around for society—they have their own families about
them and have no time to waste in running around as their
Gentile neighbors do. It is making confidants of other women

in their domestic disturbances that has brought about most of
the trouble in Polygamy, and the less people gossip the better
off they are. (*Reminiscences*, 45)

Ultimately, Jane bonded with the second wife, Elizabeth, who
became very devoted to her.

Elizabeth came into their family while Mrs Richards was very
miserable from a miscarriage and obliged to have a hired girl.
... Elizabeth at once undertook the work of the house and
said we didn't need a hired girl, and Mrs Richards directed
as before; she was but seventeen and very pretty. She had the
upper story and Mrs Richards the lower. If she was washing
Mrs Richards would do the cooking and so they got on nicely
together. ("Inner Facts," 8)

In fact, as Jane noted, sister wives offered essential support during
illness and hardship. "I was in delicate health and from the time she
first entered my house, three or four days after her marriage, she seemed
only concerned to relieve me of trouble and labor" (*Reminiscences*, 19).
Eventually, "We lived happily together and indulged no evil or jealous
feelings toward each other" (20).

Jane repaid Elizabeth for that care in 1846 when they immigrated
to Winter Quarters, Nebraska, near Omaha, on the way to Utah.
Many took ill, and one hundred died. Mr. Richards was not with them.
Elizabeth was very sick, and in her delirium screamed for Jane. Also
debilitated by illness, Jane had to be carried in to visit her. They both
recovered, but Elizabeth sickened again, and it was now Jane's turn to
take care of her. "When she talked to me of dying, I felt I could not
have it so; then I should be entirely alone; perhaps my husband would
feel that I had not done everything that I could for her" (*Reminiscences*, 26).[14] Such an interesting compression of feelings in that sentence alone. Unfortunately, Elizabeth did die. Jane's husband, Franklin,
would take ten more wives.

Even in the more open society of the twenty-first century, it can be
difficult to imagine how these women could overcome jealousy and the
desire to have the exclusive love and attention of one's partner, to be
entirely and solely "united," as Mary Isabella Horne expressed it. How
large these women's hearts and spirits must have grown, not only to

let their husbands love another—much less many others—but also to love those other wives genuinely themselves. For some, this surrender could be liberating. These families' complexity had to be fascinating to Matilda as she sought to understand the implications of polygamy.

One last story from Jane allows a glimpse of an awkward husband-sharing scene. Richards's account reveals her psychological prowess in the face of her own jealousy and that of her sister wives.

> One little incident of home life illustrates considerable.
> Mr Richards had returned to his wives after a mission in
> England, bringing with him shawls and other presents. These
> he displayed to his family asking them to take their choice.
> Of course Mrs. Richards should have her first choice as a
> right; but she was always accustomed to yielding that priv-
> ilege and as in this case she said "No, girls, you care more
> about these things than I do; take your choice and I will be
> satisfied with what is left". Although she saw at once which
> she would have selected. Something in the intimation, uncon-
> sciously given that she yielded to their selfishness aroused
> their anger and all refused the selection. She went to her
> room and cried. Her husband came in and with his man-
> nature was dull enough not to perceive the true cause and
> told her she never cared for any presents he brought her. Then
> she begged he never again would bring them all presents
> alike, but get a variety and himself make the selection and
> give it to each what was his own choice; then each would be
> satisfied. Afterwards they all met together in the room and
> she said, "Now girls, I have suggested this, which I am sure
> you will approve, and now he will distribute these according
> to his own discretion" ("Inner Facts," 6).

Between Jane's reporting and Matilda's writing, this tale presents important nuances of interpersonal dynamics, Jane's supposed self-lessness, and the other wives' selfishness. Matilda's interpretation of Franklin's "dull man-nature," such that he had no idea what a fuss he had created, is amusing. We see that Jane, as the senior wife, presented Franklin with a plan that would better resolve all the women's needs: by choosing distinct presents *himself*, Franklin could show his under-standing of each wife as an individual and thus communicate his love for her. If "God is in the details," men in plural marriage had abundant details to which they had to pay attention.

These women might have been chosen by their church to present their stories in order to display positive aspects of plural marriage. On their own, they might have written down many of these same thoughts about plural marriage. However, in Matilda they had a sympathetic and intelligent interviewer who could ask "naïve" questions from an outsider's perspective, undoubtedly helpful in prompting some of their disclosures.

LDS WOMEN AND THEIR PIONEER STORIES

These LDS women were resilient pioneers, like other women who trekked west, with families or alone, to create new lives for themselves and even new communities. Harriet Clarke enjoyed her wagon journey, but her story is unusual, given the physical hardship and privations faced by so many emigrants.

Such was the tale of Mary Isabella Horne, whose parents sold their farm in Canada and started for the Mormon community of Far West in Caldwell County, Missouri, in March 1838.

> They, with a small company of saints, took several teams—
> they also helped pay the expenses of others to emigrate. Mrs
> Horne herself drove a team hundreds of miles. She had a
> little baby girl in very delicate health and was herself far from
> strong, a boy being added to their family in July. She says she
> would many times be so exhausted at night that it seemed as
> though nature would yield; but there was no alternative—the
> men walked hundreds of miles. The roads were very bad as
> the frost was coming out of the ground. (4–5)

Even today, pregnancy and birth in a hospital can be challenging enough. But here was Horne, five months pregnant, driving a team of horses with a small child, then giving birth en route in July. Yet she considered herself lucky not to be walking with the men.

Starvation also accompanied many of the Saints, often the result of anti-Mormon bands destroying their crops and stores of food before they could escape. Jane Richards saw her mother begging for potatoes along their long walk. "A rough woman heard her story impatiently through, and putting her arms on her shoulders marched her out of the house, saying 'I won't give or sell a thing to one of you damned Mormons'" (*Reminiscences*, 24). H. H. Bancroft included this poignant story from his wife's work in his *History of Utah*.[15]

Surviving such cruelties may have contributed to the women's strength. Stories of their tribulations became part of their cultural lore. Clara Decker Young (later one of Brigham Young's fifty-five wives) told Matilda that gentile enmity forced her family to leave their farm as it burned behind them.[16]

While they were living in Davis Co, they were warned that they must leave the place immediately. Two of the children were ill from some protracted illness, but they had to be moved notwithstanding. One team was got ready, a bed placed on the bottom of the wagon and the children laid on it; as much else was piled in as could be carried and the rest of the family provided for as best they were able; there were six children.

Few of the household goods were taken, as they expected to return soon. Mr Decker returned to the house to load up another team or to look after his grain, when he was warned that he would be scourged, or his place burned if he remained. At four in the afternoon he started to overtake his family, and at 8 o'clock he saw in the distance his buildings and hay stacks in flames. The children became so ill that night, that Mrs Decker stopped the teamster two or three times, thinking one or the other was dying; they eventually recovered however.

As crowded as Far West was, every house was obliged to receive these fugitives. They were thus received themselves. While Mr Decker was gone for a load of wood he was arrested and taken a prisoner to the camp. It was a week before his family knew anything about him. He was not badly treated; with his jolly, good natured temperament he made friends everywhere. He was released and remained with his family through the winter. They had of course lost everything and had to gain their support as best they were able. Their meal, for one item of food, was of the coarsest; it had to be ground in a coffee mill much of the time, as they could get none outside the place. (1–3)

Mary Isabella Horne reported her family's confrontations with mob violence in Far West in 1838.

> The ravages and persecutions of the mob were so great that they did not [know] at any moment when it might break into their house and destroy everything. Often at night the people assembled at the beat of the drum on the square, prepared to resist invaders. The Mormons were driven into Far West and all these already overcrowded houses were made to shelter more. When the mob entered Far West they entered houses, taking what they pleased, jeering and intimidating the women. There were some 800 men, hideously painted and disguised. Some of them stopped Mrs Horne's niece on the street and asked her where were the ditches that the Mormons had dug as traps for them. They had heard and believed that the Mormons had made such ditches and had lightly covered them with earth. They would encamp by a stack of hay, use what they please and trample down more. They wantonly destroyed a great deal; they would come out at night drunk, insult the people, brandishing their knives and pistols. They would shoot down sheep, cattle and chickens for the mere pleasure of destroying them.
>
> Mrs Horne was but 20 years of age at this time, and though father, husband and brothers were in danger she said she would not humble herself to let them see she was afraid. She says she never shall forget the night when their prophet [Joseph Smith] and brethren were taken to the enemy's camp. The mob clamored with fiendish exultation over their victims through the whole night. The next day as Mrs Horne stood in the doorway several of them rode up and said: "Bid your prophet good-bye, for you will not see him again till you see him in hell." (6–8)

Horne's family, along with others, continued to make journeys further west to escape persecution. Arriving in Nauvoo, Illinois, their temporary home was a shanty overrun with rats. "The rats were so numerous in this place that they frequently carried off clothes and bit the children in bed" (13). The Hornes "had to live on boiled wheat and corn; very coarse" (15).

At last, in February 1846, the family headed for the Great Salt Lake, camping in the snow along the way. Said Mary Isabella to Matilda, "Think of the situation of women and children driven from their homes in the middle of a severe winter for no other reason than they believe in the revelations of God and in being guided by inspired men" (16).

The price paid for this persecution included the loss of family members. Martha Brown wrote,

> I feel a great delicacy in complying with your request of me to give my views and experience on Mormon life and history on account of my inability to commit my thoughts and feelings to paper not having had the benefit of an early education being born of poor parentage and more especially among a greatley dispised and persecuted people. When I should have been attending school in early childhood I was escaping with a widowed Mother and only sister and saints from the fury of a ruthless mob.
>
> . . . in 1846 My Father and only Brother were shot by a heartless mob after . . . which they ordered my Mother to leave the City. . . . Mother's life was threatened many times by the mob and in 1847 we left Nauvoo following the track of saints who left the previous year at Winter quarters Nebraska we suffered much for the want of food I my self have been glad to get a little corn bread we did not have enough of that many times not having a father to provide for us and my Mother being a sickley woman But the hand of the Lord was over us for good and for the good of his people. (3–4)

Perhaps the highest price paid was watching their children die. Jane Richards reported, "My child died beside me in the wagon, I being unable to move without being lifted." Of her despair, she said, "I only lived because I could not die" (*Reminiscences*, 24).

RELATIONS WITH NATIVE PEOPLES

Matilda's informants did not identify the Native peoples whom they encountered in the Mormon migrations across the country or in the Salt Lake City area. Despite all the struggles with gentile Americans, the Saints seemed to have met with very little conflict from Native Americans, according to Matilda's dictations, though many other accounts of persecution of Native people by LDS emigrants and their reprisals do exist. In Mary Isabella Horne's experience,

> The Indians gave them very little trouble. They brought Buf-
> falo robes and exchanged for a little corn. At one time while
> the men were thus engaged trading, the squaws stole several
> kettles and skillets. One Indian offered Mrs Horne four
> ponies for her little girl whose pretty face and red shoes won
> his admiration. (19)

Mrs. Horne declined the offer.

The relatively peaceable associations with Indians may have been owed to stories in the *Book of Mormon* about ancestral connections between Indigenous American peoples and the ancient tribes of Israel. In Horne's story we see that some Saints sought to be kind to Native people, perhaps illustrating the directive in the Mormon Article of Faith to be benevolent and virtuous and to do good to all.

> The Indians were most degraded, and naked. They were so
> nearly starved they would seize the bones thrown outside
> and break them open for the marrow. . . . They would [steal]
> at first, but the Mormons gave them some rather than have
> them steal. They were councilled not to harm them as theft
> was not a crime on account of their ignorance. (27–28)

Horne's companions even enjoyed a cultural exchange of music and dance with the Sioux Indians.

> As the company was en route for Salt Lake in '47, the usual
> plan was carried out—two companies of fifty each were
> formed. The wagons were placed in circles with tongues out,
> and the cattle corralled within to keep them from Indians.
> Then the trumpet would sound, and they would often have
> instrumental music, singing and dancing. At one time they
> and the Sioux Indians had a dance. The Sioux danced their
> national dances, and then the Mormons. (31)

Of course, not all stories about LDS encounters with Native people ended so positively.

LIFE AT THE GREAT SALT LAKE

The weary and starved emigrants finally arrived at their destination, the newly planned community of Salt Lake City. Yet the bleak scene that met Clara Young's party upon their arrival in July 1847 led to grievances. "They were terribly disappointed because there were no trees and to them there was such a sense of desolation and loneliness" (5). Young herself was among those left behind at the fort while others homesteaded further away. "Now but a small number was left and no one could tell how long it might be before they could see, or hear from, one another. But they had grown brave and stronger as they had grown accustomed to their surroundings" (6–7).

The forces of nature brought ever more challenges: infestations of bed bugs, invasions of mice—they might kill sixty before bedtime—and a swarm of crickets, the last miraculously eaten by flocks of sea gulls. Reported Isabella Horne:

> In the spring when thousands of young trees had been
> started and were several inches in height they had the plague
> of crickets.... Crickets swarmed in upon them destroying
> everything in their track. Everybody, men, women and chil-
> dren turned out to fight them; they would drive them into
> the water, or into piles of reeds which they would set on fire.
> Nothing would have been saved if Providence had not sent
> in the immense numbers of sea gulls—and whoever heard of
> seagulls here before? They would swallow them, then vomit
> them up and swallow them again and so saved the crops. (28)

And now renewed conflict with the US government arrived. The Saints hoped to practice their religion safely in their self-governing territory. Brigham Young was appointed governor of the Utah Territory in 1851, but in 1857 President Buchanan ordered federal troops to replace him with a non-Mormon, Alfred Cumming, inciting the Utah War.[17] Mrs. Horne described her escape.

> In 1858 [Col. Albert Sydney] Johnston's army came into Utah
> and Brigham Young advised the evacuation of their homes.[18]
> Mr Horne was away, and Mrs. Horne started on the 1st of
> May, to drive to Parowan [north of St. George], 250 miles

distant—her husband being somewhere in that vicinity raising cotton—some hundred miles further south. She had two
teams for herself and ten children and her husband's other
wife and baby—the whole distance she drove with her baby
in her arms. They had to sleep in wagons and cook for themselves on the way. They were one month travelling. They were
scantily provided with clothing; there was nothing to buy in
Salt Lake if there had been money to buy with.

Some people came in from San Bernardino to Parowan
with a load of dry goods; she sewed for the five months she
was there, thus earning the material and clothing her children
comfortably. They returned on the 1st of September to Salt
Lake where they found their homes undisturbed. (35–36)

The women who shared their oral histories with Matilda related
many more details of family life and the political history of their community, all contributing to our understanding of life on the social and
geographic margins for the Mormons in search of religious freedom
from the 1840s to the 1870s.

MATILDA'S ROLE AND PERSPECTIVE

How did Matilda experience these discussions, woman to woman?
She was clearly asking apt questions that prompted the many personal
details that fill these accounts. Perhaps she murmured sympathetically
as she listened to these tales of suffering.

As a straitlaced Victorian woman from a Puritan New England
home, Matilda probably held negative opinions about the complex
phenomenon of polygamy, but very few of her reactions slipped into
these oral histories—nor should they have if she were doing her "job"
correctly. In a few places Matilda's values are quite obvious; generally
her thoughts are veiled.

In Utah, when Matilda took a dictation from the brother of Brigham
Young, Lorenzo Young, she inserted her critique of his wives.[19] "They
appeared simple women, who could easily be taught to believe anything; looked good-natured folks, and as though contented with
a lot which was undoubtedly more comfortable than their mother's
had been" (1–2). Did Matilda find this simplicity in most or all of the
women she interviewed, implying that they were gullible in adopting
the Mormon faith and polygamy?

Elsewhere, Matilda's opinion can be inferred from her choice of words. In the following excerpt from Sarah Cooke's dictation, it is unclear whether Matilda is critiquing Mormons for being "evasive" and disloyal, or whether she simply conveyed Cooke's opinion.

> Mrs Cooke spoke of an evasive way they had. For instance president [John] Taylor once in France said publicly that he believed as they all believed "that one man shall have one wife and one woman but one husband"; explaining afterward that while one man shall have one wife he did not say how many in addition to that one. He himself had five wives at that time. His meaning was plain to his audience as he intended they should understand it. He said "seeing that this church has been charged with polygamy and other abominations I will say that I believe that one man" etc.
>
> They consider it no sin to make any denial or statement that will confound the gentiles. They are exhonerated [*sic*] from all blame if they lie in defence of their faith.
>
> They are not loyal to the United States Government. They teach their children to believe that our government will crumble and that theirs will supersede it. (7–8)

In "our" government, Matilda does quite obviously take sides. She is not just a disinterested scribe here but simultaneously an analyst.

On the other hand, Matilda reports approvingly of positive and even endearing aspects of polygamy. Jane Richards clarified the only "remonstration" she had ever shown her husband's second wife, when Elizabeth neglected to put on stockings when she was sick. Exhibiting real enthusiasm for Mormon familial amiability, Matilda wrote: "What a peaceable family if through such trials of sickness and privation this little irritability is the most serious that can be recalled!!" ("Inner Facts," 10).

In some of these dictations, Matilda systematically uses the first person to represent her interviewees. In others, however, she uses the third person to discuss the woman whose story she was taking down, with quotation marks for direct quotes. The question of voice—who speaks for whom—shifts from one dictation to another. For example, Matilda uses the first person in Jane Richards's *Reminiscences*, to convey Jane's perspective: "So I say positively that the Mormons live happier with their wives and more virtuously than other peoples" (45). However, in Jane's second dictation, "Inner Facts of Social Life in Utah," Matilda consistently refers to the conversation with Richards in the third person: "Mrs Richards in private conversation with me, related the following in regard to her personal experience" (1). Here, Matilda could more readily insert her own perspective about the relationship between Jane and her husband, Franklin. Not only was Jane "a very devoted wife," but Franklin was "remarkably attentive to her. To see them together I should never imagine either had a thought but what the other shared" ("Inner Facts," 14). Was Matilda dispelling a stereotype, that a man with so many wives could not really care about each individually?

> Mrs. Richards remembers that in talking of this subject of polygamy in prospective, with her husband, she told him she should expect that he would care for her in her old age, and that she should exact a promise from him to be faithful to her then. He seems remarkably considerate and kind and speaks of her with gratitude and pride, and that he wanted her to enjoy this little visit to California for she has suffered so much affliction and so many hardships that he wants whatever she can enjoy in life now to be hers. This was the way he first talked of his wife to Mr Bancroft as they first met; and his attentions and kind consideration of her are very marked. She is certainly very devoted to him, and I am imagining this trip and the one that they have just returned from East as a sort of honeymoon in middle life. (11)

Matilda also spoke to Mr. Richards himself about his initial response to the call for plural marriage.

> Mr Richards in talking of these early days, and in reply to my question as to how he reasoned about it when the matter was first considered as a personal obligation was a little evasive but at last told me, that at first it was a bitter pill but "the Lord required it, and we had to look for the explanation and reason afterward." (7)

As a gentile, Matilda would probably neither identify with nor condone this male "obligation." However, she could identify with the women's struggles, as in this first-person opinion in the Richards essay:

> I could not but . . . think of the narration of hardship I had just listened to from the one wife so illy provided for; yet she never complained of her lot being hard, though the severe sicknesses she endured, the care of delicate children, the earning of their livelihood by braiding straw hats and keeping boarders, teaching them to read and sewing for them, all combined to make a hard lot harder; and it seems as though it needed some divine grace to prevent her repining at the wisdom of dividing her little heritage with another. ("Inner Facts," 11)

Matilda concludes the Richards essay with a summary judgment on plural marriages.

> On the whole it seems to me that they considered it wholly as a religious duty and schooled themselves to bear its discomforts as a sort of religious penance; and that it was a matter of pride to make everybody believe they lived happily and to persuade themselves and others that it was not a trial; and that a long life of such discipline makes the trial lighter. ("Inner Facts," 18)

She could certainly relate to a long life of discipline. Her husband had already been engaged in such a life of discipline when she married him, and she was now following his example.

Matilda's Other Dictations— and H.H.'s Use of Her Work

Matilda was given credit for at least twenty-five dictations, and she mentions more in her journals. The stories she heard from other early settlers of the West, like those of the Saints, were filled with the struggles and even tragedies of their journeys or their hardscrabble existence in mining towns, distant homesteads, and wilderness camps. She received quite an education as an oral historian.

H. H. Bancroft had hired a battalion of researchers, writers, and agents for his thirty-eight volumes of historical description and commentary (followed by the personal thirty-ninth volume, *Literary Industries*). His wife Matilda and daughter Kate (who helped organize material but never took dictations) were sources of unpaid labor, though Matilda provided valuable information for *Bancroft's Works*. H.H. inserted a tribute to William Byers in his history of Colorado (volume 25 of his *Works*): "Mr Byers had a most important influence in shaping the history of Colorado. I am indebted to him for very valuable material, collected during a tour through the state of Colorado in 1884, in four different manuscript contributions," one of which is a manuscript in Matilda's handwriting and attributed to her by The Bancroft Library.[20]

In volume 26, *History of Utah*, H.H. utilized Matilda's dictations of Jane Richards in multiple places, reproducing a portion of her *Reminiscences* to reinforce the suffering of the Mormon emigrants in 1846. He also cites Jane's *Reminiscences* to support statements about various aspects of the LDS Church, such as the role of faith healing: "The laying on of hands for ordination, and for the healing of the sick, descends from the early to the later apostles." The associated footnote reads, "Says Mrs Richards, 'In all sicknesses we used no medicines, with the exception of herb teas that we ourselves prepared, trusting exclusively to the efficacy of the anointing with oil and prayer'" (335). H.H. also used her dictation to support his statements about the role of baptismal healing (337), and included it among his seven-page, footnoted list of articles on Utah polygamy (388–94).

In listing the sources of his history, Bancroft named those to whom he was especially indebted, including Jane Richards's husband, Franklin D. Richards, and Jane herself for both her *Reminiscences* and "Inner Facts of Social Life in Utah," the essay attributed to Jane. However H.H. did not acknowledge that the essay was actually written by Matilda.

In this same lengthy footnote, Bancroft included another dictation that Matilda took, Mrs. Clara Decker Young's *A Woman's Experiences with the Pioneer Band*. Young had played a significant role in the settling of the valley, and, "When 16 years of age she became the fifth wife of Brigham Young." Another of Matilda's dictations cited by H.H. (and cited differently than Horne's dictation is noted in the Bancroft

Library catalogue) was that of Mary Isabella Hales Horne, *The Migration and Settlements of the Latter-Day Saints* (331).

Nowhere in this volume is Matilda's name mentioned. At the same time, neither are the names of others—men or women—who took dictations, collected archives, or researched and wrote Utah history. Only in his memoir, *Literary Industries*, did Bancroft discuss the very valued contributions of all the "Men on the Fifth Floor," as he called his research assistants, and there he did indeed give credit to the three women who participated in his literary industries: his employee Frances Fuller Victor, his wife Matilda Bancroft, and his daughter Kate Bancroft.

At least in his archives, the voices of all these women—including Matilda's—became part of the record of the development of the West.

Page from Matilda Bancroft's dictation of Jane Snyder Richards's "Reminiscences," courtesy of The Bancroft Library (BANC MSS P-F 4)

CHAPTER ELEVEN

Businesswoman, Schemer, and Dreamer

By the late nineteenth century, many women were going to college and even entering medicine, law, and business—but not from H. H. Bancroft's home. His experience as an autodidact, along with his patriarchal attitudes, apparently convinced him that women did not need much formal training for their traditional work as a mother and wife. Despite that, he sought an intelligent and informed wife, especially in helping with his work. In Matilda, H.H. had a wife accomplished not only as mother, teacher, oral historian, and writer but also as businesswoman. She became adept at buying, building, and managing real estate, among other Bancroft business projects.

H.H. was quick to lavish praise on Matilda in his letters. Regarding a land transaction in Spring Valley, outside of San Diego, in October 1885, he wrote, "You will come out of our tribulation a first class business woman. You are doing first rate fixing up the Porter business" (June 28). In a later (undated) missive about building a home on that same land, H.H. wrote with characteristic humor, "When I fail here [in San Francisco], I want you to lend me some money to build my adobe palace—only it will be yours then. It strikes me, Matilda, that you are getting to be the better man of the two" (undated, box 1).[1]

Well organized and socially effective, Matilda helped juggle at least four significant properties in the 1880s and 1890s: a home in San Francisco; another in San Diego, whose construction she oversaw (along with a store there); and two working farms, one in Walnut Creek and another in Spring Valley. In addition, in 1901, when the family demolished the San Francisco house at Van Ness and Sutter[2] and replaced it with a residential hotel, called St. Dunstan's, Matilda helped her then twenty-four-year-old son Paul think through how to manage the business in terms of what guests needed and more. Matilda did the same for the Albatross Inn in San Diego, which Griffing managed.

Matilda also contributed to other important developments, including the sale of The Bancroft Library to the University of California in 1905. Although few of her schemes were realized, she was both energetic and visionary in her ideas about how to improve society, such as turning one of the family properties into a sanitarium. Matilda even guided her sons in their budding careers, giving them ideas about how to benefit from new possibilities in an ever-modernizing society. But here we will focus on her efforts regarding the family's initiatives.

The sources of the information in this chapter range from her children's memory books to letters Matilda wrote to H.H. and to son Griffing. (No letters to Lucy have survived, and very few to Paul and Philip.) Some of her husband's surviving letters richly portray how Matilda contributed to family businesses.[3]

Matilda as Real Estate Manager: San Francisco

The origin of the Bancroft home on Van Ness and Sutter is not known. Matilda's descriptions of the family's whereabouts indicate that they spent only a few months at a time in any one of their homes, including this one. The respiratory problems of both H.H. and son Philip led to the family escaping the cold and foggy San Francisco summers and the cold Walnut Creek winters.

In 1883, the Bancrofts preferred to rent out their San Francisco home rather than leave it empty while they ventured elsewhere, and so they did for seven years. They finally returned in 1890.

> Mr. Dodge gave up our house the 1st of April; they had
> rented it for the past seven years; we were delighted to take
> possession once more; the children examined every corner,
> and faint remembrances and sometimes distinct, of their old

The Bancroft home on Van Ness at Sutter, courtesy of The Bancroft
Library (BANC MSS 73/64 c)

home would strike Paul and Griffing. The younger ones were
but babies when we left here. (Philip, 247)

Just months later, the Bancrofts packed up and left it behind again,
probably returning to the Walnut Creek farm before their 1891 trip to
Mexico. In the following years, Matilda would mention intermittent
visits to their San Francisco home, as well as dealing with renters.

The Walnut Creek Farm

The children's favorite place was the Walnut Creek farm, eventually
named the Mt. Diablo Fruit Farm for the mountain at whose feet it

sat. Matilda explained in Philip's memory book how "Papa" presented the place to her as actually *hers*.

> First we drove directly to the farm, two miles distant, which certainly looked lovely to us from the hill top; a bright green valley thickly overspread with white oaks perfectly level, was stretched out before us in unbroken beauty, "and this," says papa proudly, "is yours, Matilda," for he had given me a deed to the 180 acres he had bought. The boys—Uncle Albert and papa—had bought about 360 acres in all, and it was divided equally with Aunt Fannie and mamma.[4] Papa was delighted with the purchase and said if it looked like a lovely park now with its young barley and old oaks, what would it be a few years hence covered with fruit trees and vines. May we all live to realize the enjoyment in it we are now anticipating!
>
> We drove to the old farmhouse . . ., and there saw Aunt Fannie and the children. The old weather-stained building, unpainted and even unwhitewashed, made a comfortable shelter first for Aunt Fannie's family and then for ours, for many months. There were several other buildings about the place, two granerys [*sic*], a barn, wagon house, chicken house, blacksmith shop, men's dormitory, etc. and altogether farm life and its accessories looked very inviting.
>
> The month of May we spent at the hotel. One trip we made, en deux familles, looking at Jersey cows which were afterward purchased. Then after Aunt Fannie's family left for their camp, we all moved into the house, mamma buying furniture for the building sufficient for our needs. Uncle Curtis was here as superintendent, and he has always been very kind to the children.[5] (109–11)

One of their happiest activities was building a log cabin on the farm. Matilda explains the motivation and the process, including the family outing to collect the sawn logs.

> While we were in Oregon[6] Mamma saw log cabins and wanted to have one built on our place, which papa consented to. . . . We had gone some little time before for the logs to Pacheco. They had been ordered from Duncan's Mill, on the

Russian River.[7] We went in two big wagons, while I drove in the buggy. It was no easy matter to handle those heavy logs and get them onto the wagon, and then to unload after we got home. The thermometer, too, was up about as high as it gets here, 110°. The building of the cabin has been a matter of great interest to us all. It is to be 16 x 25 in size and to be furnished with old-fashioned furniture. . . . We are also building a cistern as we don't like the alkali water for drinking or for washing. . . .

The cabin has given us some pleasant excursions. One trip was into Pine Cañon after stones for the outside chimney; the mason who came from San Francisco to build it would not make it rough as we had intended but smoothed off all the stones while we were in San Diego where we went in October. (Griffing, 342–45)

The log cabin, courtesy of The Bancroft Library (BANC MSS 73/64 c)

In Griffing's book, Matilda explained that Papa had learned to drive a four-horse wagon.

While hauling lumber for the buildings, Papa drove the four horse wagon and Paul a two-horse team. That is a new experience all around; they had been building at the farm in San Diego while papa was there, and he had had quite an experience in hauling lumber and in driving four-in-hand for the first time, so he is in practice now. He has not been very well and tries to be out in the open air as much as possible. (368–69)

In the family photo album, Matilda included a photo of a four-horse carriage.

H. H. Bancroft driving the four-in-hand, courtesy of The Bancroft Library (BANC MSS 73/64 c)

Beginning in April 1888, Matilda wrote multiple entries in Griffing's book about the farm's agricultural design and products, including the development of an orange orchard, an innovation borrowed from Southern California. "Our family orchard is all planted [with] acres of almonds, and now we have set out eighty budded oranges, the Mediterranean sweets, that came from Florida" (311–12).

Similarly, Matilda detailed what H.H., the gentleman farmer, was learning about the best agricultural methods: "He has learned how to care for orange trees; now he has a big saucer dug around every tree at least once a month and a barrel of water given to each tree, besides enriching the soil. The boys often jump on the sled and help drive or water" (Griffing, 370).

Matilda also reported on the challenges they faced with their grapes. First, birds attacked the drying Muscat grapes: "The birds made such a harvest of them that the boys were allowed to keep up a fusilade [*sic*], which they thought was jolly" (373). Then a ruinous rain:

> Just in the midst of our raisin drying, it commenced to rain, an almost unprecedented thing so early in the season, October first. . . . Our grapes spread out to dry required constant attention, piling up and unpiling the trays. One morning a shower came so suddenly that Griffing and Paul were of great help; with their mamma's insistence they had piled up nearly half of the trays and had covered them before a heavy rain commenced falling which ruined all the rest. . . . but our loss was light compared to many of our neighbors whose grapes were their dependence and who had many more to lose. (Griffing, 377–78)

How honest to acknowledge the greater misfortune of their farming neighbors who depended on their crops for their livelihood.

In Lucy's book each summer, Matilda extolled the glory of the farm, remarking on the different activities and developments that created the children's "paradise"—and their papa's.

> 1887: All the summer and fall that we spent at the farm was busily occupied with building—we completed our house, put up one for Charlie Blankenship, our foreman, built a barn and various other farm buildings. Papa seems to enjoy all the life and interests of the farm as much as the children do. (102)
>
> 1888: The first of March the children went over to the farm with their father, Fraulein Dartsch and a Chinaman to open the house, and I went to San Diego to look after things there. The farm is their paradise; so I had no uneasiness about their welfare, and papa remained there most of the time I was away. (109–10)
>
> 1889: The farm is as fascinating to the children as ever. Papa returned directly here from Colorado, nearly reaching here on my birthday, May 10th; he got here on the 11th. Grandma and Aunties had come to make a good-bye visit of a few days before going East. We had a happy time all together. Saturday

> evening we gathered in the log cabin, and the children
> repeated pieces they had learned and sang some little songs,
> Paul accompanying with his violin. (140–41)

Through the years, Matilda's supervision of the Walnut Creek farm during her husband's many absences earned his approval, as he wrote in a letter to Lucy (June 30, 1889): "Tell your mother she will make a very good farm superintendent and I do not think we want any other at present."

The four-hundred-acre farm remained in the family over many years, with Philip and then his son Philip Jr. taking over its management. Their Bartlett pears and walnuts were well known during the first half of the twentieth century. However, by the 1970s the town of Walnut Creek had rezoned the surrounding area for residential housing, so the family sold most of the land, except for the few acres that Philip Bancroft Jr. kept for the family compound and his wife Ruth's succulent garden, now public and world renowned as the Ruth Bancroft Garden.[8] Ruth herself tended the garden until the last years of her life; she passed away in 2017 at the age of 109.

The San Diego Farm

In *Literary Industries*, H.H. explained that the San Francisco Bay fog and cold invaded even their East Bay sanctuary, so he and Matilda searched much farther south for relief. The family had already followed the sun as far south as Santa Barbara and Ojai in late 1883. The following March, H.H. had discovered the glories of San Diego and bought a block of land in the city proper, even before buying the Walnut Creek property. In the fall of 1885, the couple fixed their eyes on a ranch in Spring Valley about twelve miles east of the still-small town of San Diego.

> The strong cold winds of Contra Costa Co. disappointed us,
> and papa said he was going to do better for climate if that
> was possible. We decided we would go to San Diego and see
> what we could find about there in the way of a farm. So we
> left the children in Cassie's care and spent two weeks in our
> search for a Paradise free from all the ills nature is subject

to. We made our headquarters at the Florence Hotel, and
would start out every morning at seven o'clock with a two- or
three-seated vehicle, taking some interested friends with us,
and drive till evening. In that way we went north and south
and east, until finally we decided upon the purchase of Capt.
Porter's place of 160 acres in Spring Valley at an average of
$50 an acre. It was the springs on the place that made its
greatest attraction, for who could guess their possibilities,
and everywhere water was in greatest demand. I went back to
the children before the final arrangement was consummated,
quite pleased with our purchase. The Porters are to live there
for several months, which is a convenience to them and to us.

So we came back … quite satisfied to look … upon the
San Diego Farm as a place where we could go and find freedom from everything that is rough and disagreeable. Uncle
Curtis is to take charge of this place as long as his oversight is
necessary, and then to go down there and take charge. Uncle
Albert's place adjoins ours [in Walnut Creek], as I said before;
they will probably make more of a home of their place than
we do of ours. (Griffing, 229–30)

In Philip's book, Matilda added that they had also bought "a tim-
ber claim" of 160 acres for $300 in San Diego, "the two some distance
apart."

In 1886, H.H. enlarged the Spring Valley farm: "Now we have all
been over to our Spring Valley farm, and papa just bought 180 acres
more of Smith Campbell for $3600" (Griffing, 241). The couple named
the San Diego place Helix Farm, after Mt. Helix, which overlooks
the terrain in the distance. They never constructed a full home there.
The first American land claimants had built a small two-room adobe
building in 1863 that now served the Bancroft family when they were
roughing it. That adobe house still stands as the center of the Bancroft
Ranch Home Museum of the Spring Valley Historical Society. Later,
H.H. constructed a "Rock House" on a hill overlooking the orchard
and spring, where he could write during his trips to the ranch.

Helix Farm did become productive, however.

Uncle Curtis came down about this time, in Nov. 1886, with
Lorenzo McDonald to take charge of the farm. They brought

five horses. Papa engaged 50,000 olive cuttings, and he bought enough rooted guavas to plant 5 acres at $15 per 100. Papa's plan was to put 40 acres into grapes, and 40 acres into olives. (Philip, 150–51)

By late summer of 1886, the Spring Valley orchards provided another fun activity for the children. "Paul enjoyed our trip where we picked apricots on the farm and made them into preserves" (Griffing, 240). For years the Bancrofts continued to plant. In 1889, "we sent down to the S.D. farm 15,000 olive cuttings; last year we sent 50,000" (Griffing, 302).

The family returned there in late 1889 in two groups, H.H. taking the two older boys with him first by land. Matilda, Philip, and Lucy followed by sea. "While the weather is miserable, it's safer travelling by water than by land as there are serious washouts on the Southern Pacific [railroad]" (Philip, 240). Upon arriving in San Diego,

They went out to the Farm at once, stopping over one night at the Florence [Hotel].[9] Papa is making a pretty place of it, cleaning Cactus Hill on which he has built a three-roomed

Children on the Spring Valley farm, courtesy of The Bancroft Library
(BANC MSS 73/64 c)

dormitory [the Rock House], clearing out the reservoir,
planting seventy five date palms, and doing lots of work. They
are all having a gala time, and none seems to enjoy the fun
more than their papa. . . . Among other work was the planting of ivy sent from the Library, which is to grow over all the
stone buildings.[10] (Philip, 241–42)

Though the Helix Farm could not house them all, Matilda found
ways to make the most of life outdoors, complete with guests, in 1890.

A Christmas picnic at Helix Farms was a feature. We did not
know what we were going to do with Christmas; there were
20 men and I don't know how many teams at work on the
Farm, and just in the midst of it Papa wrote me, for I was at
the Florence, and suggested a Christmas picnic. I always fall
in with his suggestions of entertaining, for we don't do half as
much of it as I should enjoy, though the how and the where-
fore were not quite clear. We had a delightful time. We char-
tered a [railroad] car and about 50 people came out, returning
on the 3 o'clock train. At noon the thermometer registered
89 degrees in the shade. We had a tent for the spread, all the
provisions being sent from San Diego, excepting the guavas
and cream which won distinguished recognition. (Philip, 256)

The San Diego Town Home

H.H. had also purchased San Diego town properties in early 1884,
following the family's visit there. One was on a steep hill near the Florence Hotel.

He immediately purchased one block just beyond the hotel;
it will have to be graded whenever it is used. . . . This property, and several other blocks that he bought later, he buys
as an investment to hold for several years, feeling confident
that property will advance, quadruple at least, after the
through railroad is built and connects with the branch now

terminating in National City. Property now is very low, and
his logic seems sound certainly. (Griffing, 158)

In Philip's book, Matilda reported on the same purchase, emphasizing H.H.'s method of investing for the long term. "Papa was so san-
guine of the rise of property in S.D. within a few years that he invested
in various blocks near the business center. He thinks that the children
will realize something handsome from this investment if it is allowed
to remain undisturbed twenty years perhaps" (Philip, 75). Ultimately,
he had Matilda supervise the construction of a store on one of those
blocks, but their home site was her masterpiece, of which she wrote
about considerably.

Matilda's home in San Diego, 1886, courtesy of The Bancroft Library
(BANC MSS 73/64 c)

In 1886, Matilda chronicled in detail the construction of what would
become a magnificent home in then downtown San Diego, despite the
challenges presented by precipitous hillsides.

We have decided to build in San Diego, as papa thinks life
there would be a benefit to us all, to Philip in particular. Our
first move was to leave S.F. about the first of March 1886 on

the steamer *Orizaba* for the Florence Hotel, S.D. . . . Almost
at once papa began work on our lot.[11] When he bought the
unpromising block, there was a high bluff on the upper part
of it, and a deep ravine on the lower part. The drainage of the
[Florence] Hotel was carried through it and deposited in the
ravine. No streets were graded anywhere about that portion
of town. . . . It was steep and at the ravine so narrow as to be
dangerous with a precipice forty or fifty feet deep on either
side. . . . Papa made his way through these streets once . . . in
a buggy to show me what would sometime be done when the
city was graded. . . .

Aunt Emily[12] has hastily built four cottages on her block
opposite ours. . . . I called papa a crazy fellow to buy such
a piece of land. At that time he also bought a half a block
opposite which was still worse; the whole for $750. He said
he thought I couldn't complain so long as he had the money
to use, and would give it all to me. On the strength of that, I
think, he deeded all his San Diego property to me; possibly
that was done earlier; a gift I didn't value at the time as worth
the giving. Later, when I appreciated its value, I considered it
a wise precaution on papa's part to secure this portion of his
property so well.

The children entered into the spirit of the work, for a great
deal was being done all at once. A cottage on the Poultry
block for Mr. Miller, a very pretty home for sister Kate [Ban-
croft], which was built first and was a music studio, and our
own foundation, were all undertaken together. Papa entered
into it all so heartily, often being out at work before seven in
the morning. (Philip, 132–34)

Matilda leaped into the project fully, becoming an amateur architect in training. "We were intending to build a house in San Diego,
so I was studying architecture while in town"—meaning in San Francisco (Lucy, 83–84). The respected architect Clinton Day (1847–1916)
designed the house, but Matilda oversaw much of its construction in
H.H.'s absences.

Meanwhile, H.H., with his ever-driving ambition, immediately put
a horde of workers to leveling the building site. "Papa lost no time
commencing our house. . . . He got 14 mule teams with scrappers and

20 men to work on the grounds for a few days, and after a while we could see where a house could be built" (239). She added later in Lucy's book, "These were happy weeks speeding along with building in the poultry blocks, on sister Kate's lots and on ours" (Griffing, 89).

The Burning Down of the Bancroft Building

The family's creative building happiness ended horrifically with a telegram on April 30, 1886. "But just in the midst of it all came a sudden misfortune—Papa's fine store in S.F. was burned to the ground in an hour or two!" (Lucy, 89). In Philip's book, Matilda explained more:

> I was downtown when someone from the telegraph office handed me a telegram which he said was for Mr. Bancroft and was very important. I said, "Is any one sick or dead?" and

The burning of the Bancroft Building, courtesy of The Bancroft Library (C-R 68 vol. 5)

he said no, it's business. Then I drove hastily back feeling that probably there was a failure. Papa stood on the hotel steps. I said, "Here is a telegram that they tell me is very important." He read it slowly and said, "I should think it was; the store is burning up and nothing can save it." He was cool and composed for some time, quietly reviewing the situation. How business matters stood he did not know; whether it would leave him bankrupt and unable to complete his history he could not tell; that seemed his greatest anxiety. He was happier in the consciousness that the San Diego property was secured to his family than in anything else, for that would make us comfortable if nothing else was saved. "But can I complete my history; that's the question," he said over and over again. Then leaving all the money in the S.D. bank to my credit, amounting to about $3000.00, he left with Kate on the night train for S.F. going at once to Uncle Albert's house.

For about three months he was dreadfully depressed. He wrote at one time "if things could only be definitely determined and we knew whether we should go under or not, it would be a relief, but as it is I feel as though I was dragging a corpse after me all the time." I did not know whether we could complete the house, but as most of our building material was ordered and payed for, papa wrote to go on with the work. Mr. [Bryant] Howard at this time said, "I should like to be worth as much as you are today; your San Diego property would sell now for $150,000."

Through all the stress that followed, papa would not allow me to sell any of that property to help him out in S.F. He said what it realized should be put in San Diego. It was a wonder how we ever were able to do what we did at this time, both in S.F. and in S.D. Papa at first was inclined to sell his land and give up all thought of renewing business. I, in my short sighted policy, urged his doing so. I thought it would relieve him of harassing business cares, and in middle life as he now is, it was much better than trying to make more money, for we all would even then have enough. The land was offered at an auction sale; papa's lowest price was $250,000, only $225,000 was offered, which he would not accept. Then he at once decided to re-build and felt much happier for so deciding.

Mr. Clinton Day furnished the plans; he was also the architect of our house in S.D. Of course papa had to borrow money from the bank to build, and placed a mortgage on our Van Ness Ave. house, library & farm. He also bought 25 ft. on the rear in Stevenson St., which had been cleared off by the fire, for $10,000. That added increased facilities for his business. The printing was removed to another building, and all the building will be rented except what is needed for the business, provided they move back again. At present they are [staying at] the "Grand Hotel."[13]

. . . Papa kept up a bright outlook, and told us not to "talk poor" nor "feel poor" and we would come out all right. I felt very proud of his ability to so recover himself. (Philip, 135–40)

The loss was tremendous, for the Market Street building was completely destroyed and along with it $500,000 worth of printed copies of *Bancroft's Works*. Bancroft had the hope of some insurance monies—despite the failure of his brother A.L. to renew the insurance completely—as well as funds in the bank and income from both the sales of his histories (via subscriptions) and from other properties (rentals and the two farms). Thus he encouraged Matilda to go on with the building of the San Diego home. In concert with this chapter's theme, the focus here will be on how H.H. and Matilda managed each other's business concerns in the face of this disaster.

Anxious about so many expenses, H.H.'s letters convey understandable emotional instability during that period. By turns he berated his wife for extravagant costs in the morning, then praised her good business sense in a letter sent later that day. This pattern of alternating acclaim and blame continued over the next year or so, further indicating Matilda's capabilities not only as a businesswoman but also as a careful manager of her husband's testy temperament.

On May 9, 1886, H.H. instructed Matilda, "Work on the feelings of Smith Campbell & get him to have his woman sign the deed," referring to extra land that H.H. sought to buy in San Diego. Perhaps he knew that Matilda had used her "womanly wiles" in previous situations and could wrangle something out of this wife. Note, too, that while he trusted Matilda, he explicitly expected her to follow his instructions: "Please write me in detail about all your affairs there & I will tell you what to do."

At times H.H. was generous in his praise: "I hope you will put the farm business through with Campbell and Porter as I write you, with your usual discretion and energy" (May 20, 1886). And: "You are making a splendid business woman. . . . You see I compliment you by talking to you as to a first class business man" (May 31, 1886). When Matilda was able to get the deed signed by mid-June, her husband wrote, "I am delighted to have the Smith Campbell business over. You are doing splendidly." He told her what to do with the deed, asked for a full accounting of the budget for the house construction, and closed with characteristic generosity and humor. "Then I am going to give you the money to spruce it all up. And after that I want you to get along without any more money as long as you live! HHB" (June 18, 1886).

Ten days later, he reprimanded her in reply to a letter probably seeking to buy more land to create a fish pond: "You have a little itch for buying real estate. . . . How could you think of such a thing now, Matilda, as fish ponds; nothing in it in the world except expense, and we as we are?" (June 28, 1886).

Months later, Matilda's management earned H.H.'s praise once again. "You did first rate on those lots, and you do first rate on every thing, and are a good woman generally" (Sept. 8, 1886).

In early December came a harangue. Matilda's husband noted that she was spending $5,000–$6,000 a month, a large sum even today, and wholly extravagant in 1886. Since the house was finished by this time, H.H. was undoubtedly referring to the store whose construction Matilda was overseeing, at the Bancroft Building at 655 Fifth Avenue in San Diego. This four-story brick building with stone trim, designed by Clinton Day, would be a rental property.[14]

> It just this minute occurred to me, but what will you have to pay your men with to-morrow? You should have thought of this before. Either you will have to borrow or I must telegraph you something to-morrow. As I told you, you must either quit work, or have money to pay your men. I had no idea you would sling away that $12,000 so quick or the last $6000. I have asked you twenty times to keep me posted, to give me at least once a month the amount of money you have on hand. . . . You make it twice as hard for me to look after you from what it would be if you keep me well informed all the time. (Dec. 10, 1886)

The next day, H.H. blew his top.

> I am roaring mad. Have been rushing around sweating &
> coughing in cold damp damned alleys (I say this to make you
> feel bad) telegraphing you money at an expense extra of $8.60
> ... all because you will not keep me posted, & went to work
> & paid out all your money without keeping any for the men.
>   I have important issues at stake. Never in my life more
> so, or more of them. And yet my affairs so far as money is
> concerned (which is as I have told you before the life blood
> of business) for the next six months, unless some panic or
> something comes on, is as clear to me as if I saw them all in a
> mirror. . . .
>   For a person new in business you are doing reasonably well.
> But you can respond to my wishes a little or a good deal more
> conscientiously to the benefit of both of us. (Dec. 11, 1886)

Matilda's eagerness to start new projects had not let up. By February
1887, H.H. was ranting again about fiscal prudence. The most important lesson he sought to inculcate in his children: *never* go into debt
if you don't have to. This time, he resorted to denigrating Matilda's
intelligence.

> I am sorry to see you so keen to go into things, anything
> that any body talks up to you, & that whether you have any
> money or not. It will ruin you if you indulge in it. Your course
> throughout your whole life is clear enough; as you get in
> money from your rents, & have a surplus, build more houses,
> but never borrow money or run in debt for any thing even
> to build houses & let all other matters alone. You can man-
> age real estate in this way well enough, but you cannot other
> things. You are not smart enough & you have had no experi-
> ence, and don't want any. (Feb. 4, 1887)

He concluded by warning Matilda not to get involved in the schemes
of "simpletons"; it's "humbug."

The very next day, H.H. unleashed his fury yet again about her "going into new things." Then he explained in softer, yet still resolute, terms his situation:

> I will admit, my dear, that when you see so much every day
> that wants doing it is hard not to do it. But you must remem-
> ber that since the fire burned up both bookstore and building,
> (whence I derived my income) 9 months ago, I have not had
> one dollar income from any source. I have had to restore the
> burned History, keep the men at the library going, run two
> farms, build a store here, & send you between $30,000 &
> $40,000 to help out on your building there. It strikes me that
> is doing pretty well. Now we have <u>got</u> to have some income,
> & we have got to stop everything else until we get it. (Feb. 5,
> 1887)

Two weeks later, H.H. was even more conciliatory.

> I think I am very good to you. I have done more for you than
> for any body in the world—in fact I have done enough, and
> am going to quit now and do something for my other girls....
> I have, I believe, cleared up all of your business here and am
> ready to go to Mexico after I pay a few more little bills . . .
> [such as for] the tile for vestibule . . . they will help to make
> your building tony & enable you to get a better rent and I
> want you to get all the rent you can, not because I expect it
> ever to do me any good but because I love you and that is
> why I say I have been very good to you, because money comes
> hard, and I have never done anything at all to speak of for any
> of my other women.

As a postscript he added: "I shall not leave you comfortless, dearest, I shall send you $5000 before I go to Mexico, darling, and I hope, darn it, that this will stop your capacious maw for a while till I can get my breath" (Feb. 22, 1887).

"Capacious maw"! As ever, H.H. Bancroft's diction was piquant.

During the year following the devastating fire, Bancroft surely had cause to worry. The farm boy who had grown up in rural poverty, unable to go to high school for lack of funds, had now become wealthy through the careful financial management that he sought to instill in his wife and children. Over and over, H.H. drummed in his "lessons" to "teach the doctrine to your children": "Don't spend your money before you get it. Know every day all the time how much you owe & where the money is to pay it. Live within your means" (Feb. 7, 1887).

However, the anger with which he delivered this and other lessons had to be hard for his wife and family to bear. In later years, H.H. regularly berated his son Griffing in his many letters to him, criticizing his son for inattentiveness and irresponsibility.[15] One can easily see how H.H.'s curmudgeonliness could alienate others, leading Griffing to remain at a distance in San Diego all his life. Matilda endured.

The Fate of the Bancroft Building

Matilda's building projects in San Diego were, of course, not the only construction that concerned H. H. Bancroft. Through June 1887, now at the age fifty-five, he was also reconstructing his Market Street store in San Francisco. Matilda reported on it when she and the children laid eyes on the new building in 1887:

> About the 1st of June papa came down [to San Diego] for us, and brought us all back to S.F. . . . We went directly to the Grand Hotel, though papa first took us to see his new store, almost completed. It is very pretty, beautiful; I felt very proud of his ability to so recover himself and from the ashes build up a more enduring and more roomy building than before. The business was carried on in a small store under the Grand Hotel; in the rear of it was the History Department. The printing was being done in another building; the retail business was carried on here in a humble way; the piano business was also in another building. It was undecided as yet whether the business will move into the store at 721 Market St. Papa wanted it in its old place and Uncle Albert did not want it there. (Philip, 158)

Ultimately, another sad outcome of the fire was the rupture in the relationship between the brothers. H.H.'s younger brother Albert (or A.L.) had been his business partner for over twenty years. Their relationship ended in bitter enmity because of A.L.'s failure to renew the insurance in full on the building. Matilda did not describe all the details of this struggle, but in 1887 she offered this story about the fate of Papa's business on Market Street.

> About the middle of June, quite unexpectedly papa bought out Uncle Albert's interest in the business for $50,000, taking all the debts, lawsuits etc. of the old firm. The trouble was that Uncle Albert didn't want the business to go back into the old store, thought the rent and other expenses would be too high, but papa thought it would ruin the business if it didn't go back. And then, too, he had a pride in having the business where he had put it so many years ago, and in the beautiful building he had just erected.
>
> When we reached San Francisco, Kohler & Chase, a music firm on Post St., had the refusal of the store for $750 a month; they stood on $725 which papa would not listen to, and this now is the result; the old business is in its old place, 721 Market St., and is called "The Bancroft Co.", papa being president and Cousin Will the manager.[16]
>
> We are enjoying seeing the moving in of books, the boys taking hold and trying to help, too. They commenced packing up books immediately the arrangement was made with Uncle Albert, which in fact was all done in half an hour.
>
> On the 25th of June 1887, the new sign, the Bancroft Co. was put up,[17] and on the 20th of July the firm received their friends and had a fine table in the history rooms; there were large tables spread in each room and small tables for people to sit around. (Griffing, 275–77)

H. H. Bancroft's bookstore and publishing company truly had been a significant San Francisco institution for many decades. H.H. himself felt the weight of its service to the community and its weight as part of his own personal history, which Matilda captured in Philip's journal:

> Papa expressed a great deal of feeling about this matter. He said he could not undertake the detail of business without a great deal of worry and anxiety which in middle life, as he now was, he was loath to undertake; but on the other hand

he could not see a business which he had created as a boy, die out. (162)

So commenced the Bancroft Building's new era, which would last less than twenty years until the "Conflagration of 1906." Following the 1906 earthquake, the building, now numbered 731 Market Street, was reconstructed again. It remained in the family, which leased out offices, until the building was sold in 2005. It retains its emblematic name, and the upper façade still bears some resemblance to its early twentieth-century construction, but is otherwise undistinguished at the street level, housing in 2021 a modern chain pharmacy.

Matilda's Schemes

Matilda's mind gravitated to organizational schemes that would help society through cultural and social improvements, and possibly benefit her family's accounts.

As the San Diego town house became less a home to live in for the family, Matilda entertained new possibilities for the property, including turning the grand house into a sanitarium in late 1888.

> We had renovated the house thoroughly, painted it on the outside, put up a new fence, fixed the garden and had made a different looking place of it. It was a pleasure to live in it again for a while. . . . We offered the house for rent, but as times were so dull nobody wanted so high priced a house. Just about Christmas time a Dr [William A.] Edwards of Philadelphia called to see if we would rent it as a sanitarium; it was to be a rest-cure like Dr. Weir Mitchell's.[18] We did not like to rent it for such a purpose but as we might not have another so good an opportunity we decided to let him have it for a year. He took it from the 1st of January [1889], at $200 a month for a year. (Griffing, 351–52)

Ultimately, H.H. found her efforts more than satisfactory. "Your head is level . . . & you talked just right. I tell them here that you are worth a dozen men looking after things in San Diego" (Nov. 7, 1888).

An advertisement placed in a San Diego newspaper to rent the building twenty-five years later provides a concise description of the allure of the mansion: "To rent, by year—Fine residence of twelve rooms and basement, in San Diego; unsurpassed for location, arrangement and size of rooms; elegant finish of interior and large sunny porch; private residence or sanatorium; summer climate unequaled. $12000 unfurnished or partially furnished. Griffing Bancroft."[19]

Ultimately, the lovely mansion whose construction and development Matilda had overseen was torn down at some unspecified time.

Hotel Manager from Afar: The Albatross Inn

By November 1900, the twenty-one-year-old Griffing was pursuing the idea of running a hotel at one of the San Diego Bancroft properties, to be called the Albatross Inn, located on the street of that name. Matilda wrote letters of dogged encouragement and guidance, but the place may have become a true albatross around Griffing's neck. In this undated missive from Matilda to her husband, she replicates the "doctrine" that H.H. dinned into her.

> It seems to me an awful responsibility for you to give to Griffing to try and run so expensive a thing as that property without experience. It's like our farms, places for continual outgo without compensating returns. To make a business pay, that requires life-long experience, is too much to expect from Griffing.

H.H. forwarded her note on to Griffing, with his message on the back. "Read carefully your mother's letter and learn all you can from her & me about how hotels are kept & what makes the successful ones."

Matilda, in Rome in March 1901 (no date), wrote with more sage advice. "I am sure it will pay to provide intellectual entertainment for our guests—a good library." Her suggestions show her broad interests, such as to incorporate lectures by eminent scholars about local culture and agriculture at the Inn. "Another time it's olives etc., another on irrigation by Prof. Woodward of Los Angeles who has been four years at NY College as a teacher and is charming."[20] She suggested that

Griffing "create a Lowell Institute," referring to the Boston institute for popular and advanced lectures founded in 1836, adding a litany of potential speakers relating to nature, "since we don't have ruins." She advised that he "localize," taking advantage of stories and photographs of the Southern California missions, including "idealizing" Father Junipero Serra. "We enjoy hearing of these good fathers here; why not in California? ... The guests will be anxious to see those missions after hearing about them—two hours on the cars is not too far."[21]

And to accommodate audiences for all these speakers, Matilda acknowledged, they would need a proper hall, "an inexpensive building large enough for dancing, for theatricals, for lectures, for a library. That is the trouble with our San Diego scheme. It's all outlay and an expensive plaything."

In closing this long recitation, Matilda balanced disapproval of San Diego society against the city's potential: "It's disheartening to see so much of the intellectual life of San Diego going out of it."

> With so little culture and so little opportunity for improvement as now is left for San Diego, it will die of inanition unless something is done in this line to bring out these interests. People who crowd Europe now seek the same things in their own country, and we must provide something. (No date, but probably Mar. 1901)

Matilda felt duty bound to help bolster her community's intellectual appetites—and her family's enterprise. But stimulating public intellectual life was not in Griffing's nature. In the summer of 1902, the Albatross Inn closed for lack of business. Griffing himself would later be drawn to more solitary intellectual endeavors, such as writing and natural history in company with his wife.

St. Dunstan's

Matilda continued in her role as hotelier adviser in later years. None of the family records indicate when or why their home at the southeast corner of Sutter and Van Ness in San Francisco was razed, but by 1905, a residential hotel called St. Dunstan's had been constructed in its place, managed by Paul. Various members of the family lived there at times, including Matilda and H.H.

A 1905 advertisement for the hotel noted its positive qualities:

> To those who are contemplating a residence in an apartment hotel, the management extends a respectful invitation to call and acquaint themselves with the arrangement and prices of the apartments, and with the quiet comfort and beautiful appointments of the completed St Dunstan's. The Lower floors of the house are furnished luxuriously and are available for transient and semi-transient guests.

Those qualities gave Matilda optimism in September of that year. "St Dunstan's is filling up rapidly, so much so that rooms are scarce. It promises well for the winter" (Sept. 7, 1905). Three months later: "Apparently St Dunstan's is going to prove an excellent investment; the character of the house as a family apartment house couldn't be better—all the rooms are taken now and the restaurant is well patronized" (Dec. 12, 1905).

But challenges persisted. Matilda weighed in widely on her sons' concerns, including intervening in the troubled relationship between H.H. (then age seventy-three) and Griffing. Comparisons to his older brother Paul likely did not help. Both St. Dunstan's and the Albatross Inn required investments in order to entice guests to stay and to return. Matilda walked a fine line: on the one hand, she did not want to further incite Griffing's resentment of his critical father and competent brother; on the other hand, she sought to help him learn how to manage the Albatross better, that he might be in his father's better standing.

> This is an expensive investment, St. Dunstan's. Paul works very hard and very faithfully over it; your father is giving it his closest attention and thought; it should prove of greatest value, and has now the highest patronage at high figures. Paul watches every outgo and holds tenaciously onto the prices. There are a great many expenses like the music, for instance, which do not show immediate returns, but add to the elegance and attractiveness of the house and to the class of patrons. . . . So don't call it a failure; we are sure it is a great success; it made your father sick to have you say that; he felt

he was giving you boys a tremendous value in giving you this property; all of it he has worked so hard upon, Paul has and is working so hard on, and you are receiving it without any work; . . . it's a tremendous undertaking and expense, but the outgo stops sometime and if we can maintain its high character and keep up its reputation, we are all right.

Advertisement for St. Dunstan's, courtesy of The Bancroft Library
(BANC MSS 77/169c, box 3)

And we work hard for it. I don't wonder at your feeling and all of us feeling reluctant to put so much cash from our big sales right into this investment, but when it stops interest money on the mortgage, it seems all right. We haven't made the big sales yet, however; the library matter isn't decided and until it is we shan't feel sure of its sale. (Oct. 8, 1905)

Resolution of "the library matter"—meaning the sale of H.H.'s library to the University of California, yet another scheme Matilda was involved in—was still uncertain.

The earthquake of April 18, 1906, and subsequent fire destroyed any chances of success for St. Dunstan's. A postquake photograph depicts the fate of what had been a family dream.

St. Dunstan's at Van Ness Avenue and Sutter Street, San Francisco earthquake and fire, 1906, courtesy of the Anne T. Kent California Room, Marin County Free Library

When the earthquake struck, Matilda and H.H. were traveling east by train on their way to Europe. On April 19, one day after the earthquake, while the fire was still raging, H.H. sent a desperate letter to Griffing in San Diego. Concerned for lives lost, he also focused on the financial catastrophe facing the family with the loss not only of St. Dunstan's but once again of his Market Street History Building. His daughters and wife were receiving annuities from real estate income, and he feared he had no way to support them or other family members and employees whose incomes were gained from his businesses. He must have been heartsick.

> We saw papers last night with news of the catastrophe. We are one day yet from New York, during which time we are destined to remain greatly in the dark. I see no other way than to rebuild in SF & to do that we may have to sell out clean in SD for what we can get.... I know nothing as to the extent of our loss, though I assume that St. D is badly damaged & the Hist bldg wiped out. I do not know that the boys are even alive.
>
> Of course your mother & I abandon our European trip for good & return to SF immediately. Please write to me there & tell me how much money you can get out of SD, say within six months. I do not know whether or not we are to get any insurance money.
>
> HHB

After signing off, H.H. asked further questions:

> Was there any earthquake or tidal wave at SD at the time?
> What do you think we had better do about everything? Give me your views freely. You see St D and Hist bldg are in the hands of trustees who have annuities to pay & therefore must make them yield an income. Your mother & Lucy would waive theirs. I don't know how Kate would look at it. We could do better were we not in debt.

Once again, now at the age of seventy-four, H. H. Bancroft was facing two massive rebuilding projects. How did Matilda respond? We do not know. No letters from her exist in the family archives from December 1905 to January 1907, probably because most of the family was together during this period in San Francisco or Walnut Creek. We can only imagine that Matilda was exhibiting the fortitude with which she seemed to have faced other challenges. Surely she kept herself busy, tending to the family and helping her husband think through what lay ahead. In fact, H. H. Bancroft indicates how seriously he took his wife's views into consideration in often stating to Griffing, "If your mother approves ..."

Over time, various buildings were erected on the Sutter and Van Ness lot, including a car dealership and the Galaxy Theater. The property remained in the family until 2005.

Projects

Ever eschewing "ennui," Matilda participated in both family and civic improvement. In December 1886, while finessing the San Diego mansion, Matilda joined in a project to beautify the city, as many middle- and upper-class women did, holding a gathering of the Citizens' Association for Improving and Beautifying San Diego, a society like others cropping up across the country. She was made vice president. Matilda noted in the children's books that they planted many trees themselves in San Diego in February 1887 before they left the city in May for a year and a half (Griffing, 261–62).

Another scheme that Matilda nurtured years later developed after hearing a lecture by Jacob Riis in San Francisco. His book *How the Other Half Lives* galvanized consciousness across the United States about abysmal urban poverty.[22] Matilda sought some way to help alleviate the problem by using their land in San Diego, doing well by doing good. In the family archives in The Bancroft Library, a *San Diego Union* clipping from August 14, 1900, reported on the health benefits of life in San Diego. Eventually, these ideas coalesced. Matilda suggested improving life for the urban poor while capitalizing on San Diego's warm climate and the Bancroft's Helix Farm.

In September 1905, she wrote to Griffing about offering the Spring Valley farm as a kind of colony for the poor. "I am reading books on charities and the prevention of pauperism from the scientific point of view and get a great deal of help from them." In fact, she had dared to write to Mr. Riis himself. Her letter illustrates the effervescence—if impreciseness—of Matilda's ideas for a veritable "movement" on the family property (Sept. 10, 1905).

I have written to Mr. Jacob Riis a strong letter which I think will carry considerable weight and enlist his sympathy and help. I told him that when he was here in S.F., I attended his lecture and was very much impressed with his ideas regarding poverty and with the responsibility of the individual in relieving or rather minimizing it and with what an individual could do. That a great power for good was clear in my mind and I would explain it in detail.

Then I told him of our plan and that I thought nothing like it had ever been undertaken; for the preservation of the family and for the prevention of sickness and of consequent pauperism—that for the rich, for those who could pay, were pursuits and exercises and recreations provided, as well as for those dependent upon their own exertions—and that to carry out the ideas hundreds of acres would be necessary and a large amount of money.

Then I went on with an enthusiasm and faith in the project that I really feel and asked him if he wouldn't come out to California and father the plan, give the project his support and so make our philanthropists have confidence in it. Select its superintendent, organize the movement, secure the right medical direction for it, and place it on a firm footing. That the land, with every possibility, was secured; that one of the largest olive orchards in the state was available with enough distinct houses on it now to furnish homes for twenty people; that everything was in readiness for the master hand and that I believed he could make it second only in importance to his great work among the tenement homes in N.Y. I enclosed my card and told him I had written to Dr. E.E. [Edward Everett] Hale, Dr. Mackenzie, friends, and to Mr. Henry Phipps of Philadelphia to whom I was a stranger—I wish you would call in the library for Jacob Riis book on <u>How the Other Half Lives</u>, if you want to know about his work. . . .[23]

I believe when this once gets into the hands of strong men who believe in it, that it will make a great sensation and "an instanteous [*sic*] success" as they say of the Health Farm in Denver. Your father has been searching for a name and now suggests Helix Health Farm, which is good, don't you think so—for we want the idea of farm prominent. Wouldn't you like to take up the work in the East? . . . Your father says you could do it, if you should work at it as you have done at the roads. We'll see how my letters are met. I am sure you could interest [Episcopal bishop Joseph H.] Johnson of Los Angeles, and through him perhaps Mrs. Rindge, the $20,000,000 widow of Los Angeles.[24] Your father says you could form a company to run out an electric line there and lay a good road which a large colony would make necessary.

Your loving mother

This letter is extraordinary in many ways: Matilda analyzes the problem and provides a solution. She knows exactly to whom Griffing should speak. She has thought through the steps, the funding, and necessary support from influential people. She has even elicited a name for this "colony" from H.H., the Helix Health Farm. But her plan was entirely impractical given Griffing's lack of interest and because it depended on the intervention of Jacob Riis and the Episcopal bishop of Los Angeles. All to no avail.

A week later, Matilda again sought to enlist Griffing's support and that of others for this idea. In an undated letter to her husband she said, "I wrote both Dr [John H.] Musser and Dr [Charles K.] Mills that we should be pleased to know of some physicians or syndicate wanting to establish a sanitarium in San Diego and said that we had property there that was now available for that purpose etc."[25]

The idea had also occurred to Matilda of locating a sanitarium at the former Albatross Inn. In March 1905, she wrote to Griffing about the idea. "I am always talking up a Sanitarium for S.D.; I wish we could sell the Albatross Inn property for that purpose—ask Dr Whiting if you think best, if he knows of anyone who would consider it—for nervous or rheumatic troubles, bronchial or otherwise." Later she informed him, "Enclosed is the address of the Secretary or the officer of the Medical Convention that meets in Portland this summer. I should advise your writing someone connected with its management regarding the sanitarium proposition for Albatross Terrace" (undated).

Matilda had enthusiasm and vision, but as a woman, despite access to her husband's small fortune, she was limited in her ability to enact her vision. She lacked the independence to take action.

H.H. was skeptical of Matilda's enthusiasms. To Griffing in early 1904, he wrote derisively, "Your mother says sell the farm to the Salvationists. They say that Booth-Tucker is there now talking about adding his filthy fad to the nests of fanatics already there" (Jan. 13, 1904).[26]

A year-and-a-half later, however, Matilda had apparently convinced H.H. that the Spring Valley ranch *could* become a health resort. He now tried to get Griffing to gain the support of local men "to the effect that Spring Valley is peculiarly adapted for a health resort," but noted that they had to avoid the topic of tuberculosis if they wanted support. "We drop talking consumptives for the present. If they ask for what diseases, say rheumatism, nervous, bronchial, etc., nothing about consumptives just now." He emphasized that this was work for the young: "It seems to me that you have united here pretty much all that is required in the hands of young men who will work for it long & strong enough to achieve the fullest success" (July 17, 1905).

An alternative scheme of Matilda's was to create a "colony" of Italians on the Spring Valley ranch, modeled on the Italian Swiss Colony in Sonoma County's Alexander Valley. It may well have been H.H.'s idea, for his letter to Griffing of November 25, 1904, suggests getting Italian farmers to take over the ranch: "They could make a fortune there in olives alone; they understand olives, eat & sleep olives in their own country. . . . If there is such a thing as an Italian boss in SD or LA see him."

Reporting from her reading, Matilda provided even more grist for Griffing's mill. On February 5, 1905, she wrote to him from her St. Dunstan's apartment in San Francisco.

> It seems to me that the colonization scheme is one worth looking into, if you could do it earnestly while here. That article in the January <u>Sunset</u> on Italians is excellent,[27] and just as accidentally I ran across another almost as good; better in some respects, in the October number <u>World's Work</u>— suppose you go to the Library and look it up.
>
> It concluded with the account of Andrea Sbarboro's work in California[28]—"he comes out to S.F. as a poor boy alone. All along he has succeeded in rising and in helping others to rise—"his special mission is to encourage immigrants and particularly Italians to settle in this country and acquire by industry the ownership of their homes. He has carried out this purpose by organizing six loan associations and all have been successful from the start. He is the organizer of the purely Italian Swiss Agricultural Colony—gives employment to over a thousand people. He is president of the Italian-American bank and Chairman of the California Promotion Committee"—this is from that article on the "Italian in the US."

He is the man Paul met on the trip South and to whom
he wanted to introduce you. Now I believe you can work up a
colonizing scheme with him and your father, which will solve
the problem of the farm. Bring up some numbers of the New
Years Edition of the Union, some printed matter on olives and
mulberry and silk-worm matters and grape raising, and see if
you won't be in business immediately. That you are going East
may be a great help, for it may put you in touch with other
organizations there to work with the Promotion Committee.

We should all be so pleased if you could work this scheme
out. You are so familiar with the matter, with the farm, its
possibilities and its limitations, that I believe you can work it
out. It would be a great thing for San Diego which feels we
have so little public spirit. I am glad that you are stepping out
of it, if only for a vacation but work combined with the vacation is best yet. This may be quickly done, while the library is
a tremendous undertaking.

Lovingly your mamma

This letter captures some of Matilda's restless energy, fertile mind,
and public spirit. We also see Matilda's fervent desire to transfer her
dreams and schemes to a son who appears to have responded very little,
if at all, to her many plans, not only for social improvement but for his
own betterment. He serves as her proxy to fulfill her neglected dreams.

Matilda's plans for development of the Helix Farm never material-
ized. Over the years, as the city of Spring Valley continued to expand,
the Bancroft family eventually sold their land. The old adobe house
that preceded their arrival continues to stand, along with H.H.'s Rock
House, and the original spring continues to flow, albeit intermittently.
The site on Memory Lane is protected from encroaching businesses
by the Spring Valley Historical Society, housed in the Bancroft Ranch
Home, which hosts tours for school groups and others to keep the
history of that area very much alive.[29]

The Bancroft Library

The grand finale of Matilda's efforts was helping convince the authorities
of the University of California, Berkeley to buy her husband's library of

sixty thousand items on the Pacific West. The letters from 1905 indicate that Matilda played a pivotal role, which H.H. acknowledged.

H.H.'s library had featured prominently in the children's journals. In Griffing's book, she reported on the construction of the new brick library building in 1881, then far south of downtown San Francisco, at Valencia and Army Streets (now Cesar Chavez Street), where Bancroft moved his historical collection. "The new Library building has been an attractive spot to the children, as well as to their parents. They have had their wheelbarrows and shovels and have done their part toward leveling the grounds. Papa delights in having them there" (47).

Knowing the significance of the library to the outside world, Matilda explained the history of its construction. "I must explain that the land on which it is built was bought in June last, the purchase happening . . . on the very day of Philip's birth, June 29th . . . Papa went there frequently with the children, generally in a phaeton, one of the children driving, the other whip in hand." She added, "Papa wants the children to enjoy the library, and they certainly do. We shall cultivate flowers and trees and grass, and papa calculates upon exercising there himself enough in digging to gain considerable strength" (Griffing, 49). She mentioned the plan to plant three palm trees in front of library, one for each son.[30]

Bancroft's Library ca. 1882, courtesy of The Bancroft Library (BANC MSS 73/64 c)

By 1890 Bancroft had finished his *Works*, yet many more projects lay ahead of him, including the sale of his library to a larger institution, such as the California State Library, the New York Public Library, or the Library of Congress. In her letter of February 5, 1905, to Griffing, Matilda had noted that "the library is a tremendous undertaking." Indeed it was. By that date, H.H. had spent almost fifteen years seeking to sell his library, hoping to recoup, even partially, the money he had spent on it for over forty years: purchasing collections; paying the many assistants who helped rifle through bookstores, copy archives, and take dictations; and funding their travel, as well as his own.

Matilda not only followed her husband's efforts but made her own on his behalf, while also seeking to enlist her sons' help. She commended Griffing's efforts. "I am glad that you are attending to library matters and hope you may strike the right clue yet" (Feb. 16, 1905). In a letter three days later, however, her tone had more bite. Matilda included a newspaper clipping about the death of Honora Sharp (1845?–1905), who had left $200,000 for the improvement of San Francisco's Golden Gate Park.[31] Matilda suggested that Griffing find someone to donate funds in order to buy Bancroft's library.

> Your father feels that if you are on the alert for the opportunity, you may run across someone who would be glad to immortalize himself by establishing some library of Americana, and that if his own sons don't care for the business, who will? You must see the library and know something about it, for it does seem as though it ought not to go out of California and that in S.F. or Los Angeles or thereabout the right man or woman might be found—Take for instance this Mrs Sharp; that would have appealed to her as strongly as the Park if Mr [R. H.] Lloyd had urged it as strongly—and there are any number of women who don't know what to do with their money. (Feb. 19, 1905)

At the beginning of March, Matilda asked Griffing to convince Professor Max Farrand, head of the History Department at Stanford, to write a positive review of the library.[32]

> Just a note to enclose these matters regarding the Library—first that Dr Max Farrand has been at Stanford for four years,

head of its history dept; is granted a year's leave of absence in May—is going to Cornell to give there a course on the westward movement of the population and other subjects. Can't you get him to visit the Library and write it up, when you are in S.F.?

Your father will be pleased if you should get that work done by someone—

Then his donation seems most timely. You know and Mr Bristol knows that Brown Univ. has the finest collection of Americana in the country. It should have the Library—talk it over with Mr. Bristol. (Mar. 1, 1905)[33]

This effort failed, as did many others.

A viable opportunity finally appeared later in 1905, with the University of California. In the following letter, it is clear that Matilda had dealt with history professor Henry Morse Stephens previously:

I spoke to you about the sale of the library—it's still a possible thing. I was in Berkeley this afternoon talking with our friend (Prof. Stevens) [*sic*]....He did n't come over and so I went there.[34] He has just written to Gov. Pardee to try and arrange a dinner to meet some of the Regents—just the best way to work them up, he says. As he, the Governor, is chairman of the Regents, his approval would carry great weight.[35] Its individual appropriations, as I understand it [*sic*; unclear in the original]—or otherwise, the professor says, he will go to Sacramento by appointment. So he is in earnest; he says he feels sure of $100,000—possibly of $25,000 more but beyond that would be difficult.[36]

So you see it may amount to something and may not. (Aug. 30, 1905)

By September 1905, the library sale was nearly final. Matilda reveled that the purchase by the University of California would bring "glory to your father's name that he deserves and for all time."

I really think the library is as good as sold; your father isn't quite as confident for he has thought that before; this time the proposition is one that makes us proud and brings the glory to your father's name that he deserves and for all time. The library to be always kept as a whole as the Bancroft Library and brought up to date and as soon as convenient. It is hoped that there will be a Bancroft chair of Pacific Coast History established—and for all this two years' work and great enthusiasm, Prof. [Henry Morse] Stevens [*sic*] says, as your father talked of compensation, he wouldn't accept for it so much as a cigar; if any money was given he would turn it over to the University which "wouldn't do either of us any good." (Sept. 16, 1905)

Two months later, Matilda provided an update.

The Library matter is in good shape; it is to be presented favorably by the committee this week to the board of Regents. . . . Pres. [Benjamin Ide] Wheeler invited us over to Berkley [*sic*] to see the University and take lunch with them—we had a charming time—all these attentions are very suggestive of appreciation and good fellowship. (Nov. 12, 1905)

An undated 1905 letter from Matilda was tucked in with the December letters from that year. "Library matter running smoothly—everything most promising tho' not yet decided—little doubt on the part of anybody as to result and as to the great honor conferred to the Bancroft name forever and forever."[37]

To H.H.'s credit, he gave his *wife* credit for her contributions to the sale of the library, exhorting his son Griffing in September 1905 to live up to his mother's example of hard work. "In a word, work—as . . . your mother [does] in selling library & farm" (Sept. 22, 1905).

In February 1906, H.H. wrote to Griffing about another real estate deal that his sister Emily was managing in San Diego: "It is possible after all that she will beat any of us selling SD property, just as your mother did selling library. HHB" (Feb. 8, 1906).

Berkeley's Bancroft Library is one of the enduring legacies of the Bancroft family, a plan that ultimately did manifest in an institution for all the world to use and enjoy. We owe much to Matilda Griffing Bancroft for her own contribution.

CHAPTER TWELVE

"Most Beloved of Women"

To come full circle in the story of Matilda as writer, we end where her writing began, in discussing her thirty-four-year marriage and the family that blossomed from that relationship. The journals she wrote during her early married life and travels, the memory books for her children, and the letters to and from H.H. together portray a woman devoted to her intellectual, driven, and mercurial husband, from whom she received ardent devotion in return for her own intellect, ambitions, and equanimity.

In *Literary Industries*, H. H. Bancroft wrote that he "longed to do great things." Matilda was equal to him in enterprise, but had to sublimate her own ambitions to the work of her husband and sons. H.H. gave her free rein when it came to overseeing the children's education, participating in his history work, and managing their properties. The two were true helpmates. Their relationship is a crazy quilt comprising pieces made from their varied writings: passages cut from the cotton mundanity of daily life observations; others, pieces of soft velvet tenderness; some rough burlap rants; and a few elegant, silky elegies.

Devoted Father

This exploration of Matilda's relationship with her husband begins with their shared parenting and his role as father, a respected "papa."

Surely wishing for children, she must have hoped that Hubert would be a caring and responsible father. As parents know, however, a couple's bond can be tested in the sleepless nights when infants fuss, or during the fright of caring for a sick child, or when facing the burdens of home and school, or when clashing over the best methods for instilling personal values.

The letter that H.H. wrote to the parents of his first wife upon the death of his and Emily's newborn daughter indicated that he had hoped for more children. Through Matilda, we see how H. H. Bancroft excelled as a father to their four offspring. Matilda's expectations for him were likely formed by the example of her own father, who had died in 1869. She memorialized for her children the grandfather they never knew:

> He would enter into all our interests, studies and pleasures
> with the same enthusiasm we felt, stimulating our improve-
> ment by questions and information, at the table particularly.
> Any expense for education was made with greatest pleasure,
> as indeed was every necessary outlay cheerfully incurred,
> although in our large family of seven children economy
> was duly inculcated in every direction but that of tuition.
> (Griffing, 3–4)

Matilda would expect Hubert to emulate that same parental dedication.

And he appeared to do just that. Matilda often reported how eagerly he would play with his young children. Matilda described Papa's visit when she and the children lived in the Napa Valley north of San Francisco. "Papa has been over here several times and always devotes his whole day to the babies. He has taken them down to the brook, and shoes and stockings off, has let them wade in the water to their great delight" (Griffing, 27). On another occasion, she emphasizes their mutual devotion. "Papa with us almost all the time in Oakville, spend-ing only a day or two of each week in the city, always returning laden with fruit and good things generally from the city. He devoted himself to the children and they to him" (Griffing, 38).

Once when Matilda had to go to San Diego to check on the build-ing project there, she left H.H. with the children in Walnut Creek. "He takes so much pleasure in being with the children on the farm, and wrote me of the comfort they were to him all the time" (Philip, 166).

However, H.H. learned his limits after keeping the rambunctious older boys on his own.

> He proposed that he should keep the children a few days after Theresa and I left Oakville, and though I remonstrated, he undertook it. Griffing was more than he bargained for, I imagine. But he took both children at night, dressing and undressing them. One day sufficed for a life-time, and he brought them back at short notice. (Griffing, 39)

The fact that H.H. was so much fun with his young children is intriguing, considering that later in life he became rather stodgy (as many of us do). He found ingenious ways to entertain the children, as when small Philip played "pretend" with his father: "He and his father carry on long conversations while Philip calls himself Mr. Jones. Papa asks about his wife and his children, his cars and his horses, and Mr. Jones is enchanted with the dialogue" (Philip, 78).

Another characteristic was Papa's generosity to his children in small ways and large. "Papa's custom is always to bring molasses candy and peanuts to the children that he gets on the boat, which I think they will always remember in connection with his homecoming" (Lucy, 102). He pampered them with gifts and adventures.

> On New Years day 1885 papa took us all to Ventura and bought for the children a big wagon which is a grand thing for them here; Philip had a smaller one and a baby horse on wheels, and with a fine drive each way and a wagon filled with toys, they had another joyous time. Papa is very indulgent to the little ones. He has taken the children all out on horseback repeatedly. (Griffing, 188)

For a Victorian gentleman, H.H. was surprisingly affectionate while they were "little ones," demanding the attention he willingly gave, even to the most boisterous Griffing, who was

> devoted to his papa. . . . He will crow and jump and make every effort to attract his attention, and if he isn't taken up by papa, will cry a most heart-broken disappointed cry. Papa will take "Jim," as he calls him, and the little fellow will nestle his

> face in his shoulder at once, as though settled down for a real
> good time. (Griffing, 19)

When Lucy and Paul became seasick on the ship to San Diego,
H.H. showed patience *and* humor:

> Papa went back to S.F. and soon returned with Griffing and
> Lucy. They came by steamer and poor little Lucy was sick
> every moment of the way. This was the first time that either
> Lucy or Paul had had such an experience; in both cases not a
> thing was retained on their stomachs until they reached San
> Diego. Papa's ability as a nurse was tested to its utmost; Lucy
> lay in his arms most of the time, he says, very patient, only
> asking frequently for water "so as to have something to throw
> up." (Lucy, 129–30).

H. H. Bancroft's Character-Building Industries

Bancroft's grand accomplishments indicate his enormous strength of
character. Matilda's journals hint at his workhorse energy and accompanying domineering personality. One story portrays his obstinacy and
self-righteousness—even when combating California's former governor, who seemed to be stealing the family's reserved room on a steamer
heading south from San Francisco.

> We found the stateroom we had engaged was already occu-
> pied with trunks and people. Papa skirmished round and
> declared that, governor or no governor, he must give us the
> room for which we had paid and held the receipt. After con-
> siderable excitement on both sides, ex-governor Downey . .
> . exhibited his ticket, found he was in the wrong room, and
> was obliged to rectify his mistake. We had very little time
> to settle it, and papa was afraid he should have to leave the
> steamer without knowing whether we had a room or not. . . .
> He is positive enough under such circumstances and will get
> what he is entitled to, though he despises such experiences.
> (Griffing, 130–31)

Matilda expected her children to be fighters as well.

One of the most positive values that H.H. and Matilda passed along was a passion for the countryside. They served as role models for healthy living. "Now we are ... going to San Rafael for about three months, to benefit the health of the family generally, but [for] papa in particular, who seems to suffocate almost for country air" (Griffing, 29). To provide his family with this country living, H.H. daily walked two miles to the train in San Rafael, which would take him to the ferry for San Francisco. Upon his return, Matilda and the boys walked to meet him at 4:30 in the afternoons. Matilda often noted how both parents incorporated regular exercise into each day, from walks along country lanes to horseback riding far out into the hills.

While H.H. indulged his children with gifts and play, he also sought to instill a taste for hard work, including physical labor. He had learned the value of industry growing up on a farm in rural Ohio, where even small children helped from sun up to sun down. Yet he knew that play could be incorporated into work, like Tom Sawyer enticing other boys to whitewash a fence for him. When stacking wood, "Papa joins in with the children, and they make play out of real work" (Griffing, 293). Or when the family went to Pine Cañon in search of grapevines for the porch of their log cabin, "Papa makes a picnic out of every such trip" (Griffing, 380). A trickster, H.H. could make work pleasurable.

Consistently, Matilda noticed how her husband wanted to strike a balance between the comforts of a good life and a strong work ethic: "He wants them to be industrious and fond of work. I think he will succeed for they never are at loss for occupation" (Griffing, 370). Finally, Matilda understood how her husband's hopes for his children contrasted with his own childhood hardships. "Papa says he intends that their recollection of this place shall be the very pleasantest; that his remembrance of his boyhood is one of sadness, but theirs must be a bright happy picture" (Griffing, 284). These qualities in her husband made her love him all the more.

H.H.'s Literary Industries en Famille

In her children's memory books, Matilda infused a sense of awe about their father's rugged regimen, of which she too was in awe. In her journal of their first year together, Matilda noted that on a camping trip to Cloverdale, he only cared to spend time reading and writing, not hunting or socializing. In later years Matilda remarked to her children how "Papa" carried a manuscript with him everywhere, even on family vacations. At a resort in Napa Soda Springs in 1882, "We have ordered a tent, which Papa will use as his, specially for writing and perhaps to sleep in. He is now writing and revising the History of Mexico. The children seem to understand perfectly they are never to touch any of his papers, and never do so" (Griffing, 66–67). Even on vacations, such as the one in Tahoe mentioned later, H.H. kept writing. He was so genuinely obsessed with work that simply sitting in thought was a rarity.

> Papa's coming to remain a week was looked forward to and welcomed with wild delight. He was intent on giving the children pleasure, and while he continued working hard he would steal off a little time every day for them. Indeed he combines work and babies wonderfully; he will take his manuscript and all the boys down to the beach, find the very best place for them to play in, and toil away in a shady [place] to work over proofreading or writing, something, anything, but it's work.
>
> There was one day weeks after this, when we were at Alameda . . ., when papa sat for an hour in a carriage holding the reins in front of the hotel while we were at dinner, and simply thinking. He said it was years since he had been unoccupied that length of time. It seemed strange to me to see him sit there so long without a paper or book in his hand. He had lived in that vicinity when Kate was a little girl, and he probably took that one hour to live over the past. Even on the cars and boat, travelling back and forth daily, he was always at work, regardless of anyone. (Griffing, 115–16)

One can also imagine that shy H.H., always reticent in company, found refuge in his work. Matilda described his discomfort when the family had to share meals in the public dining room of a boardinghouse. "Papa didn't like it very much and didn't take his meals with us very often. He don't like to wait or have to talk with people" (Griffing, 230–31). Being pressed for work was a good excuse to escape from unwanted conversations.

The children's journals not only illuminate their father's industry but also portray the social recognition he had gained as a historian. In 1883, Matilda recounted their reception on the way home from Lake Tahoe: "We returned to the vicinity of SF, stopping at Carson, Virginia City and Reno. Papa was shown a great deal of attention on account of his position as the historian of this coast" (Philip, 44).

All that work! What of leisure? Matilda does let slip a wistful desire that her husband might spend more playtime with *her*:

> I wish my boys could have any conception of how he works night and day. And all this pleasure trip he has brought his ms. (manuscript) along and worked over it so much as to make me feel unhappy sometimes that he would not take time for a row with me, or a little fishing. The truth is he enjoys work and doesn't enjoy rowing or pleasuring.
>
> And at Alameda, which was our next destination, he would go back and forth every day, ms. or proofs in hand, correcting and revising on the boat or cars, and never resting one moment. Then he would come home, catch up Phil and take him to the table for his company, and give him an ear of corn or anything else the child wanted, for his supper was already through with. Then quiet follows, and he works again over his papers after a very busy day, as long as he can keep up; then with a cigar, and I reading aloud to him a novel or whatever else is selected, there comes the first rest and quiet. This lasts for sometime after he has gone to bed.
>
> I don't believe anyone can work as he does, unless from their childhood up, they are accustomed to it. (Philip, 44–47)

Matilda surely agreed that hard work in their youth would prepare her children for a life of fruitful labor themselves, but their father's unceasing focus and labor had to be as intimidating as it might have been inspiring.

Note that Matilda only mentions her boys. Daughter Lucy would have no need to "work" at anything, though Matilda herself worked hard as mother, writer, and businesswoman—but not for pay.

Matilda's promotion of her husband's works endured for years and in many venues. In a 1905 letter to Griffing, she described a gathering of the American Anthropological Association, where she met George

Wharton James, a Methodist minister who had written many books on California history.

> He has been in Pasadena and has written your father in high-
> est appreciation of his work—and wants to meet him; he says,
> as so many others I met at the Anthropological meeting, that
> he could not get along without constant study of his works
> and wants to acknowledge his indebtedness in what he is
> going to publish on the Missions. (Nov. 12, 1905)[1]

How marvelous that Matilda attended the meeting herself, getting an education as well as cultivating an intellectual social network.

Mutual Love and Caregiving

Beyond Matilda's adulation of her husband in their children's journals, her devotion took other forms, including muted love and overt efforts to aid and comfort him in sickness and in disaster. Perhaps because of Victorian mores or simply due to their serious natures, Matilda and Hubert did not allow for romantic flourishes in their missives. More-over, few of Matilda's letters to H.H. survived at all, but some hints of sentiment provide an image of their steadfast love—complicated, like the couple, and abiding.

One such intimation appears in September 1883 when Matilda bemoaned that she and the younger children could not join H.H. on a trip to Mexico. Only his older daughter Kate would accompany him. Matilda shared her sorrow: "The trip by railroad and stage would be too severe for the children [so] my going was not to be considered. Papa went resolutely on with his plans, but we both had heart sinkings at the thought of the possibilities" (Lucy, 30–31).

Journeys with her husband would be superb bonding experiences, but Matilda had to put her children first. Elsewhere she wrote about this same separation, emphasizing her love of adventure balanced against concern for her children and for her husband.

> Never in my life have I felt a greater disappointment; if I had
> gone, I should have had to leave the children; that I could not
> do, and so my precious ones you must be to me everything

while your pap is enjoying without me sights I long to see; while, perhaps, without me he is ill, low-spirited, or in danger, and I am all unconscious of it so far away. Pray God we may indeed be brought safely together again in his own good time. (Griffing, 125–26)

In an 1890 letter from San Francisco to H.H., who had spent three weeks in San Diego with Griffing and Philip, Matilda wrote: "I am glad you are thinking of starting on the 15th. You have been away long enough. I long to have you all here. . . . Much love, Matilda" (Feb. 10, 1890). She certainly missed her children, but she also noted her "long enough" separation from her husband.

Hubert rarely shared his feelings for Matilda, though he typically signed his letters "Lovingly HHB" or "Your loving husband." However, a sense of his dependence on her and his children comes through in this letter from October 19, 1886, still only months after his beloved Bancroft Building had burned to the ground in April, and H.H. was battling depression. "You see, coming away from you all, & alone, & cold and sick, naturally I get blue."

Hubert also showed his love for Matilda by trying to lighten the burdens *she* carried. His letters implicitly reflect her more vulnerable side, which she rarely inscribed in her children's journals. Two months after the horrible Bancroft Building fire, H.H. wrote: "You are a very good woman, Matilda, and are standing up splendidly under this great affliction, which seems greater and greater to me every day. But you don't tell me of your head-aches and heart-aches" (June 16, 1886). Perhaps she did not want to burden him with her own troubles, yet he recognized that she had them.

In an undated letter, but probably from 1887, H.H. declares: "Lord of love, Matilda, don't worry so. Care killed the cat." In another missive, he encouraged her to find pleasure in her vigilance at the farm. "I am glad to have you look after the farm a little, but you must make it pleasure, not work" (Jan. 29, 1889). Three months later, H.H. admonished Matilda to lighten her load by getting a proper governess: "What is the use, my dear, of taking life so hard & killing yourself. It is a small matter whether the children have a governess; send them to the public school" (May 6, 1889). The next day he added a not very sympathetic postscript, making light of her ungovernable children:

In the meantime don't you think you are piling on that agony.
. . . You say the children are not governed. Then why do you
not govern them? You are bigger and stronger than they. You
lament my absence from the farm before you have been three
days; before you have been there much over a fortnight, I
shall be there. There is nothing terrible in this. It is not a matter of life & death to have a governess on that day. I will get
you one when I go to SF. I do not like the tutor idea just now.

You are comparatively a young woman . . . with nothing on
earth to make yourself miserable over. So dry up your tears &
hysterics & be sensible.

Your loving husband, HHB
(May 7, 1889)

Even today the charge of being "hysterical" is used to deprecate
women who exhibit strong and supposedly unwarranted emotion.
Considering the measured tone of Matilda's extant letters, it's hard to
imagine her getting overwrought very often. And of course Matilda
always had servants to help with the children and housekeeping, relieving her of many burdens.[2] Still, H.H. did wish her more peace.

"A Devilish Good Woman"

H.H. used the above phrase about Matilda in a letter to Griffing (May 2,
1906), regarding her "endorsing" H.H.'s business strictures of Griffing.
An odd phrase, it captures a fierce respect that H.H. had for his wife
in whom he had found much to love. And Matilda's writing reveals her
"devilish good" character, necessary for coping with a headstrong husband; five children; several large family properties; many long journeys
en famille; and various projects, from literary to real estate, for which
she assumed responsibility or played a significant role. She had a big
heart, simply put.

Of so many commitments that Matilda honored, sharing an intellectual life with her husband was crucial, as evidenced in this story
from September 1882.

I did not remain in bed a week, though I was imprudent. I
received visitors in my room, and even in the parlor when

baby was but two weeks old. . . . Philip was seven weeks old
before Mrs McGowan [the nurse] left me; this time she left
me when her month was up, that is when baby was two weeks
old. I had been several times to the table and was impatient to
be free from the nurse. I had already resumed reading aloud
to papa, and was reading first criticisms on the new history.
(Lucy, 5–6)

Working with H.H. was vital to her, even when it meant "abandoning" the children to their mischief. One time while Matilda was busy
working on a manuscript with Papa, the children had an egg fight in
the henhouse and overturned tomato plants (Griffing, 77). Their she-
nanigans discovered, it was Matilda who had to dispense justice, while
H.H. calmly returned to his editing work.

Matilda served as the proverbial angel of the household, smooth-
ing out life for everyone. Her mother, Mary Matilda Griffing, noticed
how capable her daughter "Tillie" was. Mother Griffing had arrived
in late September 1881 with Matilda's sister Mary, a few months after
Philip's birth, June 30. "The next two months we spent in Tillie's home.
Tillie did anything in her power to have us enjoy ourselves. We spent
a delightful winter. . . . She gave a large reception for us and also some
dinner companies" (2).[3] But Matilda's sweetest devotion was to her
husband and his work: "She is very much interested in her husband's
writings and takes the greatest satisfaction in reading and writing with
him" (11).

As we've seen throughout her journals and H.H.'s letters, Matilda
went to great efforts for everyone's comfort. In her relationship with
her in-laws, a rare comment to her own credit enables us to see how
well she had bonded with them. In November 1881, Grandmother
Lucy Bancroft fell, which led to her demise and death the following
February 1882. "I really loved her, and she loved me and my little ones
sincerely. She was so proud of your father, my boys; and well she might
be! She always told us that I 'was sent to Hubert in answer to prayer'"
(Philip, 10).

In later years Matilda continued to care for the elders in the family
and encouraged her children to do so as well. "Please see your Aunt
Emily[4] and show her some kind of attention—she is sick and lonely.
Offer her books to read. I will gladly contribute some to your library

for that purpose if you will send me a list of what you want" (undated 1907 letter to Griffing).

Facing the Biggest Challenge Together

The burning of the Bancroft Building in San Francisco in April 1886 was reported in chapter 11 as it related to Matilda in her role as a family real estate manager. Her handling of the San Diego construction at that time ignited H.H.'s fiery temperament in his fear of financial ruin. He agonized over reimbursements from his insurance policy in endless negotiations, while also producing volumes of his history based on materials rescued from the fire, and sought funds to finish building the family home in San Diego.

Despite the disaster and H.H.'s eruptions, the couple's gentler care for one another peeks through and provides a different lens for appreciating the emotional underpinning of their relationship. H.H.'s letters to Matilda reflect the *mutual* support they offered each other. H.H. knew that Matilda, too, suffered. His ultimate optimism and love for her sustained them both.

> First of all Matilda, it won't do, it won't do at <u>all</u> for either you or me to weaken now, to look too much on the dark side. Yesterday, Sunday, was one of the hardest days I ever lived through in my life. I went out to the library as I do every Sunday morning. I tried to work, or rather I did work in spite of everything. There was some Rock & Rye & a bottle of Hub Punch & a corkscrew & tumbler, all there nice and handy, & I knew some of it would do me good. But I was afraid to touch it & I did'nt. I knew if I did at this stage of the game, that I was a goner, and I thought of you & the children and said to myself, after all, what is a little suffering on my part in comparison to clearing up something for you and the children. So I went back to my tonic and kept on with my work. I feel better today. I will do as you say, take a warm salt bath three times a week. . . . Now for you it is just as important. . . . You must learn to throw off from your mind wearying trouble. Do every day, quietly and calmly, the best you can for that day & let the next day take care of itself. (June 21, 1886)

In August of that year in one of his more poignant letters, H.H. spoke of his depression. He was both unburdening himself to his wife as well as allaying her worry about him.

> But Matilda dear; things are not always as they seem, and
> they do not always seem the same, & they are not always
> the same. . . . For example, I thought yesterday & day before
> that death had called for me, but to-day I found out that he
> had'nt. For several days past I have been open to a full real-
> ization of the fact that my stand-by tonic, which has served
> me such a good turn—in my imagination at least—during
> the past four months, and which may be called the Essence of
> Concentrated Thunder, was gradually losing its grip on me or
> I on it.

So H.H. came up with another remedy: "a quart a day of quinine in pills, and the tincture of strychnine & iron mixed." Finally, he could say he was "feeling first rate again" (Aug. 31, 1886).

Always in Hubert's mind was the desire to provide well for his wife and children; yet he was also realistic about his limitations, life's limita- tions, as they loomed over him in the drawn-out process of rebuilding, along with the ongoing work of writing, publishing, and selling (can- vassing) his histories.

> You must not feel bad—my love. All the moments with me
> are not always and altogether happy. But I am just as virtuous
> all the same, Matilda. And we must content ourselves to be
> happy any way. When things go bad, I say, What is life? What
> does it all amount to? I shall die soon, and when I do you
> will not have to canvass for books. I will fix up things a little
> better if I live a little longer, if not, they are not so very bad
> now—much better than one in a thousand leave them." (Feb.
> 9, 1887)

Maintaining a positive attitude was simply his modus operandi. With his abundant energy—despite the roller-coaster ride of his mood swings—Bancroft drove forward all his plans.

Defending the Daughters

So many of Bancroft's ulterior plans concerned his *sons*. In Matilda's journal for Philip, she affirms her sons' higher status in their father's eyes. Following the fire, Matilda explained why Papa felt strongly about rebuilding his store in light of what he wanted to provide for his sons.

> He would save it for his own sake, and because his boys in years to come might be glad that their father had prepared for them so good an opening for a business life. Papa feels, however, that the future will determine the boys' career, rather than anything he may do. Only he prepares the place, in case it is wanted. He has often said that it is a magnificent career for a young man, that of an orator or statesman, to study the moral questions of the day, and to be able to stir the people to reform with a statesman's reasoning.
>
> We will give our boys the benefit of a good education, a speaking and thorough knowledge of modern languages, the benefits of travel in our own and foreign countries, and then we shall hope they will pursue careers in which we share and take pride. (Philip, 162–63)

H. H. Bancroft's sentiments on the potentially resplendent future of his sons provide a good segue to a final topic about the couple's relationship, as well as an intriguing aspect of Matilda's legacy to her stepdaughter Kate and daughter Lucy, for she also sought to defend their right to financial security.

H. H. Bancroft had a well-deserved reputation among his descendants for favoring males over females (not to mention Protestant whites over other races). He admitted to refusing to hire women for his research and writing enterprise. He stated in his autobiography that "frail and tender" women were less capable of the physical demands of writing than men. Nevertheless, Bancroft *did* employ one woman, Frances Fuller Victor from Oregon, who not only wrote much of his volume on that state but later brought suit against him for not properly crediting her for that and other works.[5]

A typical man of his time, H. H. Bancroft had little awareness of the potential for educated women to undertake intellectual and professional careers. If men were to take care of their wives, financially and otherwise, women had no need of a formal education beyond high school, nor did they require a family inheritance beyond basic support, since a future husband would supposedly provide for his wife. However, many men of his time enthusiastically supported the expansion of women's colleges and women's roles throughout society.

Ironically, H.H.'s own wife disproved his stance on the valuable and diverse contributions that women could offer, not just within the family but to society as well.

Matilda was clearly aware of her husband's prejudice. She noted her husband's patriarchal attitudes in the preface to daughter Lucy's memory book after her birth in 1882 (as explained earlier but bears repeating here): "I think papa perhaps places undue appreciation on boys, and our little one must grow into his heart and so wind herself into his love that he will wonder how he ever could think slightingly of girls" (2). Perhaps with some sorrow, Matilda reported her husband's bland acknowledgment of the arrival of a girl child in Lucy's diary: "He accepts the gift without expression of pleasure or disappointment, merely saying 'I am satisfied if you are,' but with the announcement 'it's a boy,' there is no concealing his satisfaction" (3).

A curious piece of family lore regarding Lucy's birth was passed along over subsequent decades and repeated by Margaret Wood Bancroft, the second wife of Lucy's older brother Griffing. Margaret reported: "When it came to the three boys who were born within a few years, and then his daughter Lucy, the story goes that [H.H.] said to his wife, 'Now if you're going to act that way, I'm not going to have any more children.' And they didn't" (154).[6]

In his letters to Matilda over the years, H.H.'s enthusiasm for the boys never dimmed. "Tell me about the boys, the chickens, and everything" (May 9, probably 1886). Nor did his emphasis on the future opportunities the boys would receive, drummed into them while still children, such as when H.H. wrote regarding the History Company: "There will be a business for your boys!" (Aug. 31, 1886). In later years, H.H. wrote to Griffing about his "blue" moods, but shared how he buoyed himself: "I get blue & cross, but how can a man be really unhappy with three as good boys as I have" (Nov. 22, 1899).

H. H. Bancroft's daughter-in-law Margaret Wood Bancroft recounted, "He said the men in the family would take care of the women" (154).[7] Matilda, however, insisted on ensuring that both her daughter and stepdaughter would have financial support throughout their lives.

H.H. did leave small properties and business interests to his daughters and arranged for them to receive fixed annuities.

In some of Matilda's papers, she refers to arrangements she pursued on behalf of her daughters. Kate had been separated from her husband, Charles O. Richards, and then went to live in Europe for some years with their daughters, Ruth and Katherine. When the 1906 earthquake struck, she returned immediately to California, but lived in San Diego. Because Griffing, too, ended up there, he became the de facto caretaker of Kate's affairs. In a 1905 letter to H.H., Matilda requested that Griffing arrange to give Kate property. "I would like to have him give Kate some property outright, so that while dealing justly by Kate and Lucy we shouldn't have to increase the annuities" (Oct. 8, 1905). One might interpret this as a sign that Matilda too was watching the family coffers, not wishing to give the girls a "raise." Having property in one's own name would allow the recipient to sell it if necessary and take advantage of rising property values, whereas a fixed income might not keep up with inflation.

In a letter shortly after his seventieth birthday in 1902, H.H. explained to Griffing the testamentary arrangements he had made for his five children:

> You need have no hesitation at any time to ask me about my will or any of my affairs. They are pretty well settled. I give all, or practically all, to you three boys, subject to $5000 a year each to your mother, Kate & Lucy, for the payment of which the History building is pledged. . . .
>
> This is a good will for you boys, as it gives you the property, while the women get only life income, though a liberal one. Your mother however has a good deal of her own; her will is similar to mine. I regard it as a just will, otherwise I could not live a day with it as it is. I could not live or die in peace knowing that I was influenced by ill-feeling toward any one of my children in my consideration of their interests. (May 7, 1902)

In another letter to Griffing (probably from 1906), H.H. berated Griffing's lack of industry (as he often did), and then spoke of how Matilda advocated for their daughters—as if the comparison would engage Griffing's sense of responsibility by comparison.

If you imagine that you get scant recognition for your efforts at SD [San Diego], what do I get for mine? You make me feel sometimes that you regarded it as your right for me to spend a life of economy & work & self-denial in your service & you do nothing for me in return. True, I have never asked you to do anything for me, but only for yourself, as less tobacco-poisoning & lazy luxurious living & more law oratory etc. as first agreed. All the same you get your living out of me consulting only your own will & pleasure. I have thus far placed you on a par with the other boys, securing to the three of you two magnificent income paying properties . . . to the exclusion of your mother & sister, whom I love & respect.

Why? What do I get for it, for thus laying the results of my life at your feet—a life of 50 years of continuous labor, almost every day from 6 am to 10 pm with no end of scrimping & self-sacrifice—marrying at 27, after earning with my own head & hands $10,000 & being in a position of my own making to support a family. . . .

As a matter of fact, *your mother thinks I should do more for Lucy & Kate*, [italics mine] & again, so do I. It might even things up some to give Lucy the store & 226 & Kate block 9 but then it would be a long time before you boys would get any money from St D or Hist bld to jingle in your pockets. (Undated, probably 1906, before the earthquake)[8]

Despite her husband's perceptions of female limitations, Matilda turned out to be a capable writer and outstanding business manager, but she herself was no feminist, at least in terms of women's suffrage or other political rights for women. In fact, she seemingly agreed with some notions about inherent gender differences, such as in this story of Leonie, a nurse who left soon after being hired: "My nurse showed the weakness of feminine nature, yielded to the importunities of her boy husband and returned to her penniless home" (Lucy, 7). Matilda also had her contradictions, a woman of her class and time.

"Most Beloved of Women!" Matilda's Life, Death, and Legacy

In a letter to Matilda at the end of the turbulent year 1886, H.H. lauded his wife's report and accounting from San Diego, calling her "most beloved of women!" He continued with an account of his cold, offering some of his characteristic dry wit.

> You need not trouble yourself about my cold in the least. It is better, and I am doctoring for all I am worth. . . . If the Good Lord is still so crazy for my society as not to be able to leave me in peace here & calls me home, I do not see but that you will have to be satisfied with another husband. Of course it will not be as good as the present one. . . . But with your position and prospects, you should be able to pick up some one. (Dec. 11, 1886)

Despite his mock threats of dying sooner than his wife—and he *was* sixteen years older—sadly, Matilda would die years before her husband, on August 10, 1910, of "angina pectoris," a heart attack. A short death notice was published in the *San Francisco Call* on August 9, 1910:

> ### Mrs. Hubert Bancroft Dies At Home
> ### Mother of Supervisor Succumbs to Long Illness
>
> Mrs. Matilda Griffin [*sic*] Bancroft, wife of Hubert Howe Bancroft and mother of supervisor Paul Bancroft, died at her home at 2898 Jackson street, yesterday morning after an illness of two years' duration. Mrs. Bancroft, who was a native of New Haven, Connecticut, was 63 years of age. She was prominent in charitable work, was a member of the board of directors of the San Francisco maternity home and of the Century Club. Beside her husband and son named, she leaves another son Paul [*sic*—there were two other sons, Griffing and Philip], a daughter Lucy, and a sister Josephine C. Griffin.[*sic*]

No references in the family archives help us understand the "long illness" referred to in the *Call* notice, and no other obituary is known. In 1889, while in San Diego, Matilda had had a presentiment that she would die of something like a stroke or heart attack after having had a "close call" with paralysis or a stroke. In Lucy's book she described the symptoms thus: "I was suddenly prostrated, and my tongue thickened so it was unpleasant to talk; other symptoms such as numbness, showing themselves, we knew it was no light matter" (137). The instigation appeared to Matilda to be the stress of entertaining hordes of children and adults.

> We decided to give a party and on the 1st of March had several hundred people gathered in the Institute building which was beautifully decorated for the occasion. We sent to San Francisco for some of the decorations Miss Bates uses, and with bunting, Chinese lanterns, orange boughs and flowers, the effect was most charming. Rooms downstairs with card tables and upstairs arranged for dancing gave everybody opportunity for enjoyment. A little later I gave a children's party in Sister Kate's house which was most delightful to the little ones. Then the boys went to the Farm, for all this was preparatory to our breaking up and going to S.F. All this time Grandmamma and Aunties were at the Florence Hotel.
>
> The consequence of such much social excitement and responsibility of various kinds, was that I was suddenly taken very ill. Papa was in Colorado on a business trip; I had a very severe headache, but went down town to work it off; it increased so much that I came right home and went to bed and sent for the doctor. All my symptoms threatened paralysis; and for two weeks I was in bed. It was a "close call" as Dr Edwards said, and I know very well that it was. I expect to die that way sometime but will not complain if it only will cut me off at once and not leave me a paralyzed wreck. But I want a more rational excuse for illness than parties give. (Griffing, 359–60)

What a coolly calculated analysis of her brush with paralysis and death! And as ever, the hint of her sardonic humor in hoping to have a better rationale for a stroke than throwing parties.

In 1907, H.H. wrote to Griffing implying that heart disease ran in Matilda's family. "Your mother is not at all well. She is liable to go off at any moment like her mother or sister" (fragment from 1907).

A telling account from the oral history of Matilda's daughter-in-law Margaret Wood Bancroft provides a sense of the demands put on Matilda in the context of her relationship with H.H.—"He was a very restless person"—and how *her* body ultimately suffered.

> He was very active. . . . He had this bad asthma. When it would come on him [in San Francisco], he would have his horse saddled, ride it down to the ferry, go across, and ride all the way to Walnut Creek, which took him part of the day. Then Matilda would follow in the buckboard with a driver, or tutor, or governess, whichever they had, and the children. They'd stay over there for maybe five or six days. Then he'd get another attack of asthma, and he'd go back, reverse it. They would make long trips in the buggy, and then later on with an automobile. They [drove] all the way . . . from San Francisco to Santa Barbara, one time. Just a retinue. At that time, they had two buggies and horses, and two of the children riding. . . .
>
> It was a hard life for her. And she was very small. They always had to put a box under her feet because her feet couldn't get down to the ground. Yet you read that book that I found there at the farm one day about their visit to Mexico [*Our Winter in Mexico*; see chapter 6]. I thought that was a charming book. You can see the energy that she put into those things, but it wore her out. I think she was in her early sixties when she died. She kept up with him. (36–37)

Worn out! That's the best evaluation we can take from Matilda Bancroft's own stories.

No depiction of Matilda's last days or description of her family's responses to their loss have been located. In fact, an enormous gap exists in the Bancroft family archives from April 1909 to January 1915. The paucity of information about Matilda at the end of her life seems odd, her husband being the writer and archivist he was. For a woman who had given so much to her family—especially her loving, observant,

Matilda Bancroft with her grandson Paul Bancroft Jr., July 1910, shortly before her
death, courtesy of Kim Bancroft

and thoughtful words—the silence about Matilda Griffing Bancroft at
the end of her life leaves a barren void.

Since no letters from that period have survived, it may well be that
none were ever written, with the family gathered together to be with
her, with their father, and with one another. The family home must

have been drenched in great sorrow, for Matilda's loving kindness surely gained her children's affection, as we know she had her husband's adoration. And given the intellectual and emotional intimacy evident between husband and wife, we can also imagine that H.H. was devastated by Matilda's loss. He had thought for so many years that he would be nurtured in his old age by his younger wife, who would survive him. It was not to be.

In his letters in the years following her death, before his own in 1918, H.H. made but two glancing references to this "most beloved of women." He wrote to Griffing that he had not ignited the furnace in his San Francisco home in the five years since Matilda had died.

> I am getting through the winter better than I expected & if my good health continues I shall be glad to have you & the children for a visit here any time after 1st of March, or when warm weather comes, as this house is too cold & draughty in the halls & the furnace not going. I have'nt had it going since your mother's time. (Jan. 14, 1915)

One can envisage both his stinginess and his loneliness as he rambled at age eighty-three through those cold hallways in foggy San Francisco.

H.H. penned another remembrance of Matilda—fleeting but fond—to Griffing on October 12, 1915: "Thirty-nine years ago to-day I married your mother."

Like so many women who work as mothers, as unacknowledged teachers of their children, as unpaid employees for their families' businesses, as private writers of articulate diaries and detailed reportage in letters, Matilda had many quiet accomplishments. Let them be appreciated here.

Climbing the Family Tree:
Kate, Lucy, and Their Families

Reading through the archives of Emily Ketchum Bancroft and Matilda Griffing Bancroft touched me with the excited anticipation of the miners still digging for gold when Emily herself came to California in 1859 and with the amazement of newcomers to the nascent yet cosmopolitan San Francisco, like Matilda in 1876. I was unearthing a wealth of intriguing information, from which I could construct the richly lived experiences of these women in nineteenth-century California—along with stories about the life of their husband-in-common, Hubert Howe Bancroft, as he wended his way through what would become his collecting and history-writing legacy.

But another gift emerged from this project, too, one that I call "climbing the family tree."

I had often heard about H. H. Bancroft's three boys, Paul, Griffing, and Philip, but little about his daughter Lucy and nothing about Kate. When Theresa Salazar, curator of Western Americana at The Bancroft Library, set me to reading the journals of Matilda Bancroft, I immediately came across references to "Sister Kate." I wondered who the heck she was! And why had I never heard of her? With many new questions about the Bancroft family, I turned to H. H. Bancroft's 1890 memoir, *Literary Industries*—and there was Kate, along with her mother, Emily.

Through the writings of H.H., Matilda, and Emily, as well as in genealogy reports and information tucked away in the minds and attics of various relatives, I encountered a bounty of new branches and leaves along an ancient, giant, twisting oak of a family tree. Some of these relatives were nearby in Northern California; others, far distant. To keep track of "who's who," I made my own family tree in 2012. My one-page cheat sheet became immensely helpful to me, and to others, when I'd call or arrive at the home of some newly found relative's house and they'd ask, "Now, *how* are we related?"

Of all the relatives I was learning about, I was most intrigued by the mysterious women I thought of as "the lost daughters." Who were they? Who were their descendants? How had they and their branches become neglected in the midst of the hullabaloo surrounding the celebrated patriarch, H.H., and his sons? My interest in telling the story of these lost daughters was later reinforced by the frequent questions posed to me at book readings of my edited version of H. H. Bancroft's *Literary Industries*, published in 2014: "Whatever happened to Kate and Lucy? Did *they* have children and grandchildren?"

My sleuthing into family history eventually added a veritable tree-top canopy, leafy with the names and stories of relatives I encountered in my journeys up and down California and even to the East Coast. I share here some of the roads I traveled along.

Kate Bancroft and Kin

Born August 21, 1860, in Buffalo, Kate Ketchum Bancroft was just nine years old when her mother, Emily, died. Seven years later, in 1876, at age sixteen, she met her new stepmother, Matilda, and attended her father's wedding in Connecticut. Kate did not return with them on the long trip back to San Francisco because she was attending Miss Porter's School in Farmington, Connecticut, as her mother had. When she did return to California, Kate probably traveled in the company of her Ketchum and Bancroft aunts and uncles, who had often taken her into their care.

In fact, Kate toured parts of Europe with her uncle Albert Bancroft (A.L.) and aunt Fannie Watts Bancroft between 1880 and 1882. These travels are documented in a thick volume of Kate's letters at UC San Diego's Special Collections & Archives (along with those letters to and from her mother there).

Kate met rancher and businessman Charles Olcott Richards in San Diego, where her stepmother Matilda had built a house. The two began courting, which included a trip to Alaska together among a larger party of friends in May 1887. They married in San Francisco in September 1887. (See chapter 9.)

Kate and Charles had two daughters, Ruth and Katherine. At The Bancroft Library, I found pictures of Kate and her adolescent daughters in the family album that Matilda surely initiated, *The Founding of a Family*. Handwriting in the album, not Matilda's, identifies many of the family members. Those notes were probably written in by Philip Bancroft's granddaughter, Ann Graham, herself one of the great family archivists and genealogists.

Ruth, Kate, and Katherine Richards, courtesy of The Bancroft Library (BANC MSS 73/64 c)

Answers to my curiosity about what had happened to Kate's daughters came from two sources: the letters in UCSD's Special Collections & Archives, which I first visited in 2010, and from my own father. I am indebted to Lynda Claassen, the wonderful director of UCSD's Special Collections, who told me how Emily's and Kate's volumes had come to rest in La Jolla.

Apparently, Margaret Wood Bancroft (1893–1986), the second wife of Griffing (1879–1955), knew that many of the Bancroft family papers were still tucked away on shelves and in chests of H.H.'s descendants. Margaret herself had in her possession the many letters that H.H. had written to his son Griffing; she had also seen some of Matilda's diaries at H.H.'s home in Walnut Creek where she herself also lived in the last year or so of his life after she and Griffing had married in 1917. In fact, in her oral history interview, Margaret referred to one of Matilda's books, *Our Winter in Mexico*, which, she said, "I found there at the farm."

For most of her life, however, Margaret had lived with Griffing in San Diego, where Griffing had enjoyed spending time with his older half-sister Kate and her family. Kate's older daughter, Ruth, had married Charles Lineaweaver. Their only child, also named Ruth but nicknamed Dickie, married Robert Swisher and became a successful oil painter, while raising three children herself (Lynn, Anne, and Robert). Ultimately, Margaret helped convince Ruth Richards (Dickie) Lineaweaver Swisher to donate the three valuable volumes of family letters to UC San Diego's Special Collections & Archives.

Through Lynda Claassen, I was able to make contact with Dickie, who still lives in La Jolla, near San Diego. We would visit over subsequent years of my trips to copy from Emily's letters.

More on Kate's family: her younger daughter, Katherine, nicknamed Babe, had married Edgar Allan Poe Jr., a nephew of the poet, and bore him a son, Edgar Allan Poe III (nicknamed Pudge) and a daughter Katherine (Kitty) Poe.

My second source for learning more about Emily's vanished daughter and her family was my own father, Paul "Pete" Bancroft III, the grandson of H.H. and Matilda's oldest son, Paul Sr. When I told my father that I had learned that Kate's granddaughter Dickie was living in La Jolla, he scratched his head and said, "Oh, yes, Dickie! I used to play at the beach with her and her cousin Kitty when we were kids in San Diego."

My father's stepfather, Blair Foster, had been stationed in San Diego with the navy during World War II. While living there with his mother (Rita Manning Bancroft Foster) and his stepfather, eleven- and twelve-year-old Pete Bancroft would often visit with his great-uncle Griffing and great-aunt Margaret. Those visits also allowed Pete to go romping on the beach with his first cousins once removed, Kate's granddaughters, Dickie and Kitty, all about the same age, and all visiting their great-aunt Margaret and great-uncle Griffing. Pete's memories of these family elders were very fond. Margaret in particular had a vibrant personality. He liked to share the story of sitting next to Margaret at some function and telling her, "I love you, Margaret," to which she replied, "I love you, too, Pete," without either of them realizing that there was an open microphone.

It was magical to find these seeming ghosts of the family past made real and full of their own talents and stories.

When I had the opportunity to speak with Dickie herself in 2010, I learned that the Kate side of the family still harbored hard feelings against H. H. Bancroft. Letters in his declining years showed how cantankerous he had become, disparaging various relatives—including his own children—for not living up to his high expectations or for seeming to take for granted the funds and property he had passed along, never expressing sufficient gratitude or working as hard as he had. H.H. *had* given Kate her own home, as well as a generous annuity that had allowed her to travel to Europe, where she had enjoyed the good life. But H.H. apparently did not approve of certain unnamed aspects of her life.

One story reflected H.H.'s extreme insensitivity. According to family legend, H.H. had thrown his daughter Kate out of his house when she was visiting with her very sick daughter Ruth (Dickie's mother), proclaiming—so said Dickie—"I will not have anyone die in my household!"

What really happened will never be known. Memory works in mysterious ways. H.H.'s actual words are now less important than the long-remembered force of his anger and rejection, infamous in Kate's family history.

Kate may have felt replaced in her father's heart by his second wife, Matilda, which may also have played a role in her later relationship with both of them. However, the young Kate often addressed her letters to Papa and Mama and wrote tenderly of sending love to her stepmother.

On the other hand, complex and contradictory family dynamics are evident in the many letters from H.H. that mention Kate and her husband Charles, as well as in other references to Kate's branch of the family (such as in Margaret Wood Bancroft's oral history). H.H.'s abiding love for his first daughter is evident, but so is his disdain for "foolish spendthrifts" like her. It would take another book to explore *those* archives.

For complex reasons, little love for H.H. blossomed on that branch of the family tree. Yet nearly ninety years after his death, Dickie and I formed a mutual regard, which later in 2010 extended to her cousin Kitty Poe Duer, whom I met in Maryland with my father. Kitty was most enthusiastic to reconnect to the young man she had once known as "Petie" and to explore old family connections with new information dug up from the archives.

I am immensely grateful to both Dickie and Kitty for having donated their family papers to UC San Diego, where they will be kept safe and provide opportunities for scholars and other Bancroft descendants to enjoy the very personal history they document. Because of their forethought, the details of the lives of Emily, Kate, and kin endure.

Looking for Lucy

Reading Lucy's memory book prepared by her mother, I had an odd experience of returning to my own childhood fascination with H.H. and Matilda's daughter, Lucy. A memory of a prior "encounter" with her floated up.

I was eight years old. My father had arranged a tour of The Bancroft Library for himself, my mother, my older brother Bradford, and me. I was too young to remember much, but one part of the tour remained indelible in my mind. The then director of The Bancroft Library, James D. Hart, "Jim" to my father, took us into the labyrinthine stacks below the building. As we walked and talked, he came to the collection of "dictations"—oral histories—and diaries going back to H.H.'s early work and collecting.

It seemed coincidental at the time, but Mr. Hart reached for an aged brown leather volume, and said, "Oh, look! Here's one that your great-great-grandmother wrote, Matilda Bancroft." He opened the book to a random page and began to read. It was a scene describing Lucy "raging" at her three older brothers who had all run off to Walnut Creek—when it really was a creek—to catch frogs and fish, and the boys did not want to bother with their little sister tagging behind. Lucy had been found crying in the road, alone and angry at being abandoned.

That image of the little girl unable to play with her three brothers, rejected (albeit temporarily) from their world, captured my imagination, for I too had three brothers and often "raged" at them as well. We had something in common, this ancestor and I.

However, family lore about Lucy had been as absent as the lore about her three brothers had abounded: how they had carried on the Bancroft family businesses and real estate, along with subsequent stories about the interesting endeavors of their progeny. Now I asked myself why Lucy had disappeared. Where did she disappear to?

Having dived into Matilda's and H.H.'s books and papers, I began passionately snooping into Lucy's fate in 2009. I decided to start my climb onto the Lucy branch by simply typing into my internet search engine "Lucy Bancroft, daughter Hubert Howe Bancroft." Imagine my shock when I found an online post from a Joan Bancroft.

> Lucy Bancroft, the daughter of Hubert Howe Bancroft, took a post in New York City with a children's home society as a settlement house director (or whatever she might have been called). There she took as her ward a male child whom she later called Dudley Kent Bancroft (I don't think there was a formal adoption, but there could have been some sort of legal name change). According to family legend she was unmarried, so adoption seems unlikely. This Dudley Kent Bancroft later traveled to Europe with Lucy where he met Jenny Hollard whom he eventually married. My children are the grandchildren of Dudley and Jenny Hollard Bancroft. Their father is Dudley Kent Bancroft, Jr.
>
> I would like to get a copy of the death certificate of Dudley, Sr. who died in Phoenix in February of 1972.

What?! Lucy had a child that she'd named Bancroft? And there were more Bancrofts unofficially descended from her?

I returned to my hitherto underappreciated source, my father, who laughed and affirmed the story, sending me to Margaret Wood Bancroft's oral history. Margaret indeed reported that Lucy had become the legal guardian of a child, whom she named Dudley Kent Bancroft. H.H. was angry when he learned that she had given the child the Bancroft name.

Later I read through Matilda's story-filled genealogical record of the Bancroft family going back many generations.[1] I discovered that Lucy had raided the family tree in naming her son Dudley and Kent, both names found in Matilda's book.

Back to the living descendants: I immediately contacted Joan Bancroft, who was living in Paradise, California (a town incinerated in the inferno of November 2018, though by that time Joan was living with her daughter Carolyn Benfield in San Jose). Thrilled to have discovered each other, we arranged for me to visit the very next weekend, in October 2009, since I was then living and teaching in Sacramento, only an hour or so away.

In the meantime, I dredged up from my memory yet another ghostly connection to Lucy. While attending Stanford in the late 1970s, I had gone out one evening for dinner with some friends at Henry's, a popular restaurant-bar on Palo Alto's University Avenue. The hostess asked us to provide a name to put on the wait list for a table. "Kim Bancroft," I told her.

"Bancroft! I'm a Bancroft, too, but not a real one," laughed the comely young woman.

"What's your name?" I asked, intrigued.

"Susan Bancroft."

"What do you mean, you're not a 'real' one?"

She replied, "We aren't really blood Bancrofts."

At that point, the crowd swirling around us pushed her back into her work role, and my friends pushed me to join them at a table.

I always regretted that I never talked more to that Susan Bancroft or tried to find her.

But then one day I did get to talk with her again!

When I met with Joan in 2009, she fully explained Lucy's story and that of her adopted son, Dudley, and his children and grandchildren. On this whole new branch of the Bancroft family tree, who should I find but Joan's daughter, Susan Bancroft, my Palo Alto restaurant hostess. Joan confirmed that in the late 1970s, already divorced from her former husband, Dudley Kent Bancroft Jr., she was living in Palo Alto, where Susan was hostessing at that local restaurant-bar. By 2009 when I met Joan, Susan had long since moved on and was running a Carmel Valley horse ranch that she called the Bancroft Ranch.

Joan and I had a talk fest as we regaled each other with family stories. Joan informed me that Lucy had moved to New York by 1915, when she was thirty-three, and was working on Manhattan's Upper West Side. She would bring children home from an orphanage to acculturate them to table manners and proper behavior in order to make them more adoptable. She also read them stories.

One little boy, Frederick H. Voight, about nine years old, begged not to be sent back to the orphanage. Lucy let him stay with her, eventually becoming his legal guardian and giving him the name of Dudley Kent Bancroft. Lucy provided him with a good life that included a European tour after World War I. Dudley met and married a French woman, Jenny Hollard. They all eventually moved to New Jersey, where Lucy lived in a duplex next door to her son and daughter-in-law. Dudley and Jenny had four children: Pauline, Dudley Jr., Noemi, and Lucy Anne. By the 1930s, Lucy had moved to the town of Buellton, in the quiet Santa Ynez Valley north of Santa Barbara.

Like Kate, Lucy had received a small but sufficient annuity that allowed her to live comfortably. In 1936, at the age of fifty-four, Lucy bought a small ranch in Buellton, where she worked and lived for nearly twenty years. Two of her grandchildren, Dudley Kent Bancroft Jr. (1928–2013) and Pauline (1927–2021), came to live with her. Dudley Jr. ended up living in Solvang, near Buellton, and his sister Pauline Bancroft Hinds was in Ventura. A trained nurse, she cared for her grandmother Lucy in the last twenty years of her life.

Several months after my visit with Joan, she invited me back to Paradise to meet her four children, Kent, Gordon, Carolyn, and Susan, and hear their stories. Though these were not Bancrofts by blood, Lucy's son Dudley and his children also carried the Bancroft name. His children and grandchildren knew her as their grandmother. Years later, I would know Pauline Bancroft and learn that her children had also grown up with their grandmother Lucy. They *were* family. I in turn adopted Lucy's great-grandchildren immediately as my distant cousins. Ironically, in a family with many female descendants whose children did not inherit the Bancroft family name, Lucy's descendants are some of the few "Bancrofts" left.

As I reported my investigations to my father, he became equally intrigued by my research and the new branches on the family tree.

So we embarked in 2010 on "Pete and Kim's Excellent Adventure," a drive to Southern California to meet Dudley Kent Bancroft Jr. and Pauline Bancroft Hinds, Lucy's grandchildren, as well as for Pete to meet Dickie Richards Swisher again, after almost sixty years.

We learned more about both Lucy and her adopted son from Pauline. The little boy she brought home at the age of nine had been found wandering in the streets of New York when he was only four. Family lore said that he had witnessed his father shoot his mother and then himself, a terrible tragedy for any child (assuming the story to be true). In his later years in New Jersey, Dudley had become seriously depressed. He and his wife separated, and his four children had dispersed. In 1972, in his mid-sixties, Dudley Kent Bancroft died alone in Phoenix, where he had gone to seek recovery from lung ailments.

With her parents separated, Pauline, at the age of sixteen, courageously crossed the country to live with her grandmother Lucy in Buellton. Pauline told my father and me that Grandma Lucy was an independent woman who never married but put her tremendous energies into helping others. During World War II, Lucy helped direct the Santa Ynez Valley's war support efforts, impressing the local people with her organizational skills. Pauline also fondly remembered Lucy's emphasis on reading the classics, as Lucy herself had been taught to do.

A glaring contradiction in Lucy's character is that she made Pauline work hard for everything, making her pay rent to live in her home. Meanwhile, she gave Pauline's brother money to go to Stanford but did not do the same for Pauline, an odd re-creation of H.H.'s refusal to give Lucy a college education while sending his sons to Harvard. Though pressed to account for this discrepancy in Lucy's treatment of her grandson and granddaughter, Pauline could offer no explanation, but she said that she never resented Lucy's stinginess. Rather, she appreciated having had a peaceful place to live at a difficult time in her life, and she admired her grandmother's strength of character.

She may well have modeled herself after Lucy, because Pauline Bancroft Hinds herself was a dynamo. She worked on Lucy's ranch herding cattle and also waited tables at Solvang's Valley Inn, the originator of the famous Pea Soup Andersen's. With her own hard work, Pauline put herself through nursing school and spent many years as an emergency room nurse at Ventura County Medical Center. She was the first woman to join the Ventura County Sheriff's Search and Rescue Team and learned how to jump out of helicopters while practicing wilderness medicine in the rugged hills above Ventura. My father and I were fascinated by her stories. That Pauline had had such a life and was taking care of her grandmother for decades speaks to yet another facet of Pauline's strength.

Lucy's strong personality has remained in the hearts of her descendants. Pauline's daughter Kathleen Keefe lived with Lucy in her last years and remembers reading stories to her great-grandmother Lucy, who was always hungry for literature. Lucy's other great-grandchildren, Susan Bancroft and her sister Carolyn Benfield, also had fond memories of visiting Lucy as children and listening to the stories that she would read to them with great verve, carrying on the long tradition started by Matilda in the 1880s. Admiringly, Carolyn called her great-grandmother an early Bohemian, a woman who had gone off to New York to live her own life and later became an independent rancher in a small town where she could have an impact.

The image of Lucy striding down the road in Buellton in her pants in the 1940s epitomizes her taking the world into her own hands to do with as she liked. Whether her mother would have approved her choices can only be imagined. Matilda died when Lucy was only twenty-eight years old.

Lucy Bancroft with her granddaughter Pauline, courtesy of
Pauline Bancroft Hinds and family

For Kate and Lucy, life with their father, H. H. Bancroft, must have been phenomenal in many ways, considering what a visionary he was in his understanding of the history unfolding around him and the dynamism with which he preserved that history. For Kate, the early energetic influence of her mother, Emily, lost too young, was perhaps offset by the later influence of her stepmother, Matilda, also a power-house in her own way. Lucy, the baby of the family, observed all these forces and chose her own path, away from the family, while following her parents' strong work ethic and intellectual life.

The stories of these women join those of other strong women who play multiple roles throughout their lives—as mothers, companions, teachers, intellectuals, artists, businesswomen—exuding strength of character in the endeavors to which they direct their passions and energies.

ACKNOWLEDGMENTS

This book would not have come to fruition without the help of many people.

First thanks go to members of the Bancroft family who ensured that the papers and photos of Emily Bancroft and Matilda Bancroft were preserved: Ruth Richards Swisher in La Jolla and Kitty Poe Duer in Maryland, who donated their great-grandmother Emily's papers to the UC San Diego Special Collections & Archives; Margaret Wood Bancroft, who ensured that Matilda's writings and other Bancroft papers were saved; and Ann Bancroft Graham, who literally left her handwriting on family papers and albums she preserved. I am also indebted to the families of Pauline Bancroft Hinds, Joan Bancroft, and Dudley Kent Bancroft Jr. for sharing their stories of Lucy Bancroft.

Second, I greatly appreciate Lynda Claassen, director of the UCSD Special Collections & Archives, for her help in my research and in securing Emily's papers for posterity.

Grand ovations to the many folks at The Bancroft Library (TBL) who have helped over the years on this project, including those who support researchers camped out in the Reading Room: Susan Snyder, Iris Donovan, Lee Anne Titangos, Kathi Neal, Terry Boom, Peter Hanff, José Adrián Baragán Álvarez, Jack von Euw, James Eason, Diana Vergil, Dean Smith, and Randy Brandt, among many others. Special thanks to Theresa Salazar for instigating this book and special thanks to Elaine Tennant for supporting this work since its early stages.

Will wonders never cease? TBL archivist Chris McDonald revealed he grew up close to Granville, H. H. Bancroft's birthplace. Chris generously helped my father, brothers, and me tour the region in 2017. Much gratitude to you!

I thank Judith Redfield, Jane Futcher, and Helen Falandes for feedback while the book was in process, and Fred Setterberg for his writerly mentoring.

A top wordsmithing award goes to Charles Faulhaber, the 2021–2022 interim director of TBL, who labored assiduously on my manuscript and provided valuable historical fact checking.

Of the wordsmiths and creative designers at Heyday, I thank Gayle Wattawa, Emmerich Anklam, Michele Jones, Diane Lee, Rebecca LeGates, Ashley Ingram, and Christopher Miya for their kind and expert help, among others who helped get the book out. (And special mention to my dear friend Keasley Jones, who was working there when he passed away in 2021.) I greatly appreciate the early enthusiasm for this book shown by Heyday's executive director, Steve Wasserman.

Also, Camilla Smith and the Friends of The Bancroft Library have made the book's publication possible as part of the tradition of TBL to provide "Keepsakes" of treasured primary sources stored in the Library.

Of course, I am most grateful to the conscientious contributions of Emily Ketchum Bancroft and Matilda Griffing Bancroft in scribbling away, sometimes under duress, for years and years. As much as I may have "saved" these two women's writing, they have also saved me, giving me purpose and companionship over twelve years.

Finally, thanks to Kate Black for your support in all ways.

This book is dedicated to my father, Paul (Pete) Bancroft III, for encouraging his children to cherish family history.

Kim, Pete, Greg, Bradford, and Stephen Bancroft, Granville, Ohio, 2017

1832, May 5	Hubert Howe Bancroft born, Ohio
1834, Aug. 19	Emily Brist Ketchum Bancroft born, New York
1848, May 10	Matilda Coley Griffing Bancroft born, Connecticut
1852, Apr. 1	H. H. Bancroft arrives in California to sell books for his Buffalo brother-in-law
1856, Dec. 1	H. H. Bancroft and Company founded in San Francisco
1859, Oct. 27	H.H. marries Emily Ketchum in Buffalo, New York; they return to San Francisco
1860, Aug. 21	Kate Bancroft born (d. June 20, 1945)
1861, Sept.– Aug. 1862	Emily with family in Buffalo while H.H. collects books in Europe
1864, Oct. 20	Emily and H.H.'s newborn daughter dies, Oakland, California
1866, Aug.– Apr. 1867	Emily and H.H. travel in Europe
1868, July– Aug.	In Granville, Ohio, for Emily to take the water cure from H.H.'s uncle
1869, Dec. (date uncertain)	Emily dies of kidney disease
1870, May	Construction of the Bancroft Building on Market Street in San Francisco
1876, Oct. 12	H.H. marries Matilda Griffing in New Haven, Connecticut
1877, Aug. 22	Paul Bancroft born (d. Apr. 25, 1957)
1878, Apr.– June	H.H. and Matilda travel to the Northwest (Oregon, Washington, British Columbia)
1879, Jan. 21	Griffing born (d. May 3, 1955)
1881	H.H. builds a brick building for his library on Valencia Street in San Francisco

1881, June 30	Philip born (d. Aug. 11, 1975)
1882, Sept. 28	Lucy born (d. July 1, 1980)
1884, Aug.–Dec.	Family travels to Utah, Colorado, New Mexico, Southern California
1885, Mar.	H.H. buys land in Walnut Creek with brother Albert Little (A.L.)
1885, Oct.	Matilda and H.H. buy ranch land in Spring Valley, near San Diego
1886, Apr. 30	Fire burns down the SF Bancroft Building
1887, Sept. 21	Kate Bancroft marries Charles Olcott Richards
1889, Mar. 1	Party for 600 in San Diego; Matilda experiences a stroke
1891, Oct.–Jan. 1892	Family trip to Mexico
1895–98	Family in Massachusetts (or Connecticut) while boys attend prep school and college
1901, Oct. 30	Griffing marries Ethel Works
1902, Aug. 5	Paul marries Louise J. Hazzard
1905, June	Philip marries Nina Eldred
1910, Aug. 10	Matilda dies of "angina pectoris"
1918, Mar. 2	H.H. dies in San Francisco

NOTES

Introduction

1 Quotations from Emily's writing generally come from two sources, unless otherwise noted: letters to her parents or to her sister. Quotations note an identifying date and to whom Emily was writing. These letters are located at the UC San Diego Special Collections & Archives: Emily Ketchum Bancroft, Bancroft Family Correspondence, MSS 0039, box 1, UC San Diego. The volumes are stamped in gold: LETTERS E.K.B. TO HER PARENTS and LETTERS E.K.B. TO MRS. COIT 1860–1869.

2 All references to *Literary Industries* come from this new edition.

3 John Caughey's biography *Hubert Howe Bancroft: Historian of the West* (Berkeley: University of California Press, 1946) covers Bancroft's life and work. *A Venture in History: The Production, Publication, and Sale of the* Works *of Hubert Howe Bancroft* by Harry Clark (Berkeley: University of California Press, 1973) describes controversies concerning his literary industries.

4 *Literary Industries*, 99–100.

5 Emily Ketchum Bancroft correspondence, BANC MSS 2003/281 cz v.1, The Bancroft Library, University of California, Berkeley.

6 Many thanks to Ruth Richards Swisher and Kitty Duer, the granddaughters of Kate Bancroft Richards, for donating these volumes to the UCSD Special Collections & Archives.

7 MSS BANC 75/92 m, The Bancroft Library, University of California, Berkeley.

8 "Genealogical register for Matilda Bancroft," Hubert Howe Bancroft letters to his family, BANC MSS 77/169 c, box 4, The Bancroft Library, University of California, Berkeley.

9 Hubert Howe Bancroft letters to his family, BANC MSS 77/169 c, box 1, The Bancroft Library, University of California, Berkeley.

Chapter One

1 Letter dated November 4, 1859, with salutation "Dear Kate & George," but in the volume of letters to her parents.

2 *Literary Industries*, 62.

3 Letter from John Richards, November 11, 1851, Emily Ketchum Bancroft correspondence, BANC MSS 2003/281 cz v.1, The Bancroft Library, University of California, Berkeley.

4 Emily Ketchum Bancroft correspondence, BANC MSS 2003/281 cz v.1, The Bancroft Library, University of California, Berkeley.

5 *Literary Industries*, 61–64.

6 Emily Ketchum Bancroft correspondence, BANC MSS 2003/281 cz v.1, The Bancroft Library, University of California, Berkeley.

7 See Lillian Faderman, *Surpassing the Love of Men: Romantic Friendship and Love between Women from the Renaissance to the Present* (New York: HarperCollins, 1981).

8   Manifest Destiny, an idea popularized in the nineteenth century, insisted on the US destiny to extend its range of territory from coast to coast, bringing supposedly civilizing values of agrarian democracy by American settlers.

9   From the family photo album and scrapbook "The Founding of a Family," BANC MSS 73/64 c. v.1, The Bancroft Library, University of California, Berkeley. Many photos from this book are located there.

Chapter Two

1   See the poem "Angel in the House" by Coventry Patmore, and Carol Christ's commentary that "appropriation" of the poem's title has provided "a repository for the prevailing Victorian conception of womanhood," cited in Natasha Moore, *Victorian Poetry and Modern Life: The Unpoetical Age* (London: Palgrave Macmillan, 2015), 29.

2   See "Report of A. A. Bancroft, Indian Agent, Washington Territory," 419, University of Washington, http://digitalcollections.lib.washington.edu/cdm/compoundobject/collection/lctext/id/248.

3   Louise Amelia Knapp Smith Clappe, *The Shirley Letters from the California Mines 1851–52*, edited by Marlene Smith-Barazini (Berkeley, CA: Heyday, 1998). These letters fueled the opera *Girls of the Golden West* by John Adams, performed by the San Francisco Opera in 2017, with the major stage setting at the Empire Hotel run by "Mr. and Mrs. B."

4   See John W. Caughey, *Hubert Howe Bancroft, Historian of the West* for the complete story (Berkeley: University of California Press, 1946), 337–40.

5   See Caughey, *Hubert Howe Bancroft, Historian of the West*.

6   The 1870 Portland, Oregon, census stated that Theod. Trevett, born in Maine about 1833, resided with Mary B., age thirty-one (wife), and three children. Their home, now the Trevett-Nunn House, is on the National Register of Historic Places.

7   See Bancroft's delightful description of his father in the chapter about his Granville boyhood in *Literary Industries*.

8   The October 8, 1865, earthquake is now estimated at 6.3.

9   She refers to *The Life of Trust: Being a Narrative of the Lord's Dealings with George Müller*, published in 1861.

10   Emperor Napoleon III, *History of Julius Caesar I* (New York: Harper Bros., 1865).

11   So said a reviewer in *The North American Review* 100, no. 206 (January 1865): 279.

12   See "From Bibliopolist to Bibliophile" in H. H. Bancroft's *Literary Industries*.

Chapter Three

1   William Anderson Scott (1813–1885) led this church from 1854 to 1861. See Kevin Starr's *Americans and the California Dream* (New York: Oxford University Press, 1973), 75.

2   See *Literary Industries*, 18.

3   Benjamin Griffin of the Mark Twain Papers at The Bancroft Library located this Currier & Ives print.

4 Here she probably refers to Henry Haight (1820–1869). Obituary in the *San Francisco Examiner*, March 25, 1869.

5 Kevin Starr discussed the collaboration between Tuthill and Bancroft: *Americans and the California Dream* (New York: Oxford University Press, 1973), 113–15.

6 *Bancroft's Works*, vol. 24 (vol. 8 of *History of California*, 1890), 722.

7 Writer John Ross Browne (1821–1875) arrived in California in 1849. Browne also published two pieces in 1869 with H. H. Bancroft: *Resources of the Pacific Slope* and *A Sketch of the Settlement and Exploration of Lower California*.

8 The House of Representatives approved articles of impeachment against Andrew Johnson on March 2–3, 1868 (the first impeachment of a president in US history), having to do with violation of the Tenure of Office Act. He was not convicted in his Senate trial three days later.

Chapter Four

1 See excerpt from *Literary Industries* later in this chapter in the section "A Grand Tour in Europe."

2 *The New West: Or, California in 1867–68* (New York: Putnam, 1869).

3 *Literary Industries* (2014 edition), 65–66.

4 Adelina Patti (1843–1919) was an Italian-French soprano opera singer. The opera *Crispino e la comarei* (The cobbler and the fairy), written by Luigi and Federico Ricci, premiered in 1850 in Venice.

5 Probably *I Capuleti e i Montechi* (The Capulets and the Montagues) by Vincenzo Bellini, and Giacomo Meyerbeer's *Il crociato in Egitto* (The crusader in Egypt).

6 Story (1818–1895) published this history in 1862.

Chapter Five

1 I am grateful to Dr. Lal for his correspondence and information.

2 See "Travels of Kate Bancroft through the Line of Missions of California," Hubert Howe Bancroft family papers, BANC MSS 71/18 c FILM, The Bancroft Library, University of California, Berkeley.

Chapter Six

1 Published by D. Appleton in New York in 1875–76.

2 *Literary Industries*, 152–53.

3 Announcement found in Hubert Howe Bancroft family papers, 1832–1908, BANC MSS 73/64 c, box 1, The Bancroft Library, University of California, Berkeley.

4 *Literary Industries*, 149.

5 "Genealogical register for Matilda Bancroft," Hubert Howe Bancroft letters to his family, BANC MSS 77/169 c, box 4, The Bancroft Library, University of California, Berkeley.

6 The travelogue is owned by H. H. Bancroft's great-grandson Thomas Graham.

7 Hubert Howe Bancroft family papers, BANC MSS 73/64 c, box 1, folder 10, The Bancroft Library, University of California, Berkeley.

8   All citations from the children's memory books will be cited by the first name
    of the child and the page from which the quotation comes. The children's
    books belonged to Griffing, Philip, and Lucy; Paul's book is missing. The
    existing books are held by The Bancroft Library: Childhood Memory Book
    for Griffing Bancroft, 1879–1892, BANC MSS C-D 5181; Childhood Memory
    Book for Philip Bancroft, 1881–1891, BANC MSS box C-B 851, carton 1, folder
    50; Childhood Memory Book for Lucy Bancroft, 1882–1892, BANC MSS
    C-D 5197. The Bancroft Library, University of California, Berkeley.

9   Letter dated August 5, 1889, to Mrs. John H. Coley, Emporia, Kansas, in
    letters from Matilda Bancroft, BANC MSS 99/88 cz, The Bancroft Library,
    University of California, Berkeley.

10 *Literary Industries*, 153.

11 Matilda Coley Griffing Bancroft, diary 1876, MSS 83/22 c, The Bancroft
    Library, University of California, Berkeley. Matilda generally did not provide
    specific dates in this diary. General John C. Frémont (1813–1890) was a soldier,
    explorer, and politician, controversial for his role in the Mexican-American
    War. As a US Army captain, he encouraged the formation of an independent
    "California Republic" in 1846. Frémont was court-martialed for insubordina-
    tion but later reinstated.

12 A note on transcriptions of Matilda's work: Matilda did not always use capital
    letters to start new sentences, nor did she show new paragraphs, perhaps to
    save valuable paper. In presenting Matilda's writing, I've edited her work to
    make it easier to read.

13 John Wesley Powell (1834–1902) played multiple roles as soldier, explorer,
    geologist, and anthropologist. He was the director of the Bureau of Ethnology
    at the Smithsonian Institution from 1879 to 1902, so, as Matilda noted, H.H.'s
    ethnological work would have particularly interested him.

14 George Bancroft (1800–1891) served as secretary of the navy and as foreign
    minister, and was himself a historian, writing, among other works, the
    ten-volume *History of the United States*. He and H.H. were distant cousins:
    H.H.'s great-great-grandfather, Lt. Samuel Bancroft (1711–1778), was also
    George's grandfather. H.H.'s great-grandfather, Lt. Samuel Bancroft (1737–
    1820), and George's father, the Rev. Aaron Bancroft (1755–1839), were brothers.

15 Daniel Coit Gilman (1831–1908) was appointed third president of the Univer-
    sity of California in 1872, and then in 1875 moved to Johns Hopkins University
    as its first president.

16 Twice the governor of Alta California, Pio Pico (1801–1894) was serving when
    the Americans won the territory.

17 Mariano Guadalupe Vallejo (1807–1890) was a *Californio* solider, general,
    rancher, and statesman. As the comandante general, he presided over the
    transition from Mexican California to US California, under great duress.

18 Juan Bautista Alvarado (1809–1882) served as the governor of Alta California
    from 1837 to 1842.

19 Another *Californio*, José Antonio Romualdo Pacheco (1831–1899), was
    governor of California from 1871 to 1875, among other roles, including foreign
    minister, California state treasurer, state senator, and US representative.

20 These refugees include journalist, lawyer, politician, and jurist José María
   Iglesias (1823–1891). As president of the Mexican Supreme Court, he declared
   the presidency of Sebastián Lerdo illegitimate in 1876. He then served as
   interim president of Mexico from October 1876 to January 1877 until Lerdo
   challenged him, and he fled Mexico for the US in January 1877. One of
   his supporters, journalist Guillermo Prieto (1818–1897), served as minister
   of finance under Iglesias. Palacio may refer to the Mexican journalist and
   politician Francisco Gómez Palacio.
21 William Ingraham Kip (1811–1893) arrived in San Francisco in 1854 and served
   as the California missionary bishop of the Episcopalian diocese.
22 Thomas Savage spent decades as a US consul in Cuba, then worked as a
   Spanish scholar for Bancroft beginning in 1873. See *Literary Industries*,
   103–104.
23 *Literary Industries*, 151–52.
24 Dr. Hugh Toland, a surgeon, came to San Francisco in 1854 and founded the
   Toland Medical College in 1864. The school eventually became the Medical
   Department of the University of California.
25 Alphonse Pinart (1852–1911), from France, was a scholar, linguist, and
   ethnologist.
26 According to a genealogical register later written by Matilda, the elder
   Bancrofts were married on February 21, 1822, which would have made this 1878
   celebration their fifty-sixth anniversary. In Hubert Howe Bancroft letters to
   his family, BANC MSS 77/169 c, box 4, The Bancroft Library, University of
   California, Berkeley.
27 We are indebted to Patricia Prestinary for sharing this valuable diary. University Archives & Special Collections, Rare Book Collection, Pollak Library,
   CSU Fullerton.

Chapter Seven
1 Matilda Coley Griffing Bancroft, diary 1876, BANC MSS 83/22c, The
   Bancroft Library, University of California, Berkeley.
2 The following edited version of Matilda's diary covers pp. 27–114; the diary
   ends on p. 118.
3 Matilda refers to her sister-in-law Celia Bancroft Derby Kenny, who had
   married Hubert's good friend George Kenny following the deaths of their
   prior spouses.
4 Archibald McKinlay (1811–1919) was a trader for Hudson's Bay Company
   from 1832 to 1851.
5 In 1861, Good (1833–1916) arrived from England in Nanaimo as a minister for
   the Society for the Propagation of the Gospel.
6 John B. Good, Victoria, British Columbia. "Written by Mrs H. H. Bancroft
   to Mr. Good's dictation, at the Driad House, May 1878," 106 pp, BANC MSS
   P-C 19, The Bancroft Library, University of California, Berkeley.
7 Some of these men and their works are easily identified both in history and
   in The Bancroft Library archives. William Fraser Tolmie (1812–1886), from
   Scotland, arrived in Victoria in 1833 in service to the Hudson's Bay Company,

but also worked as a surgeon, scientist, politician, and linguist. In 1884, he published his *Comparative Vocabulary of the Indian Tribes of British Columbia.*

8   James Deans (1827–1905) provided his dictation, partially written in H. H. Bancroft's hand, on the settlement of Vancouver Island. BANC MSS P-C 9, The Bancroft Library, University of California, Berkeley.

9   In many places, Matilda and others referred to Native people indistinctly, naming neither particular homelands nor the tribal identity of those described, following a typical European neglect of seeing the specificity of Indian cultures.

10 Matthew Begbie (1819–1894) served as the first chief justice of British Columbia from 1858 until his death.

11 Yale, eighty miles from New Westminster, was the head of navigation on the Fraser River.

12 Francis Pettygrove (1812–1887) helped found both Portland and Port Townsend. BANC MSS P-A 60, The Bancroft Library, University of California, Berkeley.

13 An adventurer in Pacific West gold mines, J. J. Van Bokkelen (1816–1889) eventually helped found Port Townsend.

14 James Swan (1818–1900) served as judge, ethnographer, and historian in the early Washington Territory.

15 Contemporary Native people often mourn the loss of precious cultural artifacts to early forced sales or pillagers.

16 Civil War general Oliver O. Howard, the namesake of Howard University, led the eleven-hundred-mile pursuit of Chief Joseph and the Nez Percé Indians in 1877.

17 Henry Yesler (1810–1892) dictated his recollections on the settlement of the Washington Territory and the founding of Seattle from his arrival in 1851. BANC MSS P-B 23, 1878, The Bancroft Library, University of California, Berkeley.

18 Amos Bowman (1839–1894) was a civil engineer who built the town of Anacortes, north of Seattle, naming it for his wife, Ana Curtis Bowman. *Daniel Deronda* was a novel by George Eliot, published in 1876.

19 Eugene Ellicott provided an interview to Amos Bowman. BANC MSS P-B 7, The Bancroft Library, University of California, Berkeley.

20 Elwood Evans (1828–1898) gave his manuscript, "The Fraser River Excitement, 1858," to H. H. Bancroft in 1878. BANC MSS P-B 8, The Bancroft Library, University of California, Berkeley.

21 Shanna Stevenson, "Rebecca Groundage Howard (1827–1881)," BlackPast, February 12, 2007, http://www.blackpast.org/?q=aaw/howard-rebecca-groundage-1827-1881.

22 Stephen Fowler Chadwick (1825–1895) was governor of Oregon from 1877 to 1878. He provided an 1878 interview to H. H. Bancroft on sources for Oregon history. BANC MSS P-A 16, The Bancroft Library, University of California, Berkeley.

23 See "Campfire Orations" recorded for H. H. Bancroft at a meeting of the Oregon Pioneer Association in 1878, BANC MSS P-A 14, The Bancroft Library, University of California, Berkeley.

24 Harriet T. Clarke, "A Young Woman's Sights on the Emigrant Trail," BANC MSS P-A 17, The Bancroft Library, University of California, Berkeley.

25 John McLoughlin (1784–1857), the chief factor at Ft. Vancouver in British Columbia from 1824 to 1845, enjoyed a sterling reputation later for aiding Americans on the emigrant trail.

26 Peter Crawford, "Narrative of the Overland Journey to Oregon," 1873–1893, BANC MSS P-A 20, The Bancroft Library, University of California, Berkeley.

27 Asa Amos Lawrence Lovejoy (1808–1882), "Founding of Portland," Oregon City, 1878, BANC MSS P-A 45, The Bancroft Library, University of California, Berkeley. The reference for this piece reads "Interview by H. H. Bancroft; contains some interjections by his wife Mrs. Elizabeth (McGary) Lovejoy."

28 Matthew Deady (1824–1893) served on various courts in Oregon, including its supreme court from 1859 to 1893. See "History and Progress of Oregon after 1845," an interview with H. H. Bancroft, BANC MSS P-A 24, The Bancroft Library, University of California, Berkeley.

29 William Strong (1817–1887) served on the Oregon Supreme Court from 1850 to 1853. See his "History of Oregon," an interview with H. H. Bancroft, BANC MSS P-A 68, The Bancroft Library, University of California, Berkeley.

30 William Wilson Bancroft (1805–1870) had an infirmary in Granville, the Bancroft family's home. He was the doctor in charge of the "water cure" for H.H.'s first wife, Emily, in 1868. Anna Wright Bancroft died in 1890.

31 Henry W. Corbett (1827–1903) provided various materials to H. H. Bancroft about his business and political endeavors. BANC MSS P-A 110, The Bancroft Library, University of California, Berkeley.

32 Joseph G. Wilson (1826–1873), justice of the Oregon Supreme Court, was elected to the US House of Representatives, but died before taking office.

33 Jesse Applegate (1811–1888). See J. Henry Brown, "Oregon Miscellanies," Salem, 1878, BANC MSS P-A 9, The Bancroft Library, University of California, Berkeley.

34 The Oregon Hospital for the Insane opened in Portland in 1859 as a model institution for treating mental illness in empathic ways for the time, under the auspices of Dr. James DeCossett Hawthorne (1819–1881). Hawthorne dictation, BANC MSS P-A 131:35, The Bancroft Library, University of California, Berkeley.

35 Jesse Applegate, "Views of Oregon History": Yoncalla, Oregon, 1878. Includes a biographical sketch by Matilda Griffing Bancroft. BANC MSS P-A 2, The Bancroft Library, University of California, Berkeley.

36 Joseph Lane (1801–1881), the father of Lafayette Lane (1842–1896), rose to general in the Mexican-American War and served as governor of Oregon Territory (1848–1850) and later as one of the first two senators for the state of Oregon (1859). Lafayette also served as a US representative from Oregon from 1875 to 1877. Amos Bowman recorded his reminiscences. BANC MSS P-A 43, The Bancroft Library, University of California, Berkeley.

37 Paine P. Prim (1822–1899) participated in the Oregon Constitutional Convention and served three times as chief justice of the Oregon Supreme Court. "History of Judicial Affairs in Southern Oregon," BANC MSS P-A 61, The Bancroft Library, University of California, Berkeley.

38 The précis of the 1878 *Narrative* by Benjamin Franklin Dowell (1826–1897) reads: "Describes his experiences in Oregon as school-teacher, tradesman, lawyer, newspaper publisher, and volunteer in the southern Oregon Indian wars." BANC MSS P-A 26, The Bancroft Library, University of California, Berkeley. No credit is given to Matilda for taking his narrative.

39 This dictation is John Ross's "Narrative of an Indian Fighter." BANC MSS P-A 63, The Bancroft Library, University of California, Berkeley.

40 Judge A. M. Rosborough (1815–1900) served as a judge in Siskiyou County as of 1856. He was a peacemaker in the terrible Modoc War, negotiating with Captain Jack. See Jefferson C.D. Riddle, *The Indian History of the Modoc War* (Mechanicsburg, PA: Stackpole Books, 1914, 2004). At a prior visit to a Soda Springs resort, they had met the wife of Judge Rosborough of Yreka, who gave Matilda a photograph of her husband. Some of his papers are at The Bancroft Library; see Rosborough family papers, BANC MSS C-B 677, The Bancroft Library, University of California, Berkeley.

41 Sisson's Hotel was in the town now called Mt. Shasta City. See a historical marker for this location: https://noehill.com/siskiyou/cal0396.asp.

Chapter Eight

1 Matilda rarely noted specific dates, though she did mention events, such as Christmas or the New Year, or a season, hinting as to when she was writing.

2 As noted earlier, the names of the children will precede or be appended to a quotation from their books, with the relevant page number—for example, Lucy, 19.

3 Kate Ketchum Bancroft letters to her father, MSS 39, box 4, UC San Diego Special Collections & Archives.

4 H. H. Bancroft owned a four-hundred-acre pear and walnut orchard in Walnut Creek, now the site of the 2.5-acre Ruth Bancroft Garden, created and lovingly tended by UC Berkeley graduate Ruth Peterson Bancroft, married to H.H.'s grandson Philip Bancroft Jr. Ruth died at the age of 109 in 2017.

5 The family may have traveled to mussel bed sites along the Oakland estuary or the southern shore of Suisun Bay, the latter a somewhat closer journey for the Bancrofts in Walnut Creek, but still probably fifteen miles.

6 Hubert Howe Bancroft letters to his family, BANC MSS 77/169 c, The Bancroft Library, University of California, Berkeley.

7 Philip Bancroft, *Politics, Farming, and Progressive Politics in California*, an interview conducted by Willa Baum for the Regional Oral History Project, 1962, BANC CD 531, The Bancroft Library, University of California, Berkeley.

8 H. H. Bancroft later built on the same site a hotel, St. Dunstan's, which was destroyed in the 1906 earthquake.

9 Silas Weir Mitchell (1829–1914) was a neurologist who ordered the rest cure that Charlotte Perkins Gilman described in her 1892 novel *The Yellow Wallpaper*. See chapter 2.

10 Margaret Wood Bancroft (1893–1986), "Recollections of Hubert Howe Bancroft and the Bancroft Family," 1980, BANC MSS 80/144 c, The Bancroft Library, University of California, Berkeley. Available online at http://archive .org/details/margaretwoodrecoooobancrich.

11 *Black Beauty* by Anna Sewell, published in 1877, became an immediate best seller and inspired animal rights activists, just as *Uncle Tom's Cabin* had inspired abolitionists, as Matilda noted.

12 See the final chapter on the later lives of the Bancroft daughters.

Chapter Nine

1 Five cents in 1890, after inflation, is roughly the equivalent of $1.50 in 2021.

2 Unfortunately, on discovering that one tutor, a Miss Levy, was Jewish, Matilda found reason to let her go on that basis alone. This prejudice is as inexplicable as it is inexcusable. In harboring racist ideas, she was not alone among others of her religion, race, or class, or in her marriage. In his later years, H. H. Bancroft published *Retrospection* (1912), laced with the white supremacist ideology of his time.

3 Denver's Brinker Institute was a private school at 1757 Tremont Place. The building still exists, now the Navarre.

4 Organized by Alonso Horton in June 1873, the Unitarian Society employed Rev. David Cronyn as their first minister for their church in March 1877.

5 The references are to Shakespeare's *Twelfth Night* and *Henry the VIII; Robin Hood: A Comic Opera in Three Acts* by Harry B. Smith (libretto) and Reginald de Koven (music), published formally in 1896; and *Mignon* by French composer Ambroise Thomas, the latter two performed by the Bostonians, a touring light opera company.

6 First edition in three volumes: London: Bradbury & Evans, 1852–54; reprinted frequently. The Bancroft children probably read it in the abridged one-volume edition (Boston: Houghton, Osgood, 1880). See an internet version 130 years after.

7 Published by A. L. Bancroft, San Francisco, 1883. This ninety-six-page volume had three distinguished authors: Charles Allen, principal of the California State Normal School; John Swett, former state superintendent of public instruction; and philosopher and Harvard instructor in philosophy Josiah Royce.

8 Although the book was first published in 1866, the Bancroft children might have read the 1881 edition (New York: Scribner's) of Mary Mapes Dodge, *Hans Brinker; or, the Silver Skates: A Story of Life in Holland.*

9 Henrietta Christian Wright, *Children's Stories in American History* (London: Bickers & Son, 1886).

10 Howard Pyle, *Some Merry Adventures of Robin Hood of Great Renown in Nottinghamshire* (New York: Scribner's, 1883).

11 Richard Henry Dana's *Two Years before the Mast: A Personal Narrative of Life at Sea*, originally published in 1840, had been reprinted numerous times by 1887.

12 Actor and playwright Henry Denman Thompson toured nationally with his 1886 play, *The Old Homestead.*

13 The Olympic Club in San Francisco was initiated in 1860 with informal gymnastics training, but did not have a permanent clubhouse until 1893. The first, on Post Street, was destroyed in the 1906 fire.

14 The *Oakland Tribune* for May 18, 1888, reported that "Professor G.W. James delivered a very interesting lecture on astronomy," 5.

15 "Our Winter in Mexico," MSS BANC 75/92m, The Bancroft Library, University of California, Berkeley.

Chapter Ten

1 *Literary Industries* (1890 edition), 477. Bancroft noted that Henry L. Oaks wrote the letter on his behalf.

2 See chapter 7.

3 The term *Mormon* is also commonly used today by those outside the church, whereas members of the church may more typically refer to themselves as LDS.

4 *History of Utah*, 1540–1886, in *The Works of Hubert Howe Bancroft*, vol. 26 (San Francisco: History Company, 1889). Bancroft relied on lengthy source footnotes to legitimize his research. Fn. 18, for example, begins on p. 359, runs for nine pages, and contains hundreds of references to Mormon publications on the "doctrines of the church."

5 Brigham Young's diaries, edited by George D. Smith, run to 1,296 pages in two volumes: *Brigham Young, Colonizer of the American West: Diaries and Office Journals, 1832–1871* (Salt Lake City: Signature Books, 2021).

6 Harriet T. Clarke, Salem, Oregon: 1878, BANC MSS P-A 17, The Bancroft Library, University of California, Berkeley. Matilda Bancroft was noted as being present; A. Bowman was recorded as the writer.

7 I am indebted to Camilla Smith for her assistance in clarifying the history of the LDS pioneer women and the value of Matilda Bancroft's role in taking these dictations. This chapter was bolstered by two informative books: George D. Smith, *Nauvoo Polygamy: But We Called It Celestial Marriage* (Salt Lake City: Signature Books, 2008), and Carol Cornwall Madsen, *In Their Own Words: Women and the Story of Nauvoo* (Salt Lake City: Deseret Book Co., 1994). I am also grateful to Bishop Dale Abono of Covelo, California, and Sienna Stone of Willits, California, for sharing their reflections on and experience in the LDS Church and community (interviewed in 2017).

8 "Reminiscences of Mrs. F. D. Richards," San Francisco, 1880, BANC MSS P-F 4, The Bancroft Library, University of California, Berkeley.

9 BANC MSS P-F 1-10, The Bancroft Library, University of California, Berkeley.

10 Sarah A. Cooke, "Theatrical and Social Affairs in Utah," Salt Lake City, 1884, BANC MSS P-F 19, The Bancroft Library, University of California, Berkeley.

11 Mary Jane Mount Tanner, letter to Mrs. H. H. Bancroft, Provo, Utah, October 29, 1880, BANC MSS P-F 12, The Bancroft Library, University of California, Berkeley.

12 Mrs. Martha Brown, letter to Matilda Bancroft, Ogden City, Utah Territory, August 7, 1880, BANC MSS P-F 12, The Bancroft Library, University of California, Berkeley. All subsequent references to Brown come from this source.

13 Mary Isabella Hales Horne, "Migration and Settlement of the Latter Day Saints," Salt Lake City, 1884, BANC MSS P-F 24, The Bancroft Library,

University of California, Berkeley. All subsequent references to Horne come from this source.

14   From page 16 on in this volume, the numbering changed such that page numbers are repeated, with one number at the top center of the page and the same number at the top right on the next page. This quotation is found on the second page 26, with that number at the center of the page.

15   *The History of Utah*, fn. 21, p. 246.

16   Clara Decker Young, *A Young Woman's Experience with the Pioneer Band*, Salt Lake City, 1884, BANC MSS P-F 40, The Bancroft Library, University of California, Berkeley.

17   Originally from Georgia, Alfred Cumming (1802–1873) arrived in 1858 during a fractious time to become governor of Utah Territory. His moderate stance toward the Mormons helped win his success in the role.

18   A. S. Johnston (1803–1862), who later served as a general in the army of the Confederate States of America, was killed at the Battle of Shiloh in 1862.

19   Lorenzo Dow Young, "Early Experiences," Salt Lake City, 1884, BANC MSS P-F 39, The Bancroft Library, University of California, Berkeley.

20   William N. Byers, "The Newspaper Press of Colorado," Denver, 1884, BANC MSS P-L 7, The Bancroft Library, University of California, Berkeley; Hubert Howe Bancroft, *History of Nevada, Colorado, and Wyoming: 1540–1888* (San Francisco: History Company, 1890).

Chapter Eleven

1   This letter was located near one dated February 16, 1887. Located in Hubert Howe Bancroft letters to his family, BANC MSS 77/169 c, box 1, The Bancroft Library, University of California, Berkeley.

2   This house is not likely the one built for Emily, who had indicated that it was near Franklin and California Streets.

3   Matilda Bancroft letters, 1892–1907, located in Hubert Howe Bancroft letters to his family, BANC MSS 77/169 c, box 4, folder 9, The Bancroft Library, University of California, Berkeley.

4   "The boys" are H.H. and his brother Albert Little, usually referred to as A.L. "Fannie" is A.L.'s wife, Frances Watts.

5   Curtis Bancroft was H.H.'s older brother.

6   Matilda may be referring to a trip to Portland in 1888 that the whole family made, or she may be remembering her more rambunctious journey with H.H. in 1878, when she might have seen an original pioneer log cabin.

7   The small town of Duncan's Mills near the mouth of the Russian River grew where Scottish brothers Sam and Alex Duncan built a mill in 1877. Logs were shipped by railroad to Sausalito, then by barge up Pacheco Slough, six miles north of the town of Walnut Creek at the mouth of Walnut Creek (originally Pacheco Creek).

8   See the garden's website for more history on the place: https://www.ruth bancroftgarden.org/about/history/.

9   The Florence Hotel, on the north side of Fir Street between 3rd and 4th Streets, had opened its doors January 24, 1884. Once premier lodging in San Diego, it was razed in the 1940s.

10 In 1881, H.H. constructed a brick building for his library on Valencia Street in San Francisco. Previously housed in his Market Street building, his library would have perished when that building burned down in 1886.

11 The Bancroft block was on the south side of Fir Street, one block east of the Florence Hotel. The footprint of the house can be seen in block H.227 on Image 34 of the Sanborn Fire Insurance Map from San Diego, San Diego County, California. Library of Congress, described as a "D[welling] 2.B[rick]. Veneered B. Gothic R[oo]f." https://www.loc.gov/resource/g4364sm .g4364sm_g008101888/?sp=34&r=0.423,0.799,0.522,0.293,0.

12 Emily was H.H.'s elder sister (1829–1907), married first to Harlow Palmer (d.1852) and then in 1884 to James Pierce (d. 1888). Her cottages were on the west side of 4th Street, block H.226 on the Sanborn Fire Insurance Map.

13 The Grand Hotel was located at the corner of Market and New Montgomery Streets.

14 The building cost $40,000 to construct. The first tenant was a branch of San Francisco's City of Paris department store. Over the years it housed the Cayuca Club, a secretarial college, an insurance company, a meat market, and, by 1910, a theater. In 1919, the upper three stories were razed. By 2021, it was an Urban Outfitters store. See Sandee Wilhoit, "History of a Historian," *Gaslamp Quarter Historical Foundation,* November 30, 2019, https://gaslamp foundation.org/the-history-of-a-historian/, and Sanborn Insurance Maps.

15 Griffing's wife Margaret Wood Bancroft (1893–1986) preserved and donated many letters to The Bancroft Library, located in Hubert Howe Bancroft letters to his family, BANC MSS 77/169 c, boxes 1–4, The Bancroft Library, University of California, Berkeley. See also the oral history of Margaret Wood Bancroft, "Recollections of Hubert Howe Bancroft and the Bancroft Family," 1980, BANC MSS 80/144 c, The Bancroft Library, University of California, Berkeley. Available online at http://archive.org/details /margaretwoodrecooobancrich.

16 Will Bancroft, the son of Curtis Bancroft, H.H.'s older brother, later sued his uncle. See John W. Caughey, *Hubert Howe Bancroft, Historian of the West* (Berkeley: University of California Press, 1946), 337–40.

17 In Philip's book, Matilda listed the principals of the Bancroft Company: "The company then consisted of papa as President, Mr. N.P. Stone as vice-president, Mr. Dorland & Mr. Colley, sister Kate, and Cousin Will, who was the manager" (161–62).

18 See Linda E. Miller, "San Diego's Early Years as a Health Resort," *Journal of San Diego History* 28, no. 4 (Fall 1982), https://sandiegohistory.org /journal/1982/october/health/. Dr. Silas Weir Mitchell (1829–1914) specialized in neurasthenia and related nervous disorders. He popularized the "rest cure," or quiet retreat for recovery. He was Charlotte Perkins Gilman's doctor. (See chapter 2 regarding Emily Bancroft's youthful friendship with Fred Perkins, the father of Charlotte.)

19 Hubert Howe Bancroft letters to his family, BANC MSS 77/169 c, box 3, folder 5: Clippings, 1905, The Bancroft Library, University of California, Berkeley.

Notes

20 This perhaps refers to Robert Simpson Woodward (1849–1924), civil engineer, geologist, astronomer, and mathematician, who served on the US Geological Survey (1884–1890) and on the US Coast and Geodetic Survey (1890–1893), and then taught at Columbia University (1893–1905).

21 She may have been influenced by the popularity of Helen Hunt Jackson's best-selling 1884 novel, *Ramona*, set in the Southern California missions.

22 Jacob A. Riis, *How the Other Half Lives: Studies among the Tenements of New York* (New York: Charles Scribner's Sons, 1890).

23 Edward Everett Hale (1822–1909) was a Unitarian minister and man of letters. Henry Phipps Jr. (1839–1930) was an associate of Andrew Carnegie, who, like him, devoted much of his Carnegie Steel fortune to philanthropy. In 1907, he established Bessemer Trust to manage the Phipps family assets. My father, Paul (Pete) Bancroft III, served as CEO of Bessemer from 1976 to 1988.

24 May Rindge was the widow of Frederick Rindge (1857–1905), a real estate developer and founder of the town of Malibu.

25 John H. Musser and Charles K. Mills were prominent Philadelphia physicians.

26 Frederick St. George de Lautour Booth-Tucker (1853–1929) was the son-in-law of the founders of the Salvation Army, William and Catherine Booth, and later became a senior officer of the Army himself. Working in India, Booth-Tucker adopted the ways of India's outcasts to win converts. He and his wife became territorial commanders of the US in 1896.

27 Marius J. Spinello, "Italians of California," *Sunset* 14 (January 1905): 256–58.

28 John Foster Carr, "The Italian in the United States," *The World's Work* 8 (May–October 1904): 5393–5404. Carr describes how Andrea Sbarboro organized the Italian-Swiss Agricultural Colony and later became president of the Italian-American Bank in San Francisco.

29 Many thanks to members of the Spring Valley Historical Society and in particular to Jim Van Meter, raconteur extraordinaire; Robert Case, president; and Carol Serr, longtime provider of important services to the Society.

30 After serving as a sarsaparilla factory, the building was razed to create St. Luke's Hospital in 1954.

31 An article in the *San Francisco Call* on February 9, 1905, reported that Honora Sharp, the widow of George F. Sharp (1822–1882), a lawyer, had left her fortune to various charities, including $200,000 to the park commissioners.

32 Max Farrand (1869–1945), professor of American history, later taught at Yale and was the first director of the Huntington Library (1927–1941).

33 The John Carter Brown Library, Brown University, specializes in the history of the Americas.

34 Henry Morse Stephens (1857–1919) was an Oxford-educated historian who went to Cornell in 1894 and then followed his colleague Benjamin Ide Wheeler (1854–1927) to Berkeley as chair of the Department of History after Wheeler became president of the University of California in 1899. Matilda's later reference to a cigar is telling, as Stephens was notorious for chain-smoking Owl cigars. Thanks to Charles Faulhaber for this information.

35 George Pardee (1857–1941) was governor of California from 1903 to 1907.

36 The purchase price asked was $250,000, offset by a gift from Bancroft of $100,000. Bancroft planned to use part of the proceeds to pay off the mortgage on the St. Dunstan's Hotel. See Charles Faulhaber, "The Bancroft Library 1900–2000," *Chronicle of the University of California* 4 (2000): 28–46. See also the online exhibit "Building Bancroft: The Evolution of a Library: Selling" at https://bancroft.berkeley.edu/Exhibits/bancroft/selling/selling .html.

37 The sale agreement was announced in a press release December 8, 1905.

Chapter Twelve

1 Englishman George Wharton James (1858–1923), who arrived in the US in 1881, served as a minister in Southern California and Nevada, and was active as a journalist and photographer, focusing especially on life in the Southwest. Matilda was referring to a meeting of the American Anthropological Association in Pasadena, August 29–31, 1905. In attendance were many luminaries in the field, including A. L. Kroeber. The proceedings can be found online: https://anthrosource.onlinelibrary.wiley.com/doi/pdf/10.1525 /aa.1905.7.4.02a00190.

2 Having grown up with three brothers myself, however, I attest to the ungovernability of young boys.

3 Mary Matilda Griffing's travel diary is in the possession of Tom Graham, the grandson of Philip Bancroft Sr.

4 H.H.'s sister, Emily Bancroft Palmer Pierce.

5 For more on these conflicts, see John W. Caughey, *Hubert Howe Bancroft, Historian of the West* (Berkeley: University of California Press, 1946), and Harry Clark, *A Venture in History: The Production, Publication, and Sale of the* Works *of Hubert Howe Bancroft* (Berkeley: University of California Press, 1973).

6 Margaret Wood Bancroft (1893–1986), "Recollections of Hubert Howe Bancroft and the Bancroft Family," 1980, BANC MSS 80/144 c, The Bancroft Library, University of California, Berkeley. Available online at http://archive. org/details/margaretwoodrecooobancrich.

7 Margaret Wood Bancroft, "Recollections."

8 Hubert Howe Bancroft letters to his family, BANC MSS 77/169 c, box 3, folder 12, fragments, The Bancroft Library, University of California, Berkeley.

Epilogue

1 "Genealogical register for Matilda Bancroft," Hubert Howe Bancroft letters to his family, BANC MSS 77/169 c, box 4, The Bancroft Library, University of California, Berkeley.

INDEX

ABOUT THE AUTHOR

Kim Bancroft taught for three decades at high schools, community colleges, and universities before turning her teaching and editing skills to helping others with their books. She began with the work of her great-great-grandfather, historian of the Pacific West, Hubert Howe Bancroft, condensing his 1890 memoir into *Literary Industries*, published by Heyday in 2014. She also helped tell the story of Heyday's founder with *The Heyday of Malcolm Margolin: The Damn Good Times of a Fiercely Independent Publisher*, winner of the California Book Award. Her recent editing projects include *Same School, Different Class: A Dual Memoir about School Integration*, written with David Waddell, and *Priscilla Hunter: Building a Tribal Nation*, written with Hunter (Pomo). *Writing Themselves into History* represents ten years of library research and gathering family stories from across California. She lives off-grid in a cabin in the woods in Northern California.